The Neighbourhood of Dublin

The Skellig Press

DUBLIN

First published 1912
This edition published 1988

The Skellig Press Limited,
2 The Crescent,
Monkstown, Co. Dublin.

ISBN 0-946241-03-1

Printed and bound by
Billings and Sons Limited,
Worcester and London.

Cover by Bluett.

PREFACE

DUBLIN is particularly fortunate in its surroundings. Within easy reach lies an attractive coast where in close association may be found cliff, beach and towering headland. On the south a great mountain tract provides an almost endless variety of moorland, valley and river scenery. In the matter of lakes only can the Dublin district be said to be deficient, there being nothing worthy of the name nearer than the Loughs Bray, and these, owing to their elevation, size and surroundings, must be classed as tarns rather than lakes.

The district fascinated me in boyhood, and holds its interest for me even now in maturer years after visits to many a foreign land. There is not a glen, mountainside or quiet village described in these pages that I have not visited over and over again, and always with a renewed pleasure.

It is now nearly twenty-five years since I contributed to the Press my first series of illustrated topographical articles under the title of " Rambles Around Dublin." These appeared in *The Evening Telegraph*, and were afterwards issued in book form. They were followed at irregular intervals by others in *The Evening Telegraph* and *The Weekly Irish Times*. All were the result of visits to, and observation in the localities described, coupled with such information as I was able to obtain in regard to their history and other matters of interest. As my store of topographical notes accumulated, I soon found that, owing to the exigencies of space, it was impossible to make any newspaper article as complete as I should have wished, and thus, in the course of years, the quantity of unused matter became considerable enough to suggest the placing before the public the entire result of over twenty-five years rambling, cycling and mountain climbing in the district. The plan I have adopted, in all but the two concluding chapters, is that of describing the district around Dublin in a number of one-day excursions such as would be possible to a person of average activity.

With the exception of a few hackneyed resorts easy of access, the Dublin folk in my earlier days appeared to take but little interest in the surroundings of their city. That reproach, however, can no longer be made, and nowadays on popular holidays and week-ends, considerable numbers may be seen in places where scarcely one would have been found thirty years ago. With the evolution and perfection of the bicycle, the great improvement in the roads, the construction of light railways to Blessington and Lucan, the extension of our splendid tram service to Howth, Dalkey and Rathfarnham, and last though not least, the advent of the automobile, a new interest has been awakened in the beautiful surroundings of our metropolis, and a great vogue for the country has sprung up among all classes. The knowledge of this fact has induced me to write this book in the hope that it may stimulate that interest in those who already know the charm of our surroundings, and excite it in those who do not, and that it may be the means of enabling others to enjoy the pleasures I have derived from rambling among the many picturesque and interesting places in The Neighbourhood of Dublin.

The photographs in all cases bear the dates on which I took them.

I am deeply indebted to my friend, Mr. Louis H. Brindley, for reading this work before publication, for his many valuable suggestions, and for giving me, throughout, the benefit of his literary knowledge and sound judgment.

As illustrative of the lighter side of the subject, I take this not inappropriate opportunity of publishing the following lines which were addressed to me some years ago by a friend to whom I had forwarded a copy of my "Rambles Around Dublin" :—

THE IDLER TO THE RAMBLER.

Dear Joyce, it seems strange that I never have seen a
Glimpse of Clondalkin or Bohernabreena,
Puck's Castle or Crumlin, or Swords or Balrothery,
So I fear that my ignorance fairly will bother ye ;
But before you were born I've oft picnicked gaily
At Killiney, the Dargle, Lough Bray, and old Bailey,
I've inspected the prison at Lusk, a friend's gig in,
And from Skerries have walked straight ahead to Balbriggan,
As for Ireland's Eye, and the huge " Nose of Howth,"
Quite as well as yourself, I'm familiar with both.
I have always admired your friend " Katty Gollagher,"
Whose attractions have sometimes induced me to follow her
And have " taken the Scalp "—altho' not " on the warpath."
Long ago when the Earl of Carlisle was Lord Morpeth.
The famous " Three Rocks " I so often have mounted,
That my feats might, I think, by the dozen be counted
And the toughest lump sugar in all my experience,
I found on the Sugar Loaf's peak a few years since.
Ah ! the fresh hill-side heather—whenever to that I come
I'm always disposed for a hearty viaticum,

For a mountain is clearly a part of the land which
Makes serious demands on a beef or ham sandwich,
And though I'm in general almost a teetotaler,
I shouldn't much relish a temperance hotel here.
But now I must stop, and no longer my fun try,
By rhyming about this suburban " Joyce country " ;
So good-bye, my dear friend, and proceed with your Rambles,
And ambles and gambols, o'er thickets and brambles,
And highways and byways, on foot or on bicycle—
A mode of conveyance which " awfully nice " I call.

The genial " Idler " has gone to his rest. Had we been
more nearly contemporaries, he too, might have become
a " Rambler."

DUBLIN,   WESTON ST. JOHN JOYCE.
    May, 1912.

PREFACE TO SECOND EDITION

SINCE the first edition of this book appeared eight years
ago, I have suffered a personal loss in the death of my father,
P. W. Joyce, who wrote the Introduction to the volume.

Disorganisation caused by the War has considerably delayed
the second edition. I trust the appearance in it of several
new chapters, together with the addition of numerous notes,
will compensate for any disappointment experienced by
those who have recently found it impossible to obtain copies
of the earlier issue.

I am pleased to think that my efforts have helped to
increase the number of those who take an interest in the
surroundings of our old city, and am happy in the knowledge
that the book has made many new friends for me among
its readers.

                    WESTON ST. JOHN JOYCE.

1921.

INTRODUCTION

THE neighbourhood of Dublin, from an historical point of view, presents in miniature the history of English colonisation in Ireland. Pent at first within the circuit of their wall-girt city, out of which they durst not go forth alone or unarmed the colonists at length took heart of grace and ventured to occupy outlying villages and important positions in which they built fortified houses and castles. Those who settled on the north enjoyed, for long periods, comparatively peaceful possession, protected as they were from harassing raids by the interposition of the city between them and the mountains. Not so, however, with those who established themselves in the chain of settlements and outposts skirting the southern border of the plains. These were subjected to continual incursions by the natives from the mountainous tracts of Dublin and Wicklow. Even with the advantages conferred by the possession of superior arms, equipment and defences, the hardy colonists, mostly old soldiers and men trained to the art of war, were continually obliged to abandon their homesteads and flee for safety to the city. The disparity between the ambition and the ability of the early English colony for conquest, is well illustrated by the fact that liberal as was the area of the Pale which they mapped out as their territory, there were at intervals large portions in which they could only remain by paying heavily in " Black Rents " to the

Irish, or into which, more likely, they dared not venture at all.

The menace of the mountains was one of the most serious obstacles to the realisation of English ambition. Frowning down upon the colonists was a wild and almost impenetrable tract of mountain, desert and forest, within the sanctuary of which the natives were able to organise their predatory raids with such impunity that nothing short of a formidable expedition could hope to succeed in any measure of retaliation. This struggle, on the south and south-west, went on intermittently through the centuries, and at times, in consequence of the unsettled conditions of life resulting from this guerilla warfare, large tracts of arable land had to be abandoned and allowed to lapse into desert condition.

The opening of the 17th century saw some tendency to build country residences of the dwellinghouse rather than the fortified type, in the district around Dublin, though no doubt their occupants in many cases had reason to regret the venture during the lawlessness and disturbances which accompanied the Insurrection of 1641. From this period there seems to have been a steady growth of country establishments, not merely in districts which are now suburban, but also in areas beyond them. At the time that Rocque constructed his map (about 1750), the city had not extended, roughly speaking, further than the Rotunda on the north, James's Gate on the west, New Street on the south and Merrion Street on the east, and in what are now the populous urban districts of Rathmines and Rathgar, Pembroke, Blackrock and Kingstown, small villages and stately country residences stood among tillage lands, green pastures and waving cornfields which survived in part within the memory of many now living. In the beginning of the 19th century the wilds of Wicklow were opened up by a system of military roads, and the construction of the Dublin and Kingstown Railway some thirty years later, gave a great impetus to building along the southern shore of the Bay, in time converting it into a continuous residential district as far as Dalkey, while the extension of the railway system in subsequent years through the district, brought many places which prior to that had been almost inaccessible, within easy reach of the Dublin public.

It is desirable to associate history with topography, and accordingly, all through this book, the reader will find brought under his attention the historical events as well as the traditions in connection with the several castles, mansions, homesteads, church ruins, demesnes, forts, hills, valleys, &c., together with references to the historical or legendary personages associated with them.

P. W. JOYCE.

Dublin,

May, 1912

NOTE

Since this book was written the modern designation of Kingstown has been replaced by the original name, Dun Laoghaire.

TABLE OF CONTENTS

xiii

LIST OF ILLUSTRATIONS

THE
NEIGHBOURHOOD
OF DUBLIN

CHAPTER I

RINGSEND, THE GREAT SOUTH WALL AND THE PIGEONHOUSE

RINGSEND, though now presenting a decayed and unattractive appearance, was formerly a place of considerable importance, having been for nearly two hundred years, in conjunction with the Pigeonhouse harbour, the principal packet station in Ireland for communication with Great Britain. The transfer of the packet service, however, to Howth and Kingstown in the early part of last century, deprived Ringsend of its principal source of revenue, and consigned it thenceforth to poverty and obscurity.

In its halcyon days it was a pretty watering-place, much frequented in the summer for sea-bathing by Dublin folk who wished to be within easy reach of town, and in the middle of the 18th century it was described as being " very clean, " healthy and beautiful, with vines trained up against the walls " of the houses." In after years it became the seat of several flourishing industries, long since extinct. It is difficult now to realise that such a grimy and dingy-looking place could ever have been a really pretty and pleasant suburb of the city, but such it was a hundred and fifty years ago, when it contained a number of picturesque high-gabled houses, with well-stocked

A

gardens and orchards, a few of which remain, even at the present day.

Ringsend must have sadly deteriorated by 1816, if we are to believe Lord Blayney's description in his *Sequel to a Narrative*.——" On approaching the town [Dublin] you pass

View near Ringsend.
(1904.)

" through a vile, filthy and disgraceful-looking village called " Ringsend." Other travellers who landed there about the same period, speak of it in similar terms.

The Dublin Weekly Chronicle of 15th October, 1748, contains the following quaint notice :—" Poolbeg Oyster " Fishery being taken this year by Messrs. Bunit & Simpson, " of Ringsend, they may be had fresh and in their purity at " Mrs. L'Sware's at the Sign of the Good Woman in Rings- " end aforesaid."

Various explanations have been given of the origin of this paradoxical name—one of the most plausible being that before the construction of Sir John Rogerson's Quay, a number of piles of wood were driven into the sand along the sides of the river, to many of which rings were attached for the convenience of vessels mooring there, and that the furthest point to which these piles extended became, in consequence, known as " The Rings end." It is much more probable, however, that it is a hybrid word—*i.e.*, " Rinn's end," *rinn* meaning in Irish a point of land projecting into the water, so that the whole name would thus mean " the end of the spur of land," and this etymology is borne out by the position of Ringsend in former times, as will be seen by reference to the accompanying plan showing the coastline of the Port in 1673.

Before the Dodder was confined between artificial banks, it flowed at its own sweet will in numerous streams over a considerable tract of marsh and slobland at Ringsend, and in time of flood caused much perturbation among the inhabitants—the waters of the river and the waves of the sea rolling without let or hindrance over land now covered by terraces and dwellinghouses. Gerard Boate, who wrote in 1652, after referring to the havoc wrought by the floods of this river, states :—" Since that time a stone bridge hath been built over that " brook upon the way betwixt Dublin and Ringsend ; which " was hardly accomplished when the brook in one of its furious " risings, quite altered its channel for a good way, so as it " did not pass under the bridge as before, but just before " the foot of it, letting the same stand upon the dry land, " and consequently making it altogether useless. In which " perverse course it continued until perforce it was constrained " to return to its old channel and to keep within the same."

The stone bridge referred to by Boate (built between 1629 and 1637) was where Ballsbridge now stands—the only route at that time between Dublin and Ringsend, except for those who hired what was known as a " Ringsend Car," to cross the shallows then intervening between that place and the city.

All the tract lying east of City Quay, Sandwith Street, Grand Canal Street, and north of Lansdowne Road was then washed by the mingled waters of the Dodder and the sea, and could be traversed only with danger and difficulty by pedestrians. (See Prendergast's *Life of Charles Haliday,* prefixed to the latter's *Scandinavian Kingdom of Dublin,* p. cxx.)

The difficulty of access to Ringsend is alluded to as follows in *The Dublin Scuffle* (1699), by John Dunton, the eccentric Dublin bookseller, italics being introduced into the quotation for the purpose of emphasising the allusion :—
" I had very agreeable company to Ringsend, and was nobly
" treated at the King's Head at this dear place (as all Post
" Towns generally are). I took my leave of . . . and two
" or three more friends, and now looked towards Dublin ;
" *but how to get at it we no more knew than the Fox at the Grapes,*
" *for though we saw a large strand, yet 'twas not to be walked*
" *over,* because of a pretty rapid stream [the Dodder] which
" must be crossed ; we enquired for a coach, and found no
" such thing was to be had here, unless by accident, but were
" informed we might have a Rings-end carr, which upon my
" desire was called, and we got upon it, not into it. . . .
" I pay'd 4d. for one fair of a mile's riding."

On the 14th of November, 1646, the Parliamentary forces were landed at Ringsend, and on the 14th of August, 1649, Oliver Cromwell, who had been appointed Lord Lieutenant of Ireland by unanimous vote of Parliament, landed here with an army of 12,000 men, a formidable train of artillery, and a large quantity of munitions of war.

In 1670, during a great storm from the East, the tide overflowed here, and flooding the country as far as Trinity College, invaded the low-lying parts of the city and carried away a number of houses.

In 1672, the English Government, apprehensive of an attack on Dublin by the Dutch, who a few years previously had done great damage in the Thames, sent over Sir Bernard de Gomme, an eminent engineer, to report as to what works were necessary for the defence of the Port. After a survey, he submitted a plan and estimates, now deposited in the British Museum, for the construction of a great pentagonal fortress, to occupy a space of about thirty acres, immediately south-east of the site now occupied by Merrion Square, at a cost of £131,277. It was indispensable to the utility of this stronghold that it should be capable of relief by sea, which then flowed in to where now are Wentworth Place and Grand Canal Street.

Nothing, however, was done towards providing defences for the Port of Dublin until the erection of the Pigeonhouse Fort nearly one hundred and fifty years afterwards.

In April, 1690, on Good Friday, an engagement took place in the Bay, near where the Poolbeg Lighthouse now stands, between the *Monmouth* yacht with some smaller vessels in command of Sir Cloudesley Shovel, and a frigate anchored in the Bay laden with goods for France. King James, attracted by the firing, rode out to Ringsend accompanied by a great crowd of people and witnessed the engagement. The crew of the frigate were obliged to abandon it after a loss of six or seven in the action.—(Dean Story's *Impartial History*, p. 58.)

In 1703, Ringsend having become populous owing to the presence of many officers of the Port and seafaring men, and being so far from the Protestant parish church of Donnybrook, which was often inaccessible owing to the overflowing of tides and floods on the highway, an Act was passed by Parliament authorising the erection of the church now known as St. Matthew's at Irishtown.

In 1711 the Liffey between the city and Ringsend was embanked, thereby reclaiming the North and South Lotts.

In 1782 the bridge across the Dodder at Ringsend was swept away by a flood, and communication was not restored for seven years. Ferrar in his *View of Dublin* (1796), writing of this incident, says :—" Ringsend was in a very melancholy situation " in the year 1787. It resembled a town which had experienced " all the calamities of war, that had been sacked by an enemy, " or that had felt the hand of all-devouring time. The un-

" fortunate inhabitants were in a manner excluded from all
" intercourse with Dublin. They were attacked by the over-
" bearing floods which issued from the mountains in irresistible
" torrents and completely demolished the bridge. The new
" bridge is a very handsome one, and cost only £815." The
folly of this economy is shown by the fact that the new bridge
lasted only until 1802—thirteen years—when it, like its predecessor, was carried away by floods. At their wits' end, the
authorities thereupon constructed the massive bridge which
survives to the present day, no longer indeed exposed to the
fury of the floods, the once turbulent Dodder having been
sadly tamed in recent years by the diversion of its waters into
the reservoirs of the Rathmines Township at Glennasmole.

The South Wall, one of the most remarkable and best constructed breakwaters of its kind in the world, extends from
Ringsend into the Bay, a distance of 17,754 feet, or nearly
three and a half miles. It was commenced in 1717 by a framework of wooden piles carried along the course of the river, for
a distance of 7,938 feet, to the position now occupied by the
Pigeonhouse, where the Ballast Board in 1735, placed a floating
lightship ; and in 1735 this wooden piling was replaced by a
double stone wall, the intervening space being filled with rocks
and gravel, forming a wide roadway, flanked on either side by
a massive parapet. Prior to this time all vessels approaching the
harbour of Dublin after nightfall were obliged to remain
outside the bar until the following morning, on account of the
dangerous shoals off the shore known as the North and South
Bulls, and even when vessels had entered the Port, there was
no place of anchorage until they reached Ringsend.[1]

It was soon discovered that the wall, although affording
some shelter to shipping, did not extend far enough to protect
the harbour adequately during storms and high tides, and
accordingly it was decided to supplement the work by an extension of the original wooden piles and framework to the
deep pool known as Poolbeg, near the eastern extremity of the
South Bull, and about two miles further out in the bay. This

further portion is not quite in line with the rest, but is deflected slightly to the northward so as to follow the course of the river.

At the point then known as " the pile ends," where the original line of wooden piles ended, and the Pigeonhouse now stands, the port authorities erected a massive wooden house, strongly clamped with iron, to serve as a watch house, store house and place of refuge for such as were forced to land there by stress of weather ; and between this place and Ringsend, a number of boats used to ply in summer, conveying pleasure-seeking citizens of that day to what had grown to be a favourite rendezvous while the works were in progress. A man named Pidgeon who lived in the wooden house and acted as caretaker of the works and tools, finding the place become such a public resort, fitted out his quarters as neatly as possible, and, assisted by his wife and family, made arrangements for supplying meals and refreshments to visitors. He also purchased a boat to hire to his guests, had it painted and finished in an attractive manner, and as he dealt with only the best class of visitors. his rude hostelry soon grew to be a noted resort of distinguished citizens and wits, while the owner found himself on the fair road to fortune. His house came to be known to all the Dublin folk as " Pidgeon's House," or the Pigeonhouse, and even after he and his family had gone the way of all flesh, and the old building, having served its purpose, had fallen into decay, the name was perpetuated in the title of the stronghold that in after years rose over its ruins.

When the Packet station was established here, it was found necessary to build the Pigeonhouse harbour, where the packets landed and embarked passengers, for whose accommodation a hotel was erected in 1790. After the transfer of the regular service to Howth, the Pigeonhouse harbour continued in use as an occasional landing place, especially for the Liverpool packets.

The Pigeonhouse Packet station in time becoming superseded by that at Howth, the Government in 1813, purchased the hotel and other buildings, and commenced the construction

of the Pigeonhouse Fort, which ultimately cost over £100,000.
The hotel formed the nucleus of the structure, and the submarine mining establishment, batteries and other additions
were erected by the War Department. In its later years the
Fort gradually lapsed into disuse, and was finally dismantled
and sold to the Dublin Corporation in 1897 for £65,000.

Entrance to the Pigeonhouse Fort.
(1895.)

The Pigeonhouse fort appears to have been built partly for
the purpose of a repository for State papers, bullion, and other
valuables in time of disturbance, and partly for defence of the
Port ; and in its earlier form, the construction of formidable
batteries commanding the passage of the wall from the city,
indicated that its designers were more apprehensive of an
attack from land than by sea. In anticipation of a prolonged
siege, efforts were made to obtain an independent supply of
water for the garrison by the usual process of sinking tubes,
but notwithstanding the assistance of eminent experts who

were brought over from England for the purpose, and the expenditure of immense sums of money on the operations, the influx of salt water through the sandy soil baffled all attempts and obliged the Government to abandon the project.

In *The Dublin Chronicle* of 3rd August, 1790, we read :—
" On Friday morning twenty-seven poor haymakers attending
" at the Pigeonhouse in order to be put on board ship for
" England, were seized by a press-gang and put on board a
" tender—the commander of the press-gang telling them at
" the same time that if they were able to mow hay, they could
" have no objection to mow the enemies of their country, and
" they should have passage, diet, &c., gratis." It is therefore
not surprising that in another issue we learn :—" Yesterday
" morning, at an early hour, a coach, in which some recruits
" were being conveyed to the Pigeonhouse in order to be
" embarked for England, was attacked at Ringsend by desperate
" banditti armed with swords and pistols, who after wounding
" the soldiers that accompanied the coach, rescued three of
" the men from them."

The Dublin Chronicle of 28th January, 1792, referring to a breach which had been made by a storm in the South Wall, says :—" Yesterday, his Grace the Duke of Leinster went on
" a sea party, and, after shooting the breach in the South Wall,
" sailed over the Low Ground and the South Lotts, and landed
" safely at Merrion Square. . . . Boats ply with passengers
" to Merrion Square."

Although the original account of this occurrence mentions the South Wall, it doubtless means the wall or embankment on the south side of the river along Sir John Rogerson's Quay, where a breach would have caused an inundation of the South Lotts, enabling boats to ply as far as what is now the lower end of Holles Street, near Merrion Square.

Sir Charles Hoare in his *Tour in Ireland* relates some interesting experiences of his visit to Dublin :—" Monday, 23rd June,
" 1806. Sailed from Holyhead in the *Union Packet*, Captain
" Skinner, and after a rough and tedious passage of twenty

" three hours, landed at the Pigeonhouse, from where a vehicle,
" very appropriately called ' the Long Coach ' (holding sixteen
" inside passengers and as many outside, with all their luggage)
" conveyed us to Dublin, distant about two miles from the
" place of landing." He states that in addition to the duty
which was exacted after a troublesome examination at the
Custom House on the South Wall, he had to pay no less than
twelve different officers of Customs. After leaving the Custom
House, he had to dismount from the vehicle and cross the bridge
on foot, as it was considered to be in too dangerous a condition
to drive over with a full vehicle. " There is nothing com-
" manding in this approach to Dublin ; a number of narrow
" passes and bridges barricadoed, still remind the traveller of
" the late rebellion." He adds that a most daring attack upon
the long coach above alluded to, was made a short time previously
by a gang of armed banditti, who obliged the passengers to
dismount, and then plundered them one by one, while on
another occasion the officer carrying the mails was fired at.
Sir Charles Hoare suggests that " a horse patrole " should be
furnished by the Government to escort the coach from the
General Post Office to the Packet station.

The process of exacting fees and payments on various pre-
texts, from the passengers at the Pigeonhouse, was known to
the initiated as " Plucking the Pigeons."

The statement as to the duration of the passage from Holyhead—twenty-three hours—may perhaps be considered an
exaggeration, but a perusal of the newspapers of the period
will show that this was not by any means an extravagantly
long time for crossing ; indeed, our forefathers thought themselves rather lucky if the voyage was accomplished in that
time, instances not having been at all uncommon in stormy
weather or with contrary winds where it extended to a week
or ten days. When we consider the limited accommodation
in these frail vessels, and the prolonged miseries of sea-sick
passengers, can we wonder that none but the most enthusiastic
travellers cared to leave their own shores in those days ?

Perhaps, indeed, the vigour of the language with which Ringsend has been assailed by successive writers who landed there, may to some extent be accounted for, by the condition of these unfortunate travellers' nerves and stomachs after the miseries of sea-sickness during a voyage of from eighteen to thirty hours duration in the packet boats of that period.

According to a diary kept by a Welsh gentleman in 1735, during a visit to Dublin, the passage from Holyhead took nineteen hours, and on the return journey when the packet had got within a few miles of Holyhead, a contrary wind sprung up which obliged the officers to abandon all hope of reaching land on that side, and forced them to turn back to Dublin where they had to wait several days before the wind was favourable. It is interesting to learn that the voyage cost 10s. 6d.—pretty much the same as at present—but when forced to turn back by stress of weather and make an extra voyage, as in this case, the cost of provisions only was charged. The passengers landed at Ringsend and paid 1s. a head to the boatman who took them ashore in his boat, and two of them hired a coach to drive them to the city, for which they paid 2s. 10d. The passengers complained of being kept four hours waiting before being landed.

Nathaniel Jefferys in *An Englishman's Descriptive Account of Dublin* (1810), gives the following amusing description of the proceedings at the Pigeonhouse landing stage, about a hundred years ago :—" Upon the arrival of the packets at the " Pigeonhouse, the passengers are conducted to the custom- " house ; and it would be a great injustice not to acknowledge " that the manner in which the examination of the luggage is " done (by giving as little trouble as possible to persons " frequently fatigued by a tedious passage and sea-sickness) is " very gratifying to strangers. As soon, however, as this " ceremony is over, one of a less accommodating description " takes place, which is the mode of conveying passengers to " Dublin in the Long Coach. This carriage is upon the plan " of those elegant vehicles upon low wheels, which are used on

" the road between Hyde Park Corner and Hammersmith in
" the neighbourhood of London ; and from the state of its
" repair and external appearance, it bears every mark of having
" retired on the superannuated list from that active duty,
" previous to its being employed upon its present service.
" This coach is usually very crowded, from the anxiety of the
" passengers to proceed to Dublin ; and from the manner in
" which some of the company may easily be supposed to have
" been passing their time on board the packet——from the
" effect of sea-sickness, the effluvia arising from twelve or
" fourteen persons so circumstanced, crammed together in a
" very small space, like the inmates of Noah's Ark, the clean
" and the unclean, is not of that description which can at all
" entitle the Long Coach to be considered as a bed of roses.
" Three shillings for each passenger is the price of conveyance,
" and this is exacted beforehand. . . . The inconveniencies
" of this ride are, however, of short duration, for in about half
" an hour the passengers are released from this earthly purgatory
" by their arrival in Dublin."

The average duration of the passage from the Pigeonhouse
to Holyhead was eighteen hours, and from Howth only twelve
hours, which was reduced to seven hours when steam packets
were introduced.

The Pigeonhouse has undergone considerable alterations in
recent years since it has become the generating station for the
city supply of electricity, and the tall red-brick chimney which
has been added is now a conspicuous feature in the Bay. Most
of the old buildings still remain, but the Pigeonhouse of our
boyhood days is gone—the sentries no longer guard its portals,
its deserted courtyards and dismantled batteries echo no more
to the tramp of armed men or resound with salvoes of artillery.
The monotonous hum of the dynamos has succeeded, and the
whole place, though doubtless fulfilling a more useful purpose
than during its military occupation, possesses much less interest
than it did as a link with old-time Dublin.

CHAPTER II

THE POOLBEG LIGHTHOUSE AND THE SOUTH WALL EXTENSION, IRISHTOWN, SANDYMOUNT, BEGGARSBUSH AND BAGGOTRATH.

THE maintenance of the South Wall extension beyond the Pigeonhouse, alluded to in the previous chapter, proved to be enormously expensive owing to the rapid corrosion of the timber foundations by the salt water, and besides, the structure was insufficient in bulk to shield the harbour effectually from the force of the waves when the wind blew from the south or south-east. Great quantities of the loose and shifting sands of the South Bull were constantly being blown or drifted across the breakwater into the river bed, materially interfering with its navigability, and seriously affecting the trade of the port.

It was accordingly resolved to replace the wooden piles on this portion by a solid stone breakwater of massive proportions, and so the Poolbeg Lighthouse was begun in 1761, and finished seven years later. The present granite causeway was then gradually built inwards towards the city until it had joined the earlier portion of the structure. In many places along the south side of the wall may still be seen remains of the original wooden piles.

At certain exposed points, to protect it from the violence of the sea, the sides were formed of blocks of granite, dovetailed into each other, so that no single block could be detached without breaking, and the intermediate space between the sides was filled with gravel for about half the height, above which great blocks of granite were laid in cement. The wall when thus constructed formed a solid causeway 32 feet wide at the base and tapering to 28 feet at the top. The only place where these original dimensions now remain is from the outfall of the Pembroke Main Drain to the Poolbeg Lighthouse. Towards the eastern end where the water is deep, the wall had to be strengthened by iron clamps and bolts, while approaching the Lighthouse, so great is the fury of the sea in a south-easterly storm, that it was found necessary to raise it some five feet higher, and to protect it for a considerable distance, by an

The Poolbeg Lighthouse in its original form.

additional breakwater of huge boulders on the outside. How necessary this was, is shown by the rounded condition of many of these great rocks, which are often tossed about like pebbles during easterly gales, and in some instances cast up on the wall itself. Even with all these precautions to ensure the stability of the wall, repairs are constantly necessary.

Few townsfolk have any conception of what a south-easterly storm means along the coast, and I would strongly recommend anyone who is not afraid of rough weather, to select a day when there is a gale from this point, and arrange to reach the Pigeon-house about high tide ; it would be inadvisable to go further, but ample view can be obtained therefrom of the action of the sea along the wall.

Gerard Boate, writing in 1652, gives the following quaint description of the Port of Dublin :—" Dublin haven hath a
" bar in the mouth, upon which at high flood and spring-tide
" there is fifteen and eighteen feet of water, but at the ebbe
" and nep-tide but six. With an ordinary tide you cannot go
" to the key of Dublin with a ship that draws five feet of water,
" but with a spring-tide you may go up with ships that draw
" seven or eight feet. Those that go deeper cannot go nearer
" Dublin than the Rings-end, a place three miles distant from
" the bar, and one from Dublin. This haven almost all over
" falleth dry with the ebbe, as well below Rings-end as above
" it, so as you may go dry foot round about the ships which lye
" at anchor there, except in two places, one at the north side,
" half way betwixt Dublin and the bar, and the other at the
" south side not far from it. In these two little creeks (whereof
" the one is called the pool of Clontarf and the other Poolbeg)
" it never falleth dry, but the ships which ride at an anchor
" remain ever afloat ; because at low water you have nine or
" ten feet of water there. This haven, besides its shallowness,
" hath yet another great incommodity, that the ships have
" hardly any shelter there for any winds, not only such as come
" out of the sea, but also those which come off from the land,
" especially out of the south-west ; so as with a great south-
" west storm the ships run great hazards to be carried away
" from their anchor and driven into the sea ; which more than
" once hath come to pass, and particularly in the beginning
" of November, An. 1637, when in one night ten or twelve
" barks had that misfortune befaln them, of the most part
" whereof never no news hath been heard since."

The Pool of Clontarf is now called The Pool, and the other the Poolbeg, or little pool.

Poolbeg, which lies in the channel between the Pigeonhouse

and the Lighthouse, was in former times a recognised anchorage
for vessels. In the accompanying reproduction of an old print
of Dublin Bay, about one hundred and seventy years old, a fleet
of large fishing vessels is represented riding at anchor there.

The Poolbeg Lighthouse is a handsome and conspicuous
feature in the bay, in which it occupies an almost central
position, though its picturesque appearance has been somewhat
marred since it was painted black by the Port authorities some
twenty years ago. It is nearly equi-distant from Dublin,

View of Beggarsbush and Dublin Bay 170 years ago.
(From an engraving in the National Gallery, Dublin.)

Kingstown, and Howth, and commands extensive views of the
whole shores of the bay, with an unbroken panorama of the
mountains on the south. Howth with its heather-clad hills,
its bright green fields and rugged reaches of sea cliffs, looks
particularly attractive from this point.

An interesting effect of the isolated position of this spot
which can hardly escape the notice of the casual visitor, is the
impressive silence which prevails here on a calm summer's day,
though surrounded on all sides by evidences of bustle and
activity. Occasionally the stillness is broken by the rythmical
beat of some steamer gliding gracefully past, as she leaves or
enters the port, or at intervals one may faintly distinguish the

whistle of a far off train so softened by distance as to mingle
with the cry of the sea birds and the gentle plash of the water
against the rocks.

The lighthouse when originally constructed, presented an
entirely different appearance from what it does at the present
time. It was not so high as the existing structure, it sloped
much more rapidly towards the top, and was surmounted by
an octagonal lantern with eight heavy glass windows. A stone
staircase with an iron balustrade led to the second storey, where

The Poolbeg Lighthouse.
(1902.)

an iron gallery surrounded the whole building. The alteration
to the present form was made in the early part of last century,
and was, beyond doubt, a decided improvement so far as the
appearance of the structure is concerned.

The foundations consist of immense blocks of stone and
cement, bound together with massive iron bands, interwoven
so as to form great cages ; and the base thus formed is
strengthened by sloping buttresses all round.

Returning along the Wall, we take the turn on the left
along the Rathmines and Pembroke Main Drain embank-

originally designed to protect this locality from the ravages of the sea.

The most conspicuous object in this neighbourhood is the belfry tower of St. Matthew's Church, before alluded to, which is still in good preservation and is thickly mantled with ivy.

The strand at Irishtown was at one time noted for its cockles and shrimps, the shrimps being found in great quantities at certain states of the tide, but after the severe winter of 1741, known as " The hard frost," they completely disappeared and never since returned to this coast. The cockles, however, still remain for those who have the courage to eat them, and occasionally yield a rich harvest to the professional cockle pickers. Going to Sandymount on Sunday to pick cockles was a favourite amusement of the Dublin folk a hundred years ago.

Cranfield's Baths, for many years a well-known institution in this neighbourhood, were established by Richard Cranfield, who died at Irishtown in 1859.

In former times the tract along the sea from Ringsend to Sandymount was known as Scal'd Hill, or Scald Hill. In the middle of the 18th century there was a village called " Brick-" field Town " on the site now occupied by Sandymount Green, deriving its name from Lord Merrion's brickfields, which extended along the shore from there to Merrion. A well-known inn called " The Conniving House " then stood where the modern Seafort Avenue West, meets the shore. It was a famous old hostelry, noted for its dinners of fish and its excellent ale, and is referred to as follows in *The Life of John Buncle, Esq.* [Thomas Amory], Vol. I., p. 87 :— " I set " forward (1st May, 1725), and in five days arrived from the " western extremity of Ireland at a village called Rings-end " that lies on the Bay of Dublin. Three days I rested there, " and at the Conniving House, and then got my horses on " board a ship that was ready to sail, and bound for the land " I was born in, I mean Old England. . . . The Conniving

" House (as the gentlemen of Trinity called it in my time
" and long after) was a little publichouse, kept by Jack
" Macklean, about a quarter of a mile beyond Rings-end, on
" the top of the beach, within a few yards of the sea. Here
" we used to have the finest fish at all times ; and in the season,
" green peas and all the most excellent vegetables. The ale
" here was always extra-ordinary, and everything the best ;
" which with its delightful situation, rendered it a delightful
" place of a summer's evening. Many a delightful evening have
" I passed in this pretty thatched house with the famous Larry
" Grogan, who played on the bagpipes extreme well ; dear
" Jack Lattin, matchless on the fiddle, and the most agreeable
" of companions . . . and many other delightful fellows
" who went in the days of their youth to the shades of eternity.
" When I think of them and their evening songs——' *We will*
" ' *go to Johnny Macklean's to try if his ale be good or not*,' *&c.*,
" and that years and infirmities begin to oppress me, what
" is life ! "

Sandymount, though now a populous suburb of the metropolis, is remembered by many old people as an isolated village
standing around Sandymount Green. In the early part of last
century—about 1810 to 1820— it came into great favour as a
watering place ; there was a well-equipped hotel here, and a
range of lodging-houses was built at the north-eastern side of
the Green, continuous with Newgrove Avenue, for the accommodation of visitors. The extent to which it was patronised
in consequence of its fine strand, pretty beach and depth of
wave at full-tide, excited the ambition of the residents to make
it an aristocratic resort, and in order to attain the desired degree
of exclusiveness, the fee charged for bathing there was 2d., which,
of course, restricted it to the nobility and gentry, the common
people betaking themselves to Irishtown, where the fee was
only 1d., and where there was a larger array of bathing boxes
with plainer accommodation.

At the corner of Sandymount Avenue,[3] on the main road
to Kingstown, was an inn and snack-house called " The Bird

" House "—a cosy thatched tavern where travellers arriving late in the evening sometimes stayed the night rather than risk the remainder of the journey to town in the dark.

On the 21st of April, 1826, the Rev. George Wogan was murdered in his house in Spafield Place, off Sandymount Avenue. The murder created a great sensation in Dublin, as the victim was widely respected and known. The murderers were duly hanged, not for the murder, however, but as the result of conviction for a highway robbery in the same neighbourhood.

Up to about 1840 there was a famous concern known as Haig's Distillery on the banks of the Dodder immediately eastward of the present Herbert Bridge, but I believe it had ceased working for several years prior to that date. It was approached from Haig's Avenue and Watery Lane (now Lansdowne Road) by a stone weir across the river, and the buildings extended a considerable distance along the banks, surrounded by meadows and grass lands. This establishment had become notorious by reason of its frequent conflicts with the Revenue authorities, and the audacity with which its operations were conducted both by day and night. Many strange stories were told as to encounters with excise officers in its earlier years, and the rumour was current in the neighbourhood that several of these unpopular functionaries had mysteriously " disappeared " in the establishment. The proprietor undoubtedly fought the Revenue both physically and legally by every means that his ingenuity could devise, but being beaten, he had to succumb in the end, and his concern was ultimately dismantled. A local builder purchased the old buildings some years afterwards, and it was understood that he had effected an excellent bargain, as the debris included a great quantity of copper tubing and machinery. The stones of the old building were utilised in laying down the foundations of the two roads constructed across the distillery fields—viz., Herbert Road and Newbridge Avenue.

Watery Lane, now represented by the portion of Lansdowne

Road between Pembroke Road and Shelbourne Road, was little better than a wet ditch with water constantly oozing out from its mud banks, and was passable only by means of a line of stepping stones laid along it.

Lying immediately inland from the coast, though no longer designated by their ancient titles, are the localities formerly known as Beggarsbush and Baggotrath, now almost entirely merged in the suburbs. In the old print of Dublin Bay, already alluded to, which appears to have been sketched from a position somewhere near the present Haddington Road, the origin of the name of Beggarsbush is clearly shown, for there, prominently in the foreground, is the bush under which the beggars of that day used to find a temporary shelter before descending on the metropolis. Three beggars appear in the picture, two of them—a man and a woman—of tattered and disreputable aspect, are standing up, looking towards the city, and apparently in consultation as to the route to be pursued in their campaign. A third, of more placid temperament, is reclining at ease in this arboreal beggars' rest, and to all appearances, waiting, like Mr. Micawber, for something to turn up.

Many of the worthies who used to avail themselves of this friendly shelter were doubtless, when opportunity offered, highwaymen, as the neighbourhood had acquired an evil reputation in this respect, and numerous robberies are recorded in the newspapers of the time as having taken place there.

In the print referred to, not one building of any description is shown between Beggarsbush and Ringsend, the intervening space being open country through which the Dodder flowed over a wide tract of waste and slob land. Judging by the relative positions of the various objects in the picture, the original " bush " must have stood a little to the north of the modern Beggarsbush Barracks, though Duncan's map of the County Dublin, made about ninety years ago, assigns the name of Beggarsbush to a hamlet or group of houses which stood at the intersection of what are now known as Lansdowne Road and Shelbourne Road.

The view in the picture at first sight appears unduly extensive, and it is probably somewhat exaggerated so far as the height of the standpoint is concerned, but even allowing for only a few feet of elevation where the " bush " stood, a very considerable view of the Bay must have been obtained therefrom. Even at the present day, with all the buildings intervening, the higher portions of Howth Head are clearly visible from the middle of Haddington Road, opposite the barracks.

In the early part of last century—down to about 1820, or thereabouts—there stood in a field at the spot now occupied by the north-eastern corner of Beggarsbush Barracks, an old vaulted building in ruins, covered with a dense growth of ivy, nettles and brambles, called Le Fevre's Folly, which was utilised as a refuge and point of reconnaissance by highwaymen, robbers and smugglers, then abounding in the neighbourhood, as the ruins commanded a view along the five roads radiating from this point.

The inhabitants of all the adjacent localities—Ringsend, Irishtown, Ballsbridge, Donnybrook, and Sandymount, seldom ventured out of doors at night time without being fully armed, as they were almost entirely dependant upon their own arrangements for the protection of themselves and their homes, the whole district at that time being in a most lawless state, and burglaries and highway robberies of almost nightly occurrence.

The only house of any note in the neighbourhood at that time was Pembroke Lodge, which now in its old age, may still be seen a few paces from the railway bridge, on the northern side of Bath Avenue, then Londonbridge Road. It will be readily recognised by its great projecting eaves, owing to which it was popularly known as " The Umbrella House."

This house, about 1825, was occupied as a residence by the proprietor of adjoining chemical works which covered the whole area bounded by the Dodder, Bath Avenue and Ringsend Road. Isolated as it was, and containing the ordinary valuables to be found in a house of its size occupied by well-to-do people, it was naturally an object of much interest to the burgling confraternity. Attempts were frequently made to enter the premises, and on one occasion the inmates, immediately before retiring, observed an ill-looking individual peering over the wall and evidently reconnoitring with a view to a night attack. Thus put on their guard, they received the expected visitors on their arrival with discharges of slugs from blunderbusses, causing an immediate retreat. A number of burgling implements were left behind by the robbers in their hurried flight, and a trail of blood was traced next morning the whole way to Halpin's Pool, Ringsend, where it ceased. Two familiar faces were missed from the gang after this occurrence, and it was supposed that the party dropped the dead bodies of their comrades into this pool.

The whole incident doubtless attracted little notice at the time, having been but one of many such, as will be seen by reference to newspapers of the period, and it is related here merely for the purpose of illustrating the extraordinary condition of lawlessness then prevailing in the immediate neighbourhood of the city—a condition now to be found only in some wild mining camp or semi-organised community.

When the delta or slobland formed at the confluence of the Swan Water, the Dodder and the Liffey was embanked and reclaimed in 1792, it became known by the name of New Holland, possibly on account of the desperadoes resorting there, the original New Holland having been a convict colony. This old name has now almost passed out of living memory, but is commemorated in the names " New Holland " in Newbridge Avenue, and " New Holland Lodge," until recently in Bath Avenue.

The ancient district of Baggotrath was an extensive one, and included a considerable portion of the lands on which are now built the south-eastern part of the city, and the adjoining suburbs of Donnybrook and Pembroke. It derives its name from the family of Bagot or Bagod, who came into possession of the Manor of Baggotrath in the 13th century, and soon afterwards erected thereon a castle which they occupied as their residence. The Castle of Baggotrath stood on the ground now occupied by 44 and 46 Upper Baggot Street, down to the early part of last century, when it was taken down on the extension of the suburbs in this direction. *Lewis's Dublin Guide*, published in 1787, gives the following particulars in regard to this old ruin :—" The upper part, " which threatened immediate destruction to all who should " approach its base, was in 1785, taken down ; and what small " fragment of the tower was left was entirely filled up with " stones, earth and other matters, and the whole closed at the " top, so that it is now almost as solid and compact as a rock, " and may bid defiance to the shocks of time."

This castle played an important part in the Battle of Rathmines (see Index), where in August, 1649, the Royalist forces under command of the Marquess, afterwards Duke of Ormonde, were decisively defeated by the Parliamentary garrison of Dublin, commanded by Colonel Michael Jones.

For a long time after the battle, the ruin was a resort of desperadoes and highwaymen, and was considered a dangerous place to pass after dusk.

The office of Governor of Baggotrath Castle, though a sinecure from a remote period, was filled from time to time until the Union, when this appointment, with a number of similar ones, was abolished, and a commutation of the salary paid to Sir John (afterwards Lord) de Blaquière.

The following authorities have been consulted in the preparation of this chapter :—Blacker's *Sketches of the Parishes of Booterstown and Donnybrook ;* Gerard Boate's *Natural History of Ireland ; St. Catherine's Bells*, by W. T. Meyler ; Rocque's and Duncan's *Maps of the County of Dublin ;* Wakeman's *Old Dublin ;* Warburton, Whitelaw and Walsh's *History of Dublin ;* and *The Scandinavian Kingdom of Dublin*, by Charles Haliday.

CHAPTER III

THE ROCK ROAD — BALLSBRIDGE, MERRION, BOOTERSTOWN, BLACKROCK AND MONKSTOWN

LEAVING town by the Kingstown tram route—Lower Mount Street, Northumberland Road and Pembroke Road—we reach Ballsbridge, a name which, originally attaching to a bridge here, at length became extended to the adjacent locality. As the road to Blackrock, Kingstown and Dalkey *via* Stephen's Green and Baggot Street, represents one of the most ancient highways from Dublin, it is highly probable that even from the earliest times, the Dodder was spanned by a bridge at this point, though, no doubt, long periods often elapsed between the decay or destruction of one bridge and the erection of its successor. During the 15th and 16th centuries when, owing to the difficulty of navigating the Liffey, Dalkey was the Port of Dublin, there must have been a continual traffic with passengers and merchandise along this road, and, as the river Dodder can hardly ever have been fordable here, it would have been impossible to convey the heavy cargoes of goods into Dublin in the absence of a bridge of some description.

In *An Historical Sketch of the Pembroke Township*, published in connection with the Dublin Exhibition of 1907, Dr. F. Elrington Ball states that bridges stood here with the names of Simmonscourt and Smothe's Court, and that in the beginning of the 17th century there was a dwelling called " Ball's House " on the site now occupied by Ballsbridge Bakery. This, he considers, is the origin of the name, Ballsbridge.

The maps of the Down Survey (1650, &c.) show no bridge here, but according to Rocque's Map, about one hundred years

later, the river was then spanned by a narrow bridge at this
point, and the immediate neighbourhood was known by its
present designation.   A substantial stone bridge, which was
probably preceded by a wooden one, was erected in 1791, and
this structure was successively rebuilt in 1835 and 1904.

On the way to Ballsbridge, we pass near the site of an
eminence known as Gallows Hill, where the old city gallows
stood, and where the Marquess of Ormonde, in 1649, planted
his artillery to support the party he had told off to fortify
Baggotrath Castle prior to the Battle of Rathmines.[4]

Ballsbridge.
(1905.)

In the early part of the last century Duffy's celebrated
calico print works at Ballsbridge gave employment to some
five hundred hands from this neighbourhood, and the bleach
green extended along the western side of the Dodder the whole
way to the Fair Green at Donnybrook.   The concern was
ultimately purchased by a syndicate of Manchester firms, who
closed and dismantled it to crush out Irish competition.

All this locality was quite rural up to about fifty years ago,
and the Dodder flowed through the fields between sloping
green banks instead of, as at present, between stone embankments.

Besides the main road to Blackrock, &c., *via* Ballsbridge

there appears to have been an equally ancient route *via* Donnybrook bridge or the ford that preceded it, and thence by an
old field-path and double-ditch that ran through the fields
a little south of Aylesbury Road as far as Nutley Lane, where
it turned to the southward, and emerged on the Rock Road at
Old Merrion churchyard. Although in its later years only a
field path, it seems to have been the route taken by the Dublin
Corporation in former times on the occasions of the annual
ceremony of riding the franchises or boundaries of their municipal jurisdiction. The accounts of this ceremony state that on
the way back from Blackrock along the main road to Merrion
Church, the corporators turned up to the left along an ancient
mearing that ran through the fields by the Well of the Blessed
Virgin, to Simmonscourt, and thence to Donnybrook.

This ancient pathway, through the meadows, commanding
charming views of the mountains, was used until about twenty-
five years ago, and the old track and double-ditch can still be
distinctly traced the whole way from where it started at Seaview Terrace, near the upper end of Aylesbury Road, down to
Nutley Lane. Beyond this point nearly all traces of it are lost
for some distance, but indications of a track are again discernible in the grounds of Nutley, behind the boundary wall of
St. Mary's Asylum, and joining Churchyard Lane, which was
probably portion of the old roadway. The Well of the Blessed
Virgin, otherwise called Lady Well, stood beside the path
exactly at the point where the Parliamentary boundary turns
abruptly to the north-west, but it has now disappeared, its
source having probably been disturbed by drainage operations.
This well is marked on Duncan's Map (1820), and its site can
be found on the six-inch Ordnance Survey Map by following
the Parliamentary Boundary to where it turns at right angles,
one hundred and fifty yards south of a point about midway
on Aylesbury Road.

The fact that the line of this old field path coincides for a
considerable portion of its way with the ancient franchise
boundary and the present Parliamentary boundary, would go

to show that some well defined landmark must have existed here from early times.

It is to be regretted that no public interest was taken in this ancient roadway, and that after having been in existence for probably over a thousand years, the extinction of the right-of-way was so recently permitted.

Down to the early part of the last century, the strand from Merrion to Kingstown was the scene of frequent shipping disasters, most of which were probably due to the few and inefficient lighthouses then along this coast.

A traveller's description of the Bay of Dublin, written in 1800, states that the locality is a most dangerous one to shipping, and that :—" The numerous wrecks which take place every " winter, apparent from the masts, which are seen every here " and there peeping above the surface of the water, as it were, " to warn others by their fate, are convincing proofs of the " truth of this assertion " (*Blacker's Sketches*).

Besides the casualties to shipping, however, there were numerous drowning accidents, which cannot be so easily accounted for, as the water in most places is shallow, even at high tide.

After the disasters to the troopships, *Rochdale* and *Prince of Wales*, in 1807, the strand between Merrion and Blackrock acquired such a terrible notoriety by reason of the number of mutilated bodies cast up along it, that a tract was published that year, entitled *The Ensanguined Strand of Merrion*, or a " Stuffing for the Pillow of those who could have prevented " the recent calamity in the Bay of Dublin." This publication drew attention to the dangerous condition of the coast, and advocated improvement in the lighthouses of the Port.

At Merrion there formerly stood, on ground nearly opposite the railway crossing, Merrion Castle, the ancestral home of the Fitzwilliam family, who settled in this locality early in the 15th century. The castle, which was one of the largest structures of its kind in the County Dublin, fell into decay early in the 18th century after its owners moved to Mount Merrion, their new residence, and was partly taken down in 1780. Duncan's Map of the County Dublin (1820) represents the castle as still existing, from which it would seem that portion of the ruins survived until the early part of the 19th century.

A survey of 1654 states that Merrion had been the property of the Lord of Merrion, " an Irish Papist," and that on the lands were an old decayed castle and an extensive rabbit burrow.

Opposite Merrion crossing there was, until about twenty years ago, an inn called " The Coach and Horses," which was

Merrion.
(1897.)

adorned in the old fashion, with an imposing pictorial representation of its title. The building, or portion of it, still remains on the roadside, forming part of the out-offices of the Blind Asylum.

In 1807 this inn was visited one night by ten highwaymen, who robbed the proprietor of all the ready money he had in his possession, amounting to £60, and leisurely proceeded to divide the spoils. They then adjourned to the bar parlour, where they remained for about an hour drinking, and the health of the host was proposed and drunk with much enthusiasm, after which the unbidden guests departed with many apologies for their intrusion.

On the south side of Churchyard Lane, and close to the

main road, is the Old Merrion churchyard, now neglected and
forgotten, enclosed by a high wall, and exhibiting no outward
indications of its existence. Of the thousands of people who pass
within a few yards of it every day, probably not a dozen have
ever heard of it. Yet it was well known in former times, before
this locality was so extensively built over, and many a prominent
citizen of his day sleeps within the circuit of its mouldering
walls, undisturbed by the modern innovations that have grown
up around his last resting-place. Dalton, writing in 1837,
states that " the old church presents some few but insignificant
" remains, in the middle of a graveyard most scandalously
" open to every species of insult and desecration."

No remains of the church are now distinguishable in the
jungle of weeds and brambles with which the place is overgrown, but a number of headstones, some of them a couple of
hundred years old, remain in excellent preservation. In the
churchyard are some ancient trees, and the trunks of others
blown down by storms. Immediately inside the wall, next the
lane, is a headstone erected to the memory of the soldiers who
perished in the transport packet *Prince of Wales* in 1807. It
bears the following inscription :—

> " Sacred to the memory of the soldiers belonging to
> " His Majesty's 18th Regiment of Foot, and a few belonging
> " to other corps, who, actuated by a desire of more ex-
> " tensive service, nobly volunteered from the South Mayo
> " and different Regiments of Irish Militia into the line
> " and who were unfortunately shipwrecked on this coast
> " in the *Prince of Wales* Packet, and perished on the night
> " of the 19th of November, 1807. This tribute to their
> " memory has been placed on their tomb by order of
> " General the Earl of Harrington, Commander of the
> " Forces in Ireland."

Walsh's Impartial News Letter of 16th May, 1729, contains
the following curious item of news in regard to this neighbourhood :—" This morning we have an account from Merian that
" a parcel of these outlandish Marramounts which are called

" Mountain Rats who are now here grown very common . . .
" walk in droves and do a great deal of mischief." The account
then goes on to relate how these mysterious pests devoured a
woman and a nurse-child in Merrion, and that the inhabitants
" killed several which are as big as Katts and Rabbits. . . .
" This part of the country is infested with them. Likewise
" we hear from Rathfarnham that the like vermin destroyed
" a little Girl in the Fields."

Passing out of Merrion, we presently enter Booterstown, a
locality held in high repute as a fashionable summer watering
place, and the scene of much gaiety a hundred years ago. In
1435 the name appears as Ballybothyr, or town of the road,
from its position on the ancient road to Dunleary and Bray,
and this name, by a translation of the first portion, resolved
itself in time into Butterstown or Booterstown.

Ferrar, in his *View of Dublin* (1796), writes enthusiastically
of the strand here :—" To ride over the extensive strand from
" hence to Booterstown, while the waves roll over the horse's
" feet ; to see numerous ships with expanded wings passing and
" re-passing the azure main ; to see so many groups of men,
" women and children bathing, walking, jaunting, coaching,
" in pursuit of that inestimable blessing, health ; to consider that
" we are within ten hours' sailing of Britain's favourite isle,
" added an indescribable gaiety to our spirits."

Thirty years later, in 1826, Brewer in his *Beauties of Ireland*
describes the road at Booterstown as being " enlivened, par-
" ticularly at a time of bathing, with numberless carriages of
" various descriptions, from the well appointed equipage, at
" once convenient and superb, down to the jaunting car of
" passage, drawn by one miserable garron, so ill-fed, so ill-
" groomed and lean, that it would appear to be scarcely
" capable of accelerating its own dissolution by an effort
" towards speed of foot. . . . The street of transit, thickly
" lined with houses of an ordinary description, holds forth no
" charms, and independent of some agreeable and ornamental
" dwellings retired from the busy thoroughfare, the sole

" inducement to visitants is found in the facility of bathing on
" the soft and gently sloping strand."

.   .   .   .

" Going to the County of Wicklow, the road to Blackrock
" is evidently the pleasantest, most frequented, and level.
" At Booterstown the fields are disposed in a style of judicious
" husbandry, the villas are neat and commodious. . . . The
" elevation of the road contributes greatly to the pleasure of
" the traveller. The vast expanse of the prospect, opening on
" the wide expanse of the ocean, the steep, indented shore,
" the strand stretching three miles to the lighthouse, the
" fertile, verdant banks, everywhere fringed with wood and
" hanging gardens."

This delightful picture became completely altered by the
construction of the railway in 1832–1834, and the old sea-wall,
over which, prior to that time, the storm-driven waves had
often swept on to the road, thenceforth became the boundary
of a foul-smelling salt marsh, the exhalations from which in
time drove everyone out of the neighbourhood except those
whose circumstances obliged them to reside there.[5]

The road next passes through Williamstown, until recently
a ruinous and miserable looking village, but now improved out
of all recognition, the removal of the houses on the inland side
of the road bringing prominently into the view the imposing
buildings of the French College. There is nothing of interest,
topographical or historical, to chronicle here, and we next
enter Blackrock, once a fashionable watering place, but, like
Booterstown, ruined as a seaside resort by the railway, which
did the double damage of cutting off access to the shore and
at the same time bringing more attractive places within easy
reach of the city. For many years Blackrock languished in a
dilapidated condition until it was constituted into a township,
when great improvements resulted, and from a decayed village
it rapidly grew into a prosperous suburb, while an attractive
park replaced the malodorous swamp enclosed by the railway
embankment.

No vestige whatever of the " black rock " (calp limestone), which originated the name of this locality, can now be discovered *in situ*. It is said that some few feet of it remained above the sand before the People's Park was laid out, but if so, the deposits of rubbish to raise the level have long since covered it. The original vein of this rock was extensively used in connection with the railway, and some of it may be seen in the walls near the station, as well as on the top of the sea wall along the railway near Williamstown. Although not of a dark colour in a dry condition, it becomes when wet almost black, and in its original position on the shore, wetted by the waves and spray, must have presented, from the sea, so striking a contrast to the granite beside it, as inevitably to command attention.

In *A Narrative of an Excursion to Ireland*, by members of the Honorable Irish Society of London, privately circulated in 1825, the writer, referring to a journey from Dublin to Blackrock, says :—" There are some very neat cottages on the road, " the thatching of which is the very best work of the kind I " have ever seen, and although I had heard much of the neat- " ness of these buildings, they far exceeded my most sanguine " expectations. I looked out in various directions for the " Black Rock, expecting to see some stupendous mass—

> " ' Huge as the tower which builders vain
> " ' Presumptuous piled on Shinar's plain.'

' but could find nothing more than a dark coloured limestone " crag, just peeping above the surface near the water's edge."

From this it would appear that even so far back as 1825, the original Black Rock had nearly disappeared, either as the result of artificial removal or long continued erosion by the sea.

The " Rock " was under what is now the Park-keeper's lodge, formerly the Peafield Baths. Between forty and fifty years ago these baths were fairly well patronised, and a row of bathing boxes stood on the shore, now portion of the public park, a culvert through the railway embankment allowing the water to enter and pass out with the tide.

Blackrock, some hundreds of years ago was variously called
Newtown-at-the Black Rock, Newtown on the Strand by the
Black Rock, Newtown Castle Byrne, or simply Newtown, so
that " Blackrock " is simply an abbreviation of one of its ancient
titles.

At the upper end of the main street, upon a pedestal, stands
the ancient cross of Blackrock, which, from a remote period,

Blackrock Cross.

marked the limit of the municipal jurisdiction in this direction.
This relic of the olden time was owned and kept in repair by
the Byrne family, from whom the name Newtown Castle Byrne
is derived.   The Dublin Corporation, when riding the franchises, crossed the sands from near Poolbeg to " the Black Rock,"
and thence by low water mark to a point opposite the cross,
where one of the party waded out as far as he could, and cast
a javelin into the sea, to indicate the limit of the boundary
eastward.   The procession then rode by old Bath Street to the
cross, and thence along the main road to Old Merrion churchyard, already alluded to.

In 1865 it was proposed to replace the cross by a new one, but public opinion in the locality declared itself in so unmistakable a fashion against such an act of vandalism, that the project was abandoned.

Blackrock in the 18th century was a great social centre, and the residence or resort of many distinguished people. Conway's Tavern, the scene of many a brilliant function, stood in the main street, on the right-hand side entering George's Avenue, and the annual melon feast held there was an event of great local interest, gold and silver medals being awarded to the producers of the best melons grown in the neighbourhood.

An article on Blackrock which appears in Walker's *Hibernian Magazine* for 1783, states that :—" This is a noble village, " situated about three miles from the north-east corner of " Stephen's Green, on a rising ground south of the Bay of " Dublin ; it consists of a considerable number of elegant " country houses, and in summer it is much resorted to by the " citizens for the purpose of bathing. In fine evenings it is as " much crowded with carriages as the most populous streets in " the city ; and as there is a number of genteel families residing " here at this season of the year, they have drums and assemblies " as in town, whereby it is very sprightly and agreeable to such " as have nothing to do."

The Vauxhall Gardens, which were opened here in 1793, were, for a time, a favourite place of public amusement until the fickleness of fashion consigned them to obscurity. The house had previously been called Fort Lisle by the first Lord Lisle, who built it as a residence for himself. The following notice of the gardens appears in *The Dublin Chronicle* of 29th June, 1793 :—

" VAUXHALL GARDENS, BLACKROCK, FORMERLY OCCUPIED BY LORD
" LISLE.

" The proprietors of the above place respectfully inform " the nobility and gentry residing at and visiting the Rock, " that they have engaged a complete military band to attend

" on Tuesday next, and every Tuesday and Monday from 5 to
" 9 p.m. They humbly solicit public patronage and support,
" which they will anxiously endeavour to deserve. Admittance
" on the music nights, 6½d. The house is laid out in a style
" of elegance as a hotel and tavern, and provided with every
" accommodation, equal to any house in England or Ireland."
A further advertisement in the same journal states that
" the house is furnished with everything in season—bowers,
" grottoes, interspersed through the dark, shady walks—make
" the garden truly romantic, and the effect the music has on
" the sea, which flows at the foot of the garden, can better be
" imagined than expressed."
Notwithstanding these alluring announcements, Vauxhall
Gardens failed to obtain the patronage and support so humbly
solicited by its proprietors. In 1804 the place was advertised
for sale, and after experiencing a succession of changes and
vicissitudes as a private house, boarding school, and industrial
school, it was at length demolished when the People's Park was
being laid out. The house stood on the ground now occupied
by the entrance gate to the Park, and the grounds sloped down
to the water's edge.

Perhaps the most interesting house from a historic point of
view in this neighbourhood is Frascati, formerly the seaside
seat of the Leinster family, and the favourite residence of the
unfortunate Lord Edward Fitzgerald. Here he spent many
happy years with his talented young wife, and appears to have
been greatly attached to the locality. After his death Frascati
became the residence of the Dowager Duchess of Leinster, and
was subsequently sold to Sir Henry Cavendish, Receiver-
General for Ireland. In 1804 it became a boarding school, and
afterwards underwent considerable alterations on being divided
into two dwellinghouses.

In 1787 the state of the Rock Road became so dangerous
owing to highwaymen, that a special meeting of the Blackrock
Association was held in Jennett's Tavern, with Lord Ranelagh
in the chair, to consider the best means of ridding the road of

these pests. They offered £20 reward to anyone prosecuting to conviction persons guilty of highway robbery or burglary on the road between Dublin and Dunleary, and, finding the local watch useless, established a nightly patrol from Blackrock to Baggot Street to protect passengers.

The following extract from *The Chronicle* of 5th July, 1792, throws an interesting sidelight on the means of communication with Dublin in those days :—" Sunday night an affray happened " at Blackrock. The new carriage, called the Royal George, " which passes between Dublin and the Rock, and carries, with " perfect accommodation, sixteen passengers, was the object of " an envious attack, made by the drivers of jaunting cars, " noddies, &c. Fortunately, some gentlemen of rank and spirit " were passengers in the George, who, aided by the gentlemen " resident in the village, not only protected that useful vehicle " but made two of the assailants prisoners."

After the exodus of the gentry from Dublin and its neighbourhood consequent upon the Union, Blackrock fell rapidly into decay, and many of the large houses were untenanted or abandoned for years, until there was a slight revival of the place as a bathing resort in the early part of the last century.

This neighbourhood was in 1807 the scene of a fearful tragedy, almost without parallel in shipping disasters on the Dublin coast. On Wednesday afternoon, the 18th November, two transport vessels, the *Prince of Wales* and *The Rochdale*, sailed in company of some others from the Pigeonhouse harbour with volunteers for foreign service drawn from Irish militia regiments. A snowstorm set in soon after their departure, accompanied by a violent easterly gale, and on the following morning they were observed labouring in the heavy sea outside the Bay to the southward, endeavouring, as it was believed, to return to the harbour. As the day advanced the snow fell so thickly that it was impossible for them to see their way, while the sea was so violent that they could not come to anchor. After a long and futile struggle, the *Prince of Wales* was driven on to the rocks behind Sir John Lees' residence, Blackrock House.

The long boat was launched, and Captain Jones, the crew, two soldiers and the steward's wife and child jumped into it and rowed off as speedily as possible. In the darkness of the night they seem to have rowed for some distance along the shore, of the proximity of which they were ignorant, until one of the sailors falling overboard, found that he was in shallow water. Upon this the whole party walked ashore and made their way to Blackrock, where they found shelter. Extraordinary to relate, they made no effort whatever to rescue the passengers on board (about 120 in number), who were left to their fate and perished without exception.

The fate of *The Rochdale* was even worse. On the day after her departure she was observed from Blackrock, labouring heavily in the offing, burning blue lights and firing guns as signals of distress, but the weather was such that no succour could be afforded. She threw out several anchors, but they dragged and snapped their cables, and she then drove with bare poles before the storm. Driven gradually towards the shore in the direction of Sandycove, she swept in the darkness past the old pier at Dunleary, and struck on the rocks under the Martello Tower at Seapoint, half a mile from where the *Prince of Wales* struck. Of the troops on board, their families, and the ship's officers and crew (some 265 in all), not one escaped, and their mutilated bodies were found in great numbers next morning strewn along the shore.

When the ill-fated vessel was driving past the pier at Dunleary, the inhabitants of the adjoining houses could hear the cries of the terrified passengers and the reports of the muskets which they fired to attract assistance. Some people on the east side of the old harbour seeing the flashes and hearing the reports, ran round to the westward in the hope of affording help, but on reaching the road at Salthill, they were obliged to lie down behind the parapet abutting on the sea to protect themselves from the bullets fired in the dark by the despairing troops on board.

The wrecked vessel was poised in an extraordinary manner

on the rocks at the foot of the tower, and lay so close to the shore that a twelve-foot plank sufficed to reach to her quarter-deck, but at the time she struck, the night was so dark and the snowstorm so dense that the unhappy passengers were doubtless unable to see anything off the vessel, and were consequently unaware of their proximity to the land. The Martello Tower, which is shown in a contemporary print of the disaster, was probably unoccupied at the time.

Nearly four hundred lives were lost in this double disaster, and for days afterwards the bodies of men, women and chi'dren were cast up by the sea along the coast from Merrion to Kingstown. The bodies of *The Rochdale* victims were in almost every case unrecognisable owing to the violence with which they were dashed to death on the rocks or torn to pieces by the action of the sea in the hold of the vessel after she commenced to break up. Most of them were interred in the old Monkstown churchyard, while those from the *Prince of Wales* were buried at Merrion as already stated.

Owing to the plundering of the bodies and the thefts of articles from the wrecks, a detachment of soldiers was stationed at intervals along the shore for some days after the occurrence.

The bottom of *The Rochdale* was completely smashed, but the decks to a great extent remained unbroken. The entire of the following Sunday was spent in removing the bodies from the holds of both the wrecks.

At the inquest on the thirty-seven bodies found in the wreck of the *Prince of Wales*, which were laid out in Sir John Lees' coachhouse, Captain Jones deposed that on Thursday morning when the snowstorm was in progress, he commenced to back, facing towards Howth. About 7 o'clock in the evening the vessel struck, and the waves broke over her, whereupon they launched the boat.

One of the witnesses, a soldier, stated that the Captain, after he had assured them that there was no danger, proceeded to hoist the boat, and that when he, the witness, got into it, the Captain endeavoured to throw him overboard. It was also alleged that the Captain, with a view to facilitating his own escape and that of the crew, removed the ladder communicating from the cabin to the deck, thereby depriving the unfortunate passengers below, of any chance of escape. Another witness deposed that he heard the Captain say that " he did'nt care " a —— who were lost, provided that his own men were saved."

An inquest was also held on the seventy-three bodies found on *The Rochdale*, but nothing of importance transpired, as the

Scene of "The Rochdale" disaster, Seapoint.
(1911.)

completeness of the disaster had deprived the proceedings of all material testimony.

After the inquests had concluded, the captain, mate and steward of the *Prince of Wales* were arrested on a charge of murder, for having removed the ladders communicating from the hold to the deck, while the crew were escaping from the vessel. The remainder of the crew were detained as witnesses pending the trial, but when the case came on in December, the Crown abandoned the proceedings, finding, presumably, that the evidence was insufficient.

The Martello Tower at Seapoint at the present day looks a rather unlikely place for a shipping disaster, but it must be remembered that all the coast along here was much altered by the construction of the railway, and that many of the sharp rocks which proved so fatal to the victims are now covered over by the embankment and by the adjoining road and houses ; moreover, in 1807, the immediate locality was so lonely and unfrequented that a vessel might easily be wrecked there at night without attracting notice. The scene of the *Prince of Wales* wreck is a reef of dark, jagged rocks projecting from the shore immediately behind Blackrock House, and easily identified by an ornamental embattled structure overlooking this spot of tragic memories. It is accessible on foot at low water only, and is visible from Seapoint Martello Tower, from which it is distant almost exactly half a mile.

The rocks all along this portion of the shore are so sharp and irregular that even in fine weather it is a difficult task for an active person to climb them without injury, so that it is not surprising that at night during a snowstorm, in a furious sea impelled by an easterly gale, not even one of the unfortunate passengers cast ashore on these cruel crags escaped.

Passing out of Blackrock by the main road, we reach Temple Hill, a little beyond which, on the right, is Montpelier Parade, one of the first terraces built in this locality. An illustration in *The Hibernian Magazine* represents this place as it appeared in 1802, the terrace having been completed a few years earlier by a Mr. Molesworth Green, with the idea of making this a residential neighbourhood. At the time it was built, this terrace must have enjoyed an uninterrupted view of the sea, as there were no houses to the south or east of it ; but notwithstanding its attractive situation, it is surprising if any city people lived so far away from town in those days, when we consider the dangers of the road to Dublin owing to highwaymen, as well as the absence of any regular means of communication with the Metropolis.

In the picture referred to, also appears the tower of old Monkstown Church, taken down in 1832 to make room for the nondescript edifice which now disfigures its site.

Turning to the right at Monkstown Church up Carrick-brennan Road, we arrive at Monkstown Castle, situated within the grounds of the modern residence of the same name, and forming a picturesque and extensive ruin. It is enclosed by a grove of trees, and must originally have been a large building.

It is not certain when this castle was built, but it is recorded

Monkstown Castle.
(1905.)

that in 1546 it was granted to Sir John Travers for his services to the Crown, and that in 1565 Sir Henry Sidney, the Viceroy, passed the night here after his debarkation. From 1650 to 1660 the castle was in possession of General Ludlow, one of the regicides, who constantly alludes to it in his memoirs (*Ludlow's Memoirs*), and mentions the details of several conversations he had with the Protector's son, Colonel Henry Cromwell. Describing one of these, he writes :—" There on " a subsequent occasion, after a short collation, walking in the

" garden, I acquainted him with the grounds of my dissatis-
" faction with the present state of affairs in England, which I
" assured him was in no sort personal, but would be the same
" were my own father alive, and in the place of his. He told
" me that his father looked upon me to be dissatisfied upon a
" distinct account from most men in the three nations, and
" thereupon affirmed that he knew it to be his resolution to
" carry himself with all tenderness towards me."

Monkstown is mentioned in that famous hunting song of
the 18th century, " The Kilruddery Hunt " (see Index), as
being one of the places through which the fox passed during an
exciting hunt in the winter of 1744. Needless to say, the
locality must have been thoroughly rural at that time, when
the fox considered it safe to make his route through it, and the
huntsmen were able to follow him in hot pursuit across the
country.

Close to the Castle is the old Monkstown or Carrickbrennan
Churchyard, where are buried many of the victims of the
shipping disaster of 1807.

The following authorities were consulted in the preparation
of this chapter :—" The Antiquities from Kingstown to
" Dublin," by the late Rev. Dr. Stokes, published in the
Journals of the Royal Society of Antiquaries for 1895 and 1900 ;
Hill's *Guide to Blackrock ;* Ball's *History of the County of
Dublin ;* Dalton's *History of the County Dublin ;* Wakeman's
Old Dublin ; Blacker's *Sketches of Donnybrook and Booterstown ;*
Brewer's *Beauties of Ireland,* and various Dublin newspapers
and magazines of 1807.

CHAPTER IV

DUNLEARY, KINGSTOWN, AND DALKEY

PASSING in succession through the various localities along the Rock Road, we enter Kingstown, known prior to 1821 as Dunleary, and still having portion of it distinguished by that ancient designation. Since that time the town has advanced from an obscure fishing village and watering place to one of the most important seaports in Ireland—a change in its fortunes due to two distinct causes—namely, the establishment of the Mail Packet station, with its fine harbour of refuge, and the connection with Dublin by rail.

The carrying out of the great works in connection with the Dublin and Kingstown Railway in the years 1832-4, excited an extraordinary amount of interest in Dublin, as it was the first railway constructed in Ireland. On the conclusion of the undertaking, *The Dublin Penny Journal* published a number of illustrated articles on the subject, in one of which, inspired by the importance of the occasion, it magnificently observed :—

" Hurried by the invisible but stupendous agency of steam,
" the astonished passenger will now glide, like Asmodeus,
" over the summits of the houses and streets of a great city—
" presently be transported through green fields and tufts of
" trees—then skim across the surface of the sea, and taking
" shelter under the cliffs, coast along the marine villas and
" through rocky excavations, until he finds himself in the
" centre of a vast port, which unites in pleasing confusion the
" bustle of a commercial town with the amusements of a
" fashionable watering-place."

When we consider the importance of the railway as a factor in the development of Kingstown, it is not a little amusing to learn that when it was proposed to build the terminus in its present position, the inhabitants offered every opposition to the proposed desecration of their town by this vulgar and democratic mode of conveyance, and ultimately succeeded in obtaining an alteration in the Bill for the construction of the railway, so as to prevent the company from bringing it nearer than the commencement of the West Pier. The terminus accordingly was erected at this point, and the grateful inhabitants, all danger being then over, presented Mr. Gresham, of hotel fame, with an address and five hundred sovereigns in recognition of his valiant and successful defence of their town against the attempted invasion by the railway company. In after years, when the inhabitants had grown accustomed to the innovation, the railway was extended to the point occupied by the present station.

Wisdom comes frequently after the event, and if we feel inclined to laugh at what looks like folly on the part of the good folk of 1834, let us remember that a few years ago, when the electric trams first ran to Kingstown, the cars had to start from Northumberland Road, and that there was fierce opposition to the proposal to run them through the streets of the city.

The old picturesque name of Dunleary, meaning Leary's Fort, was originally applied to a dun or rath, standing on ground where a Martello tower, long since taken down, was erected in the last century, and where the Coastguard Station now stands. This dun and many other interesting relics were ruthlessly swept away during the construction of the railway through the district.

This neighbourhood was in vogue as a summer wateringplace so far back as the beginning of the 18th century, and although communication with England was, at that time, principally made from Ringsend direct, a considerable number of packets also sailed from Dunleary. Arthur Young, in his *Tour in Ireland*, relates how on 19th June, 1776, he embarked at Holyhead on board *The Claremont* packet, and arrived the next day at Dunleary. A hotel and coffee-house for the reception and entertainment of travellers then flourished at this place, and an illustration of it appears in *The Hibernian Magazine* for 1803. The old building, though much altered, still remains, overlooking the Monkstown gas works, and contains the original inn kitchen.

About 1760, a harbour was formed at Dunleary by the construction of a small pier about 200 yards in length, which although insufficient for the requirements of the locality, un-

The Dunleary Coffee House in 1803.
From "The Hibernian Magazine."

doubtedly afforded effective protection against the east and south-easterly gales, so full of evil memories along this coast. In a few years, however, the harbour began to fill with sand, and in time became quite useless.

After some years of agitation, stimulated by the failure of Howth Harbour as a packet station, the necessary Parliamentary authority was obtained for the construction of a harbour of refuge, and in 1817 the first stone of the East Pier was laid by the Lord Lieutenant, the pier being finished four years later, when the visit of King George IV. was made the occasion for superseding the old name of the town by the modern one. The construction of the west pier followed, together with many minor alterations and improvements which were not concluded until 1859.

The stones for this great work were drawn from Dalkey Hill on lorries running on a tramway, still owned by the Harbour Commissioners, and locally known as "The Metals." The immense amount of stone taken from the hill materially decreased its bulk and quite altered its appearance, and so ex-

Kingstown Harbour and George's Monument.
(1897.)

tensive were the various works in connection with the undertaking that the employment of a small army of workmen became necessary, descendants of whom remain to the present day near the original settlement beside the quarries.

About the time that Kingstown first assumed its modern title, a person standing on the ground now occupied by Sandycove Railway Station, and looking along the open country road towards the newly-named town, beheld a view which, except for its setting, would scarcely be recognised by a modern inhabitant. Not a house intervened between the observer and a group of cottages around the Royal Marine Hotel ; and about

midway on the inland side a massive rock surmounted by a
half-moon battery overhung the road, forming a conspicuous
object in the view. Only one pier, the eastern one, sheltered
the new packet station, and as yet no pier lighthouse showed
its welcome beams to the storm-tossed mariner seeking the
refuge of the port. To the right of the main road, fields sloped
down to the sea, where a few cottages and cabins were scattered
at intervals along a rough bridle path that skirted the rocky
shore. Opposite the Royal Marine Road, Patrick Street and
Mulgrave Street were represented by a few small terraces,
while to the right of these, rising through its scaffolding, was
the tallest building in the neighbourhood, the Royal Marine
Hotel, then in course of erection, towering high above the
humble dwellings adjoining. In the distance might be seen the
South Wall and the squat form of the old Poolbeg Lighthouse,
with Howth and the northern shores of the Bay.

Immediately in the foreground to the right was a Martello
tower, surrounded by a kind of circumvallation, partly artificial
and partly natural, and situated on a slight eminence overlooking the harbour. This tower has long since been taken
down to make room for building, but indications of the eminence
on which it stood may be seen in the rising ground on the left
hand side of Martello Avenue, close to Sandycove Railway
Station.

The rock on which stood the battery was removed by blasting
some fifty years ago, and while the operations were in progress,
passengers and traffic were warned by a bell rung on the road
some minutes before the firing. The name Stoneview, applied
to the portion of Upper George's Street now occupying its
site, commemorates the existence of this almost forgotten
landmark.

At the present day, instead of the rural aspect described
above, houses extend the whole way from Kingstown to Dalkey,
with the exception of a short open space beyond Bullock ; and
the once detached villages intervening have become absorbed
in the adjoining townships.

Shortly after passing out of the main street of Kingstown and crossing the railway, we enter Glasthule, where may be seen traces of the original village which derives its name from a little stream (*Glas*) flowing into Scotch Bay, and Tuathail or Toole, a surname, the whole name meaning Toole's stream.

Immediately adjoining Glasthule is Sandycove, a name which originated with the little haven there, and was subsequently applied to the rocky point on which a battery or fort, now dismantled, and a Martello tower were erected. The fort was, until a few years ago, occupied by the military,

Sandycove Point.
(1904.)

and at certain seasons of the year was utilised for artillery practice, the firing causing much havoc among the windows of the adjoining houses.

About the beginning of the last century an extravagant scheme was propounded to construct a ship canal from Sandycove by Monkstown and Stillorgan to Milltown, where it was to cross the Dodder valley by a gigantic aqueduct, proceeding thence in a direct course to James's Street Harbour. The object was to connect Kingstown with the canal traffic through the interior of the country, but it is not clear what commensurate advantage could have been anticipated from so costly and chimerical a project as compared with sailing up the Liffey as far as Ringsend Canal Docks.

D

Beyond Sandycove is Bullock, a town of some note in ancient times, where the ruin of a fine castle stands in a commanding and conspicuous position over the harbour. The castle is an oblong building, originally two storeys high, flanked by towers of unequal height, rising above the body of the structure at the ends. One of these towers, upon its ground floor, contains the original doorway and inner porch. A spiral staircase communicates with the upper apartments and leads to a series of small rooms in the same tower. There is a garderobe on the first floor, and the upper walls are gracefully battlemented. There was formerly a rocking stone at Bullock, which was sketched by Gabriel Beranger in 1777, but was removed about the beginning of the last century.

Goshawks—so-called from their habit of preying on wild geese—were found in the neighbourhood of Bullock until about a hundred years ago.

The port or harbour of Bullock was known from a very early period, and as far back as 1346 the Cistercian Monks of St. Mary's Abbey, Dublin, who built the castle there, established their right to exact from every fishing boat entering the harbour a toll of one of their best fish, herrings excepted ; and from every herring boat a meise (about 600 fish) annually.

Bullock in early times seems to have been a self-contained settlement, enclosed by a wall, strongly fortified, besides being equipped with a church, so as to avoid any unnecessary risks to the inhabitants entailed by attendance at places of worship outside. (Ball's *History of the County Dublin.*)

In 1402, Prince Thomas of Lancaster, the King's son, landed at Bullock as Lord Lieutenant, and in 1559 the Earl of Sussex, as Lord Deputy. In 1611 the town and lands of Bullock are described as consisting of one castle, one ruinous tower, thirty dwelling-houses, 10 acres of meadow, 200 acres of pasture and furze, with the fishing and haven to the main sea. (Dalton's *History of the County Dublin*).

Clarendon's *History of the Rebellion and Civil Wars in Ireland* contains the following reference to Bullock :—

" In the same week [2 November, 1641] fifty-six Men, Women
" and Children, of the village of Bullogge (being frighted at
" what was done at Clontarff) took boats and went to sea, to
" shun the Fury of a party of Soldiers come out of Dublin,
" under the command of Colonel Crafford, but being pursued
" by the Soldiers in other boats, were overtaken and thrown
" overboard."

The incident at Clontarf referred to is the burning of the
village by Sir Charles Coote in 1641.

A serious affray between a party of smugglers and the local
Revenue officers occurred here in 1735, and is described as
follows in *The Dublin Weekly Journal* of 26th April, 1735 :—

" Last week some of the King's officers made a seizure of a
" large quantity of tea and brandy at Bullock ; and next
" morning several persons attempted to rescue it from the
" officers, which occasioned a great battle, in which several
" were wounded on both sides ; one Mr. Brown, an officer,
" was shot through the thigh, and 'tis thought two of the
" smugglers were killed."

As we pass the little harbour, the road rises considerably,
affording an extensive view of Dublin Bay, and we now enter
on the only remaining bit of wild rocky country between
Dublin and Dalkey—a gap which doubtless, within the next
few years, will be filled by terraces and dwellinghouses.

We next reach Dalkey, formerly a port of great importance,
to which most of the goods consigned to Dublin by sea were at
one time shipped, owing to the difficulty of navigating the
Port of Dublin before the construction of the great South
Wall.

In 1306, it appears that the King made a complaint that the
wines sent to him from Ireland arrived in a sour and deteriorated
condition, and an inquiry upon oath was thereupon instituted
to ascertain the cause. The commissioners found that the wines
in question were shipped from Bordeaux to Dalkey where they
were reshipped to Skinburness on the Solway Firth, and that
the deterioration complained of was caused, not by any default

of the mariners or merchants, but by the tempestuous nature of the latter voyage, which was usually from one to two months in duration.

In 1369 one Reginald Talbot was sued in the Court of Exchequer for delivering therein, as the rent of his estate at Dalkey, one goshawk, which on inspection and examination proved unsound, unfit, and of no value, and inasmuch as the same was a fraud on the Court, and a grievous damage to the King, the said Reginald Talbot was fined.

Goshawks were highly prized in the days of falconry as being a large and powerful variety of hawk.

Many passengers of distinction landed here from time to time, and in 1396 the place had become of such note that King Richard II. granted to the Archbishop of Dublin the privilege of exercising the rights of Admiral or Water Bailiff of this port. A contemporary document on this subject states that " there is no anchorage or good lying for great ships " coming into the Port of Dublin with wines, salt, corn, and " other merchandises, freighted for Dublin from foreign parts, " only at the Port of the Archbishop of Dublin in the town " of Dalkey, which is six level miles from Dublin, and out of " the port and liberties of the city, at which place they are " bound to unload, and there is no other port in the neighbour- " hood where they can ride so safe from storm, and the mer- " chants were wont to buy their goods at said port of Dalkey " as well as in the port of Dublin and other ports, to land same " and to bring it up on cars or in boats to the city, and there " land same and pay the customs." (Dalton's *History of the County Dublin*).

It was at this period of its history that the castles of Dalkey, originally seven in number, were built for the storage of the merchandise and valuables landed there, where they could be protected against the predatory incursions of " the Irish " enemie " until such time as they could be safely escorted to Dublin.

In 1451 the King appointed as bailiff of Dalkey, James Prendergast, portion of whose duties was to receive all customs and dues, payable to the municipal authorities of Dublin, arising out of the sale of merchandise and wares at the fairs of Dalkey, of which seven were annually held ; such customs, &c., to be applied towards walling and paving the city of Dublin, of which Dalkey was then the port.

In 1538 Walter Cowley landed here with treasure for the King's service in Ireland. An account of his disbursements in this behalf is preserved in the State Paper Office, and the treasure is certified to have been conveyed in two hampers on pack horses to Holyhead *via* St. Alban's, Brickhill, Towcester, Daventry, Coventry, Lichfield, Vyleybridge, Stone, Nantwich, Chester, Conway, Rhuddlan and Beaumaris.

For further information in regard to this locality and Dalkey Island, see next chapter.

CHAPTER V

CARRICKMINES CASTLE; THE VALE OF SHAN-
GANAGH; DALKEY, KILLINEY AND BALLY-
BRACK HILLS

THE three above-named hills, which so gracefully sentinel
the southern shores of Dublin Bay, are seen to great
advantage from the inland side, for which reason
Carrickmines has been selected as the starting point for this
excursion. Carrickmines can, of course, be most readily
reached by train from Harcourt Street, but those desiring a
longer walk might, perhaps, get out at Dundrum, proceeding
thence by Sandyford, after which the third turn on the left
should be taken. Just at the turn is a high whitewashed wall,
in the masonry of which, over a former entrance door, is a
tablet bearing the quaint inscription :—" Content in a Cottage,
"and Envy to no One. BD. M. 1771." A secluded road about
two miles in length, conducts us thence to Carrickmines,
formerly Carrigmayne, a locality of great historic interest and
the site of a castle, portion of which still remains.

During the Insurrection of 1641, a strong body of the insurgents established themselves in the castle, to dislodge whom a
small body of cavalry was sent out from Dublin on a Saturday
in the month of March, under command of Sir Simon Harcourt,
an officer of experience and distinction. When he arrived there,
however, he found that the castle and its garrison were much
stronger than he had expected, and that to attack would be
hopeless with the force at his disposal, the smallness of which
excited the derision of the defenders on the battlements ; and,
accordingly, he sent to Dublin for reinforcements. As these
did not reach the place until late that night, he decided to

defer the assault until next day, encircling the castle meanwhile with his forces, and placing musketeers and horsemen alternately in the cordon, with the view of preventing the escape of any of the garrison.

Signal fires were lit on the battlements after dark, and others answering them on the surrounding mountains, revealed the proximity of the insurgents in such numbers that Sir Simon

View from Sorrento.
(1900.)

Harcourt hesitated to make the attack even with his reinforcements, and sent into town for further assistance. During the interval the garrison were not idle, utilising every opportunity that presented itself, by sorties and musket fire, of inflicting losses upon the besiegers. In repelling one of these sorties, early on Sunday morning, Sergeant-Major Berry was mortally wounded by a shot in the side. At this time Harcourt with some of his officers, had taken shelter behind a thatched cabin, but incautiously exposing himself to give commands, he was picked out by one of the sharpshooters in the castle armed with a long piece which had already done great execution, and shot in the breast under the neck bone. He attempted to walk away, assisted by two of his men, but had to desist from weakness, and as it was then seen that he was seriously wounded, a vehicle was procured, and he at once set out for Dublin accompanied by an escort. The jolting on the way, however, occasioned him such pain that the party decided to break the journey at Merrion, leaving him at Lord Fitzwilliam's castle, where he died next day.

Further reinforcements with artillery having now arrived, Lieut.-Colonel Gibson, the next in command, ordered a bombardment and general attack, which was met with desperate resistance by the defenders, but the superior numbers and equipment of the besiegers prevailed, and they at length succeeded in making a breach sufficiently large to effect an entry into the building. The first two that entered were killed, but they were followed by others who, acting under orders, deliberately proceeded to slaughter the entire garrison, with a great number of women and children who had taken refuge in the building, to the number of about 200 to 300 in all. The castle was then blown up. The besiegers lost about 40 altogether in this action.

The authorities from which this account has been compiled are :—A tract, entitled *The Last True Intelligence from Ireland* " (1641), and Borlase's *History of the Irish Rebellion*.

In Lord Clarendon's *History of the Rebellion and Civil Wars in Ireland* (p. 343), however, it is stated that quarter had been given by Lt.-Col. Gibson before the slaughter :—" After " quarter given by Lt.-Col. Gibson, to those of the Castle " of Carrigmayne, they were all put to the sword, being about " three hundred and fifty, most of them women and children, " and Col. Washington endeavouring to save a pretty child of " seven years of age, carried him under his cloak, but the child " against his will was killed in his arms, which was a principal " motive of his quitting that service."

A totally different account of this siege is given in the

Aphorismicall Discoverie, Vol. I., p. 24, which is, however, un-supported by any authority. According to this version, the castle was garrisoned by 15 men only, who repelled the attack with a loss of 500 of the besiegers, and after capturing, by a sortie, a quantity of powder with which it was attempted to blow up the castle, stole out by a back door and escaped with a loss of only two of their number.

The last of Carrickmines Castle.
(1906.)

On approaching Carrickmines Station by the road already referred to, on the right will be seen a farmhouse entered from the Glenamuck road. The castle stood on the site of this house and adjacent buildings, and although no definite trace can now be discovered of the foundations other than the great quantity of stones about the place, there still remains, incor-porated with one of the outhouses, portion of the western wall containing a light or window and constructed with great strength and solidity. Some fifty yards to the south-west is the remnant of a square watch tower that evidently formed part of the outworks. Portion of the moat lies eastwood of the farm buildings, and still contains water supplied from the stream that flows through the adjoining fields. An old lane, now closed, probably the original entrance to the castle, leads to the Kilgobbin road.

Resuming our journey, we cross the bridge at Carrickmines Railway Station and turn immediately to the right over a stile. We now keep to the laneway beside the railway wall as far as the first hedge, after which we follow the pathway through the fields, passing to the left of Barrington's Tower, an ornamental castellated structure, erected by a local proprietor.   The district between Carrickmines and Foxrock has come greatly into favour in recent years for residential purposes, and now contains quite an extensive settlement of handsome detached houses, many of them built in the old English style of architecture. As we reach the road close by the tower, to the right will be seen the dense woods of Glendruid, within whose dark shades is concealed a large cromlech, or Druid's altar, as these structures were formerly called, that originated the name of this glen.

Keeping to the road for about half a mile, we reach Cabinteely, whence we proceed along the main road towards Bray for a little over a quarter of a mile, till a slated cottage is seen on the left. Here cross the stile beside the iron gate, pass between the wooden posts, and keep to the pathway along the hedge down to the bottom of the field, where cross the foot-bridge over the stream. Now take the pathway uphill to the swing-gate at the corner of the field, proceed along by the wall of Kilbogget Farm, cross the low wall into the lane, and emerge by the stile on Church Road, Ballybrack. Ballybrack hill, easily identified by its flagstaff, with its bright green golf links, stands prominently in view all the way from Cabinteely.

In the grounds of St. Columba's at Ballybrack, is a pyramidal limestone monument commemorating the death while hunting,

at the early age of twenty-one, of the 4th Duke of Dorset.
It bears the inscription :—

> THIS PILE
> WAS RAISED TO MARK THE FATAL SPOT
> WHERE AT THE AGE OF 21
> GEORGE JOHN FREDERICK,
> The 4th Duke of Dorset,
> Accidentally lost his life 14th Feb. 1815.

On reaching Church Road turn to the right, and proceed
for some distance until an entrance gate is seen on the left,
bearing the names " Balure " and " Larkfield " ; pass through

Memorial to Duke of Dorset at Ballybrack.

this entrance into the laneway and pathway uphill through the
swing gate into the golf links, and thence towards the boundary
wall at the top of the hill, where another swing-gate and stile
will be seen, leading out on a lane which joins the main road to
Dalkey near the entrance to Victoria Park.

The view of the mountains and of the district inland is seen
to better advantage from Ballybrack hill than from Killiney

hill, the westward view from which is frequently obscured by the smoke from Killiney village and the numerous houses adjoining it.

We now enter Victoria Park by the entrance gate, and proceeding by the steep pathway up the hill, we presently come in view of the sweep of coast extending map-like from the base of the hill on towards Bray, fringed in rough weather by a long

Killiney Obelisk 80 years ago.
From " The Dublin Penny Journal."

white selvage of foam. On reaching the Obelisk, at an elevation of 512 feet, we obtain what is probably the finest coast view in the county, comprising the Dublin and Wicklow Mountains extending from south to west, Kingstown and its harbour below the hill, to the north Howth, Sutton, and Portrane, and to the left of these the South Wall, the Poolbeg Lighthouse, and the metropolis enveloped in its smoke.[6]

The Obelisk, which gives such a distinctive character to this hill, has undergone so many repairs and alterations since it was erected, that it may be said to resemble the traditional Irishman's gun, of which the only portion of the original left after the many alterations was the touchhole, and, in consequence, the drawings made at different periods vary considerably in their representations of it. The masonry work is of a very rough description, probably carried out by unskilled workmen, so that it is not surprising that it required frequent attention. It seems to have been at one time surrounded by a circular walled enclosure, entered by a massive gateway, which in time gave place to a railing that was ultimately removed to allow visitors access to the structure. Then, again, a flight of steps formerly led up to a balcony over the lower portion, and the upper part, which is now conical, is represented in one of the older pictures as curved at the sides, giving it somewhat of the appearance of a gigantic sugarloaf. Two marble slabs on the side facing the sea bear the inscriptions :—" Last year being hard with the " Poor, the Walls about these Hills and This etc. erected by " John Mapas, Esq, June, 1742." " Repaired by Robert " Warren, Esq., MDCCCXI."

The winter of 1741-2, known as " the hard frost," was a time of such distress and suffering among the working classes, that wealthy proprietors all over the country erected fanciful structures merely to give employment to the poor.

The flat, well wooded tract extending along the coast from Killiney to Bray, including portion of the valley of the Loughlinstown river, is known as the Vale of Shanganagh, and owes its attractions to its environment rather than to the possession of picturesque features.

From any of its higher points the views are strikingly beautiful. To the north and north-east are Ballybrack, Killiney and Dalkey hills with Dalkey Island and the Muglins, to the east is the sea dotted with various craft on their way to and from Dublin, southward the bold form of Bray Head rises precipitously out of the water, and on the west are seen Carrickgollogan with its conspicuous chimney and the higher mountains of Dublin and Wicklow in the background.

Situated on the very bank of the Loughlinstown river are

the ruins of the ancient castle of Shanganagh, the ancestral home of the Walsh family, whose connection with the locality lasted over three centuries.

The name Shanganagh, which should be accented on the first syllable, the other two being pronouced very short, means a place abounding in ants, and at the present day these insects are found in great abundance in the district, especially along the sandy banks of the river. (See Joyce's *Irish Names of Places*," Vol. II., p. 293.)

On a high cliff immediately south of the flat stretch of shore where the Loughlinstown river flows into the sea, are the remains of a battery erected about a hundred years ago in what appears to be a very ill-chosen position, for although elaborately loop-holed, no portion of the structure, owing to the rising ground in front, commands a view of the shore, or even of the sea, except in the distance. Remains of the dwelling for the accommodation of the garrison may still be seen, and underneath is a vaulted chamber, probably the ammunition store.

Adjoining Shankill Railway Station is a village now known as Tillystown or Chantilly, but which seems to have originally been called Shanganagh, as evidenced by a tablet dated 1830 in the wall on the main road. No indication of a village or even house, however, appears here in the Ordnance Survey Map of 1837.

In 1751 a lead mine was opened at Killiney, which contained some silver, but, proving unremunerative, it was abandoned after a considerable sum of money had been wasted on the project. Small garnets have occasionally been found among the sands of Killiney strand.

The descent from the Obelisk should be made by the pathway leading down to the Vico Road, along which we proceed towards Sorrento, turning to the left up the flight of stone steps leading to the Torca Road so as to reach the road at the back of Dalkey hill. This hill was originally much larger and higher on the northern side than it is at present, the quarrying away of the rocks to build Kingstown Harbour having greatly reduced its bulk, and rendered it so precipitous that in places it is steep and rugged enough to test the agility of even an experienced Alpine climber. The ornamental castle on its summit is fashioned out of a semaphore station which stood there in the old days, before the invention of the electric telegraph, when the hill was generally known as " Telegraph Hill "—a name not yet extinct among the aboriginal inhabitants. The castle, which is substantially the same structure, was nearly undermined by the quarrying operations.

The Castle on Dalkey Hill.
(1906.)

Early in the last century, up to about the time the building of Kingstown Harbour commenced, the whole coast from Dunleary to what is now called Sorrento, but then generally known as " The Land's End," presented an almost uniform appearance of wildness and solitude, with open expanses of sward and heather, broken by masses of granite rocks amid thickets of golden furze, and, except for the villages of Glasthule, Bullock and Dalkey, was almost uninhabited. The portion known as the Commons of Dalkey, lying between the village and Sorrento, was a place of singular beauty, much in vogue as a holiday and Sunday resort for the Dublin folk of that day.

A few cottages standing on the shore, with a solitary cabin originally built by miners, were then the only habitations in this neighbourhood, all of which has now been built over with the exception of a small portion remaining in its original condition of wildness on the hill over Sorrento.

Up to the close of the 18th century there stood on Dalkey Commons a cromlech enclosed by a circle of granite stones, and almost concealed by a luxuriant growth of ferns. This interesting relic was unfortunately removed during the Martello Tower epidemic, and the stones utilised in the construction of one of these ungainly edifices in the neighbourhood. This cromlech was such a conspicuous landmark on the Commons that they were generally known as "Dalkey Stone Common," and as such are referred to in the famous old hunting song, "The Kilruddery Hunt" (see Index.)

In consequence of Dalkey having been for so long the port of Dublin, quite a number of distinguished historical personages landed there from time to time, and a metal tablet, setting forth their names and the dates of arrival, was formerly attached to a large rock at Coliemore harbour.

In 1385 the Lord Deputy, Philip de Courtney landed here, and Sir John Stanley, the Deputy of the Marquess of Dublin, two years later. In 1414 Sir John Talbot, afterwards the renowned Earl of Shrewsbury, landed here as Viceroy, and in 1488 Sir Richard Edgecombe embarked from this harbour for England, after having taken the homage and oaths of fidelity of the nobility who had espoused the cause of Lambert Simnel. Here also landed Sir Edward Bellingham as Lord Lieutenant in 1548, Sir Anthony St. Leger in 1553, and Sir John Perrot as Viceroy in 1584; and it was also from this harbour that the Earl of Sussex, in 1558, embarked a large expeditionary force to oppose the invasion of the Scots at Rathlin Island.

In 1834 numbers of persons attracted by rumours of buried gold, flocked to Dalkey where they worked and mined, day and night, at the rocks, under the directions of a young girl who claimed to have had the place of concealment revealed to her in dreams. When the craze had gone on for a time, some wags let loose among the operators at night, two black cats covered with phosphorescent oil, which scattered the gold seekers in all directions, and effectually put an end to the proceedings owing to the ridicule provoked by the incident.

A land craze immediately succeeded the gold fever, and a number of modern residences were soon afterwards erected at Dalkey, the old squatter tenants selling their holdings for high prices in consequence of the enhanced values produced by the construction of the railway.

Dalkey Island, so conspicuously in view from all points along this coast, is of nearly oval form, with a long reef of rocks extending in a north-westerly direction, and has a very irregular surface, partly rocky and partly consisting of fertile pasture land. It contains several springs of fresh water, one of which, within a few yards of the shore on the western side, was in former years considered to possess valuable sanative properties, and was much resorted to for the cure of scurvy and cutaneous diseases. On the verge of the cliffs, and often washed by the spray from the raging surf, is the ruin of an ancient church dedicated to St. Begnet or Benedict, the patron saint of the parish. At the south-eastern extremity of the island there is a dismantled battery, and adjoining, on high ground, is a Martello tower, the entrance to which was originally constructed on the top with a view to affording extra security, but was subsequently altered to the side.

To the northward of the island are three small rocky islets called Lamb Island, Clare Rock, and Maiden Rock, and to the north-east is the group of rocks known as the Muglins, on which, in 1766, were hung in chains, the bodies of the pirates MacKinley and Gidley, who were executed for the murder of Captain Cochrane, Captain Glass, and other passengers of the ship *Sandwich*, on the high seas in the previous year.

Dalkey Island, in 1575, became a refuge for a number of the Dublin citizens who fled from a terrible outbreak of plague in the Metropolis. At a later period it was the scene of the

E

annual coronation of the King of Dalkey, a burlesque ceremonial continued up to 1797, when owing to the political
troubles at the time, the promoters voluntarily discontinued
the proceedings. An interesting description of the scene on the
island on one of these occasions, is given by an eye-witness,
surviving in 1840, who communicated it to *The Irish Penny
Journal* in that year. According to this writer, both Dalkey
Island and the Commons, on the occasion of this festivity, were
covered with dense masses of people, gaily dressed and arranged
into groups of happy parties, each with its own musician. The
dresses of the women were almost invariably white, with green
silk bonnets—a costume that lent a brilliant effect to the scene.
A large marquee was erected about the middle of the island
for the use of His Majesty and Officers of State, and a cordon
was drawn around it to prevent intrusion by unauthorised
persons.

A military band was generally in attendance to provide music
for dancing—the noblemen and ladies of the Court remaining
within the cordon, whilst the ordinary subjects of the monarch
danced outside. For the Dalkey boatmen it was a red-letter
day—they were kept busy from morning till night, and generally
reaped a harvest sufficient to maintain them in idleness and
inebriety for a considerable time afterwards.

The ceremony of coronation was performed in St. Begnet's
Church, on the island, with a mock gravity which was irresis-
tibly humorous, and as the various functionaries were chosen
for their known wit and eloquence, it can readily be imagined
what a treat it was for the audience. The long coronation
sermon was one of the principal events of the day, and produced
effects such as sermon never produced before.

During this august and imposing ceremony the church was
not only crowded to its utmost capacity, and its ruined walls
covered by anxious listeners, but it was also surrounded by a
dense crowd, most of whom could hear little or nothing of the
proceedings beyond the loud bursts of laughter that punctuated
the various speeches and addresses.

Towards evening the people commenced to return from the island, but it took many journeys by the boats to convey them all back, and it was generally late at night or early in the morning before all his loyal subjects had reached their homes after paying their respects to, and drinking the health of " His Facetious Majesty (Stephen the First), King of Dalkey, " Emperor of the Muglins, Prince of the Holy Island of Magee, " Elector of Lambay and Ireland's Eye, Defender of his own " Faith and Respecter of All Others, Sovereign of the Illustrious " Order of the Lobster and Periwinkle."

The ruined Church of St. Begnet, apart from these proceedings, was subjected to very irreverent treatment about a hundred years ago, when the tower and battery were being constructed on the island. The masons and other workmen finding it inconvenient and often dangerous to cross the Sound to their lodgings, fitted up the ruin as a dwellinghouse, added a fireplace, and enlarged a doorway and some of the windows.

Distances—From Dundrum to Carrickmines Station, $4\frac{1}{2}$ miles ; Carrickmines Station to Killiney Village, $3\frac{1}{2}$ miles (approximately by route described above); Killiney Village over the hill to Dalkey by Torca Road, about $1\frac{3}{4}$ miles.

CHAPTER VI

BALLYMAN GLEN, CARRICKGOLLOGAN, BALLY-CORUS, TULLY, AND BRIDE'S GLEN

LEAVING Bray Station, we walk up the Quinsborough Road, cross Bray bridge into Little Bray, and after about half a mile, turn up the road on the left, presently entering the village of Old Connaught, where may be seen the ruin of an ancient church overgrown with ivy and elder trees. The name of the locality is properly Old Conna, but the only instance in which this form has been preserved is the name, Old Conna Hill, a modern residence about three-quarters of a mile to the north of the village.

Early in the 16th century the lands of Old Connaught came into possession of the Walsh family of Shanganagh, who maintained a residence on the site of the present Old Connaught House until after the Treaty of Limerick, when they finally severed their connection with the locality and went abroad.

As we reach the higher portion of the road above Old Con-raug'it, a stile will be seen on the left, from which a pathway leads down to the secluded glen of Ballyman or Glenmunder watered by a little stream that rises in the Scalp and here forms the boundary between the counties of Dublin and Wicklow. This glen is well wooded, and on portions of its southern slopes may be seen in the springtime such a wonderful profusion of primroses that their pale, delicate tint quite dominates the colouring of the banks on which they grow. At the bottom of the glen, not far from the stream, is the ruin of a very ancient church, dating probably from a period not later than the 12th century. Only the eastern portion of the

68

building remains, enveloped in a luxuriant growth of ivy, and the eastern and southern windows exhibit marks indicating that they were at one time protected by upright bars, while traces of concentric carving may be seen on the southern one. A few old tombstones, scarcely recognisable as such, lie scattered around the ruins.

Not far from the church, and situated on the banks of the stream, though almost entirely concealed by the wild tangle o brushwood, is St. Kevin's holy well, still honoured by the observance of the old custom of tying rags and ribbons to the adjacent bushes. This well enjoys a high reputation among the people in the neighbourhood for its curative qualities, the fame of which has extended through the surrounding districts, whence persons come occasionally to take away some of the water for use in affections of the eyes.

Retracing our steps to the road, we continue along it, until, at a distance of nearly a mile from Old Connaught, we meet a narrow lane on the right, the enclosing banks and hedges of which are so high as to shut out all view, the foliage in places meeting overhead. After about half-a-mile, the lane sweeping to the right, affords a view of the rounded rocky " hump " of Carrickgollogan (popularly corrupted into " Katty Gollagher "), and just at this point two cottages will be seen on the right, opposite which is a gateway opening in on the mountainside, where a marble slab, bearing an inscription to that effect, has been placed by some friends to commemorate a Dr. Alcock. By a short, steep ascent through the bracken and heather we arrive at the cairn which marks the top, 912 feet high, from which a fine view is obtained of Bray, Howth, Dalkey, and Killiney, the vale of Shanganagh, and Bray Head and town. Between the observer and the sea will be seen Loughlinstown, looking very closely built from this point, like the towns of mediæval times, which were built within as small an area as possible, so as to reduce the circuit of the enclosing wall. To the westward will be seen the wooded hill of Barnaslingan, forming the eastern side of the Scalp, beyond that the Two and Three

Rock Mountains, and south of these the higher Wicklow hills—War Hill, Douce, and Duff Hill. Having finished our observations from the top, we may make our way towards the tall chimney, which is such a conspicuous feature on the hill and gives it an individuality by which it can be readily identified at a distance. A descent from the summit, equally steep as that by which we reached it, conducts us

The Chimney on Carrickgollogan.
(1905.)

to the wilds of fern and heather beneath, intersected by pathways in various directions.

The chimney is about 80 feet high, terminating a flue nearly a mile in length, which is carried up the whole way from the Ballycorus Lead Works in the valley below. A winding flight of stone steps ascends for about two-thirds of the height of the structure. These works were established about ninety years ago, at which time sufficient ore was found on the spot, supplemented by that taken from the company's mines at Glendalough, to keep a large staff of workmen constantly employed.

Dr. (afterwards Sir Robert) Kane, in his *Industrial Resources of Ireland* (1844), " states that ' the dressed ore ' (from the " Luganure Mine at Glendalough) is brought in cars to the " company's smelting works at Ballycorus, where it is worked " up along with ores from other sources by processes to which " I shall, after a little, return.

" The lead mine situated on the hill of Ballycorus, contains " two lead veins, which at the surface are nearly parallel, and " cross the junction of the granite and mica slate, which takes " place at its summit. In the workings these veins have been " found sometimes to diverge, and at others to coalesce, and " were then in every case found to contain valuable bunches " of ore. These veins have latterly, however, become unpro- " ductive, and although some limited explorations are still " carried on by the Mining Company, this mine cannot be " reckoned as being at the present time in action. In its " vicinity are situated the Mining Company's smelting works " to which all their lead ores are brought for the purpose of " their reduction and manufacture."

At the present time a considerable business is carried on by the company at their works, where the ore is smelted and converted into ingots, the silver separated and refined, and litharge, red lead and shot manufactured. The flue, which was remodelled and extended about fifty years ago, at the cost of about £10,000, is a unique structure, in Ireland at least, and is stated to be one of the best constructed of its kind in the United Kingdom. One of the various purposes it serves is the carrying off and depositing of all poisonous products, delivering the almost purified vapour at an altitude of nearly 900 feet above sea level, thereby relieving the works and neighbourhood of the usual deleterious effects resulting from lead smelting. The deposits, chiefly in the form of sulphate of lead, are removed periodically by workmen with barrows, after the flue has been thoroughly ventilated by opening the various doors, &c.

The shaft of the mine runs westward from the chimney, under the adjoining wood, where considerable quantities of native silver were found when the mine was started. The shot tower, a conspicuous object in the valley, is a handsome and substantial structure, having a spiral stairs within, terminating in an artistic iron verandah on the outside, nearly 100 feet from the ground, overlooking the adjoining pond, water-wheel, machinery, and shot premises, while in the immediate vicinity are a number of cottages, built for the employes of the company.

Puck's Castle.

(1905.)

On leaving the chimney, by heading towards Loughlinstown, we can again reach the narrow lane we had previously left, presently observing on our right the square fortified dwelling known as Puck's Castle, constructed with great strength and solidity, and still in excellent preservation. It has three entrances, two of which appear to be modern ; the northern side is dashed, and the whole edifice bears evidence of many minor alterations carried out after it had ceased to be used for its original purpose, the brickwork fireplace in particular, on the eastern wall, presenting a distinctly modern appearance. This castle is one of the many buildings credited by popular tradition with having afforded shelter to King James for a night during his flight southwards after the Battle of the Boyne.

From here a short journey across the fields in an easterly direction conducts us to the ruins at Rathmichael, consisting of the remains of a church and the stump of a round tower, the latter, locally known as " The Skull Hole," being a receptacle, as the name suggests, for skulls and bones from the adjoining burial ground. These ruins stand on the slopes of Carrick-gollogan, almost in the centre of a large caher or rath, doubtless the original Rathmichael, while on an adjoining eminence are the remains of a similar enclosure. Their situation is most picturesque, overlooking the hills of Dalkey, Killiney and Ballybrack, and the blue waters of Killiney Bay. The ruins are maintained in excellent order, showing, perhaps, rather obvious evidences of repair, and are approached by an ancient roadway exhibiting traces of paving, and known as Rathmichael lane.

Continuing our journey by this lane until we reach the main road at the head of Bride's Glen, a sharp descent conducts us to that romantic wooded defile, doubtless deriving its name from St. Brigid or Bride, to whom the adjacent church at Tully was dedicated. Although in the 18th century this glen was called Cherrywood Glen, and as such is referred to in " The Kil-ruddery Hunt," this name is probably one of comparatively modern origin, which has been discarded in favour of the original one. The name of Cherrywood, however, still remains as the designation of a modern residence at the lower end of the glen. The slopes are thickly planted with larches, Scotch firs, limes, and Spanish chestnut trees, and among them may be seen a few old cherry trees—remnants, perhaps, of the original cherry wood which gave name to the glen. Beneath the shade of the trees a fresh green sward slopes down to the Loughlins-town river, and, as we approach the village of Loughlinstown, the railway is carried across the valley by an imposing stone viaduct, built before iron bridges had come generally into vogue for such purposes.

From Bride's Glen the return home can be made by Shankill

Station, three-quarters of a mile distant, but a much more interesting and picturesque route is to return from Carrick-mines Station, visiting on the way the ancient church and cross of Tully, and thence walking by Carrickmines golf links to the station.   If this latter is desired, we turn back from Bride's Glen, ascending the hill and taking the first turn to the right at a place called Hearnsford or Heronford, whence a short sharp rise conducts us to an iron gate and stile opening on to a pathway across the furze and heather.   On approaching the venerable ruins of Tully, the cross will be seen on a high pedestal, standing in the middle of the road, which was formerly on a level with the base of the plinth.   A few paces from the cross is the church, darkly shaded by trees and presenting little appearance of intrusion.   Tully was anciently known as Tullagh-na-Nespuc, or the Hill of the Bishops, and a legend relates how seven of these holy men went from this establishment to pay a visit to St. Brigid at Kildare.   The cross on the road is that commonly known as the Celtic pattern—*i.e.*, a cross within a circle, and is of plain design, with little attempt at decoration, while that in the adjoining field is of the Maltese pattern, very tall, and embellished with rude carving, though much more dilapidated than the other, the right arm being missing.   The carving consists of a full length figure in high relief, in the conventional attitude of a saint.   Both crosses are supposed to date from about the eighth or ninth century.

In the churchyard is a monumental stone curiously inscribed with three sets of concentric circles, and almost identical in pattern with that of similar stones in Rathmichael churchyard. These stones have been rather a puzzle to antiquarians, being conjectured by some to be of early Christian origin, and by others to be of Pagan origin converted to Christian purposes.

Having seen these interesting relics, it will be necessary to turn back a short distance along the road, and indeed it is advisable for those not familiar with the locality, to inquire at the adjoining farmhouse for the track across the fields by the golf links to Carrickmines Station.   The distance from Bride's Glen to Carrickmines Station is about two miles.

The comparatively short circuit described in this chapter, about seven miles, including the ascent of Carrickgollogan, is, of course, practicable only to pedestrians, but cyclists desirous of following it as closely as possible, should proceed to Little Bray, thence to Old Connaught, and by the lane skirting Carrickgollogan to Puck's Castle, Laughanstown, Tully Church and Cross, Cabinteely, and home by the Bray road. Many portions of these lanes are, however, too rough for cycling, and must be walked.

CHAPTER VII

THE BRAY ROAD—DONNYBROOK, STILLORGAN, LOUGHLINSTOWN, OLD BRAY AND ITS SMUGGLERS

LEAVING town by what was formerly known as the Donnybrook road, but which, since its accession to respectability, has become the Morehampton Road, we enter Donnybrook, now almost merged in the populous district around it, though still retaining its distinctive character as a village. Few of its old features, however, now remain, its quaint inns are gone, its thatched cottages have vanished, and the whole place has assumed a less rural appearance than it possessed in the days when the " glories " of its Fair shed around it their halo of renown. It must be confessed, however, notwithstanding the glamour with which prose and ballad writers have endeavoured to invest Donnybrook Fair, that for many years prior to its abolition, it had forfeited every claim to recognition as a national festivity, and in its final stages had grown to be a gigantic public nuisance and disgrace.

This Fair was established by Royal Charter in 1204 to compensate the Dublin citizens for the expense of building walls and defences around the city, and was for centuries the most important fair in Ireland. It is now, indeed, difficult to realise that the deserted, low-lying field on the left as we pass out of the village, is the historic ground where for over six hundred years was held the world-renowned Fair of Donnybrook, so famed for fighting, dancing, love-making, and drollery, and so long associated with the name and character of the Irish people.

Only a brief reference can here be made to the circumstances which led to the abolition of this historic festivity. For several

weeks in August every year, all business in Dublin was more
or less paralysed in consequence of the general demoralisation
caused by the Fair. An agitation commenced by the Press
led to the inauguration of a public subscription to purchase the
patent from the owners, and this having been satisfactorily
arranged in 1855, the Fair was allowed to lapse, and the
" glories of Donnybrook " were thus quenched for ever.

Donnybrook.
(1906.)

Memories of its vanished revels still linger in the locality,
and in the minds of strangers the place is still associated with
the Fair, the name conjuring up visions of shillelaghs, dancing,
whiskey drinking, and skull cracking, but these frolicsome days
are gone, never to return, the generation that witnessed them
has nearly passed, and Donnybrook, repenting of its evil ways,
has now settled down as a respectable suburb of the city, anxious
to atone in its later years for the faults and follies of a disreputable past. [7]

Lewis's *Dublin Guide* (1787) contains the following notice

of Donnybrook :—" A large and pleasant village, two miles
" from the Castle of Dublin, and much frequented by the
" citizens of Dublin, on account of the good accommodation
" to be had here, particularly at the two principal tea-
" houses, one at the sign of the Rose at the entrance of the
" place, and the other a little further on, kept by Mrs.
" Darby."

A " Fair " Fight.
(From a sketch by Samuel Lover.)

The Rose Inn, so frequently alluded to by writers in connection with old Donnybrook, was situated at the end of
Church Lane, and occupied premises which had originally been
the glebe house.

Crossing Anglesea Bridge over the Dodder, we enter on a
rather uninteresting stretch of road, three miles long, to
Stillorgan, anciently Tigh-Lorcan, meaning Lorcan's house or
resting-place. Opposite Mount Merrion Avenue will be seen
the entrance gate to Mount Merrion, the Irish residence of the
Earl of Pembroke and Montgomery, representative of the

Fitzwilliams of Merrion, whose ancestral castle stood near the
site now occupied by the Blind Asylum at Merrion.

We next enter Stillorgan, situated in a hollow, and well
sheltered by its surrounding woods.   There is little of interest
to notice in the village, but a short distance east of it there
stood until some twenty-five years ago, the manor house of

Donnybrook Fair.
(*From " The Dublin Penny Journal."*)

Stillorgan, a stately mansion, formerly the home of the Barons
Allen of Stillorgan.   Here many a gay company assembled in
the early part of the 18th century during the lifetime of the
second Lord, and in after years, when it had passed out of
possession of the Allen family, it had many distinguished
occupants, and was a social centre of considerable importance
in the 18th century.

A conspicuous object for a considerable distance around is
the fine obelisk standing in grounds which formerly were

portion of Stillorgan House Park, but now belong to Obelisk Park. This obelisk was erected in 1741 during the severe winter known as " the hard frost," to give employment to the poor.

In Ware's *Antiquities of Ireland* it is mentioned that in 1716 a sepulchral chamber was discovered at Stillorgan, lined with flag-stones and covered over with one massive, flat stone of such a size that ten men were unable to lift it. In the interior were fragments of human bones, accompanied by an urn containing what appeared to be loose earth. It was evidently the grave of some chieftain or person of distinction, though no tradition has been handed down to us as to his identity, and it may be that he was the Lorcan commemorated in the ancient name of the locality, which has been modified into the modern designation of Stillorgan.

The road now ascends to Galloping Green, a small village deriving its name from a miniature race-course which existed here many years ago, and about half a mile further, the highest point of the road is reached, 303 feet over sea level. The road now begins to descend, and we presently reach the village of Cornelscourt, where up to a few years ago stood the remains of the ancient castle or fortified dwelling which gave name to this hamlet. Of this old building only portion of an end wall now survives, the rest having been taken down to make room for two new houses at the far end of the village.

A mile beyond Cornelscourt we enter Cabinteely, in which there is nothing calling for notice ; and in a mile and a half further along a pleasant open road, we reach Loughlinstown, situated in the sheltered valley of the Loughlinstown river. In the middle of the road leading into the village will be seen a fine tree with seats around it, beyond which, to the left is a waste sandy tract along the bed of the river. At the far end of the village, in a commanding position above the valley, is the Rathdown Union Workhouse, an extensive establishment which, with its out-offices and grounds, covers a considerable area.

Loughlinstown House, to the left of the village, has been in possession of the Domvile family since the Restoration, and although it has undergone considerable alterations since that time, portion of the original structure still remains.

In the 18th century, Loughlinstown was the centre of a great hunting district, and was much patronised by devotees of the chase. There was then in the village a well-known hunters' inn, owned by one Owen Bray, which, according to Dr. Ball's *History of the County of Dublin*, has since been altered into the modern residence known as Beechwood, opposite the entrance to Loughlinstown House. These sporting times have been commemorated in the fine old hunting song, " The Kilruddery Hunt," which is reproduced at the end of this chapter. It is interesting by reason of its allusions to many places where fox hunting would now be utterly impossible, but which at that time were wild and unenclosed.

During the troublous period at the close of the 18th century, the lands lying for a considerable distance to the west of the village were the site of a great military camp, which extended over 120 acres, and accommodated 4,000 soldiers. Notwithstanding the scenes of bloodshed and misery which were of frequent occurrence in the neighbourhood, the troops found ample opportunities for amusing themselves, and contemporary writers describe the camp as being a constant scene of gaiety, a ballroom having been specially erected for dancing. Vivid traditions of this camp still survive among the people of the locality.

Passing out of the village by a steeper hill than that by which we entered it, in about a mile we reach Shankill Station situated at the junction of the Bray and Killiney roads.

Crossing the high railway bridge, we enter the village of Tillystown, not far from which, to the left of the road, are the almost indistinguishable remains of the ancient Church of Kiltuck. Just before entering the portion of Bray town called Little Bray, formerly included in the County Dublin, we pass, on the left, the modern residence known as Cork

F

Abbey, in the grounds of which is shown the site of an old burial place, together with a well, said to have belonged to an ancient monastic establishment.

Passing through Little Bray, the only object worthy of notice is the Castle, which is probably only portion of a much larger structure, as so important a position, commanding the passage of the road from Dublin and of the only practicable ford across the river for miles, would require to be defended by an extensive and strongly fortified building. Walter de Ridelesford, a renowned Anglo-Norman warrior, was, in 1173, granted the lands of Bray and the surrounding district by Strongbow, and in all probability built the castle here. In 1213 King John granted to de Ridelesford a charter entitling him to hold a fair in the town every Thursday.

In 1402 John Drake, Mayor of Dublin, marched out with a well-equipped force against the Irish tribesmen, whom he encountered and defeated near Bray, for which service he was re-elected to the Mayoralty for the following year. Bloody Bank, now changed to Sunny Bank, on Bray Common, is said to derive its name from having been the burial place of those who fell in this battle.

The two portions of Bray divided by the river (formerly the county boundary at this point) were anciently known as Much Bray and Little Bray, of which names it is curious that the latter alone has survived.

It is somewhat interesting to read in a " regal visitation " of 1615, that one Maurice Byrne was then the Vicar of Bray, that the value of the benefice was £7, that he read the service in Irish, and that the Book of Common Prayer in use in the Church was printed in the Irish language. It would thus appear that the native language was in general use at the time in this district, irrespective of religious or racial distinction, as the records of the time would go to show that there was a fair sprinkling of persons of English descent dwelling in the locality.

In 1690, on the day after the Battle of the Boyne, King James, in his flight from Dublin, arrived in Bray early in the morning,

and learning that he was closely pursued, posted a strong force
at the bridge, with instructions to them to remain until noon,
to oppose the passage of the pursuing party, while he and his
retinue made their escape through the mountains of Wicklow,
on the way to Waterford. A skirmish is said to have taken place
in consequence, but no details are forthcoming on the subject,
and it must have been only a trifling affair.

Bray, as a watering place, may be said to date from the
extension of the Dublin and Kingstown Railway to the town

Bray Bridge.
(1905.)

in 1851. In the earlier part of the century there was no
esplanade extending by the shore—nothing but the heaped
sand, shingles and low sand dunes, along which a rude raised
pathway led to the Head, interrupted by numerous hollows
and irregularities caused by the digging and carting away of
the sand by farmers and others in the neighbourhood. All the
space now occupied by the Esplanade was swept by a fierce sea
during easterly gales, and the present line of house frontage
marks, roughly speaking, the extreme range of the waves on such
occasions.

The few persons who went in the summer to enjoy the sea
breezes had to pick their way as best they could among the
slippery pebbles and sand heaps that strewed the shore. The

route from Bray Bridge towards the beach was the old road which runs beside the river, and the present Quinsborough Road was represented by a pathway through fields, while Quin's Hotel possessed a splendid garden extending the whole way down to the sea.

At this period there were only two habitations along the sea front—one a small, pretty cottage where Bray Head Hotel now stands, whilst somewhere on the ground occupied by Claddagh Terrace was the other, a mud hovel, so diminutive, so wretched and so miserable as to earn for it the local soubriquet of " The Rat Hole." This strange dwelling was tenanted by an equally strange occupant—an eccentric, solitary, tar-begrimed old fisherman, who was a well-known character in the neighbourhood, and who took a delight in surrounding his unattractive abode with ill-smelling heaps of manure, offal, seaweed and every other abomination that came within his reach, until at last it became difficult to distinguish between the dwelling and these strange accessories. To what end he accumulated these malodorous tumuli none who knew him could surmise ; but that he enjoyed the possession of them could be open to no doubt, as he was to be seen there daily, during his leisure hours, regaling his nose and eyes on their perfume and proportions.

In the other cottage near the Head lived an elderly woman and her daughter, whose ostensible means of livelihood were seeking and selling the pebbles peculiar to the locality, known as Wicklow pebbles, but who really were engaged in the profitable business of smuggling, and, in conjunction with others, acted as agents for the various overseas craft that then frequented this coast for the contraband trade.

The mother was a woman of great courage and strength of character, and always went about armed ; she was known to have amassed a considerable fortune by her operations, and was, at least on one occasion, engaged in an affray with the Preventive men. When she died many years afterwards, her daughter found herself a rich woman.

The wild and lonely coast of Wicklow offered so many facilities for smuggling that the efforts of the Government were unable to accomplish more than barely to interrupt and at most delay the well-laid schemes of the contrabandists.

The usual plan adopted by smuggling vessels plying here was, under cover of night or misty weather, to send their contraband goods ashore in boats to the preconcerted places of concealment on the coast, and then to sail openly with their legitimate cargo to Dublin or other port, and thus hoodwink the Revenue authorities. There can be little doubt, however, that corruption was rife among the Revenue and Customs officers at that period, and that they could, when necessary, look in the wrong direction.

The natural conformation of the coast around Bray Head lent itself readily to the adaptation of places of concealment, of which there were several, but the principal one was that known as "The Brandy Hole," half a mile along the shore from where the road crosses the railway on the Head. Here was an immense cavern, with its entrance opening to the sea, and its many ramifications extending far in under the hill, affording ample accommodation for the cargoes of all the vessels plying their risky trade here. Into this great natural storehouse, fully laden boats were easily able to make their way by the light of lanterns, and discharge their contents high and dry into the numerous receptacles prepared for them.

Immediately over this cavern, and adjoining the rude goat track that then encircled the Head, was a shaft sunk in a slanting direction into the earth, communicating with another subterraneous chamber—a sort of second storey to the lower one—but showing no trace of its existence on the surface, as the entrance was carefully concealed by a thick growth of brambles and bracken. This provided for the initiated a ready means of access from the land to the cavern, which was furnished where necessary with steps and platforms whereby a person above could, by means of a rope, assist those below to climb out on top, or if need be, drag up bales of goods for storage in the upper chamber.

In after years, when reports began to be whispered abroad as to the existence of this Ali Baba's cave, the locality became the scene of some fierce struggles between the Revenue men and the desperadoes engaged in the contraband traffic. It was a time when a Revenue officer's life was one of constant excitement; he needed to be a man of courage and determination, and the risks of his avocation were almost as great as those of a soldier's in the field.

Both the caves mentioned were utterly obliterated during the construction of the railway, but the name of " The Brandy Hole " still attaches to an inlet in the cliffs, and is the sole memorial of this great smugglers' rendezvous, the very tradition of which has been lost among the modern population.

With the advent of steam, telegraphs and police, smuggling has been shorn of much of the romance with which it once was associated; the picturesque figure of the bold smuggler with his slouched hat and feather, jack-boots and huge pistols, has disappeared from the stage of modern life and survives only in that of melodrama, and the Dublin folk of to-day, whirled rapidly along the railway around Bray Head, look down on his former haunts with scarcely a thought for the desperate scenes enacted there a hundred years ago.

THE KILRUDDERY HUNT

The author of this spirited song was Thomas Mozeen, an actor and singer, who also wrote " An Invitation to Owen Bray's at Loughlinstown," and was a well-known patron of that hunters' hostelry. Before the publication of " The Kilruddery Hunt," and only a few days subsequent to the event which it commemorates, it was sung for the first time at the house of one of the sportsmen who took part in the hunt, at his house on Bachelor's Walk, Dublin.

Hark! Hark! jol-ly sportsmen, a - while to my tale, Which to pay your at-ten-tion I'm sure cannot fail; 'Tis of lads and of horses, and dogs that ne'er tire, O'er stone walls and hedges, through dale, bog and briar; A pack of such hounds and a set of such men, 'Tis a shrewd chance if ev - er you meet with again; Had Nimrod, the mightiest of hunters, been there, 'Fore God he had shook like an as - pen for fear.

" Hark ! Hark ! jolly sportsmen, awhile to my tale,
Which to pay your attention I'm sure cannot fail ;
'Tis of lads and of horses, and dogs that ne'er tire,
O'er stone walls and hedges, through dale, bog and briar ;
A pack of such hounds and a set of such men,
'Tis a shrewd chance if ever you meet with again ;
Had Nimrod, the mightiest of hunters, been there,
'Fore God, he had shook like an aspen for fear.

" In Seventeen Hundred and Forty and Four,
The fifth of December, I think 'twas no more,
At five in the morning by most of the clocks,
We rode from Kilruddery in search of a fox.

The Loughlinstown landlord, the brave Owen Bray,
And Johnny Adair, too, were with us that day ;
Joe Debil, Hal Preston—those huntsmen so stout—
Dick Holmes, some few others, and so we set out.

" We cast off our hounds for a full hour or more,
When Wanton set up a most terrible roar,
' Hark to Wanton ! ' cried Joe, and the rest were not slack,
For Wanton's no trifler esteemed in the pack.
Old Bonny and Collier came readily in,
And every hound joined in the musical din ;
Had Diana been there, she'd been pleased to the life,
And one of the lads got a goddess to wife.

" Ten minutes past nine was the time of the day,
When Reynard broke cover, and this was his way ;
As strong from Killegar as if he could fear none,
Away he brushed round by the house of Kiltiernan ;
To Carrickmines thence, and to Cherrywood then,
Steep Shankill he climbed, and to Ballyman Glen ;
Bray Common he crossed, leaped Lord Anglesea's wall,
And seemed to say ' Little I care for you all.'

" He ran Bushe's Grove up to Carbury Byrne's——
Joe Debil, Hal Preston, kept leading by turns ;
The earth it was open, yet he was so stout,
Though he might have got in, still he chose to keep out.
To Malpas high hill was the way that he flew ;
At Dalkey Stone Common we had him in view ;
He drove on by Bullock, through Shrub Glenageary,
And so on to Monkstown where Larry grew weary.

" Through Rochestown wood like an arrow he passed,
And came to the steep hill of Dalkey at last ;
There gallantly plunged himself into the sea,
And said in his heart, ' None can now follow me.'

But soon to his cost, he perceived that no bounds
Could stop the pursuit of the staunch-mettled hounds;
His policy here did not serve him a rush,
Five couple of Tartars were here at his brush.

" To recover the shore then again was his drift;
But ere he could reach to the top of the clift,
He found both of speed and of daring a lack,
Being waylaid and killed by the rest of the pack.
At his death there were present the lads I have sung,
Save Larry who, riding a garron was flung,
Thus ended at length a most delicate chase,
That held us for five hours and ten minutes space.

" We returned to Kilruddery's plentiful board,
Where dwell hospitality, truth and my lord;
We talked o'er the chase and we toasted the health
Of the men who ne'er struggled for places or wealth.
Owen Bray baulked a leap——says Hal Preston ' Twas odd,'
' 'Twas shameful,' cried Hal, ' by the great living——.'
Said Preston, I halloo'd ' Get on though you fall,
' Or I'll leap over *you*, your blind gelding and all.'

" Each glass was adapted to freedom and sport,
For party affairs we consigned to the Court;
Thus we finished the rest of the day and the night,
In gay flowing bumpers and toasts of delight.
Then till the next meeting, bade farewell each brother—
So some they went one way, and some went another;
And as Phœbus befriended our earlier roam,
So Luna took care in conducting us home."

EXPLANATION OF NAMES OCCURRING IN THE SONG.

Wanton, Bonny, and ..Favourite hounds in Lord Meath's
Collier   pack.
Killegar ....On western side of the Scalp.

The House of Kiltiernan..The residence of " Johnny Adair,"
referred to in the song——near the
Scalp.

Cherrywood...........Bride's Glen, near Loughlinstown.

Ballyman ....A sequested glen near Old Connaught.
(See Index.)

Steep Shankill.........Carrickgollogan Mountain.

Carbury Byrne's........A well-known residence at that time
near Cabinteely.

Malpas high hill.......Killiney Hill, the obelisk on which was
erected by Colonel Malpas or
Mapas.

Dalkey Stone Common...Between Dalkey and Sorrento. (See
Index.)

Rochestown Wood.......Between Ballybrack and Glenageary.
Some of the wood still remains.

Garron ....(Irish) a worthless old horse.

My Lord..............The 6th Earl of Meath.

Shrub Glenageary.......An old name for Glenageary.

CHAPTER VIII

RATHDOWN, GREYSTONES, KILLINCARRIG, DELGANY AND THE GLEN OF THE DOWNS

CYCLISTS and pedestrians desirous of making this excursion should proceed to Bray, making their way up the main street and keeping to the left at the Markethouse, whence the road gradually ascends to Kilruddery, the entrance gate of which will be seen on the right, bearing in high relief the motto, " Vota vita mea," and surmounted by the arms of the Meath family. Immediately opposite this gate, at the other side of the road, is the entrance to the walk and carriage drive round the top of the Head, admission to which can be obtained by signing one's name at the gate lodge, and, if accompanied by a bicycle, paying a toll of 3d. Entering at the gate, we pass a succession of plantations, largely composed of Scotch firs and other evergreens, and continuing the track, at length reach the open mountainside, where in summer may be seen in profusion the purple splendour of the heather, interspersed with the gay colouring of the gorse, the brilliant contrast enhanced by the varying shades of sward and bracken. The track now sweeps to the seaward, and looking over the adjoining wall, we can see, far below, the railway and path overhanging the deep green water, with, perhaps, a border of white surf showing boldly against the dark rocks. From this point, our view comprises Dalkey and Killiney, Dublin city under its pall of smoke, portions of the southern suburbs, and the familiar forms of the tall twin chimneys at Ringsend, a conspicuous landmark even at this distance. As we proceed, an extensive view inland is obtained, including the Two and Three Rock Mountains, Prince William's Seat, the Scalp and

the Sugar Loaves, with the long open valley of Glencree.
Not far off is Bray Head summit, on which stands a small
monument, erected to commemorate the Jubilee of the late
Queen Victoria.

Continuing the ascent, we arrive at a high ledge, where we
unexpectedly come into view of the entire coast as far as
Wicklow Head, readily identified by its three lighthouses, while
on the curve of the coastline may be dimly discerned the town
of Wicklow. From this point the pathway begins to descend,
considerable portions being practicable for cycles, and we
presently enter another pine plantation, ultimately reaching
the exit on the main road, where the key of the gate can be
obtained at the adjoining lodge.

On reaching the road we turn to the left up the hill, presently
arriving at the little hamlet of Windgate on the very summit,
about 400 feet over sea level, and from here a long descent of
about two miles conducts us to Greystones. About half a mile
from Windgate, a laneway called Rathdown Lane will be seen
on the left, leading down to the site of the ancient castle of
Rathdown. For pedestrians it is somewhat of a short cut to
Greystones, but cyclists will find it rather difficult, and
would be well advised to avoid it and keep to the main
road.

Near the end of the lane will be seen in a field a little to the
southward, the ruins of the church of St. Crispin, thickly
enveloped with ivy. The adjacent ground now shows no indication of having been a graveyard, although it certainly was
such during the period when the church was in use, and the
last interment known to have taken place there was that of
the body of a sailor which was washed ashore early in the last
century. When the ancient village of Rathdown in course of
time disappeared, the local proprietor removed all the tombstones, disinterred the bones, and buried them in one heap
at the eastern end of the church. Some tradition of this
act of vandalism survived when Eugene O'Curry visited the
place in 1838.

The church is 23 feet long by 14 feet wide, and the entrance was by a porch at the western end. In the eastern gable is a window 6 feet square, and in the southern wall there is another about 3 feet square. The ruin bears several indications of comparatively recent repair, and does not look more than about three hundred years old, having been probably used as a chapel during the existence of the village of Rathdown.

A short distance north-east of the church, on a slight eminence, and facing the lonely sea-beaten shore, stood the ancient castle of Rathdown that in time gave name to the barony. No portion of the building now remains, and its site is partly occupied by a limekiln, which, as well as the adjoining railway bridge, was probably constructed out of the materials of the walls. The ruin, which is still marked as existent on the Ordnance Survey maps, was taken down some sixty years ago, and at that time consisted of some massive outer walls from 5 to 8 feet in height. The castle was built on an ancient fort or rath, portions of which are yet discernible to the south and east of the site.

The village of Rathdown stood a short distance to the north-west, and in draining one of the fields there during the last century, the remains of a paved street were discovered. Adjoining the site of the castle is a clear spring well which probably supplied the household with water.

Resuming our journey, we presently enter Greystones, some thirty years ago only an insignificant village consisting of a group of cottages around the Coastguard station, but now bidding fair to become one of the first watering-places in Ireland.

The following interesting notice of this place appears in Atkinson's *Irish Tourist*, published in 1815, and it should be remembered that there was then no village here, and that the name Greystones applied only to the reef of rocks still called "The Grey Stones," jutting out into the sea immediately north of the railway station. "Between Bray and the village "of Killincarrig, I looked at a spacious indenture in the coast,

" which I had heard spoken of as the native outline of a harbour,
" and which, considering its favourable position, and the ad-
" vantages which would result to that neighbourhood from
" the suitable accommodation of shipping, I was not surprised
" to hear had become an object of attention to some public
" spirited gentlemen in that neighbourhood.   Some idea may

The Beach, Greystones.
(1906.)

" be conceived of the character of this half-formed harbour,
" from the circumstance of a vessel in distress having been
" towed in there, as the best which was to be met in that part
" of the coast, and though incapable in its present form of pro-
" tecting a ship from the effects of a storm, its favourable
" position for a harbour may in some degree be inferred from
" the above circumstance."   The hopes entertained by the
writer of the above, have unfortunately not been realised, and
the harbour, as it now stands, may be regarded for all practical
purposes as useless.

Greystones possesses an irregular sea frontage of nearly a mile in length, and extends inland from the sea in a south-westerly direction to within a short distance of the hamlet of Killincarrig, which it threatens to absorb, as also, in time, the more distant village of Delgany. The sea is visible for a considerable distance inland, as the ground gradually rises from the shore. There is ample accommodation for bathing, both off the rocks, and at the pretty strand immediately south of " The

Killincarrig.
(1906.)

" Grey Stones " already alluded to. The houses are for the most part detached or semi-detached, instead of being built in terraces.

The great charm of Greystones consists in its unconventionality and the absence of the features which go to make up the typical modern watering-place, while its golf-links, its picturesque surroundings, and the pleasing combinations of rural and seaside scenery in its neighbourhood, combine to render it a most attractive and restful holiday resort.

From the top of the Killincarrig road a field-path leads by the golf-links, through a wood, to the village of Killincarrig, entering the latter beside the grim, ivy-clad ruins of an old mansion popularly known as "Killincarrig Castle," which appears to date from about the Elizabethan period. There was a tradition current that Cromwell slept a night in it, which may have had some foundation in fact, as his troops were engaged in several skirmishes in this neighbourhood during the troubled times of 1641-2.

Killincarrig stands upon a considerable eminence, commanding views both of the sea and of the mountains inland, and although the village is of considerable antiquity, the old houses have nearly all disappeared, and have been replaced by dwellings of a modern type.

In 1641 some troops were quartered in a temporary barrack in this village to protect the property of residents in the neighbourhood. In connection with the sojourn of this garrison, it is recorded in Dudley Loftus's minutes of the Courts Martial at Dublin Castle, that one Kathleen Farrell was arrested at Killincarrig as a spy, taken to Dublin, and sentenced to be hanged, which sentence, it may be presumed, was duly carried out. Another case from the same locality was that of John Bayly, a soldier, who was tried for desertion. As the penalty for this offence was usually death, there must have been some extenuating circumstances in his case, as he was merely sentenced to run the gauntlet of the soldiers stationed at Killincarrig, the soldiers armed with switches, and the culprit with his back bare and his hands tied behind him. The carrying out of this sentence probably provided a pleasant day's amusement for the inhabitants of the village, who doubtless had anything but friendly feelings for the soldiers quartered there, and were heartily glad when the time came for their departure.

At a distance of about half a mile from Killincarrig is the pretty village of Delgany, picturesquely situated on a rising ground, in the midst of an undulating and richly-wooded country, and adjoining the southern entrance to the Glen of the Downs. Immediately below the village is the deep wooded valley of the Three Trouts river, a small stream, which, after flowing through the Glen of the Downs, empties itself into the sea a mile south of Greystones. Delgany possesses a new Catholic Church attached to the convent, as well as a Protestant Church built in 1789, by Peter La Touche, the tower of which forms a prominent feature in the view of the village, as seen from various points in the surrounding country. The La Touche family, who have been connected with this locality since their purchase of the lands of Bellevue in 1753, settled in Ireland with many other Huguenot refugees after the revocation of the Edict of Nantes. They were originally a family named Digges who left England in the reign of Henry II. and settled on their estates at La Touche near Blois, from which circumstance they derive their second name. David Digges La Touche, the first of the family who came to this country, was an officer in La Caillemote's regiment of French refugees in the service of William the Third during the Irish War of the Revolution. When the war was over he entered into business as a banker in Dublin, in the concern known as " La Touche's Bank," which he managed for many years, and at length died suddenly, at a ripe old age, in 1745, while attending service in the Chapel Royal. (*Lodge's Peerage.*)

The ancient name of Bellevue was Ballydonough, which was changed to its present one in 1753 on the purchase of the lands by David La Touche.

Atkinson, in *The Irish Tourist* " (1815), above quoted, makes the following reference to Delgany :—" The village of Delgany, " situate about fifteen miles south of Dublin, and ten north " of Wicklow, forms a feature too significant to render its in- " significant extent an adequate apology for wholly neglecting " it, in a description of the beauties of this county. It is " composed principally of thatched cottages in the English " style (something similar to the village of Abbeyleix), and of " these, in which the parsonage house, a large stone edifice, and " the church of Delgany, a very ornamental structure, are not " included, there may be from fifteen to twenty habitations in

G

" the village. The influence of Delgany Church (which stands
" suitably elevated above the valley) on the scenery of that
" neighbourhood, is well known to the numerous visitors of the
" district."

At the time the above was written, there was a straw hat
and bonnet factory in the village, which articles were, according
to the same authority, sold at prices varying from one to thirty
shillings, and the writer adds that some hats which were shown
to him at eight shillings, made of Irish straw, were of exceptional
quality.

It may be mentioned that one or two of the original
" thatched cottages in the English style," referred to in
the above description, survived until a few years ago,
and the parsonage house is still the largest building in the
village.

The original name of this place was Dergne, the pronuncia-
tion of which would be represented in English by the spelling
Dergany, and this by the change of the liquid *r* to *l* became
converted to the modern designation of Delgany. The name
Dergne, meaning a little reddish spot, took its origin in the red
colour of the clay and rock underlying the surface soil around
the village, which is more noticeable after heavy rain.

In the older authorities the place is referred to as Dergne-
Mochorog, the latter portion of which is the name of the local
saint, a Briton by birth, who settled here about the end of the
6th century, building his church on the site now occupied by
the old churchyard at the lower end of the village. (See *Irish
Names of Places*, Vol. II., p. 26.)

Local tradition avers that an ancient town of Delgany stood
some four miles out to the seaward, where there is now a shallow
and rock called Delgany Bank, and that one stormy night it
was entirely submerged by the sea.

Delgany to a great extent owes its popularity to its proximity
to the Glen of the Downs, and to the fact that it lies in the
direct route between the latter and Greystones Railway Station.
The Glen of the Downs, which is too well known to require a

detailed description, is a ravine a mile and a half in length, the sides of which, rising to a height of some 700 feet, are so densely wooded that with the exception of the roadside, scarcely a glimpse of the ground is visible the whole length of the Glen. The views from the road are very soft and pretty in the summer-time, looking up along the apparently fathomless mass of foliage, relieved in places by dark patches of pines. It has been customary to admit visitors on Mondays to the eastern side, which forms portion of the demesne of Bellevue, but permission must be obtained for admission on other days. The principal attraction at this side is the octagon house at the top, from which an extensive view is obtained.

One of the best short excursions from Delgany for either cyclist or pedestrian is to go through the Glen, and after emerging at the upper end, to take the first turn on the right up the steep hill, keeping to the right throughout, and again entering the village by a well shaded road down a long decline. This will entail a journey of a little over four miles.

Cyclists arriving in Delgany *via* Bray and Greystones, should return by the Glen of the Downs, Enniskerry, and the Scalp.

Distances from G. P. O. (for cyclists) :—Bray Bridge, 12¼ miles ; Greystones by route described around Bray Head and *via* Rathdown, 18¾ miles ; Killincarrig, 20 miles ; Delgany, 20½ miles ; back to G. P. O. *via* Glen of the Downs and Enniskerry, 41 miles.

Distances from Bray Railway Station (for pedestrians) :— Greystones by route described, 6¾ miles ; Killincarrig, 8 miles ; Delgany, 8½ miles ; back to Greystones Railway Station, 10¼ miles.

CHAPTER IX

TINNEHINCH, THE GREAT AND LITTLE SUGAR LOAF, KILMACANOGUE AND POWERSCOURT

THE district described in this chapter can be most readily visited by means of cycles, but it will be necessary to leave them at the top of the Rocky Valley while ascending the Great Sugar Loaf, and at Kilmacanogue during the ascent of the Little Sugar Loaf. We first proceed to Enniskerry by the Scalp, continuing straight ahead at the upper end of the village street, passing on the left the church, the spire of which is such a conspicuous feature in pictures of Enniskerry, and on the right, one of the entrance gates to Powerscourt Demesne. As we turn the corner just opposite the entrance to the Dargle, we descend a very steep decline down to the bed of the Dargle River—a very dangerous descent in the old cycling days before the invention of rim brakes. At the bottom of the hill is the entrance to Powerscourt known as the Golden Gate, with its pretty lodge, and beside it, Tinnehinch Bridge over the Dargle. Near the bridge, and situated in the sheltered vale of the river, is Tinnehinch, for some time the residence of the distinguished patriot and statesman, Henry Grattan, who spent his declining years in the seclusion of this romantic retreat. Twiss in his *Tour Through Ireland* (1775), states that this house was designed and erected by the then Lord Powerscourt as an inn, and that it was for some years the leading hostelry in this district, and Arthur Young spent some days there, as stated in the quotation further on, during his tour in Ireland in 1776.

After crossing Tinnehinch Bridge we turn to the right along

ι road which gradually ascends through a wooded district, glimpses being obtained at intervals of the surrounding mountains through the trees. Having reached the top of this road we turn twice in succession to the left, and are now facing the Great Sugar Loaf, which looks very high and abrupt from this point of view, in consequence of being seen across the intervening valley of the Killough river. A steep descent conducts us to a bridge over that river, beyond which an equally

Tinnchinch House.
(1906.)

steep ascent rises to the head of the Rocky Valley, where we turn to the right up a long ascent, properly Killough Hill, which must be walked the whole way to the top, a distance of about a mile. This ascent is commonly, but erroneously, called the Long Hill, which is at the opposite side of the Killough River valley.

As the elevation increases, the area of our view extends, and we can see to the north the Scalp and the steep sides of Glensink through which flows the Glencullen or Cookstown River; then Prince William's Seat, the Glencree Valley, with the low hill of Knockree midway, and the Reformatory at the far end, and to the left of these Tonduff, Douce, and War Hill. Between us and Glencullen will be seen Powerscourt House standing on the summit of a rising ground, and enclosed within its extensive demesne. We at length reach the summit level of the road, at a group of cottages, 850 feet over sea level, and here cyclists must arrange to leave their machines pending their return from the ascent. From this point the pathway can be seen the whole way to the top—an easy ascent through stunted furze and heather until the peak is reached, where the gradient becomes much steeper, and the difficulty of ascending is enhanced by the loose condition of the stones under foot.

Viewed from below, the peak presents an imposing appearance, denuded in patches by the winter rains, and rising to so sharp a point that there is no more than room for a small party of visitors there.

From the summit, 1,650 feet high, may be seen Lugnaquillia, Roundwood and its reservoir, Croghan Kinsella Mountain on the borders of Wexford ; Douce, Tonduff, Glencree Reformatory and the Military road ; Wicklow Head, the Scalp, Dublin Bay, and Howth, while the country in the immediate vicinity presents the appearance of a map.

Descending the mountain, we again reach the road, and return as far as the head of the Rocky Valley, which, as its name indicates, is a defile strewn on all sides with jagged and precipitous rocks, overhanging the road in a threatening manner. On the southern side of the road will be seen a well called the Silver Springs, under the shadows of a rocky cliff, and opposite is a pretty cottage enclosed by a grove of trees. Below this point the sides of the valley become very irregular and precipitous, and small patches of reclaimed ground may be seen at intervals, with little cottages nestling among the rocks. Continuing the descent, we reach the scattered hamlet of Kilmacanogue (pronounced *Kilmakanik*), with its church on a conspicuous eminence off the main road ; and from here we may either return home at once, *via* Bray, or ascend the little Sugar Loaf.

If the latter be decided on, cycles should be left at Kilmacanogue, and the ascent commenced by turning aside from the
main road at the post office, into a lane which rises steeply
between high hedges, through which occasional glimpses are
seen of the valley below, and of the Great Sugar Loaf and the
mountains beyond it. The lane sweeps somewhat to the left
at a farmhouse beside a grove of firs, after which a wooden gate
is met, from which the ascent may be made either direct up the

Summit of the Great Sugar Loaf.
(1906.)

slope of the mountain, or by following the track to the right—
a somewhat longer, but easier route. As we ascend, the little
hamlet of Kilmacanogue appears to great advantage below,
embosomed in its sheltering woods at the foot of the Rocky
Valley; while overshadowing all, rises the Great Sugar Loaf,
and beyond it the great range of mountains, of which Douce
is the centre. To the northward are Killiney Bay, the Hills of
Dalley and Killiney dotted with their pretty villas, and further
off, Howth, the Poolbeg and Pigeonhouse; underneath is the
town of Bray, and at the foot of the hill Kilruddery House—an
extensive establishment—while to the right of that is the small

group of cottages called Windgate, at the summit of the long hill between Bray and Greystones. Right under the mountain is Bray Head, looking low and flat from this point of view ; to the right is Greystones, with its houses scattered and detached, and then a long uninteresting sweep of flat shore extends away towards Wicklow town, beyond which rises Wicklow Head.

On reaching the top of the Little Sugar Loaf it will be observed that there are three distinct summits a couple of hundred yards apart, but when seen from the north-west or south-east it appears to have only two, and it is by this latter appearance, as a double-topped mountain, that most Dublin people recognise it.

The following extract from Arthur Young's *Tour in Ireland* (1776–9) is of some interest, as showing the impressions of a stranger visiting the district at that period :—" Took my leave " of General Cunninghame, and went through the Glen of the " Downs on my way to Powerscourt. The Glen is a pass " between two vast ridges of mountains covered with wood, " which have a very noble effect. The vale is no wider than " to admit the road, a small gurgling river almost by its side, " and narrow slips of rocky and shrubby ground which part " them. In the front all escape seems denied by an immense " conical mountain [the Great Sugar Loaf], which rises out of " the Glen, and seems to fill it up. The scenery is of a most " magnificent character. On the top of the ridge to the right " Mr. La Touche has a banqueting-room. Passing from this " sublime scene, the road leads through cheerful grounds all " under corn, rising and falling to the eye, and then to a vale ' of charming verdure broken into inclosures, and bounded by " two rocky mountains [the Great and Little Sugar Loaf]— " distant darker mountains filling up the scene in front. This " whole ride is interesting, for within a mile and a half of " ' Tinnyhinch ' (the inn to which I was directed) you come to " a delicious view on the right ; a small vale [the Dargle] " opening to the sea, bounded by mountains, whose dark shade

" forms a perfect contrast to the extreme beauty and lovely
" verdure of the lower scene, consisting of gently swelling
" lawns, rising from each other, with groups of trees between,
" and the whole so scattered with white farms as to add every
" idea of cheerfulness."

After breakfasting at the Tinnehinch inn, Young drove to see
Powerscourt Waterfall, and thence to the Dargle, his description of which, pitched in a high key, extends to a considerable

Kilmacanogue.
(1906.)

length. Of Powerscourt he writes, that " it presently came in
" view from the edge of a declivity. You look full upon the
" house, which appears to be in the most beautiful situation
" in the world, on the side of a mountain, half-way between
" its bare top and an irriguous vale at its foot. In front, and
" spreading among woods on either side, is a lawn, whose
" surface is beautifully varied in gentle declivities, hanging to a
" winding river."

The celebrity of Powerscourt is almost entirely due to its
Waterfall, which, although of great height, possesses but a

small flow of water, except after heavy rain. It has been described by successive writers in such extravagant terms, that
the tourist who visits it in fine weather is apt to be much dis-
appointed.

The Wingfields, the ancestors of the Lords Powerscourt,
derive their name from the manor and castle of Wingfield in
Suffolk, of which the family was possessed before the Norman
Conquest. Sir John Wingfield, Lord of Letheringham, served
the Black Prince in the wars in France, and afterwards wrote a
history of the campaign. Coming down to the reign of
Elizabeth, we find that Jacques Wingfield was appointed Master
of the Ordnance and Munition in Ireland, and in 1560 was
commissioned to execute martial law in the territories of the
O'Byrnes and O'Tooles. Twenty years later he accompanied
Lord Grey of Wilton, on his ill-starred expedition against the
Wicklow tribes, which culminated in the Battle of Glenmalure,
where the English troops becoming entangled in the dense
forests, met with signal defeat at the hands of the Irish clansmen
under Feagh MacHugh O'Byrne and FitzEustace, Earl of
Baltinglass.

In 1600 Sir Richard Wingfield was appointed Marshal of
Ireland by Queen Elizabeth in recognition of his services against
the French at Calais ; for his further services in Ulster he was
granted the district of Fercullen, containing nearly the whole
parish of Powerscourt, and in 1618 he was created first Baron
Powerscourt.

The district of Powerscourt takes its name from the De la
Poer family, who came into possession of it through a marriage
with a daughter of Strongbow, and who it is believed, built a
castle on the site now occupied by the present Powerscourt
House. That this latter house incorporates some of the ancient
structure would appear probable from the fact that some of
the walls in the central portion are from eight to ten feet thick.

According to the Down Survey, Sir Richard Wingfield was
granted the lands of Powerscourt, " five miles in length by four
" miles in breadth, in the territory of Fercullen in the County

" of Wicklow, by James the First, said land being mostly
" mountainous and stony, and with a ruinous castle."

Pedestrians desirous of ascending either of the Sugar Loaf
Mountains should take the train to Bray, walking thence to
Kilmacanogue and back, a distance of seven miles for the
double journey.

The distance from the G.P.O. to Kilmacanogue *via* the
Scalp and Enniskerry is 15½ miles.

CHAPTER X

RATHFARNHAM, WHITECHURCH, KELLY'S GLEN AND KILMASHOGUE MOUNTAIN

TO reach Rathfarnham, we either proceed there direct in the tram *via* Harold's Cross, or take the Rathmines tram as far as the top of the Rathgar road, walking thence along Orwell Road to Orwell Bridge, and then turning to the

Rathfarnham.
(1906.)

right along the grassy bank of the Dodder. Orwell Bridge was built about sixty years ago, replacing a wooden footbridge which had done duty for a number of years, and had at length become unsafe.

Prior to the erection of Orwell Bridge, vehicles had to cross by a ford, which is still to be seen about half way between the bridge and the Dartry Dye Works. There are some large stones in the river near this point, which appear to be the remains of a line of stepping-stones. Orwell Bridge was formerly called "Waldron's Bridge," from the name of a former proprietor of the mills adjoining.

The Dodder from Rathfarnham Bridge.
(1903.)

The portion of the river between Orwell and Rathfarnham Bridges is extremely picturesque ; a high wooded bank rises above the northern side, crowned by modern residences, while adjoining the road is the densely wooded demesne of Rathfarnham Castle. The entrance gate, in the form of a Roman triumphal arch, was erected in the early part of last century by Charles, Lord Ely, who, for his vote and influence in connection with the Act of Union, received a step in the peerage and £45,000 in cash.

This quiet spot was, in 1841, the scene of a crime which excited an extraordinary degree of interest in Dublin. On the night of the 27th February, an Italian named Domenico

Garlibardo, an organ-grinder, was murdered, and his body thrown on the waste ground in front of Lord Ely's gate, where it was found next morning by a policeman. The inquest was of a protracted character, lasting no less than eight days, and resulted in a verdict of wilful murder, accompanied by a rider attaching strong suspicion to a tinker and his wife from Rathfarnham. These two were in due course placed on trial, but during the proceedings the evidence of the principal witness (Patrick Bryan) broke down on cross-examination, and he contradicted himself to such an extent that he was arrested in court for perjury, and the prisoners were consequently acquitted. It was understood, however, that the police had another informant named Delahunt, who, for reasons unexplained, was not produced at either the inquest or trial ; but no further developments took place, and the mystery seemed as far from solution as ever, although public opinion strongly inclined to the suspicion that Delahunt was the guilty party.

A few days before Christmas of the same year, the Dublin folk were horrified to hear of another murder, that of a boy named Maguire, whose body, still warm, was found in Pembroke Lane, at rear of Pembroke Road. About an hour after the body was discovered, Delahunt turned up at the police headquarters with the story that he had seen a murder committed at the spot, adding incriminating details as to the conduct of the victim's mother, but his strange demeanour and shifty answers excited the suspicions of the police, and he was detained. Inquiries being set on foot, a mass of damning evidence was soon obtained against him, principally from his own immediate relatives, and after a brief trial he was found guilty and executed on the 5th February following.

Before his execution he acknowledged having murdered the boy, Maguire, but denied the murder of Garlibardo. Many of the public, however, continued to believe that he was guilty of both murders, and that the motive was the hope of getting a reward from the authorities for evidence leading to a conviction.

Less than a mile south of Orwell Bridge, and situated on a
by-road, is a strange-looking, conical shaped structure, called
" Hall's Barn " after a local proprietor who erected it during
" the hard frost " in the winter of 1741-2, to give employment to the poor, then in great distress. It was obviously
built in imitation of " The Wonderful Barn " near Leixlip,
and like it, is ascended by a winding staircase. (See Index.)

Hall's Barn.
(1900.)

Gerard Boate, in his *Natural History of Ireland* (1652),
writing of this neighbourhood, says :—" No country in the
" world is fuller of brooks than Ireland, where the same be
" numberless and water all the parts of the land on all sides.

· · · · · · ·

" The brooks—beside the great good they do the land in
" watering the same, and beside the commodity they afford of
" drenching the cattle and other beasts—do also greatly serve
" the inhabitants for another good use—to wit, the grinding

" of their corn, whereunto the windmills are very little used in
" Ireland, because they have the conveniency, through the great
" number of brooks, to erect watermills in every quarter where
" it is necessary : which bring a great profit to the owners
" being kept and maintained with less cost and labour. . . .

" Of these dangerous brooks there are two hard by Dublin,
" both running into the haven somewhat more than a mile
" from the city—the one at north side thereof, a little below
" the village Drumcondra, which is seated upon the highway
" from Dublin to Drogheda ; and the other at the south side,
" close by the Rings-end. This, called Rathfarnum water
" [the Dodder], of the village by which it passeth two miles
" from the sea and the same distance from Dublin, is far the
" worst of the two, as taking its beginning out of those great
" mountains southwards from Dublin, from whence after any
" great rain, such abundance of water is descending to it that
" the same, which at other times is of very little depth, groweth
" thereby so deep, and exceeding violent that many persons
" have lost their lives therein. Amongst others Mr. John
" Usher, father to Sir William Usher that now is, who was
" carried away by the current, nobody being able to succour
" him, although many persons, and of his nearest friends, both
" a-foot and horseback, were by on both the sides.

．　　　．　　　．　　　．　　　．　　　．　　　．

" To go from Dublin to Rathfarnum, one passeth this river
" upon a wooden bridge ; the which although it be high and
" strong, nevertheless hath several times been quite broke,
" and carried away through the violence of sudden floods ;
" although at other times, and when that brook doth only
" carry its ordinary water, a child of five years may easily and
" without danger wade through it ; and a tall man on horseback
" riding underneath it [the bridge] not being able to reach it.
" In the great floods the water many times riseth so high as that
" it doth not only touch, but floweth quite over the bridge."
The statement as to the drowning of Sir William Usher's

father is incorrect. Boate probably confused him with the elder son and heir of Sir William Usher—*i.e.*, Arthur Usher of Donnybrook, who was drowned in the Dodder on the 2nd March, 1628.

At a distance of less than half a mile from the Dodder we reach the village of Rathfarnham, a sort of outpost in former times to menace the mountaineers, but now almost a suburban village. At the terminus of the tram line, on the left, will be seen a lofty though ungraceful entrance to the demesne, while the battlements of the castle itself may be observed towering high above the humbler structures in the village street. This imposing edifice was built towards the close of the 16th century by Archbishop Loftus, who had previously acquired the adjoining lands by grant or purchase.

During the troublous time of 1641, Rathfarnham Castle was first used for the purpose for which it was primarily intended—namely, that of interposing a strong military station between Dublin and the mountains, on the principal road leading southwards. One of the incidents of the military occupation that year was an explosion of gunpowder which nearly killed one John Ogilby, a Scotchman, who was Master of the Revels in Ireland, and had built two theatres in Dublin. Eight years later, during the war between the Royalists and the Parliamentarians, and a few days before the Battle of Rathmines, the Castle was stormed by the Royalists, in command of the Marquess of Ormonde, who took all the garrison prisoners, without loss of life on either side, from which it would seem that the defence was not of a very resolute character.

At this period the village was the scene of so many skirmishes and encounters between the Dublin settlers and the mountaineers, that it became a very undesirable place of residence and fell into a decayed condition.

Adjoining Rathfarnham was in former times a village named Butterfield, of which no vestige has been left beyond the name, which still attaches to the lane on the right, at the southern end of Rathfarnham. This village probably stood in Butterfield

Lane, possibly extending along the bank of the Owen Dugher, which at this point is spanned by a bridge.

In 1692, the Castle of Rathfarnham passed by marriage into the possession of the Marquess of Wharton, and in 1723 it was sold by his son to the Right Hon. Wm. Conolly, Speaker of the Irish House of Commons. In 1767 it was purchased by the 2nd Earl of Ely, and thus reverted to the possession of the family that built it. In 1852 the Castle was bought by Lord Chancellor Blackburne, in whose family it still remains.

Passing through Rathfarnham village, with Mount Pelier conspicuously in view in front, we pass on the right Butterfield Lane, where Robert Emmet resided for a time in 1803. Presently we reach the new Catholic church, where a turn to the right leads to Willbrook, now in a rather decayed condition, but gradually being replaced by new dwellings built by the rural district council.

At Willbrook we turn to the left along the Whitechurch road, following for some distance the course of a small stream which forms a series of pools where a few wary trout may at times be seen disporting themselves. On the left, at the cross roads, and just inside the grounds of " Hermitage," is a monument, erected by a former owner, Major Doyne, to a horse which carried him through the Battle of Waterloo.

As Whitechurch is approached, the view opens and the road winds considerably, following the course of the pretty stream which here flows between gently sloping banks diversified by tufts of furze and whitethorn. To the left of the road near the Moravian cemetery is a plantation of fine Scotch firs, which, it will be observed, are all inclined towards the east, owing to the force of the prevailing west and south-west winds at this point.

The tall spire of a church presently appears in view, and in a short distance further the structure itself will be seen on a grassy knoll to the left, sheltered by a grove of trees and enclosed in prettily planted grounds.

From very early times a church stood in this locality, and was variously designated as " Alba," " The Church of Balgeeth," or " The Church in the Marches ;" the " Marches " being the name applied to the hinterland or border lands of the Pale. About half a mile nearer Dublin, approached by a narrow laneway, may still be seen the remains of the ancient church, in the graveyard of which certain families still retain the right of burial.

Immediately beyond Whitechurch we cross a bridge over the Little Dargle river, and turn immediately to the left, passing a group of mill buildings in ruinous condition, beside which is the local national school. We now enter a narrow lane rising steeply up the slopes of Kilmashogue Mountain, and towards the upper part, sheltered between high hedge-banks covered with a luxuriant growth of herbage and wild flowers. On the left are the well wooded grounds of Kilmashogue House, planted with firs, larches and yew trees.

As the top of this lane is approached, an extensive view is obtained westward towards the Bog of Allen, and northward to the low range known as the Naul or Man-of-War hills which form the northern boundary of the county. In the immediate foreground are the church and the scattered hamlet of White-church embosomed in trees, while to the right are the extensive buildings of St. Columba's College. In the distance will be discerned the Pigeonhouse, with its conspicuous new red brick chimney, Clontarf, Dollymount, Sutton, and Howth Hill, while to the left lies the city under its canopy of smoke, the southern suburbs alone being clearly distinguished. The lane now bending to the right, ascends more steeply and enters upon a wilder track fringed by growths of bracken and furze, the heights to the left being crowned by the woods of Kilma-shogue, while to the right the road is bordered by a plantation of firs and larches, below which in the valley, is the picturesquely situated residence known as Larch Hill, now a sanatorium, surrounded and almost concealed by its pine woods. At this point we may enter the fields to the left of the road and make our way among the rocks and furze bushes until the road is again met higher up the mountain, but in damp weather the

mountainside is apt to be swampy, and it will be better to keep
to the road, even though the distance may be somewhat longer.
Here overshadowed by the larches, the road becomes highly
picturesque, bordered by a selvage of grass on either side, and
with a rocky tract on the left through which a murmuring
rivulet threads its course.

After passing the larch plantation, the road ascends very

On Kilmashogue Mountain.
(1906.)

steeply, and in consequence of sweeping to the eastward the
view of the Dublin plain is cut off by the upper part of the
mountain. Almost directly in front is the Two-Rock Mountain,
the summit of which is marked by the pointed carn known as
" Fairy Castle," and to the left, but at a lower elevation, the
familiar forms of the Three Rocks will be observed. The road
here becomes little more than a bridle track along the side of
the mountain, and almost at its highest point is closed by a
wooden gateway, which, however, presents no obstacle to the
pedestrian. A short distance beyond this point is a lane known
as " Kelly's Lane," leading down to a small slated house almost

at the bottom of the valley, and at the opposite bank of the stream beside the bridge, is a chalybeate spa that enjoyed a considerable share of popularity among the Dublin folk about one hundred and fifty years ago. It will easily be identified by the reddish-yellow deposit with which it is surrounded. All this valley between Kilmashogue and Tibradden is called Kelly's Glen, and the precipitous little gorge through which the stream runs at the bottom, was supposed by Gabriel Beranger to have been caused by an earthquake, to which agency he also attributed the displacement of the top stone of Mount Venus cromlech. The stream is spanned by two bridges, erected by a proprietor named Caldbeck about the middle of the last century, one bearing the inscription " De la Sophannie, 1850," and the other " A suore amabile "—said to have been intended as memorials to his deceased sister.

The spa here came into vogue about 1750, immediately after the decline of Templeogue Spa at Spawell House, but its distance from town and the height at which it stood, greatly militated against its popularity. Dr. Rutty in his *Natural History of the County of Dublin* (1757) has the following interesting notice of it :—" This spring was first taken notice of about " the year 1748, being in my opinion superior to that of Temple- " ogue, even when this last was in its utmost perfection, though " not so easy of access. It is a perennial spring, about nine " inches deep, and about twelve inches over, situate in a small " glyn on Kilmashoge Hill, a mile south from Kilmashoge, " and five miles from Dublin, and consequently, Templeogue " spring now failing, is the nearest of any to the city, and not " unworthy the notice of our citizens, who though probably " by the badness of the road they may be deterred from going " to the fountain, may be daily supplied with this water con- " veyed to them early in the morning in bottles well corked, " and so it deserves a cover from the rain."

Dr. Rutty himself took this water for three seasons, and gives a detailed account of the beneficial effects he experienced from it. For some years it was brought to the city daily, and the house adjoining the spa is said to have been originally built to accommodate visitors desirous of staying there to take the water.

Retracing our steps to the head of " Kelly's Lane," we leave the grass-grown track and ascend the wild mountainside, making our way as best we can through the furze and heather, perhaps startling an occasional grouse, and possibly equally startled ourselves by the loud whirr with which it rises from its hiding place. After a fairly easy climb of a few hundred feet we reach the summit, 1,339 feet high—the nearest of the mountain summits to the city, from the centre of which it is, in a straight line, just six miles distant.

Kilmashogue Mountain possesses no very striking feature, its outline is rounded, and it has no carn or other mark to indicate the exact summit as in the cases of some of the higher mountains around. Having viewed the extensive prospect from the top, the descent should be made down the south-eastern side, so as to visit the ruined remains of Caldbeck's Castle—a most unpicturesque structure, which, although called a castle, was evidently nothing more than an ordinary dwelling-house. It is said that it, like the house lower down the valley, was built to accommodate visitors to the spa. The ruin lies almost exactly in a line from the top of Kilmashogue to the top of the Two-Rock Mountain. What remains of the building shows that it had a number of cramped and curiously arranged apartments such as might be expected in a lodginghouse or hotel of limited dimensions. It is now enclosed by a loose stone wall and stands in a slight hollow on the mountain, possibly made for its reception.

Some forty years ago there stood on the northern slope of Kilmashogue, a diminutive church ruin with little of the walls standing, but recent search failed to discover any trace of it, and probably it has long since either fallen down or been dismantled for building purposes. In all likelihood it was the original Kil-mashogue (the Church of Saint Moshamhóg or Mashoge).

The return journey may be made by going round to the northern side of the mountain, and then following a path leading back to the lane over Whitechurch, by which the ascent was made. A more varied and interesting route, however, for the return journey is to cross Kelly's Glen and make for a solitary farmhouse which will be seen half-way up the side of Tibradden Mountain on the opposite side of the valley, from which a rough roadway, crossed by a couple of gates, leads into a most picturesque winding lane, affording exquisite views of the Dublin plain and the blue waters of the Bay. This is one of the prettiest lanes in the Dublin mountains, but it is difficult to reach it in damp weather by crossing the valley, as the intervening low ground is sure to be marshy and almost impassable after rain. This lane ultimately leads out on the road known as " Mutton Lane " from Whitechurch to Rockbrook, close to the latter hamlet, from which there is a direct road to Rathfarnham, not quite three miles distant.

Distances :—Rathfarnham to Whitechurch cross-roads, $2\frac{1}{4}$ miles ; Whitechurch to Caldbeck's Castle, 2 miles ; Caldbeck's Castle back to Rathfarnham, 4 miles. Total, $8\frac{1}{4}$ miles.

If Kelly's Glen is crossed, and Rathfarnham is reached by Rockbrook, it will add about a mile and a quarter to the journey.

CHAPTER XI

A DAY ON MOUNT PELIER

THERE are few places more attractive for a ramble on a summer's day than the green, rounded hill of Mount Pelier, with the ruined shooting lodge on its summit, its extensive views over land and sea, and the various residences in its immediate neighbourhood, which in former times were associated with personages of social and historic importance. We start by taking the steam tram as far as Tallaght, turning to the left by the Oldbawn road at the end of the village, then crossing in succession Oldbawn Bridge and the Bohernabreena road, and continuing straight ahead into Oldcourt lane. Immediately on the left is Allenton, an old-fashioned house of the 18th century with high-pitched gables, deriving its name from Sir Timothy Allen, Lord Mayor of Dublin in 1762, who made it his residence, and whose monument may be seen in Tallaght church. At the rear are the remains of an ancient building, consisting of a narrow square tower, which looks like a belfry, and on the opposite side of the road are the ivied ruins of a massive entrance gate, apparently of very ancient date.

Following the devious course of this pretty country lane, in about three-quarters of a mile we reach a disused avenue on the right, opposite to which is the entrance to Oldcourt, a very ancient farm residence, with remains of an old garden, now overgrown and wild, and an extensive quadrangle of out-offices served by a water conduit taken from the adjoining stream. This house, which is mentioned in numerous inquisitions and grants for hundreds of years past, bears evidence of numerous alterations at different periods, but being untenanted, is gradually falling into decay.

We now enter the old avenue opposite, leading up to a building popularly known as "The Long House," originally called "Dollymount," and at a subsequent period "Mount Pelier House"—a name which has caused it to be confounded with the ruin on top of the hill. The original heavy gate pillars and stone walls along the avenue still remain, as also a couple of stiles constructed for the use of foot passengers when the approach was closed during the absence of the proprietors. The house is two storeys high in front, with six windows on each side, and over the hall-door are the arms of the Ely

Mount Pelier House.
("Dollymount.")
(1912.)

family, surmounted by a coronet. The rooms had marble chimney-pieces and stuccoed ceilings, some portions of which yet remain; and the windows commanded a beautiful view of the County Dublin, the city and bay, with Howth, Ireland's Eye and Lambay. On each side of the house was a large arched gateway, from which extended a long wing of out-offices, servants' apartments, stables, &c., terminating at each end in a square three-storied tower with embattled top and pointed windows. Over the door of the left hand tower was, formerly, the date 1763, inscribed on the key-stone of the arch—probably the date of erection or commencement.

This establishment was built as a hunting residence by Henry

Loftus, Earl of Ely, the Count Loftonzo figuring so prominently in *Baratariana*, whose wife, Frances Munroe, was aunt of the celebrated beauty, Dolly Monroe, after whom the place was called " Dollymount." It was originally surrounded and sheltered by a fine plantation of trees, some of which, mostly chestnuts, may still be seen to the left on approaching the building, and on the slope of the hill above it was a splendid wood of firs and larches, as dense as a tropical forest, not a trace of which now remains, the trees having been cut down and sold by a tenant who occupied the place after it had been abandoned as a residence by the owners.

Half a mile to the north-east is Orlagh College, formerly Footmount, now owned by the Augustinian Fathers, and easily identified by its spire peeping above the surrounding woods. This house was built about 1790 by Mr. Lundy Foot, the celebrated snuff manufacturer, of Westmoreland Street and Essex Street, who subsequently altered the name to Orlagh. He was an active magistrate, and as such was instrumental in bringing to justice the three Kearneys, who were hanged at Bohernabreena in 1816 for the murder of the gamekeeper of Friarstown. He was afterwards fired at, receiving desperate injuries, from which, however, he recovered, and ultimately was murdered in 1835 on his estate at Rosbercon, in the County Kilkenny, it was supposed by some relatives of the Kearneys, although this was only surmise, as the murderers were never discovered. His remains were some years afterwards removed to St. Matthew's Church, Irishtown, where a tombstone records the manner of his death.

This Lundy Foot constructed the road from Ballycullen House to the entrance gate of Orlagh, and planted the fine woods around the house, as well as the trees on the roads adjoining it. After he went to the County Kilkenny, Orlagh was taken by Carew O'Dwyer, a prominent citizen and social figure in his day, who built a large banquetting hall in the house, and entertained with lavish hospitality.[8]

Making our way over the gorse and heather up the slopes of the hill from Mount Pelier House, we at length come into view of the old ruin on the top—an interesting and conspicuous object from afar, but proving a most unprepossessing structure on closer acquaintance. It is variously known to the Dublin folk as the Hell Fire Club House, the Haunted House, and the Shooting Lodge, although it really possesses no valid claim to any of these designations, it having been built, apparently as a mere freak, for use as an occasional summer residence, by the

Ruin on top of Mount Pelier.
(1904.)

Right Honourable William Conolly of Castletown, Speaker of the Irish House of Commons, about the year 1725, shortly after he purchased the Duke of Wharton's estate in this neighbourhood. Up to that date, there had stood from remote times upon the summit of the hill, a large carn similar to those on the tops of some of the adjacent mountains, consisting of a kind of rude wall or circumvallation of large flat stones set edgewise, within which a great quantity of smaller stones were collected into a heap. In the centre was a large monolith, 9 feet high, 6 feet wide, and 3 feet thick, and a similar stone about 5 or 6 feet high stood about sixty yards to the south-west. Nearly all these relics of a prehistoric age were utilised in building the house, which, it will be observed, is constructed of very rough and irregular materials, ill calculated to remain long in good repair. The building contained two large apartments and a hall on the upper floor, underneath which was the kitchen, where the jambs of the great fire-place may still be seen, a servants' hall, and a small room at each end under a lean-to roof. The halldoor was reached by a lofty flight of steps, which with most of the other cut stone work, was taken away and used in the building of Mount Pelier House lower down the hill. In front was a semi-circular courtyard, enclosed by a low stone wall and entered by a gate.

Shortly after the house was built, the slated roof was blown off one night in a tremendous storm—by the agency of the devil it was popularly believed, on account of the sacrilegious conduct of the builder in desecrating the old carn. But Squire Conolly was not a man to be easily beaten, and so he set to work and built a massive arched roof of stones keyed together as in a bridge, and of such impregnable strength that it has effectually withstood the efforts of wind or devil—whichever it was—from that day to this. This roof is perhaps the best built portion of the whole structure, consisting of flat stones set edgewise and the irregularities then filled in with gravel and mortar until brought to a uniform surface.

With regard to one of the names which seems to have taken the fancy of the public, it is to be observed that while the Hell Fire Club may have held some of its meetings in this house, it is tolerably certain that it was never one of the regular meeting-places of that mysterious and iniquitous body, the ordinary rendezvous of which was the Eagle Tavern, on Cork Hill.

The windows all face the north, evidently for the sake of the view, which must have been one of the chief attractions in selecting such a site. Standing in front of the building and looking eastward, one sees in succession Kilmashogue, the Three Rock and Two Rock Mountains, Tibradden, the dense woods of Glendoo, and then Cruagh and Killakee Mountains, due south lies Kippure, with the infant tributaries of the

Dodder in deeply-sunk furrows by which they can be traced to their respective sources; and trending away in a southerly direction across the heather-brown slopes of Killakee is the great Military road, like a white ribbon flung across these desert solitudes—the sole mark of man's dominion in that wild region. Westward is Knockannavea or Tallaght Hill, beyond which may be discerned with a glass, the Bog of Allen and the serrated ruin of Carbury castle standing out boldly on the horizon. Farther off may be seen the double-topped Croghan Hill in Westmeath, with a number of lower elevations in its neighbourhood, while in the same direction, but much closer at hand, is the picturesquely wooded hill of Oughterard. North-east lies Howth with its bright fields and pretty villas, set in the sapphire waters of the bay, to the left is the greyish blur of smoke marking the position of the city, and then in succession along the coast, are Kingstown Harbour and the hills of Dalkey and Killiney.

There can be little doubt that this hill possessed an Irish name, like the other hills around it, and it is highly probable that this name was known to the Irish-speaking race who were to be found in Glennasmole down to the early part of the last century, but all trace of it has now, unfortunately, been lost among the country folk in the neighbourhood, to whom it is universally known as "Mount Pelia." The modern name originated with the house on its summit, which was called Mount Pelier by the builder.

The descent may be made either directly down to the road near Killakee House, or through the steep little defile at the back of the hill, keeping to the left through the wood, and reaching the Military road beside the old reservoir. Turning homeward we pass the woods of Killakee House, and if desired, can take the private road through the demesne to Rockbrook. If, however, the road is adhered to, we presently pass on our left, the extensive stables of Killakee House, about a mile beyond which is the lofty gateway leading into the grounds of Mount Venus, a roomy old country house standing on the summit of a prettily wooded round hill enclosed by splendid trees.

A short distance from this house, and adjoining the by-road leading to Rockbrook, is Mount Venus cromlech, standing within a walled enclosure, and nearly concealed by a grove of trees. The table stone has slipped from its original position, and only two of the supporting stones now remain upright. As stated in another chapter, the displacement of this top stone was attributed by Gabriel Beranger to an earthquake, which he also considered responsible for the formation of the precipitous little gorge at Kelly's Glen.

A little lower down the road, inside the dashed wall so liberally inscribed with the names of excursionists, is Woodtown, now a school, built by George Grierson, King's printer in the 18th century, who received £100,000 compensation for the loss of his office at the Union. With portion of the money he set up a wonderful farming establishment here, where he raised prize cattle and crops that brought him great renown at the agricultural shows, but made such inroads on his capital that, with the aid of a few similar enterprises, he soon succeeded in dissipating the whole of it, and died considerably in debt.

Resuming our journey, we next pass the Rathmines auxiliary reservoir, and crossing Billy's Bridge, we join the Rockbrook road, passing in succession through the hamlets of Ballyboden and Willbrook before reaching Rathfarnham, from which the tram can be taken to town.

For those desirous of a somewhat longer walk than that *via* Tallaght, it will be an agreeable alternative to start instead from Rathfarnham, proceeding thence by Butterfield lane and the Bohernabreena road to Oldbawn, whence the route already described should be followed.

If Tallaght is made the starting point, and the return made by Rathfarnham, the total distance to be walked is 7½ miles, while if both start and finish are made at Rathfarnham the distance would be 10¼ miles.

The route described in this chapter for ascending Mount Pelier has been selected for the purpose of seeing Oldcourt, Mountpelier House and Orlagh, but the easiest and most usual route is from the Military road near Killakee House (Lord Massey's), from which there is a pathway up to the ruin on the summit.

Cyclists might arrange to leave their machines at one of the cottages at Killakee, and then walk over the mountain.

In the preparation of this chapter much information has been obtained from Handcock's *History and Antiquities of Tallaght*.

CHAPTER XII

HAROLD'S GRANGE, THE THREE ROCK, TWO ROCK AND TIBRADDEN MOUNTAINS

RATHFARNHAM has been selected as the starting point for this excursion on account of the facility with which it can be reached by tram from nearly all parts of the city and suburbs, but Dundrum is a more direct route, and, for those residing near the railway, will be found more convenient. Those who make Dundrum their starting point should walk thence to Tiknock cross-roads, from which they should follow the route described further on in this chapter.

Having reached Rathfarnham, we turn to the left at the end of the village street, passing in succession the new Catholic church and the dilapidated locality known as "The Ponds," where a large square-framed gateway stood until last year, bearing the inscription "Nutgrove School, Established 1802," and leading into a pretty avenue shaded by a row of tall trees. The schoolhouse was in former times the dower house of Rathfarnham Castle, and its grounds are now utilised as a flower farm. In the old playground is a tree, on the trunk of which are carved the names and initials of many of the former scholars.

The road turning to the right at the Ponds, passes the extensive buildings of the Loreto Convent, the central portion of which was a residence of Mr. Grierson, King's printer at the time of the Union. Nearly opposite is the row of dwellings called St. Patrick's Cottages, recently erected by the district council, and forming with the new terrace behind them on the Whitechurch road, a considerable addition to the old village of Willbrook. Beyond this point the road is enclosed between walls, and presently ascends past the grounds of "Hermitage" to a fantastic embattled structure known as "The Fortification," which, owing to its mantle of ivy, has acquired an appearance of age beyond its years. It probably dates from about the middle of the 18th century, as during that period it was the fashion for the wealthy gentry to have in their grounds some form of ruin, cromlech or other fabricated antiquity.

On the opposite side of the road, and enclosed by woods, is "The Priory," for some years the residence of John Philpot Curran.

Beyond "The Fortification" occasional glimpses of the Bay are obtained through the trees on the left; a long stretch of road then follows, enclosed by walls, until after passing the entrance to the course where the Rathfarnham races were formerly held, the road sweeps to the right, affording the first view of the open country, and of the Two Rock and Three Rock Mountains from their bases to their summits.

We next reach the locality known as Harold's Grange, deriving its name from a grange or farm house, probably fortified, of the Harolds, a powerful Anglo-Norman sept who were territorial proprietors in this neighbourhood for hundreds of years, and whose dominion is also commemorated in the more familiar designation of Harold's Cross.

On the banks of the stream, a little beyond the cross-roads, and almost concealed by lofty trees, is the ruin of a small square turret or watch-tower, which, probably belonged to the original grange, and was connected with it by a bridge across the stream. It is entered by a pointed arched door, the cut keystone over which appears to be more recent than the rest of the structure. On the opposite bank, vestiges of an ancient building may be distinguished in the masonry of some cottages and outhouses, which would point to the probability that they have been incorporated with the remains of the ancestral home of the Harolds.

At this point we turn to the left along a road which gradually ascends for about three-quarters of a mile to Tiknock cross-roads, from which on a clear day, an extensive view is obtained

I

to the north and east. We here turn to the right along the
Tiknock road, with heather and gorse-clad heights on either
side.   A few hundred yards further on, a cottage will be seen
in the fields to the right, behind which is the once famous
Grumley's Well, where a patron was formerly held, and where
even now an occasional pilgrim comes to pay his devotions
In front of the well are two willow trees, and over it a stunted
thorn bush, with a few rags tied to its branches in accordance

View on the Three Rock Mountain near Ballyedmonduff.
(1905)

with the time-honoured practice. In the covering stonework
is a recess, which probably at one time held the pediment of a
cross, while in front are engraved two chalices, and on top a
rude 'representation of a cross with the letters I.H.S.   A
remarkable head of water originates at this well which forms
the source of a pretty stream flowing through the fields and
crossing the road from Harold's Grange.

As we continue our journey, the view extends eastward, and
we presently obtain a view of Kingstown and its harbour, after
which we cross a spur of the Three Rock Mountain by a steep
ascent, where the road is very rough and loose in consequence of

being torn up by the torrents in rainy weather. To the right
will be seen a precipitous rocky eminence rising over the group
of cottages known as Stackstown, to which there is a pathway
through the fields from the road.

Just as this steep part of the road is passed, and we again reach
level ground, a lane, entered by an iron gate, will be seen on
the left—follow this lane past the farmhouse, and pass through
the latched wooden gate at the end beside the rifle club
house, after which bear well to the left—in a south-easterly
direction—over rocks, gorse, and heather, resplendent with
colour in blossoming time, until at length the tops of the rocks
are seen peeping above the sky-line in front. A wire fence
will then be observed, with a conspicuous stile for the convenience of visitors.

An alternative but scarcely so easy a route as the above, is
to proceed to the inn which occupies so conspicuous a position
half a mile south-east of the Tiknock cross-roads, taking the
road at the back of the house and almost immediately diverging
by a rough but well defined track on the right. Keep to this
track until it reaches the quarries, where go straight ahead and
bear well to the left until a low stone wall or mearing is seen,
on the left side of which a grassy track leads straight up to the
stile near the summit.

The three groups of rocks which give name to this mountain
are nearly in a line, running south-east by east, and are only
partially visible from the Dublin plain. The following scientific
description of them, by Mr. G. V. Du Noyer, an eminent
archæologist and painter, is taken from a memoir published in
1835 by the Geological Society of Ireland, to explain their
map of the Dublin district :—" The remarkable-looking bosses
" of granite on the summits of the Three Rock and Two Rock
" Mountains are not perched blocks, but the solid granite
" weathering in places ; and this weathering is solely the result
" of long-continued atmospheric action—rain, frost, and snow.
" The rock being evenly jointed in vertical as well as horizontal
" planes, has weathered on the line of separation ; and some of

" the rough cubical masses thus formed have resisted the action
" of the weather more completely than the others. In this way
" are left those great table-like masses, having their edges
" moulded along the horizontal joints."

A much more fanciful description is that of Gabriel Beranger,
who wrote about 1780 :—" This mountain has on its summit
" three huge heaps of rock, piled one on another, and seen at
" some miles distance, from which the mountain takes its name.
" I take them to be altars on which sacrifices were offered.
" The plate [a sketch made by Beranger of the group of rocks
" visible from Dublin] represents one of the most entire ; it
" rises about 18 feet above the ground, and is accessible by
" an easy ascent. It has several basins cut in the rock on its
" top, of the size of the inside of a man's hat ; but one more
" remarkable than the rest, being of an oval form, and measures
" 2 feet 6 inches in length by 2 feet broad, the depth in the
" centre, 9 inches. Another of these, but less entire, is at some
" distance. I have copied every stone as they are fixed, and the
" regularity which is observed in piling them convinces me
" that they are the work of man, as they could not grow in that
" position. The sea is seen, though more than 6 miles off.
" The extensive summit of this mountain, the parched ground
" and its solitude, make it the most awful spot I had ever seen."

Beranger probably considered that the " basins," of which
he took such particular notice, were intended for the reception
of the blood from the victims sacrified.

Sir William and Lady Wilde, in their *Memoir of Beranger*
(p. 170), notwithstanding the fact that they had the advantage
of Du Noyer's opinion, strangely enough, assent to Beranger's
preposterous surmise as to the human origin of these piles of
rocks, and describe them in an introductory reference to the
foregoing account as " a Druid monument on the Three-rock
Mountain."

It will be observed that Beranger has not a word to say in
regard to the beauty of the prospect from the top, having
apparently been impressed only by feelings of awe for his surroundings. This attitude is quite usual with old writers, by

whom mountains were usually regarded as objects of horror, while in still earlier times the inhabitants of the plains so peopled them with fabulous monsters and malevolent spirits, that they were regarded as extremely undesirable places of resort. It is only in quite recent times that a perception of their beauty or grandeur has been evolved.

These rocks have been worn by the action of the weather into so many nooks and crannies that it is possible to find shelter

Summit of the Three Rock Mountain.
(1905.)

from the wind, no matter from what point it blows, and numerous initials and other inscriptions, contributed from time to time by visitors, appear all over the more accessible portions. The view from this commanding height, 1,479 feet over sea-level, extends over a vast tract of mountain, sea, and plain, comprising, to the north, the blue waters of Dublin Bay, with Clontarf and Howth, the Naul or Man-of-War hills, and the Mourne Mountains; eastward, Kingstown, Dalkey, and Killiney, and then in succession the fertile vale of Shanganagh, Carrickgollogan, the Scalp, Bray Head, the Sugar Loaves, and the slopes of Prince William's Seat. In clear weather Holyhead and the Welsh mountains may frequently be discerned, Snowdon and the Llanberis Pass being usually the most conspicuous, but occasionally the elongated outline of Cader Idris may be observed some distance to the right. [9]

From the Three Rocks a long and easy slope of about a mile conducts us to the top of the Two Rock Mountain, 1,763 feet high, the rocks from which the mountain derives its name, lying about half a mile to the south-east, at an elevation of 1,699 feet, and consequently not being visible from the Dublin side. On the summit is a carn of loose stones, called " Fairy " Castle " on the Ordnance Survey maps, which assumes varying shapes from year to year according to the vagaries of the summer excursionists who find their way up here. The view, although more extended towards the west and south-west, is, on the whole, less pleasing and varied than that from the Three Rocks.

The walk from here to Tibradden along the ridge between the two mountains should not be attempted except in thoroughly dry weather, as the ground is inclined to be swampy, and after rain is often impassable. If it be decided to visit Tibradden, keep along a mearing running westward from the summit of the Two Rock Mountain for a considerable distance, and when it ends, bear to the right towards a plantation of firs and larches ; and from this, take a straight course through what will be found to be a very rough and difficult piece of country, to the top of Tibradden, now immediately in front. The ground to be traversed immediately before reaching the rocks on the summit is very boggy, and in a pool which forms here in wet weather small lizards or newts are occasionally to be seen. The narrow defile of Glendoo appears from this point darker than it really is, deeply shadowed by its woods, with the brown slopes of Cruagh Mountain rising on the opposite side, while to the left will be seen the open valley of Glencullen and the road extending away over the hill beyond Glencullen Bridge.

On the southern side of one of the rocks on top of Tibradden is a rude carving of a cross and a human face, which, judging roughly by the growth of moss upon it, would appear to be at least a hundred years old. Adjoining are the remains of an ancient carn and beehive burial place, in which, when opened many years ago, was found an urn now preserved in the National Museum. Tigh-Bradden means Bradden's house or resting-place, and this name, which was no doubt in the first instance applied to the carn, in all probability commemorates the name of the old chieftain buried there, to whose memory the mountain is now an imperishable monument.

Barnacullia.
(1911.)

It should be mentioned that the summit of Tibradden is exactly in line with Rathmines Road, which, when viewed from here through a glass, presents with its trams and other vehicles a curious appearance of exaggerated width owing to the fore-shortening. The descent into Glendoo may be made either directly to the road underneath—through the heather and forest, or by making one's way to a low wall northward of the summit, and thence descending by a rough, steep track joining the road just at the entrance to the wood. The direct descent from the top is rather dangerous, as the heather is high, and the slopes of the mountain abound in deep holes where one might easily suffer serious injury. The alternative route is in parts nearly as bad, so that any person coming here would do well to be provided with a stout stick, and to proceed very cautiously.

Should the Three Rock Mountain only be ascended, the return journey might with advantage be made down the eastern slope, towards the straggling village of Barnacullia, situated about half way up the mountain, from which point either Dundrum or Rathfarnham can readily be reached.

The total distance to be walked in this excursion—viz., from Rathfarnham to the Three Rock Mountain, Two Rock Mountain, Tibradden and back to Rathfarnham is 12 miles; if Tibradden is omitted and the descent made from the Two Rock Mountain to Tiknock and back to Rathfarnham, the distance would be 10 miles, while the excursion to and from the Three Rock Mountain only, would entail a journey of 9 miles. These distances will vary according to the directness of the tracks taken, and on this account must be regarded as only approximate.

Persons starting from Dundrum should take the turn to the right at the end of the village and keep straight ahead until Tiknock cross-roads are reached, following thence the route described.

The " Memoir of Gabriel Beranger," by Sir William Wilde, is published in the *Journal of the Royal Society of Antiquaries of Ireland* for 1876-8.

CHAPTER XIII

CRUAGH, KILLAKEE AND GLENDOO MOUNTAINS

THE three mountains whose names form the title of this chapter would be more correctly described as three elevations in the desert plateau lying between the valleys of Glendoo and Glennasmole, and wholly comprised within the limits of the ancient Manor of Cruagh. These points, although marked as mountain summits on the Ordnance Survey maps, are of so indeterminate a character, and differ so little in altitude from their immediate surroundings as to be almost incapable of identification, except by careful observation with an aneroid and compass. It is, perhaps, owing to this absence of striking features, that the tract in question has never been a favourite one for mountain climbers, and it must be confessed that except in the finest and driest of weather, it is not an attractive one for the excursionist. From the earliest times a sparsely inhabited district, it possesses, with the exception of the Mount Venus cromlech and the ancient church of Cruagh, but few objects of historic or antiquarian interest. The northern confines of this wild region are well marked by a fine belt of wood, extending from the Military road on the west to the summit of the Glendoo valley on the east, and by a mountain road constructed at so great an elevation above the plain as to afford a seemingly illimitable prospect over land and sea.

There are few historic events of interest recorded in connection with this locality, and the earliest mention we find of it is in 1184, when Prince John (son of Henry II.) granted Creevagh or Cruagh with its churches to the See of Dublin, a gift which was successively confirmed by Edward III. in 1337, and by Richard II. during his visit to Dublin in 1395. Nothing further of interest appears until the year 1620, when Peter Talbot demised to Patrick Travers " the towns, villages, and " hamlets of Cruaghnaclough and Newtown, in the parish of " Cruagh in Harold's Country," with all houses, lands, commons, turbary, and pasturage on the moors, mountains, and bogs of Cruagh and Tibradden. All this neighbourhood was, at that time, known as " the Harolds' Country " from the powerful clan of that name, who, for centuries, dominated the district

Winter Scene on Cruagh Mountain.
(1899.)

south of Dublin on the borderland of the Pale, and left their name impressed on the localities known as Harold's Grange and Harold's Cross.

The excursionist who desires to explore this region should proceed by Rathfarnham, Willbrook, Ballyboden, Edmondstown, and Rockbrook. A short distance beyond the last hamlet will be seen on the right, the road, entered by two massive gate pillars, leading through the demesne of Killakee House. This is the old Military road, and is still open to the public.

Immediately beyond the entrance to this road is the ancient churchyard of Cruagh, with its curious watch-tower described in another chapter. (See Index.)

A short descent from here leads to a bridge, beyond which, after an ascent of about three-quarters of a mile, we enter the picturesque woods of Glendoo, presently crossing another bridge over that turbulent little mountain stream, the Owen Dugher, and turning to the right at the far side where the road branches. A long ascent through the over-arching woods conducts us to the mountain road already mentioned, over 1,000 feet above sea level, from which there is so striking a view of the plain and Bay of Dublin. Once the higher part of this road is reached, the ascent of the mountain may be commenced at almost any point by entering the pine wood on the left, afterwards, however, bearing to the right, until the bed of a little stream is seen, to the left of which the highest point is Cruagh summit. As we ascend through the trackless heather and furze, looking back, our view extends over the top of Mount Pelier to the plains of Meath, Kildare, and Westmeath, and on our left may be observed the bed of the little stream that joins the Owen Dugher at Rockbrook, its course marked by stunted rowan and elder trees, amid rank herbage and thickets of bracken. A slight further ascent over some marshy ground takes us to the summit marked as Cruagh on the Ordnance map, 1,714 feet high. From here we may observe to the eastward the Two Rock Mountain, with the carn on its summit and the rocks on its southern slope ; to the left and farther off, the Three Rock Mountain, and through the gap between the latter and Kilmashogue, Kingstown and its harbour. Beyond the blue waters of the Bay is the familiar form of Howth, with the Poolbeg, the bright sands of the North and South Bulls, and the Clontarf shores intervening. To the north lies the flat Dublin plain, in which numerous familiar objects may be distinguished with the aid of a glass. Nothing distant can be seen southward, as Glendoo mountain shuts off all view in that direction.

As stated, Cruagh Mountain has no distinguishable summit, and it slopes almost continuously to Glendoo Mountain, over a somewhat difficult and broken tract of country interspersed at intervals with patches of marsh. The further climb to the top of Glendoo is amply rewarded by the extensive prospect to the southward, comprising Shanganagh valley, Carrick-gollogan, Bray Head and town, Windgate, the Little Sugar Loaf with its bigger colleague peeping out over the side of Prince William's seat, then the valley of the Glencree and Dargle River, rising over which are Douce, Tonduff, and neighbouring elevations, while immediately underneath, to the eastward, is the valley of Glencullen. It will be noticed that for some reason, the Great Sugar Loaf appears to be considerably higher than the observer, although it is actually 270 feet lower—an interesting illustration of how easily the eye may be deceived. Standing on this summit, 1,929 feet high, the eye ranges over a scene of wild moorland solitude, where the silence is broken only by the whistling of the wind through the long bog-grass and heather, or by the hoarse voice of the grouse as they wing their way across these wind-swept wastes. Here, on the modern county boundary, we can look down into the ancient district of Fercualann, now Powerscourt, an impregnable fastness of the "Irishry" in the days of the Pale, where prisoners, cattle, and other spoils were taken for safety after the raids upon the plains. Southward, on the slopes of Kippure, may be seen the deep recess in which are hidden Upper and Lower Loughs Bray, as well as the Military road winding up the steep hill over the Upper Lough, and trending away towards Sally Gap.

Glendoo Mountain is called "Garrydow" in Duncan's Map of the County Dublin, 1820.

Having sufficiently observed the view from this point, we next make our way over the coarse mountain grass, in a westerly

direction towards the flat, bare tract that forms the summit of
Killakee Mountain, the view from which differs little from that
visible from Glendoo, except that it is less extensive. Looking
westward from this point across the deep valley of Glennasmole,
we can see in succession, Seechon, Corrig Mountain, Seefingan,
and Seefinn, the two latter intervening between us and the

Gamekeeper's Lodge on Cruagh Mountain.
(1906.)

Kilbride rifle range, from which, in calm weather, may frequently be heard the sounds of firing. On the top of Killakee
Mountain the turf is carved into the most fantastic shapes by
the combined action of rain and wind, and the granite that once
covered it has, in the course of ages, become disintegrated until
nothing has been left of it but grains of quartz, with occasional
garnets, which are, however, of no commercial value on account
of their small size. This mountain was formerly known as
" White Sands Mountain " on account of the quantity of quartz
sand found there.

Descending from this point, we continue our course westward, coming into view of the Rathmines Waterworks reservoirs at the bottom of the Glennasmole valley, and at length, striking the Military road, along which we make our way homeward by the well-known route to Rathfarnham.

Instead, however, of taking the direct route by Ballyboden and Willbrook, it will be an agreeable change without adding much to the return journey, to turn to the left by Oldcourt road, after passing Mount Pelier, and take the first turn to the right opposite the avenue to Orlagh College, leading by Ballycullen House and Knocklyon to Firhouse. The lands of Knocklyon, originally formed portion of the grant to that famous warrior and territorial proprietor, Walter de Ridelesford, and after numerous changes of proprietorship, came into possession of the Loftus family of Rathfarnham. The Castle of Knocklyon, which is over five hundred years old, now consists of a square three-storied edifice, with two towers at opposite corners, incorporated in a modern dwellinghouse, further modernised by the construction of new windows, door and roof. The original entrance was an arched door leading direct into the principal room, at the end of which was an immense fireplace.

From Firhouse the road leads to Butterfield Avenue, conducting the excursionist into the village of Rathfarnham, from which the tram can be taken to town.

The distance to be walked in this excursion, starting from and returning to Rathfarnham, is about 13 miles according to the directions of the routes taken across the mountains. If the return journey is made *via* Knocklyon and Firhouse, it will add about 1¼ miles to the distance.

Cyclists might arrange to leave their machines at one of the cottages on Cruagh mountain; they will have to walk the greater part of the way there from Edmondstown, but will be able to return home in little over half an hour.

CHAPTER XIV

SEECHON OR SLIEVEBAWN MOUNTAIN, KILBRIDE AND CLOGHLEAGH

IF this journey be undertaken by cyclists, one of them must be prepared to wait at the summit of the road on Seechon Mountain to take charge of the bicycles while the others make the ascent, for which about an hour will be required ; but should the whole party wish to visit the top, arrangements might be made to leave the machines at a house some distance further along the road, although this will entail a considerable addition to both the journey and the ascent. For pedestrians the best plan is to proceed from Terenure by the steam tram to Tallaght, from which the ascent is often made, returning home from either The Lamb or Brittas. Cyclists and pedestrians alike should make their way to Ballinascorney Gap, described in another chapter, the cyclists proceeding by Templeogue, Firhouse, and Bohernabreena, and the pedestrians by the Oldbawn road from Tallaght. The Gap, which may be said to commence at Bohernabreena Bridge (called " Fort Bridge " on the maps), is a long, steep incline, somewhat trying in warm weather, but the picturesque wildness of its surroundings will amply repay for the exertion of climbing it. Cyclists will have to walk nearly the whole way to the summit level of the Kilbride road, a distance of three and a half miles, it being a mile and a half from Bohernabreena Bridge to the top of the Gap, and two miles from that to the highest point of the road across Seechon Mountain.

At the top of Ballinascorney Gap is a large plain granite cross, erected some sixty years ago, and at this point we turn to the left along a well-kept road, bounded by low hedges, interspersed with fern, foxglove and other wild flowers, and passing through a partly cultivated country, with occasional meadows and stunted trees. Some distance further, a pretty ford leading to a farmyard, crosses the little stream beside the road which here begins to rise sharply, having already attained an elevation of over 1,000 feet. As we continue the ascent, the character of the country becomes wilder, the white-thorn and hazel hedges give place almost entirely to those of furze, and rising majestically to the left of the road in front is Seechon or Slievebawn—the great mountain dominating all this region, its rounded summit seared and scarred by the winter torrents, and its brown, heather-clad slopes variegated by patches of soft green sward. It will be noted that those portions of the top denuded of vegetation assume a whitish tint in dry weather, which circumstance may have originated the name of Slieve Bawn (the White Mountain). It should, however, be mentioned that the name Slievebawn, which has now disappeared from the maps, is quite unknow to the country people in the neighbourhood, by whom it is invariably called Seechon (the seat), corrupted by the Ordnance Survey in the more recent maps, into Seahan.

Looking back towards the Dublin plain, it will be observed that the view is greatly limited by the slopes of the valley through which we have passed, but as the summit of the road is approached, the prospect extends, and we enter upon a wild tract of moor, swept by mountain breezes redolent of the turf and heather, with little to remind us of our proximity to civilisation except the white road and the telegraph wires to Kilbride military camp. To reach the top of the mountain, we leave the road at its highest point, and follow the course of the little stream up towards the summit—500 feet above the road—over a rather rough stretch which will take about half an hour to climb.

The chief attraction of this ascent is the extensive view due to the great elevation—2,131 feet—as the summit is entirely devoid of any characteristic feature, and is simply a tract of

bare mountain bog, surmounted by a small carn recently
fashioned into a pillar by the Ordnance Survey. Viewed from
this point, Howth, Ireland's Eye and the Bay look very distant
and insignificant compared with their appearance from the
mountains nearer home ; to the right are the Three Rock,
Two Rock, Cruagh, Killakee and Glendoo Mountains, then the

Seechon Summit in Winter.
(1908.)

two Sugar Loaves, and still further southward a number of
high summits, the most conspicuous among which are Tonduff,
War Hill, and Douce—all over 2,000 feet high. Considerably
nearer is Kippure—dark and gloomy—300 feet higher than
where we stand, while almost due south and quite close is
Seefingan, covered with green sward to the top. Away to the
north will be observed the bold and rugged outline of the
Mourne Mountains in County Down, and to the left of these
the rounded form of Slieve Gullion in County Armagh. To
the right of Kippure, but farther off, is Mullaghcleevaun, one

of the highest summits in this region, then Moanbane and a number of lower elevations extending over towards Bally-knockan and Poulaphuca. Below, on the slopes of Seefinn and Seefingan will be seen the tents and huts of Kilbride Military Camp ; westward, the Brittas ponds will be distinguished among the low hills around Brittas, and to the north, the whole Dublin plain, a great flat expanse, cut up into thousands of irregularly shaped fields.

Just at the top, beside the carn, is a well—the source of a small stream that runs down the western slope of the mountain—generally dry during drought ; and on the south-western side, near the summit, is what appears to be the remains of an ancient sepulchral chamber, long since rifled of its contents.

Descending again to the road, which, it may be mentioned, is 1,602 feet over sea level at this point, we continue our journey now down hill, over a rather rough surface, to the Camp, a little over a mile distant, where the road crosses the head waters of the Shankill river. About half a mile further on, we turn to the right by the road leading to Ballinascorney, again crossing the river by a bridge on the site of the old Shankill ford. If, however, the excursionist is on foot, or if he is not afraid of taking his bicycle along a rather rough track through the heather, it will be well worth while to diverge from the road on the left, by the pathway which crosses the river, and leads to the Cloghleagh iron mine. The high mountains, Gravale, Mullaghcleevaun, and Moanbane present an imposing appearance from this point, traces of snow often remaining on their summits as late as mid-summer. Keeping to the pathway, we presently reach a curious-looking stone house, which was erected as a residence for the manager of the iron mine some fifty years ago. It would seem that no earnest attempt was ever made to work this undertaking to a successful issue, as the great stone segments of the crushing wheel, now lying beside the river, and other machinery obtained from England, were never put together, so that the whole concern was a failure from the start. Just beside the house is the entrance to the mine, the shaft of which, now closed up, extended a considerable way under the hill.

A short distance beyond the house we reach a wooden gateway leading by a pretty bridge to a picturesque little defile, planted with firs and larches, through which the Shankill river tumbles and splashes along its rocky bed to join the Liffey a few hundred yards below Cloghleagh Bridge. This little glen is so pretty that I would strongly recommend persons who are not disposed to reach it by the route described above, to do so by proceeding to The Lamb station on the Blessington tram line, from which it is distant about three miles. It can also be reached from Brittas, whence it is about a mile and a half farther. In either case the road should be asked to Cloghleagh Bridge, which is also well worth a visit.

Some years ago a hermit took up his abode in this glen above Cloghleagh Bridge, and lived in a small, roughly-fashioned hut on a precipitous bank overhanging the river.

The lane passing through the glen leads out on the main road, just beside the bridge, where we turn to the right to reach the Lamb or Brittas Station on the tram line. It should, however, be noted that at Kilbride glen the road to the right leads to Brittas, and that to the left to The Lamb.

On leaving Kilbride Camp, if it be decided to proceed by the road instead of the pathway to Cloghleagh, our route lies for about a mile across a boggy mountain tract to Ballyfolan, where the road, sweeping to the right, enters a grassy country much tamer and less interesting in character than that through which we have passed. A little beyond this point on the roadside will be seen a massive stone cross bearing the inscription :—

I. N. R. I.

✠

I. H. S.

P. B.

1804.

This monument was erected to mark the spot where a resident of this neighbourhood named Bealis lost his life in a snowstorm in 1804. He was riding at the time, and both horse and rider were overwhelmed in a deep snowdrift on the side of the road, where they were discovered stiff and lifeless next day by a rescue party.

The road gradually rising from this point, crosses a high ridge on the western slope of Butter Mountain, and passing for a considerable distance through a pine plantation, descends sharply into the valley, where it joins the road from Ballinascorney. To avoid a needless descent to the bottom of the valley, turn to the left through a gateway beside an unoccupied gate lodge, into an avenue of yews leading up to Talbotstown House—an old country residence, with extensive gardens and orchards, now in a somewhat neglected condition. This avenue leads out upon a by-road, passing through a boggy and sparsely inhabited district, and at length joins the Ballinascorney road about half a mile from Brittas Inn, an old-time hostelry accidentally burnt in 1911, but since rebuilt. At Brittas, which is the junction of the new and old Blessington roads, the old road will be observed extending away to the right over Tallaght Hill or Knockannavea.

About a mile and a half further, the pretty police barrack is reached which marks the summit of the picturesque Slade of Saggart, and from here cyclists have an easy journey home *via* Jobstown and Tallaght to either Dolphin's Barn or Terenure, according to the part of the suburbs to be reached.

Distances from G. P. O. :—Bohernabreena, 8¾ miles ; highest point of road on Seechon, 12½ miles ; Talbotstown, 16½ miles ; Brittas, 18½ miles ; G. P. O., 31 miles.

CHAPTER XV

ROCKBROOK, GLENDOO AND GLENCULLEN

STARTING from Rathfarnham, we take the road through Willbrook and Ballyboden, small hamlets in semi-ruinous condition, with the Owen Dugher flowing on the right, and at length reach Billy's Bridge, rebuilt and widened some twenty years ago. No record survives as to the identity of the individual who has been commemorated in the title of this structure, but it is possible that the name may be an irreverent abbreviation for " King William's Bridge." Along the river bank under the trees is a track called " The Ghost's Walk," enjoying the local reputation of being haunted.

Leaving the bridge on our right, and keeping straight ahead past a row of cottages sheltered by lofty trees, we presently enter Edmondstown, a village of modern growth, which probably originated with the cloth mill established here early in the last century. As we leave the village, we pass the national school, situated on the very edge of the stream and at the foot of a steep ascent, where cyclists generally dismount and walk the rest of the way to Rockbrook.

Mount Venus, embosomed in its woods, now comes into view on the right, and as we reach the higher portion of the road, to the north will be seen the flat expanse of country extending away towards the County Meath, while on the coast are Howth, Sutton, Clontarf, the Poolbeg and the Pigeonhouse with its tall red chimney. West of the city are the Phœnix Park, readily identified by the wide green expanse of the Fifteen Acres, the Liffey valley, beyond that Dunsink Observatory, and in the distance the hill of Garristown surmounted by its square ruin.

The village of Rockbrook, like Edmondstown, is of recent
date, and was originally built to accommodate the employes
of the various mills which existed in this locality in more
prosperous times. Very little of the original village now remains
in a habitable condition, and the people are gradually leaving
it for the new cottages which are rapidly springing up in the
vicinity. Yet the site is a healthy and well chosen one, and it is
to be hoped that as the older houses fall into decay they will be
replaced by new ones, so that this picturesquely-named village
shall not wholly disappear.

Passing Mutton Lane branching off on the left to Larch
Hill and Whitechurch, we reach the police barrack, a building
with projecting eaves, under which the swallows have built
their nests for many years past, returning year after year. A
few hundred yards further will be seen on the right, two massive
stone pillars and a stile, forming the entrance to what appears
to be a private road, but is really the old military road, constructed after 1798, and subsequently altered to its present
route by Billy's Bridge, Stocking Lane, and Mount Venus.

Immediately to the right, inside the entrance to this old
road, lies the ancient churchyard of Cruagh, surrounded by a
high wall, and now closed as a burial place. It contains a number
of very old tombstones, some of which, made of granite, are
so worn and weather-beaten as to be almost illegible. Small
portions of the end walls of the church remain, and adjoining
is a strongly built, low tower, so close to the site of the old
edifice that it is impossible to believe that it can have existed
during the period when the church was in use. The appearance
of the masonry would also suggest that this building is of much
later date, and portions of it bear evidences of comparatively
recent repair. An iron-plated door leads into a low arched
chamber some feet below the level of the ground, while above
is a similar apartment entered by an upper door, to which
there is no access.

According to local tradition this curious structure was
originally erected as a watch-house or shelter for the guards,

who were necessary in the olden time to protect the graveyard from body-snatchers.

A short descent now leads to a bridge over the Owen Dugher, whose murmuring song has accompanied us the whole way from Rathfarnham, and whose rocky bed doubtless suggested

View in Glendoo, looking towards Dublin.
(1905.)

the name for the village of Rockbrook. From this bridge the cyclist must walk the whole way to the summit level—a distance of nearly a mile and three-quarters through the woods, which completely overshadow the road for a considerable portion of the valley and extend high up the mountain slopes enclosing it. The locality, however, is so beautiful that the visitor need not regret the fuller opportunity which the walk will afford him of observing his surroundings.

Shortly after entering the wood, we cross by a bridge to the opposite side of the ravine, and turn to the left up a short steep ascent overlooking the bridge and stream below, which make a pretty picture in the winter time, but are shut off from view by the dense foliage in summer.

Almost within a stone's throw of the preceding one we meet another bridge, which was badly damaged by the floods some years ago, and was the scene of a sad cycling fatality in the early days of that pastime when brakes were all but useless.   The unfortunate cyclist was riding one of the old high machines down the hill towards this bridge with his hind wheel brake hard on, when the cable snapped and the machine ran away with him.   He ran against the grassy wall on the right, perhaps deliberately, in the hope of saving himself, but was dashed with fearful force against the stone parapet and instantly killed. A rude cross in the masonry is intended to commemorate this tragic incident.

This bridge is a favourite subject for artists and photographers, although the felling of some fine trees which formerly stood beside it has somewhat detracted from its picturesque appearance.

A straight stretch of road bordered with bracken, and shaded by firs and larches, leads to the top of the glen, where the Owen Dugher, here a small moorland stream, comes plashing and tumbling through a little ravine down the side of Cruagh Mountain.   The slopes over this stream are noted for their abundant growth of fraughans or whortleberries in the early autumn.

A few hundred yards beyond this point is the summit level of the valley—interesting as forming here the watershed between the basins of the Dodder and the Bray rivers—and if the streams on the roadside here are closely examined, it will be seen that their waters, though apparently continuous, really divide, and flow in opposite directions.

The country now becomes wilder and more rocky ; the pine-woods continue along the heights to the left, and here and there may be seen some recently planted shrubs of that gaudy

View in Glendoo.
(1903.)

Entrance to Glendoo from the South.
(1905.)

exotic, the rhododendron, whose brilliant blaze of tropical splendour contrasts harshly with the subdued tints of our native landscapes. Strange to say, the rhododendron seems to be disliked by every form of animal life ; so much so, that any plantation dominated by it is shunned by birds, flies, and insects of every description, while it is, perhaps, the only shrub which is proof against the nibbling teeth of the rabbit.

As we pass the last clump of the pines, the road sweeps slightly to the left, and, emerging suddenly from the close defile, we enter upon an open valley, with wide wastes of moorland and rough marsh pasture, interspersed with the humble homesteads of the cottiers who inhabit this wild and inhospitable region. In front will now be seen the long, flattened form of Bray Head, to the right of that the Little Sugar Loaf, and presently the conical top of the Great Sugar Loaf, over the side of the mountain known as Prince William's Seat. Some short distance further will be observed at the opposite side of the valley, a couple of diminutive, red-roofed cottages nestling beneath the friendly shelter of a pine plantation, and appearing at that distance like a pair of painted toy houses placed on the hillside.

The road, now sweeping to the left, brings us within view of the southern slope of the Two Rock Mountain, with the rocks conspicuously showing near its summit, and after passing in succession the remains of the hamlets of Ballybrack and Brockey, we enter the village of Glencullen, where the turn on the right conducts us to Glencullen bridge. Before descending the steep hill, on the left will be seen Carrickgollogan and the more distant hills of Dalkey and Killiney, while in front lies the richly-wooded valley in which is concealed the pretty village of Enniskerry. At this point cyclists will do well to dismount, as the hill leading down to the bridge is probably the steepest in the whole county, and would severely tax even the most powerful of brakes. At the bottom of this long descent is Glencullen bridge, spanning the Glencullen river, which, in consequence of the broken and mountainous character of the district through which it passes, is very liable to sudden floods. Along the left bank a rough pathway leads to Enniskerry, but it is rather difficult in parts, and, having been closed at the Enniskerry end, is not to be recommended.

Having crossed Glencullen bridge into the County Wicklow, we must patiently toil up a long ascent to where the road—a rather rough one—crosses a high ridge of land commanding

Glencullen Bridge.
(1902.)

extensive views of the surrounding mountains, with the higher summits of Douce and Maulin in front, and Bray Head and the sea to the left. About a mile and a half from the bridge we reach the main road from Glencree to Enniskerry, entering the latter village by a descent so steep that cyclists, unless their brakes are in the best of order, had better walk down it. The return journey may be made as desired through the Scalp or by Bray and the Stillorgan road home.

As an alternative to the round by Enniskerry—rather long for pedestrians—the return might be made by turning to the left at Glencullen along the Ballyedmonduff road, which, after ascending the heights over Glencullen, skirts the eastern slopes of the Two Rock and Three Rock Mountains at a great eleva- tion, affording extended views of the Bay and coast. At a distance of a mile and three-quarters from Glencullen cross- roads, we reach a somewhat sharp turn in the road, where, turning to the left up the hill, we at length come into view of the scattered village of Barnacullia, with the city and suburbs in the distance below, and Kingstown and its harbour away on the right. A mile and a half beyond this, we reach Tiknock cross-roads, whence the return to the city may be made either by Dundrum or Rathfarnham.

Distances :—Rathfarnham to Glencullen cross-roads, 8 miles ; Glencullen cross-roads to Enniskerry, 3¼ miles ; Ennis- kerry to Bray Bridge, 3¼ miles ; Enniskerry to Nelson's Pillar *via* Dundrum, 12¾ miles ; Bray Bridge to Nelson's Pillar *via* Stillorgan and Donnybrook, 12½ miles ; Glencullen cross-roads *via* Ballyedmonduff to Dundrum, 5¾ miles, or to Rathfarnham, 7 miles.

CHAPTER XVI

RANELAGH AND CULLENSWOOD, DUNDRUM
THE SCALP AND ENNISKERRY

LEAVING the city by Charlemont Bridge, we enter the
district of Ranelagh, a name of modern origin, dating
from the establishment of the Ranelagh Gardens
towards the close of the 18th century. On crossing the Canal
Bridge, the houses on the right-hand side will be seen to be
much below the level of the road, which was raised many
years ago to ease the gradient to the bridge, when trams were
first introduced into this neighbourhood. In the addition to
the name-plate on the corner house, bearing the modern name
of the road, there will be observed, on close inspection, a tablet
below it, exhibiting the almost obliterated inscription :—
" Upper Charlemont Street "—a name which does not appear
to have ever been generally adopted.[10]

Rocque's map shows that in the 18th century a large country
house named Willbrook stood on the ground now occupied by
the Convent of St. Joseph at Ranelagh. It was, for some time
the residence of the Bishop of Derry, and becoming vacant
about the year 1770, was taken by an English speculator, and
converted by him into a place of public entertainment called
" The Ranelagh Gardens " in imitation of the London Gardens
of that name, of which they purported to be a copy. These
gardens were a favourite resort for some years, largely attended
by the rank and fashion from the city, for whom bands, fireworks, and other attractions were provided, and from them in
1785, Crosbie made his famous balloon ascents. The Gardens,
however, enjoyed but an evanescent popularity, and, after a
run of less than twenty years, closed altogether ; the place was

then acquired by the Carmelites, who converted the buildings into the Convent of St. Joseph; but the name of Ranelagh has ever since clung to the locality, which prior to that had been comprised in the district bearing the historic designation of Cullenswood.

It would seem that the village of Ranelagh derived its origin as well as its name from these gardens, as no trace of a village or even a house, with the exception of Willbrook, is shown on Rocque's map, the date of which is about 1753. There were, however, at the time of the Gardens, probably a few residences about the triangle of land where the tram turns westward to enter Charleston Road, as well as a terrace in Sallymount Avenue, either new or in course of erection.

Cullenswood is memorable as the scene of the massacre by the mountain septs, on Easter Monday, 1209, of the Bristolian settlers who had assembled here for holiday sports, the chief item of which was to have been a great hurling match between two parties of the citizens.

All this neighbourhood was then wild country, covered with forest, brushwood, and heather, affording excellent facilities for an ambuscade.

Stanyhurst, who wrote in 1584, gives the following quaint account of this sanguinary episode of the early settlement of Dublin :—" The citizens having over great affiance [confidence] " in the multitude of the people, and so consequently retchless " [reckless] in heeding the mountain enemie that lurched under " their noses, were wont to roam and royle in clusters, some- " times three or four miles from towne. The Irish enemie, " espying that the citizens were accustomed to fetch such odd " vagaries on holydays, and having an inckling withal by means " of some claterfert [traitor] or other that a company of them " would range abroad on Monday in the Easter week, towards " the woode of Cullen, they lay in a state very well appointed, " and layde in sundry places for their coming. The citizens " rather minding the pleasure they should presently enjoy than " forecasting the hurt that might ensue, flockt unarmed from

" the citie to the woode. Where being intercepted by their
" lying in ambush, were to the number of five hundred, miser-
" ably slayne. The citizens, deeming that unlucky tyme to be
" a cross or dysmal day, gave it the appellation of Black Monday.
" The citie being soon after, peopled by a fresh supply of
" Bristolians, to dare the Irish enemie, agreed to bancket yearly
" in that place. For the mayor and the sheriffs, with the
" citizens, repayre to the Woode of Cullen, in which place the
" mayor bestoweth a costly dinner within a moate or roundell,
" and both the sheriffes within another, where they are so well
" guarded by the youth of the citie, as the mountain enemie
-' dareth not attempt to snatch so much as a pastye crust from
" thence."

For hundreds of years afterwards the colonists kept up the
tradition of the tragedy by marching out on the anniversary,
thereafter called Black Monday, to Cullenswood, fully accoutred
and armed, headed by a black standard, and formally challenging
the mountain tribes to combat. In 1316 the O'Tooles
attempted a similar surprise of the settlers, who, however,
sallied forth in numbers from the city, with their black
standard, and routed their assailants, pursuing them for miles
into the mountains. It has been generally stated by modern
writers that the actual scene of the massacre of 1209 is the
locality known as " The Bloody Fields," now almost entirely
built over, though some hold that this name originated with the
Battle of Rathmines in 1649, when considerable fighting took
place in the neighbourhood.

In ancient times the district south of Dublin was known as
Cualann, and the wood which covered a considerable portion
of it was known as the wood of Cualann, or Cullen, while the
most conspicuous glen in it was called Glencullen. By the
colonists the district appears to have been called Nova Colonia,
Boscus de Colonia and Colon (Dalton's and Ball's *Histories*),
the latter name being probably an Anglicised form of the native
designation.

Just where the railway crosses Charleston Road, there

formerly stood jutting out elbow-wise into the road, a curious old house, the removal of which was necessitated by the exigencies of the traffic when the electric tram service was established. In this old country house—for it was in the country in those days—the celebrated John Wesley used to stay when visiting Dublin in the latter half of the 18th century. He had many distinguished friends in the Irish capital, and was a welcome guest at the houses of many of the leaders of society. The district about Ranelagh was then quite rural ; the Wellington orchard, still remembered by many, covered the ground now occupied by Charleston Road, and a few scattered residences, standing in their own grounds, were probably the only indications of suburbs that Wesley could see from the windows of this quaint old house.

One of the oldest avenues in this neighbourhood is Sallymount, which was laid out about 1770, and was, for many years afterwards, only about a furlong in length, and closed at the end by an iron gate. Between this avenue and Ranelagh, in the early part of last century, was a fine whitethorn hedge, opposite to which was Toole's and Mackay's (afterwards Toole's) Nursery, while the fields now occupied by Sandford Terrace were noted for their blackberries. In Sallymount Avenue resided for a time the well known Rev. Dionysius Lardner, no less renowned for the pursuit of scientific research than for that of the fair sex, and whose doings occasioned much gossip in the neighbourhood. It was he who proved satisfactorily, for the time at least, by calculations based on the consumption of coal, that no vessel propelled by steam could ever cross the Atlantic. He was the guardian of the distinguished dramatist and author, Dion Boucicault.

Down to about 1830, snipe, plover, and other wild fowl were shot in the winter time in " The Bloody Fields "—where now are the M'Geough Home and Palmerston Park ; even Mountpleasant was then quite rural, and the newly enclosed square, in which plantations had just been started, was surrounded by a rubble wall and ditch.

Immediately beyond Annavilla, and on the same side, is an avenue known as " Major's Lane," deriving its name from the notorious Major Sirr, whose house stood there within living memory, and traditions of whose doings lingered until recently in the locality. Some of the older inhabitants who have spoken to his contemporaries, state that he was described as a big, corpulent man, most unpopular with every class on account of his spying and interfering in matters which should have been delegated to his subordinates. It may be here mentioned that Major Sirr's title was not a military one, but an abbreviated form of " Town Major," a corporate office long since abolished. While he lived in Cullenswood he used to walk to and from his office in town every day.

The name of Sandford, attaching to the district immediately beyond Cullenswood, originated with Sandford Church, called after Lord Mountsandford, while the name of the adjoining country house, " Merton," would appear to have been suggested as the correlative of Sandford by the title of " Sandford " and Merton."

Turning to the right from the tram route by the Milltown road, we presently enter the village of Milltown, situated almost on the very bed of the Dodder, and formerly subject to frequent inundations from that river. This rather prettily situated village was at one time much resorted to by the citizens for recreation ; coaches and " noddies " used to ply thither from town, and the wants of the visitors were provided for by an old-fashioned hostelry which may still be seen in a ruinous condition at the far side of the old, and probably the oldest, bridge over the Dodder. The most conspicuous feature in modern Milltown is the great stone viaduct of nine arches by which the Dublin and South-eastern Railway is carried across the Dodder valley.

Crossing by either the old or new bridge, we presently reach Windy Harbour, a scattered village, the inhabitants of which in former times were extensively engaged in the silk industry ; and a short distance further, to the left of the road is the Dun-

L

drum Criminal Lunatic Asylum, enclosed by formidable walls and occupying a considerable area.

About half a mile beyond this point we enter the village of Dundrum, formerly much frequented by invalids to enjoy the salubrity of its air, and to drink the milk of the mountain goats. Brewer, in his *Beauties of Ireland* (1826), quaintly writes :—

Dundrum Castle.
(1905.)

" Dundrum is in a sheltered declivity, sheltered from the harsh 'winds. The village is the fashionable resort of invalids for " the purpose of drinking goats' whey. At early hours of the " morning numerous jaunting cars convey from the city large " parties of visitors to partake of that sanative beverage amidst " the reviving scenery over which the animals have browzed. " In this rural hamlet are many romantic cottages, whose " white fronts and low proportions would appear to harmonise " with the wishes of those who frequent the place, by holding " forth the soothing invitations of retirement and peace."

In 1816, and for some years afterwards, while this neighbourhood was in vogue among the citizens, communication between Dundrum and the city was carried on by a service of coaches, on which the fares were 1s. 3d. inside and 10d. outside, for the single journey. These somewhat high charges materially assisted in maintaining the air of exclusiveness so dearly prized by the fashionable invalids and hypochondriacs who patronised the place.

The following interesting advertisement appears in the *Freeman's Journal* of 27th February, 1813 :—

" MEADOW BROOK BOARDING HOUSE, DUNDRUM.

" The second Whey season having commenced, Ladies " and Gentlemen are respectfully informed that there are " a few Vacancies in the House ; the accommodation will " be found agreeable, and terms very much reduced— " respectable Society in the House."

Not far from Dundrum is Goatstown, which claimed a special excellence for its breed of goats, and where still may be seen some of the houses which accommodated the visitors who resorted thither to drink the " sanative beverage."

Near the southern end of the village of Dundrum, within private grounds, and almost entirely concealed by trees from the eye of the wayfarer, is the ancient castle of Dundrum, believed to have been erected by one of the Fitzwilliam family, who came into possession of these lands towards the close of the 13th century. The ruin is kept in excellent order, and is almost covered with ivy.

From Dundrum the road rises almost continuously to Sandyford, where it branches right and left, either way leading to Stepaside, and taking the right hand turn as being the most direct, the country presently becomes more open, and we come into view of the Three Rock Mountain in front, with the straggling village of Barnacullia scattered irregularly along its slopes about half way up the mountain, while farther off and

to the left will be seen Carrickgollogan and the hills of Dalkey
and Killiney. After about a mile the ruin of Kilgobbin Church
will be seen on the left, standing on a sharply defined eminence,
which is probably the remains or site of an ancient rath, and in
the adjoining laneway is a fine granite cross, about ten feet
high, of very ancient date. A short distance across the fields
to the north-east of the church, is Kilgobbin Castle, a tall,
narrow structure entirely devoid of bawn or outworks, which
might be described as a fortified dwellinghouse rather than a

Sandyford.
(1905.)

castle. It originally belonged to the Walsh family, from whom
it passed by forfeiture or otherwise, in the reign of Charles I.
into possession of Sir Adam Loftus, of Rathfarnham.

Returning to the main road, on the opposite side will be seen
a steep by-road leading up the side of the mountain to Bally-
edmunduff, and adjoining is the picturesque entrance to the
demesne of Fern Hill, through which the public are admitted
as a short cut to Barnacullia. The road hence falls slightly
to Stepaside, a village which acquired a temporary notoriety in
the last century as the scene of a miniature battle during the
Fenian rising in 1866. High over the village to the right, the
dark foliage of the pine woods lends a softening effect to the

brown mountainside, and in front will be seen the rocky heights of Killegar, overhanging the Scalp, and partly covered by the dense wood of Ballybetagh.

A little over a mile from Stepaside we reach the high ground at the head of the Glenamuck road, from which may be seen the Bay as well as the district intervening between us and the coast, and shortly afterwards we enter the small village of Kiltiernan, consisting of a row of neat slated cottages. Here, in a sequestered position are the ivied ruins of an ancient church, surrounded by thorn and elder trees, and presenting evidences of great antiquity. A castle also stood in the village in the 17th century, but no trace of it now survives, and even its site has been forgotten. Down to about sixty years ago there were paper mills and a cotton factory in Kiltiernan affording considerable employment in the neighbourhood.

About half a mile west of Kiltiernan, on the wild mountainside, surrounded by fern and heather, is one of the largest cromlechs in Ireland, commonly known as "The Giant's "Grave," the table stone of which is 22 feet long by 13½ feet wide, and is estimated to weigh about 40 tons. The supporters, judging from their irregular positions, would appear to have suffered some considerable disturbance.

Passing out of the village we enter upon a highly picturesque portion of the road shaded on both sides by trees, approaching what was known as "The Novice's Hill" in the early days of cycling, when that pastime was deemed suitable only for athletes or acrobats. In the springtime this place is seen to its best advantage, the young pale foliage of the deciduous trees contrasting finely with the dark blue-green of the pines, while scattered here and there through the woods are open patches all ablaze with the blossoms of the ever-flowering furze.

A sharp descent in the road conducts us to the picturesque defile known as The Scalp, formed on the west by the rocky heights of Killegar, and on the east by the wooded hill of Barnaslingan. This place is so well known, and has been so frequently described, that there is no necessity to enter into

any detailed account of it here ; it should be mentioned, however, that the rocky side is well worthy of ascent, which should
be performed, not by climbing straight up from below—a
somewhat trying task—but by continuing along the road
towards Enniskerry, until a perpendicular wall of rock is passed
on the right, when a pathway will be observed ascending

The Scalp and the Little Sugar Loaf
(1903.)

through the furze and heather to a patch of soft green sward
at the top. From this point of vantage will be seen away to the
north, Dublin Bay with the South Wall, the Pigeonhouse, the
white sands of the South Bull, Howth, and the Bailey, while
close at hand is the rugged little defile of Glenamuck, like a
miniature Scalp ; to the left of that and nearer is Ballybetagh
Wood, and then in succession are the Three Rocks, Two Rocks,
the mountains forming the southern outposts of Glencullen
valley, Douce, Powerscourt, the Sugar Loaves, Bray Head

and town, and to the left of these the rough and rocky hump of Carrickgollogan.

At the bottom of the valley below are the remains of the old road, now grass-grown, with some portions of the enclosing walls still standing, although this route was superseded by the modern one over seventy years ago. The whole defile is much more imposing when viewed from this old roadway, and an illustration of it in *The Dublin Penny Journal* was evidently taken from this standpoint.

Immediately before reaching Enniskerry, the road branches right and left, either way leading into the village. The left-hand road, being the older one, is much steeper than the other, and was the scene of many a serious accident in the old cycling days. Between the two roads is a dark wooded gorge, where a small monastery stood in ancient times, the site of which is still remembered in tradition. Viewed from the heights above it, the little village of Enniskerry presents a very striking appearance, embosomed in its pine woods and situated in a well-sheltered hollow, with the Great Sugar Loaf rising majestically over it.

From Enniskerry the reader must be left to his own choice as to the route to be pursued homeward, a favourite one being the road to Bray, and thence by the Bray and Stillorgan road to town.

Distances from G. P. O. :—Dundrum, 4½ miles ; Stepaside, 7 miles ; The Scalp, 10½ miles ; Enniskerry, 12 miles ; Bray, 15½ miles ; G. P. O., 28 miles.

CHAPTER XVII

RATHMINES AND RATHGAR, TEMPLEOGUE AND ITS SPA, BOHERNABREENA AND BALLINA-SCORNEY GAP

PORTOBELLO Bridge, which connects the city with the populous districts of Rathmines and Rathgar, was the scene of a terrible tragedy on the night of the 6th April, 1861. One of the " Favourite " omnibuses, returning from Rathgar to Nelson's Pillar, where it was due at 9 o'clock, p.m., stopped in the middle of the bridge to allow a passenger to alight. When the driver endeavoured to re-start the horses, they found some difficulty in proceeding, and backed slightly towards the Rathmines side. The old bridge being very steep, he then turned the horses' heads eastward so as to take the incline at an angle, but they still continued to back in spite of the driver's efforts, and at last forced the heavy vehicle round in a semicircle against the wooden paling which then stood between the road and the canal lock on the south-western side of the bridge. The frail paling gave way under the heavy weight, and the vehicle rolled over into the lock on end, with the door underneath. The horses falling between the omnibus and the bridge, by their weight on the traces, pulled the front of the vehicle down on its wheels, and thus caused it to right itself There were only a few feet of water in the lock, and no difficulty should have arisen in extricating the passengers, had not the lock-keeper turned on all the upper sluices in the hope of floating the bus, with the result that in the darkness and confusion, the passengers, six in number, were all drowned, the driver alone being rescued. In a few moments when the mistake was realised by the spectators, the upper sluices were closed and the lower ones opened, speedily emptying the lock, but it was then too late, and the passengers when taken out were all dead.

Among those who perished on this occasion was Mr. Michael Gunn, father of the late Messrs. John and Michael Gunn, the founders and proprietors of the Gaiety Theatre, Dublin.

About the beginning of the last century, Rathmines was quite a rural neighbourhood, and was considered too far out of town for residential purposes, except for people who were in a position to keep vehicles for their own use.

Down to about 1820, Rathmines Road, from Portobello to Castlewood Avenue, was fenced on the eastern side by a ditch with thorn hedges at intervals, and the sentry box of the night watchman was usually about half way, while the only houses on the road were Mount Anthony and Williams Park on the western side. Castlewood Avenue was then a narrow country lane, without a house of any description, leading to " The " Bloody Fields " (near the modern Palmerston Road), and Cullenswood Avenue, now Oakley Road, was a rustic avenue with a turnstile at the upper end opening into the meadows and cornfields south of Dunville Avenue. The older houses on the southern side of Dunville Avenue are among the earliest built in this neighbourhood.

At this period Rathgar Road was not properly finished, although it had been laid out some years previously, and the usual route from Rathmines to Terenure or Roundtown was by Upper, or as it was then called, Old Rathmines, and Highfield Road.

Rathmines village commenced opposite Rathgar Road, and in addition there was the portion known as " The Chains," which occupied the site where the Belfast Bank and surrounding buildings now stand. " The Chains " were so called, because a number of dilapidated shanties at this point were enclosed by chains hung from stone pillars such as now surround Stephen's Green. These old rookeries were really an unsightly and insanitary slum, and were swept away some twenty-five years ago, much to the advantage of the neighbourhood. The Swan Water, now almost entirely a subterraneous river, flows past this point, and has given name to the avenue known as " Swanville Place."

To connect Rathmines with Harold's Cross, Leinster Road was opened up about 1835 through what was then Mowld's Farm, and the old farmhouse, which stood on the northern side of the road close to Rathmines Road, was taken down about 1840. Its site is, I believe, occupied by the two stucco houses near the Rathmines end of Leinster Road.

Close to where is now the western end of Leinster Road there was, about eighty years ago, Clandaube Bridge, by which the Harold's Cross road spanned the Swan Water, then an open river, flowing through the fields.

In Wright's *Guide to the County of Wicklow* (1822), this locality is referred to as——" the village of Rathmines, chiefly " inhabited by invalids, in consequence of the supposed purity " and wholesome quality of its atmosphere." This should be comforting to the modern inhabitants.

The ancient Castle of Rathmines, originally an extensive building erected by Sir George Radcliffe in the 17th century, stood on the site occupied by the house known as " The " Orchards," Palmerston Park, and when Rocque constructed his map of the County Dublin in 1776, was the country residence of Lord Chief Justice Yorke. On Duncan's map of the County Dublin (1821) it appears as " Rathmines School," and in *The Dublin Penny Journal* of 1833 it is described as " an " irregular, uninteresting building, so far modernised as to " have the appearance of an old whitewashed farmhouse. It " is now occupied as a boarding-house for invalids, and un- " fortunately is seldom empty." The entrance was opposite the end of Highfield Road, beside what is now the terminus of the Palmerston Park tram line.

The old Castle of Rathmines must not be confounded with the modern edifice of that name in Upper Rathmines, which, owing to its recent origin, possesses no historic interest.

The Rathgar Road was constructed early in the last century, and for some years remained without a single building to relieve its monotonous straightness or interrupt the view of the open pastoral country through which it passed. At its upper end, on the older portion leading from Highfield Road to Terenure, there then stood a few thatched cottages and an inn, the latter a favourite hostelry for country people going into and out of town by that route. This group of houses became in time known as " The Thatch," and even at the present day this name, though locally forgotten owing to the many changes and shifting population, is still the designation by which the place is best known to the older country folk in the southern part of the county.

The Cusack family became resident proprietors in this locality in 1609, and remained in possession of the lands of Rathgar for about a century. The extensive ruins of their old castle or mansion survived up to a late period in the 18th century, and were visited in 1782 by Austin Cooper, the well-known antiquarian, and described in his " Note book."

According to Rocque's Map of the County (1776), which, however, is so inaccurate in parts as to render identification difficult, it would seem that these ruins stood on the ground immediately south of the upper end of Rathgar Road, and the Ordnance Survey Map of 1837 shows that there was then near this point a house called " Rathgar Castle Cottage "—a name which was probably intended to commemorate the site of this old mansion, whose ruins may have survived within the memory of the builder.

Up to about thirty years ago a tradition remained among some of the older residents, that the castle had stood in this position.

A roadway, now represented by Rathgar Avenue, probably a private avenue in its original form, led to Rathgar Castle from the Harold's Cross Road.

Geoghegan, the author of *The Monks of Kilcrea*, probably

either saw the ruins himself or obtained a description of them
from some one who had seen them, when he wrote :—

> " Rathgar, upon thy broken wall,
> Now grows the lusmore rank and tall—
> Wild grass upon thy hearthstone springs,
> And ivy round thy turret clings ;
> The night-owls through thy arches sweep,
> Thy moat dried up, thy towers a heap,
> Blackened, and charr'd and desolate—
> The traveller marvels at thy fate ! " [11]

The Castles of Rathmines and Rathgar must both have
suffered considerable injury at the Battle of Rathmines, having
been occupied and defended by parties of fugitives from Lord
Inchiquin's portion of the Royalist army.   This battle is fully
described in the succeeding chapter.

In March, 1798, a brutal murder took place at Rathgar House,
which stood on the site now occupied by Oaklands, Highfield
Road.   The gate-lodge of that house, situated in what was
then a very lonely neighbourhood, was attacked in the middle
of the night by three men, who having some grudge against the
occupant, a gardener, after some ineffectual resistance on his
part, forced their way into the lodge and murdered him.
The story of the murder was told in the *Freeman's Journal* of
March 17th, 1798, in the following words :—

> " Yesterday morning, about two o'clock, a numerous ban-
> " ditti, said to be forty in number, attacked the country house
> " of Charles Farren, Esq., which is situated near Rathmines
> " Road, adjoining the avenue that leads to Rathfarnham Road.
> " They first entered the gardener's lodge, in which was a poor
> " man, in the service of Mr. Farren, named Daniel Carroll,
> " who giving what resistance he could to the barbarians, they
> " cruelly put him to death, and which we since understand was
> " the chief purpose for which they came to that place."

The murderers were tried, found guilty, and publicly hanged

at the cross-roads of Terenure, where the Rathmines tram now stops. The *Freeman's Journal* of November 1st, 1798, gives the following description of the execution :—

" Yesterday were executed on Rathfarnham road, at the
" entrance of the avenue leading to Rathgar and Rathmines,
" Kelly, Rooney, and O'Donnell, who had been gardeners to
" gentlemen in that neighbourhood, and had perpetrated a
" most barbarous murder on a poor, inoffensive man, named
" Carroll, carter to Charles Farren, Esq.

" The above malefactors were conducted from Kilmainham
" Jail along the Circular Road, and through Rathmines, to the
" place of execution by the High Sheriff of the County of
" Dublin, accompanied by troops of the Rathfarnham and
" Crumlin Cavalry. The peasantry who were spectators
" seemed to have no pity for them, and believed they were
" guilty, though these criminals denied the fact. The bloody
" shirt of poor Carroll, who had been murdered, was placed in
" front of the cart before them on the way to the place of
" execution. Just before they were turned off, Kelly and
" Rooney shook hands ; the former appeared in much trepida-
" tion. After hanging the usual time, they were cut down,
" and their bodies conveyed to Surgeons' Hall for dissection,
" consonant to the letter of the law."

The " numerous banditti " described as participators in this crime existed only in the imagination of the prisoner Kelly, who was Mr. Farren's gardener ; and it would appear that after the murder, the ruffians who had been engaged in it, plundered the wine cellar and carried off a quantity of liquor to their homes. The origin of the foul deed seems to have been a complaint made against Kelly to his employer by the murdered man, Carroll, whom Kelly when slaying him, described as " an Orangeman."

Mr. Farren was Deputy Clerk of the Pleas in the Court of Exchequer.

The imposing presence of " the Rathfarnham and Crumlin " Cavalry," troops of which it is stated formed the escort in

the procession, was probably considered necessary to overawe
any of the " peasantry " of Rathmines and Rathgar who might
have been sympathisers or friends of the condemned men, as
the crime attracted a great deal of attention in the locality,
and appears to have been, to some extent at least, tinged by
the heated political feelings of the period.

It should be observed that the route of the procession was by
Rathmines Road, Upper Rathmines, Highfield Road—past the

The Old Ford near Templeogue.
(1906.)

scene of the murder—to the cross-roads at Terenure, Rathgar
Road not being then in existence.

The whole occurrence with its incidental surroundings
affords an interesting glimpse of the methods of justice which
prevailed at the close of the 18th century, as well as of the
condition, at that time, of the now populous and flourishing
suburbs of Rathmines and Rathgar.

Adjoining Rathgar is the village of Roundtown, the name
of which has, in recent years, being almost entirely superseded
by " Terenure," the ancient title of the locality. The name
" Roundtown " is of modern date, and evidently originated

with the circle of small cottages close to the cross-roads.   From
this point we follow the route of the Blessington Steam Tramway
along a straight and somewhat uninteresting road to Templeogue, a village of small cottages on the roadside, beyond which
the country is more open and the mountains come into view.

The route from this point should properly be across Templeogue Bridge to the left, but in order to visit the old ford across
the Dodder, used before the bridge was built, it will be neces-

Spawell House, Templeogue.
(1906.)

sary to continue along the tram road for about a quarter of a
mile further, where the old road will be seen sloping down to
the river bed.   Templeogue Bridge was not built until about
1800, and before that time, all vehicles going to or coming
from the neighbourhood of Firhouse, had to ford the river
here, which was, however, at that time much wider, its bed
having been subsequently restricted by the Drainage Commissioners.   Crossing here by the stepping-stones, we enter an
ancient roadway, whose moss-grown, ivy-clad walls attest
its antiquity, and after crossing a stile, we emerge upon the
main road to Firhouse.

If desired, before crossing the river, a visit may be paid to Spawell House, a quaint, old-fashioned dwelling, with numerous windows and high chimneys, on the grounds of which, as the name indicates, is situated the once famous spa of Templeogue, where the wealth, the beauty and the fashion of Dublin were wont to assemble one hundred and eighty years ago.   The entrance to the grounds is now by an iron gate on the Tallaght road, but was then opposite the old church of Templeogue, and a long avenue of stately elms led up to the house.   The Dodder did not then flow so close to the place, a long bend in its course having been straightened by the Drainage Commissioners in 1846.   The site of the spa is marked by a semi-circular amphitheatre, where there was formerly a large white-thorn tree that has gone the way of its companions, the elms, but a circular stone seat which surrounded it still remains. The spa is now covered over, a slight depression in the ground marking the actual spot, and the water flows underground to the bank of the river adjoining, where it can be seen and tasted if desired, but its chalybeate qualities for which it was once so noted have entirely disappeared.   According to Dr. Rutty, the naturalist, it lost its properties as a spa between the years 1749 and 1751.

This place was, in its hey-day, of such fashionable importance that there was a weekly paper of eight pages, called *The Templeogue Intelligencer*, devoted to the doings and frolickings of the spa drinkers, which it often chronicled in what would be considered very plain speaking nowadays.   A few numbers of this curious production are preserved in the *Haliday Pamphlets* in the Royal Irish Academy, as also a ballad, of which the following verses are extracts :—

THE TEMPLEOGUE BALLAD.

(Printed at the Cherry-tree, Rathfarnham, 1730, and dedicated to the worthy Manager, Mr. Benson.)

To the tune of " To you fair ladies now at hand."

" Ye Dublin ladies that attend
    This place of mirth and fame,
    My song or praise or discommend,

As you approve my theme ;
'Tis you that make the poet sing,
The subject's but a trivial thing.
>   With a fal, lal la, &c.

" Those damsels that were used of late
To rise when some had dined,
Now leave their toilets pleasing seat
For air that's unconfined.
On Mondays rise by six, oh strange,
What stubborn hearts can't music change !
>   With a fal, lal la, &c.

" The coxcombs that officious wait
With kettles in their hands,
And walk about from seat to seat
To see who 'tis commands,
If smiles wont pay for all their pain,
Another time the rest they'll gain.
>   With a fal, lal la, &c.

" My brother bard, whose honest heart
Still props our falling state,
And strives with judgment and with art,
T' avert impending fate ;
Who speaks so much, so little gains,
Just honour claims for all his pains.
>   With a fal, lal la, &c.

" To him, O Templeogue, is due
Thy praise and fame renowned,
Had he not been thy patron true,
Thy well had not been found ;
Thy waters might have silent sprung,
Nor yet by him or me be sung.
>   With a fal, lal la, &c.

" Ye Dublin Citts, whose thoughtless souls
 Incline ye to be blind,
Whose knowledge ends in brimming bowls,
 These my last sayings, mind—
Where fops unnumbered pay their court,
Let not your pretty girls resort.
   With a fal, lal la, &c."

Nearly opposite Spawell House, on the other side of the
river and close to the old ford, there was, in the eighteenth
century, a small house beside the old road, known as Cherry-
tree.   Long afterwards it was enlarged and partially rebuilt,
whereupon the name was altered to Cherryfield, its present
designation.   This,   doubtless,   was   "The   Cherry-tree,
Rathfarnham,"   where   the   above   ballad   was   printed,
Rathfarnham   probably   having   been   the   postal   address.
The house can be seen from both the Firhouse and Tallaght
roads.

The hour for assembling at the Spa was eight o'clock a.m.,
and as the journey from town occupied about an hour, its
patrons had to rise soon after six, so that in addition to whatever benefits they derived from drinking the waters, it obliged
them to keep regular hours and to go to bed early instead of
spending half the night gambling and drinking, as was customary
in these hard-living times.

Leaving Spawell and the memories of its vanished revels,
we cross the Dodder by the old ford, already alluded to, leading
to the Firhouse road, and next pass, on our left, Delaforde
House, a roadside hostelry in the eighteenth century, but now
a considerable distance from the road, which was altered
about a hundred years ago by a Mr. Bermingham, who bought
the place, converted it into a private residence, and made
the alteration to leave room for a lawn in front of his house.
He laid out the grounds in ornamental fashion, and changed
the old name of the place from Clandarrig to Springfield,
which was in turn altered to its present name.

Immediately beyond Delaforde House is Firhouse, containing little of interest to notice, and in the course of another mile along a pleasant open road with Mount Pelier conspicuously in view on the left, we arrive at Oldbawn cross-roads, beside which a massive though unpicturesque bridge of one span crosses the Dodder. From Firhouse to near Bohernabreena,

Bohernabreena Bridge.
(About 1895.)

the river bed comprises whole acres of waste land, overgrown with brushwood and furze, and cut up into gravel pits.

After passing Oldbawn cross-roads the most prominent object in the view is Knockannavea Mountain—a long rounded hill, devoid of any striking features, but prettily interspersed with pastures, cornfields, and little white cottages peeping out from their sheltering groves of trees. The road now ascends

considerably till it reaches Bohernabreena Chapel, picturesquely situated on an eminence over the river.

From the Chapel a steep descent conducts us to Bohernabreena Bridge, formerly a picturesque structure, but disfigured
in recent years by an iron water main laid across it, and by
the consequent loss of its ivy, which gave it an appearance of
respectable antiquity, although it is only about 80 years old.
There is a remarkably pretty view from this bridge looking
up the Glennasmole valley, with its wooded and furze-clad
river slopes, the towering form of Seechon, and the little
cottages nestling along the mountainside.

On the left is Friarstown House, in the grounds of which
a little stream descends through a densely wooded glen, abounding in miniature grottoes and cascades, and having at its head
an artificial lake.

After leaving the bridge, the road at once commences to
ascend through Ballinascorney Gap, and we obtain a more
extended view of Glennasmole and the adjoining mountains.
At the far end of the valley is Kippure, on whose dark, deeply-
furrowed slopes the infant Dodder, and its tributary streams,
Slade Brook and Cot Brook, take their origin. The Dodder
valley from here appears to great advantage, just before the
slopes of Slievenabawnogue shut it off from the view.   The
road now rises continuously, amid surroundings which grow
wilder and wilder as we ascend, while almost the whole way
to the top can be heard the plash and murmur of a turbulent
little stream that empties itself into the Dodder opposite
Friarstown glen.   As we approach the top of the road, to the
right will be seen the track of an older one, forming a loop
with the modern road, the alteration in its course having been
made to graduate the ascent.

The view from the top, eastwards, includes only the tract
visible between the hills of Knockannavinidee and Slievenabawnogue, comprising the southern portion of the Dublin
suburbs, the whole South Wall from Ringsend to Poolbeg;
beyond these, Howth, with the Bailey just shut out of view,

Ireland's Eye, Sutton with its bright rows of pretty villas; and to the left, Lambay Island. Nearer, and to the right, is Mount Pelier, surmounted by its conspicuous ruin.

At the top of the Gap, where the road branches off on the left to Kilbride Camp, is a granite cross, evidently of modern date, but of whose origin nothing is known in the neighbourhood. Some distance beyond the top will be seen, lower down on the opposite side of the valley, Ballinascorney House, pleasantly situated in the shelter of its woods, over which rises what is locally known as " The Black Hill." This house was formerly called Dillon Lodge, having been erected as a shooting lodge by the Dillons of Belgard early in the eighteenth century. Some of Robert Emmet's party took possession of it in 1803, to the great alarm of the inmates, who were, however, treated with the greatest courtesy by the party, and suffered no further injury than the consumption of the contents of their pantries. About 1860, Major Knox, the proprietor of the *Irish Times*, lived in this house, and gave numerous entertainments there, taking his guests out from town in a four-horse drag, and providing music for the festivities by a brass band organised by himself.

From the summit of the Gap the road winds along the northern slope of a fine open valley with the Black Hill and the towering form of Seechon on the left, and Knockannavinidee and Tallaght Hill on the right.

At a distance of ten miles from Terenure, by the route described herein, the road meets the Blessington Steam Tramway at Brittas Inn, whence the return journey to Terenure may be made by tram.

The following authorities were consulted in the preparation of this chapter :—Handcock's *History and Antiquities of Tallaght*; *St. Catherine's Bells*, by W. T. Meyler; Wakeman's *Old Dublin*, Part II. ; Petty's, Rocque's and Duncan's *Maps* and the *Ordnance Survey Map of* 1837.

CHAPTER XVIII

THE BATTLE OF RATHMINES AND BAGGOTRATH

THE most notable event in the annals of Rathmines was the battle in 1649, during the Civil War between the Royalists and the Parliamentarians. Dublin was then a small city—much smaller, indeed than the Rathmines Township at the present day—and, if we take Speed's *Map* of 1610 as a guide, may be said to have been almost wholly comprised within a boundary drawn as follows :—Bow Street, St. Michan's Church, Mary's Abbey, and thence obliquely across the river to the College, Grafton Street, Peter Street, St. Patrick's Cathedral, Francis Street, Thomas Street, and James's Street.

In those days Rathmines was far out in the country, laid out in fields, pastures and tillage lands, with perhaps occasional waste patches covered by furze or bracken. There does not appear to have been any village there at the time, and we may suppose the district between Rathmines Castle and the city to have been interspersed with cottages and farm houses adjoining the two highways now known as the Rathmines and Ranelagh roads. Viewed across the open country to the south-ward was an unbroken panorama of the mountains, which, however, peaceful looking, were full of menace to the lowlands, owing to the spoils exacted by the " mountainy men " in their frequent raids upon the fertile tract lying between them and the metropolis.

The roads which traversed the district in which the battle was fought coincided almost exactly with the modern routes from the city through the following localities :—(1) Portobello, Rathmines, Upper Rathmines, Dartry Road, Milltown ;

(2) Charlotte Street, Charlemont Street, Ranelagh, Clonskeagh ;   (3) Stephen's Green, Lower and Upper Leeson Street, Morehampton Road, Donnybrook ;   (4) Stephen's Green, Baggot Street, Pembroke Road, Ballsbridge, Merrion. Besides these there was a path or track diverging from Rathmines Road, following the route of the present Mountpleasant Avenue, Palmerston Road, and the foot passages therefrom, *via* Richmond Avenue to Milltown Station and Milltown. This old field-path survived in part up to about forty years ago, and is still remembered by many.

Routes (1) and (2) diverged at the place formerly known as " The Bleeding Horse," from an old inn that stood at the junction of Charlotte Street and Camden Street.[12]

These routes will be found tolerably well marked in Petty's *Maps of the Down Survey* (*circa* 1650), and Rocque's *Maps of Dublin and its Environs* (1756, &c.). Although the survey for Rocque's *Map* was made about 100 years after the battle, there is no reason to suppose that any great alteration had taken place in the main roads during that interval.

No cross roads are marked in either of these maps, and communication between the main thoroughfares was probably by means of rough lanes and tracks across the fields, used principally by farmers and others residing in the district. An allusion to these lanes is to be found in a letter written by Sir James Dyve, a Royalist, who fought in the battle, to the Marquess of Newcastle, in which it is stated that the only way of reaching the camp at Rathmines from the city was by a number of " avenues."

When the Marquess of Ormonde, as Commander in Chief of the Royalist Army in Ireland, took the field in 1649, Dublin was held by a Parliamentary garrison under command of Colonel Jones, a skilled and experienced officer. Naturally the metropolis was the first place which Ormonde selected for attack, and with that object he marched from Kilkenny, reaching Castleknock on the 21st June, and moving next day to Finglas, from which he carried on some desultory operations against the north side of the city. According to a statement in a letter to King Charles II., written by Ormonde after his defeat, the total forces which he had at his disposal for the investment of Dublin, numbered 28,000 horse and foot. But, in the First Appendix to Walsh's *Irish Remonstrance*, &c., Ormonde mentions that after the defeat he sent word to the portion of his army at Finglas to retreat to Drogheda and Trim, from which it would appear that his entire forces were not engaged in this action. He also states that his army " encamped at Rathmines " was not more numerous than that of Jones, and Ludlow in his *Memoirs* estimates the strength of Jones's force engaged to have been between 4,000 and 5,000.

The city was then in a very unfit state to sustain a prolonged siege—it was not properly fortified, and the garrison was in serious straits for provisions, besides being much inferior in point of numbers and equipment to the total forces of their adversaries. One of the officers of the garrison, in a letter written to his brother in London, states that wheat was selling at £5 10s. a quarter (504 lbs.), rye at £4 10s. a quarter (480 lbs.), and cheese at 9d. a pound ; and he adds that there was a great scarcity of provisions even at those prices, and less money wherewith to buy them. It should be remembered that money was then some four or five times its present value. This officer estimated the strength of the garrison at about 7,500, including the inhabitants (he probably meant those bearing arms), and that of the besiegers at about 10,000.

Ormonde may have been unaware of the serious plight of the city ; indeed it is difficult otherwise to explain his prolonged inactivity which allowed time for supplies and reinforcements to be sent from England, and enabled the beleaguered garrison to strengthen their fortifications. Whatever may have been his reasons, however, he took no decisive steps until the close of July, when he marched to Rathmines and encamped some-where on the high ground lying between the localities now known as Palmerstown Park and Ranelagh. He then cut off the water supply—*i.e.*, the old city watercourse which starts from the Dodder at the weir of Firhouse—thereby further increasing the straits of the city by depriving it of drinking water and stopping its corn mills. (Jones's letter to the Council of State, and Ormonde's letter to Charles II.)

On the 27th July a Council of War was held by Ormonde in his camp at Rathmines, as a result of which Rathfarnham Castle, held by a small force of Parliamentarians, was, next day, taken, the garrison offering little or no resistance. Another Council of War was held on 1st August, and it was there decided to fortify the old castle of Baggotrath, standing on the ground now covered by the houses 44 and 46 Upper Baggot Street, opposite Waterloo Road, with the object of preventing the besieged garrison from grazing their horses on the pasture lands lying between Baggotrath and the city.

This would, it was thought, in a short time deprive the garrison of the use of their cavalry, and greatly hamper them in their operations. As the sequel shows, however, Ormonde had waited too long, the beleaguered force having now been relieved by the arrival of several vessels from England bringing reinforcements of cavalry and infantry, as well as considerable supplies of arms and ammunition.

On 1st August, in pursuance of the decision arrived at, Major-General Purcell was sent after dark with 1,500 men to fortify Baggotrath Castle, little over a mile distant, but as there was no direct route, he had to seek the aid of guides.

At daybreak on the 2nd August, Ormonde rode over to Baggotrath to ascertain how the work of fortification had proceeded, but, to his surprise found that very little progress had been made, and that Jones had forestalled him by dismantling the castle, leaving it in such a condition that it was scarcely worth fortifying. On demanding an explanation of the delay, Purcell informed Ormonde that the party had arrived there only an hour before daybreak, having been treacherously misled by the guides, and, seeing that the distance was so short, it would seem that treachery was at work somewhere.

When Jones recognised the object of the besiegers' movements near the castle, he considered the risk of delay so great that he determined to strike at once, and with that object deployed a large force of cavalry and infantry behind his fortifications at Lowsy Hill, now Townsend Street.   Ormonde, observing this movement, drafted the bulk of his troops over towards Baggotrath, planted some artillery on Gallows Hill (now Mount Street), and issued orders to the whole army to prepare for action.   He then assigned posts to his commanding officers, and, having been up all the previous night writing despatches, rode back to his camp, which he reached about 9 o'clock, to take some rest, in order that he might be ready for the action which he expected that day. (Ormonde's letters to King Charles II.)

Meanwhile Jones, by making the utmost haste with his preparations, was enabled to commence his advance by 9 o'clock, and about an hour later, suddenly attacked and utterly routed the right wing of Ormonde's army at the castle, some of the fugitives flying towards the main body and others towards the mountains; Ormonde, awakened by firing, which as he states himself, he judged to be much nearer than Baggotrath, rushed from his tent, but before he could even mount his horse, learned that his men had been beaten out of Baggotrath, that Sir William Vaughan had been killed, and the cavalry under his command who were supporting the operations at the castle, routed. This body of cavalry, Sir Lewis Dyve in his letter states, had been stationed " upon a large plowed " field looking towards the Castle of Dublin."

The portion of the army nearer to Ormonde's camp, except the two regiments commanded by his brother and Colonel Reilly, became demoralised when they saw the others in retreat, and ran away without even facing the enemy, notwithstanding the efforts of Ormonde and his officers to rally them, and the Parliamentary troops gained field after field until at last they reached the artillery.   Here Ormonde with the regiments mentioned, together with a force of infantry under Colonel

Gifford, appears to have made a last desperate stand, facing the Parliamentarians as they came out from the city, when a party of Jones's cavalry that had got on the Milltown path or road, by riding round or crossing the country unobserved, attacked them in the rear, while a further body of infantry advanced against them in front, and then, to use Ormonde's own words " Some called for quarter, some threw away their arms and " some continued shooting. Then we quit the field, and " endeavoured (but in vain) several times to rally the horse." He adds that he followed the cavalry for twelve miles in the hope of checking their retreat. (Walsh's *Irish Remonstrance*, 1st Appendix, p. III.) He then felt that he had no alternative but to make good his escape westward, leaving his artillery, ammunition and treasure in the hands of the enemy. During the engagement he was struck by a musket ball, but the superior quality of his armour saved him from injury.

In one of Ormonde's letters to the King, in which he almost claims the victory, he mentions the fact that his men were greatly agitated by the rumour that Cromwell had landed in Dublin, although he (Ormonde) knew that the story was baseless, and had been circulated with the object of demoralising his men.

Jones, in his despatch dated 11th August, 1649, reporting the result to the Council of State, gives a detailed list of the artillery and prisoners captured in the battle, and states that the engagement lasted two hours. Among the prisoners mentioned are :—

" William Cunningham, a noted rebel." [Each party called the other rebels in this war.]

" Mr. Baggot, Deputy Paymaster.

" Mr. John Herbert, servant to the pretended King, who " landed at Galway about six days since with the King's house- " hold goods."

Two of the cannon captured are described as follows :—

" One square brass demi-culverin, weighing two thousand " eight hundred pounds, her length eleven feet four inches, " her bullet weighing twelve pounds."

" One brass mortar piece, weighing nine hundred and twenty-
" seven pounds, her shell weighing one hundred pounds."

Owing to exaggeration and misrepresentation on both sides
is is not easy to form an accurate estimate of the number killed—
it was probably between 1,000 and 1,500.

A number of the Royalist troops under Lord Inchiquin's
command, who had taken refuge in the castles of Rathmines
and Rathgar, surrendered on being offered quarter, and
" promising faithfulness," took up arms in the Parliamentary
service. (Jones's letter to the Council of State.) Of this
incident, Ludlow gives the following account in his *Memoirs* :—
" Colonel Jones pursued him [Ormonde] close, finding little
" opposition, except from a party of Lord Inchiquin's horse
" that had formerly served the Parliament, who defended a pass
" [*i.e.*, a passage] for some time, but were after some dispute
" broken and forced to fly. Having routed these, he marched
" with all diligence up to the walls of Rathmines [Castle],
" which were about sixteen feet high, and containing about
" ten acres of ground, where many of the enemy's foot had
" shut up themselves ; but perceiving their army to be entirely
" routed, and their General fled, they yielded themselves
" prisoners. After this, our men continued their pursuit,
" found a party of about two thousand foot of the Lord
" Inchiquin's, in a grove belonging to Rathgar [Castle], who
" after some defence, obtained conditions for their lives ;
" and the next day most of them took up arms in our service."

As stated in the preceding chapter, the castle of Rathmines
stood on the site now occupied by the house known as " The
Orchards," Palmerston Park, and that of Rathgar, on the ground
immediately adjoining the top of the modern Rathgar Road
and the beginning of the Orwell Road.

The principal grounds for supposing the site of Ormonde's
camp to have been between Palmerston Park and Ranelagh
are —(1) the statements of both parties that he encamped
at Rathmines, and (2) that his camp was a mile (Irish measure)
from Baggotrath Castle. (*Irish Remonstrance*, Sir Lewis

Dyve's letter, &c., &c.)   No mention is made on old maps
or elsewhere, of the existence of any village at Rathmines
at that time, and the statement that he encamped " at
Rathmines " would probably mean that his camp was somewhere in the neighbourhood of the castle which was then the
most important object in the district.   Now the highest
ground fulfilling the conditions (1) and (2) is that immediately
east of Palmerston Road, from time immemorial known as " The
Bloody Fields," which would naturally be selected by Ormonde
as commanding the best view—possibly extending to Baggotrath
castle itself, as there were then no buildings intervening.

The name " The Bloody Fields " would at first sight appear
to suggest that this must be the scene of portion of the conflict,
but as the massacre of the Bristolian settlers in 1209 occurred
in the same locality, it cannot with certainty be stated to
which event this name is attributable.

These fields, now nearly built over, would be the most
probable place where numbers of the fugitives in their flight
to Rathmines and Rathgar Castles were overtaken and slain
by Jones's cavalry, the dead bodies afterwards being buried
where they fell by the peasantry of the neighbourhood.

Sir Lewis Dyve, in his letter to the Marquess of Newcastle,
states that no effort was made to defend the lanes leading
from Baggotrath to Ormonde's camp, although they could
have been held with little risk or difficulty, and that, owing
to treachery, some of these lanes had been purposely left open
and unguarded for the convenience of Jones's soldiers.

The manner in which Ormonde kept his camp is thus alluded
to in the ninth article of " The Declaration of Jamestown,"
in Walsh's *Irish Remonstrance* :—" Nothing happened in
" Christianity more shameful than the disaster at Rathmines
" near Dublin, where His Excellency, as it seemed . . .
" kept rather a Mart of Wares, a Tribunal of Pleadings, or
" a great Inne of play, drinking and pleasure, than a great
" camp of soldiers."

The conclusion to be drawn from a perusal of all the

correspondence and narratives in connection with this battle is that from the outset the result was a foregone conclusion, Jones's forces being well disciplined and skilfully handled, while those of Ormonde's were honeycombed with treachery and dissension, commanded by inexperienced officers, and lacked the cohesion and enthusiasm essential to success. There even seems to have been a suspicion that the Confederation of Kilkenny, with which Ormonde was then co-operating, was desirous that he should not achieve too great a success, and that this was the explanation of the many acts of treachery that came to light in connection with this engagement. It should also be remembered that a large portion of Ormonde's army must have been composed of men who had fought against him in the Insurrection of 1641-2.

The victory of the Parliamentarians was complete and decisive ; it broke up the Royalist army and raised the siege of Dublin. Ormonde abandoned all hope when Cromwell landed in Dublin a fortnight later, and the following year retired to the Continent where he remained until the Restoration.

The following authorities have been consulted in the preparation of this chapter :—Dr. Elrington Ball's *History of the County of Dublin ;* Dalton's *History of the County Dublin ;* Carte's *Life of Ormonde ;* Ludlow's *Memoirs ;* Walsh's *Irish Remonstrance,* &c. ; Ormonde's two letters to King Charles II., written after the battle ; Colonel Jones's letter to the Council of State of 11th August, 1649 ; Two letters from a Colonel in Dublin during the siege to his brother, a merchant in London, and other tracts in the Thorpe Collection.

CHAPTER XIX

HAROLD'S CROSS, CRUMLIN, THE GREEN HILLS, TALLAGHT AND OLDBAWN

THE earliest information available concerning Harold's Cross would go to show that it formed portion of the possessions of the powerful sept of the Harolds, whose house or castle stood at Harold's Grange, near the foot of Kilmashogue Mountain, and that from ancient times a common or green existed here on which a gallows was maintained by the Archbishop of Dublin for the execution of criminals.

After the invasion, as soon as the country lying immediately outside the city walls had become sufficiently settled to live in, this neighbourhood began to be colonised by some of the poorer classes from the city, whose descendants, for hundreds of years afterwards, lived in the manner of the original settlement—viz., with their cabins all round the common, on which they reared their children, their cattle, their goats, and their poultry.

About the middle of the 18th, and well into the 19th century, Harold's Cross began to improve considerably in consequence of its reputation as a rural sanatorium. In the " Diary of a Dublin lady in the reign of George I.," published in the *Journal of the Royal Society of Antiquaries* for 1898, it is stated that she took lodgings there in 1754, paying 15s. a week, for which she had " two middle rooms, the street closet, use of the parlour " and kitchen, with a bed for my man servant, the dairy, and " leave to walk when we please in the garden." Many of the townsfolk sent delicate children there to be nursed, and the parents going out on Sundays to visit them, and perhaps dining in rustic fashion there, initiated a close intimacy between the city and the rural village of Harold's Cross as it then was, with its invigorating breezes blowing straight down from the mountains.   In due time some of the citizens purchased the interest of villagers, erecting comfortable houses on the sites of the old mud cabins, and thus commenced the conversion of Harold's Cross into a suburb—a process that might have continued to the present day had it not been for the establishment of Mount Jerome Cemetery, which acted like a blight on the neighbourhood, and arrested all further progress.

Harold's Cross in 1832.
(*From "The Dublin Penny Journal."*)

As might be expected with a locality like Harold's Cross, which has become all but incorporated with the city, very little of its ancient individuality, either in customs or traditions, has survived to the present day.   A Maypole formerly stood on the Green, and the May sports were annually held there amid much enthusiasm, a ceremonial which may possibly be remembered by some of the older inhabitants.   The original pole stood beside the road, opposite the entrance to Mount Jerome Cemetery, and remained there until 1820, when it had to be taken down in consequence of its decayed and dangerous condition.   It was replaced by a tall poplar pole of unfinished appearance, which, however, served its purpose for several years afterwards.   In 1836, the publicans of the locality, desirous, from interested motives, of reviving the ancient glories of the May sports, subscribed the cost of a new Maypole, which was gaily decorated with ribbons and streamers in the orthodox fashion, but the sports were carried on only in a half-hearted fashion, and in a few years ceased altogether, in spite of all efforts to revive them.

Harold's Cross Green remained, until 1894, in the wild state of nature in which it had existed for hundreds of years, affording a precarious livelihood to a number of horses, donkeys, goats, and other animals, which were rudely dispossessed of their ancient patrimony when the Green was taken over by the Rathmines Commissioners and converted into a public park.

In the earlier part of the last century there was a Yeomanry corps called " The Uppercross Fusiliers," many of whom were workingmen from this neighbourhood ; but the uniforms and equipments of these warriors were of a very crude description and made the wearers seem fitter subjects for the ridicule than the admiration of the inhabitants.

Harold's Cross derives some interesting associations from having been, for a time at least, the residence of the two leaders of the insurrectionary movements of 1798 and 1803—namely, Lord Edward Fitzgerald and Robert Emmet. Lord Edward is stated to have remained for a month in the house of a Mrs. Jameson, at Parnell Place, on the Canal, although some hold that it was an old house near Lennox Street in which he made his brief sojourn in this neighbourhood. In the case of Robert Emmet it is tolerably certain that he resided in the house of a Mrs. Palmer at Harold's Cross in March, 1803, under the name of Hewitt. The house, which is mantled with ivy, and can be seen from the passing trams, stands near the western end of Mount Drummond Avenue, a little further out of town than the Canal bridge.

On the western side of the Green is a tall, conspicuous house, rejoicing in the unsavoury soubriquet of " The Buggy Barracks," which was occupied by the military for some years in the early part of the last century.

Leaving Harold's Cross by the Kimmage Road, at the south-western extremity of the Green, we almost immediately emerge into the open country, though, indeed, new houses

are so rapidly springing up in this neighbourhood that it
cannot hope to retain much longer its rural character. We
take the second turn to the right on this road, and enter a
narrow winding country lane called "The Captain's Lane,"
from which are obtained glimpses of the mountains on the left
and of the western portions of the city on the right. At the
end of this lane we turn to the right into Crumlin, still a country
village, notwithstanding its proximity to the city, and formerly

Drimnagh Castle.
(1900.)

noted for its horse races, which ceased on the enclosure of the
extensive commons by Act of Parliament early in the last
century. In 1594 Walter Reagh Fitzgerald, in command of
the Wicklow insurgents, raided and burnt the whole village,
plundered the church, and carried away the lead off the roof
to make bullets. The glare of the conflagration attracted
notice in Dublin, from which troopers were despatched with
all possible haste, but they arrived too late either to save the
village or capture the despoilers. An ecclesiastical report,
dated 1615, on the condition of the parish, states that the
parishioners were so poor, in consequence of the destruction

of their property in the raid alluded to, that they were unable yet to repair the church.

Crumlin was one of the four ancient manors in the County Dublin which were the property of the Crown, and in *Hollinshed's Chronicle* (1577), we read the following quaint notice of it as such :—" The Manor of Crumlin payeth a " greater chief rent to the prince than any of the other three, " which proceedeth of this : the Seneschal, being offended " with the tenants for their misdemeanour, took them up very " sharply in the court, and with rough and minatory speeches, " began to menace them. The lobbish and desperate clob- " beriousness, taking the matter in dudgeon, made no more " words, but knocked their seneschal on the costard, and left " him there, sprawling on the ground for dead. For which " detestable murder their rent was enhanced, and they pay " at this day ninepence per acre, which is double to any of " the other three Manors."

It appears, according to a document of 1496, that a cross was then standing in the village, but no tradition of its existence or site has reached the present day. It may, however, be mentioned in this connection that, from time immemorial, it has been the custom in the neighbourhood for funeral processions to walk bareheaded round the little triangular plot of grass just where the road from the village meets the Dolphin's Barn and Drimnagh road. No reason is assigned for this practice, and it may possibly be the case that this spot is the site, if not the place of concealment, of the village cross, buried, perhaps, during troublous times, as in the case of the old cross at Finglas, to save it from injury and desecration.

It was from his camp at Crumlin that King William issued his proclamation stopping the currency of the brass money coined by King James, except at a reduced valuation.

Passing out of the village and turning to the left at the far end, we almost at once come in view of the castle of Drimnagh, which is in so much better preservation than most of its contemporaries that it can hardly be described as a ruin. Traces of its once broad and deep fosse, and of its battlemented roof, are still readily distinguishable, while its ancient doorways and balustrades, its massive walls and staircases, proclaim its original purpose, notwithstanding its modern conversion to the uses of a dwellinghouse. Standing in a picturesque position at the head of the winding Lansdowne Valley, through which the Camac river threads its devious course, the castle commands an unbroken view of the mountains and of the fertile country extending to their bases.

The Lansdowne Valley is the original Cruimghlinn (Crumlin), meaning a crooked glen, from which the village of Crumlin derives its name.

In 1215 Drimnagh with its lands came into possession of the great Anglo-Norman family of Barnewall by a grant from King John, and was held by them for about 200 years, when it was leased to Sir Adam Loftus, nephew of Archbishop Loftus, who built Rathfarnham Castle. It is recorded that Loftus cut down some of the woods around Drimnagh, contrary to the covenant in the lease, and that the King expressed his disapprobation thereat upon complaint being made to him by the owner, Peter Barnewall.

In 1649, immediately before the Battle of Rathmines, the Marquess of Ormonde was about to occupy and fortify this castle in pursuance of his operations against the Parliamentarians who held the city, but was ultimately dissuaded from the project by his principal officers. Leaving Drimnagh and turning back a few paces along the road towards town, we turn to the right along a road, which, in conjunction with that passing through Dolphin's Barn, formed the ancient highway to Tallaght for hundreds of years before the construction, in the early part of last century, of the more direct route, from the southern side, through Terenure and Templeogue. A cross-roads is presently passed, after which a long ascent commences, and the road at length attains a height of over 200 feet, affording a comprehensive view of the flat country to the north and west. Up to about twenty-five

years ago, there was, around this point, a range of grassy sand
hills called " The Green Hills." over which the road was carried ;
the highest of these, standing immediately to the left, rose
to a height of 300 feet, and formed a most picturesque object
in this neighbourhood, clothed to the top with a short green
sward as smooth and as close as a carpet. Gabriel Beranger
(1780) thought that the Green Hills were artificial tumuli like
those at Dowth and Newgrange. These hills have gradually
been excavated and carted away for sand, until the only portion
of them which survives at the present day is that over which
the road passes, but their memory is perpetuated in the name
of the adjoining village of Green Hills.

Instead of proceeding the whole way to Tallaght by the
foregoing route it would be well to go by Tymon Lane, a
pretty secluded by-road which diverges to the left from the
main road at the entrance to the village of Green Hills, and
entails an addition of only about a mile to the journey. This
is a very ancient road, running along the ridge of the sandhills so as to avoid the marshes which formerly surrounded
Tymon Castle. From the highest point, overlooking the
village, the prospect is a striking one—the meadows and bright
green fields in the immediate vicinity, the blue waters of the
Bay in the distance, flecked here and there with a sail or the
blur of smoke of a passing steamer, Howth and the Bailey,
Killiney, and the whole range of mountains trending away
to the westward.

From this point the road descends to the course of a little
stream close to which is a slight elevation called " The Fairy
Hill," and beside it " The Fairy Well," surrounded by
luxuriant vegetation and a wealth of wild flowers. A few
paces further along this sequestered by-way will be seen the
picturesque ivied ruin of Tymon or Timothan Castle, situated
on a grassy knoll in a commanding position above the adjoining
road. It is a rather small edifice, but, standing as it does on an
eminence rising from the plain, is a conspicuous object for
some distance around. It had apparently only two apartments,

one above the other and both arched, communicating by a winding staircase. It must be remembered, however, that this class of castle was merely intended as the fortress of the household, for defence in case of attack, and that its limited accommodation was usually supplemented by a number of wooden structures beside it for the use of the family and servants.

Over the entrance to the castle, on its western side, is a small machicolation or projecting gallery for pouring melted lead, boiling water, or other suitable matters on the attacking party. No trace of bawn, fosse, or outworks can be distinguished, and if such ever existed they were probably very small, as the surrounding land was in ancient times an impassable marsh, making approach to the castle, except by the road, so difficult a matter as to render outworks almost unnecessary. The little stream flowing in a winding course through the adjoining fields now drains the locality and forms a tributary to the Poddle.

There is little of interest to chronicle in regard to Tymon. In 1247 it was constituted a prebend of St. Patrick's, and in an Inquisition of 1547 it is referred to as being in a ruinous condition, so that it is remarkable that it has lasted so long even as a ruin.

In 1798 a party of soldiers attacked Ballymanagh House, near Oldbawn, occupied by insurgents, and killed one of them. The defending party then left the house and crossed the fields in the direction of Tymon Castle, leaving the body of their comrade on the way. The soldiers followed, and finding the body, hung it from one of the windows of the castle.

Emerging on the steam tram road at Balrothery, there is nothing worthy of notice until we reach the ancient village of Tallaght, about a mile further. The earliest notices of Tallaght date from a period when historical narrative was largely blended with fable, and so remote that it is impossible to place any reliance upon their authenticity. It seems, however, that at some early date in the world's history, the whole population of the adjacent country, consisting of a colony from Greece, were wiped out by pestilence, and that they were buried wholesale in this neighbourhood. These pestilential outbreaks, which are so frequently recorded in the early histories of most countries, were doubtless due to the insanitary conditions under which people lived in those rude times.

Tallaght.
(1900.)

Some confirmation of these traditions about Tallaght is to be found in the great number of burial mounds, stone circles, cairns, and other ancient places of sepulture which, from time to time, have been discovered on the Tallaght and Saggart hills.

Tallaght is interesting as having been for a time the country residence of the Protestant Archbishops of Dublin. In 1729 Archbishop Hoadley took down the extensive ruins of the ancient Castle of Tallaght which stood on the site of an earlier monastic establishment, and with the materials built a large episcopal mansion, thus described by Austin Cooper, the antiquary, in 1779 :—" For a thing of the kind it is the poorest " ever I saw. It is a large piece of patchwork, so devoid of

" either order or regularity that it is past describing."
Brewer in his *Beauties of Ireland* (1826), gives the following
account of it as it existed shortly before its demolition :—
" The present structure is a spacious, but long and narrow,
" building, composed of the grey stone of the country, and is
" destitute of pretensions to architectural beauty.   The interior
" contains many apartments of ample proportions, but none
" that are highly embellished.   The hall into which the visitor
" is conducted by a lofty flight of double stone steps in the
" centre of the building measures 21 feet square, and is lighted
" by two tiers of windows. . . .   The date is 1729, and above
" is the crest, a hawk perched upon a round ball.   Underneath
" the coat of arms is the following inscription—' Johannes
" Hoadley, hanc domum reficit.' . . .   The library is a small
" apartment, having a large window, from which, as from
" all the windows of the reception rooms, fine views
" are obtained of Mountpelier Hill and the surrounding
" country."

Having regard to the above descriptions by such writers
as those mentioned, it is impossible not to conclude that the
well-known engraving in possession of the Dominican Fathers
at Tallaght, and reproduced on opposite page, representing
this structure as a lordly pile of imposing proportions, was
largely due to the imagination of the artist who depicted it.

The palace having fallen into ruinous condition early in the
last century, and there being no funds wherewith to repair it,
an Act of Parliament was passed in 1821 divesting the See of
the responsibility for its maintenance.   It was thereupon
sold to a Major Palmer, who took it down and built himself
a large house out of the materials.   In 1842 the site was leased
to the Dominicans, who established a large monastery here,
and in more recent times erected the handsome Church as
a memorial to Father Burke, the eloquent and distinguished
member of that Order.

Tallaght village or town as an outpost of the Pale, was, in
early times, enclosed by a wall, towards the construction of

which the inhabitants in 1310 received a grant from the Crown, while fourteen years later the Archbishop of Dublin received a similar grant in consideration of building a castle for the defence of the place.

Situated as Tallaght was, on the borders of a wild mountain tract, with a small population, these defences availed little against the fierce Irish septs, who for hundreds of years preyed ruthlessly upon the colonists, despoiling them of their cattle,

Archiepiscopal Palace and Castle, Tallaght.
(Taken down about 1825.)

plundering their dwellings, and laying waste the adjoining country.

In 1331, O'Toole of Imaal with a numerous force swooped down from the fastnesses of his native hills upon Tallaght, looting the castle and taking away three hundred sheep, besides killing a number of the Archbishop's servants, and defeating in a pitched battle Sir Philip Brett and a body of Dublin citizens who had marched out against him. After this incident, efforts were made to put the town into a better state of defence, and the inhabitants ceaselessly kept watch and ward, so as to be in readiness for any future attack, but ultimately, recognising the insecurity of their position and the inadequacy of their defences, they came to an agreement with the O'Tooles, whereby the latter undertook not to molest the Marches, from Tallaght to Windgate, at Bray, and to defend them if necessary from any of the mountain septs.

This compact with the O'Tooles does not seem to have been a success, as we read that in 1378 Mathew de Bermingham was sent to Tallaght with 120 hobillers (cavalry) to resist the attacks of the O'Byrnes, and it is recorded that in the same year John de Wade received £20 compensation for the loss of two horses and other property burnt here by the O'Nolans.

In 1538, Archbishop Browne, who resided here for some years, made bitter complaint to the Government, of the treatment he received from Lord Leonard Gray, the Lord Deputy, and of the oppression of his tenantry by the O'Tooles. In 1540 that powerful sept devastated Tallaght and the adjoining royal manors of Crumlin, Saggart, and Newcastle, laying waste the whole countryside.

This raid was provoked by a gross breach of faith on the part of the Lord Deputy, who, having appointed a meeting with Turlough O'Toole, on the borders of the County Dublin, proceeded thither with an armed force, and after a pretence of parleying with the Irish chieftain made an attempt to take him prisoner. This piece of treachery, however, failed, owing to the fleetness of O'Toole's horse, which outdistanced his pursuers after a chase lasting till dark.

This discreditable act was one of a number of charges subsequently brought against Lord Deputy Gray in connection with his government of Ireland. (State Papers, Hen. VIII.)

In 1662 the Churchwardens of Tallaght were, on petition to the House of Lords, awarded £100, to be levied off the estate of a Captain Alland, who wantonly wrecked the church when quartered here with his troop.

In 1691, according to Dean Story's *Impartial History*, " a " party of rapparees, coming near Tallaght, took away several " horses and four men belonging to Colonel Donep's regiment " of Danish horse. This being easily believed could not be

" done without the knowledge of the inhabitants of the adjacent
" villages, the Colonel ordered several of them to be taken up,
" and threatened to hang them all, unless the horses and men
" were brought back by such a day, which was accordingly
" done, and some of the men that stole them delivered up."

The ancient cross of Tallaght formerly stood at the end
of the village in the middle of the road leading to Oldbawn,
and on account of the traditions attaching to it was greatly
venerated by the people; but in 1778 Archbishop Fowler
removed it for the purpose of using it as building materials
in the construction of a bathroom attached to the palace.
It was only when the building was being dismantled about
1826 that this act of vandalism was brought home to the right
person, through the discovery of the shaft and pedestal among
the ruins of the bathroom.

The extensive gardens of the old palace still remain, and
are kept in good order as an appanage of the monastery. They
contain an immense walnut tree hundreds of years old, called
St. Maelruan's tree after the Patron Saint of Tallaght.

The Protestant Church, at the far end of the village, is
built on the site, and partly of the materials of a much more
ancient edifice, which seems to have been originally enclosed
by a kind of circumvallation, traces of which still remain. The
old ivy-clad belfry tower beside the modern structure is portion
of the old church which was taken down in 1829. In the
interior of the church are a monument and memorial tablet
to Sir Timothy Allen, who was Lord Mayor of Dublin in
1762, and who lived near Oldbawn in a house which has since
been called Allenton.

St. Maelruan's patron, or "pattern," was every year
celebrated here from a remote period on the 7th July, but
in later years the original Saint's name was lost sight of
altogether, and replaced by the corrupted form, "Moll
Rooney," under which title the "pattern" continued to be
annually held, until it came to be such a nuisance, owing to
drunkenness and debauchery, that it was suppressed in 1874.

The proceedings consisted in making a kind of effigy, supposed to represent the Saint, and carrying it about from house to house in procession, headed by a fiddler or piper. The occupants of each house then came out as they were visited, and danced to the music, after which a collection was made to be spent on drink. Few went to bed that night ; many slept in ditches on the way home, and drinking, dancing, and fighting went on intermittently till morning. Another item in the performance in recent times was to visit the grave of an old village piper named Burley O'Toole, who had expressed a dying wish to that effect, and to dance and fight around his grave.

The degeneration of this patron is unfortunately only typical of others throughout the country, which explains why so many of them have been discontinued through the influence of the clergy and others.

At the far end of the village where the road turns to the right, it crosses a small stream that supplied the castle and palace with water This place is called Talbot's Leap from a tradition that when Cromwell was on one of his marauding expeditions in this neighbourhood he paid a visit to Talbot's castle at Belgard while the owner was out, and helped himself as he pleased. When Talbot returned he was naturally enraged, and collecting a few retainers gave chase to Cromwell and his soldiers, overtaking them at Tallaght. Finding, however, that the Ironsides were more than a match for his company, he hastily retired, and finding the drawbridge, which then stood here, raised, he, by a supreme effort, jumped his horse across the fosse, and thus saved his life.

In the 18th century there appears to have been a considerable number of parish officers in Tallaght, and one cannot help wondering where all their salaries came from, even considering that rates were struck on the acreage of districts so distant as Whitechurch and Cruagh to provide the necessary revenue. There was a special vestry whose function it was to issue licences to paupers to beg, and a parish officer, known as " Bang-beggar," was appointed to supervise the practice of this profession in the town, and to repress sternly any poaching by unlicensed members of the craft.

Leaving Tallaght by the road to the left at the end of the village, we cross Watergate bridge and presently reach a rough stony lane on the right, leading up to Oldbawn, an interesting old house, now in very ruinous condition, built about 1630, by Archdeacon Bulkeley, to whom the lands had been ceded

Oldbawn in 1890.

some years previously by grant of Charles I. In the dining room was, until recently, a very remarkable stucco chimney-piece, now in the National Museum, Dublin, bearing the date 1635, representing the building of Jerusalem, as told in the 3rd and 4th chapters of Nehemiah. The accompanying illustration is from a photograph which was taken about 20 years ago, when the place was in a much better state of preservation than at present. Many of the figures have since been somewhat defaced, and the whole overmantel, which reached to the ceiling, was becoming so much blackened by smoke that it would, in a short time, have been worthless as a relic, if it had not been removed to a place of safety. Considering that the figures are in such high relief, it is wonderful that this interesting piece of work has lasted so long.

This house was originally surrounded by orchards and plantations, as well as a deer park, the enclosing wall of which is still to be seen beside the road along the Dodder. In the grounds are a number of evergreens and hollies of immense size ; one of these, a large cypress, is called " The Informer's Tree," from the fact that in 1798 a rebel, who was about to be-hanged on it, was pardoned for giving information. The stumps of three other trees, where his companions were hanged, are still pointed out by the people.

According to popular traditions of this neighbourhood, the ghost of Archdeacon Bulkeley at times revisits his patrimony in a cumbrous, old-fashioned coach, drawn by six headless horses. But woe to the luckless wayfarer who looks on this fearsome equipage, for within a year and a day he passes to that shadowy land from whose bourn no traveller returns.

At the time that Oldbawn was in its prime, a great number of persons were employed in connection with it, and a village of the name, now only represented by a few cottages, stood here adjoining the Dodder.

A paper mill was for many years worked in this place, but was eventually burnt, and the remains of the sheds and machinery may still be seen beside the old house. Nearly all the original plantations have been cut down for firewood—the fate, unfortunately, of many plantations and orchards attached to old Irish mansions. An eccentric resident in the 18th century imported a herd of reindeer from Lapland, and kept them in the deer park ; but, almost needless to say, they died out rapidly, as the climate was much too warm for them.

About a quarter of a mile from Oldbawn bridge, on the bank of the Dodder, will be seen a little old house, nearly concealed by trees. The adjoining fields were the scene of a remarkable concourse in 1816, when thousands of the country people assembled to witness the execution of three men named

Kearney—a father and his two sons—for the murder of one John Kinlan, steward to Ponsonby Shaw of Friarstown, Bohernabreena. The conviction was not, strictly speaking, for murder, but for conspiracy to murder under an Act then newly passed. Kinlan had somehow incurred the enmity of the Kearneys, who, on the Sunday prior to the victim's dis-

Oldbawn Chimneypiece, now in National Museum.
(1892.)

appearance, were heard to say that they would have his life. A hatchet was found in the vicinity of the Kearneys' house with blood on it, and hair that resembled Kinlan's, but the body was never found, and it was said at the time that it was burnt to ashes. It is more probable, however, that it was buried in one of the bogs in the neighbourhood.

On the night of the murder, Kinlan was in the house of one of Shaw's gamekeepers, who remonstrated strongly with him as to the folly of going home alone and his refusal to accept an armed escort of his friends. He, however, ridiculed the suggestion of danger, and set out alone. He had not gone more than five minutes when the stillness of the night was disturbed by a shot, whereupon the occupants of the house hastily seized their arms and rushed out along the road in the direction from which the sound proceeded. Not a human being was to be seen, however, but, on a subsequent examination of the road by the light of a lantern, one spot appeared much disturbed as if a struggle had taken place there, and part of a suspender was found which was afterwards identified as belonging to Kinlan.

Lundy Foot, of the well known tobacco firm, an energetic magistrate in this neighbourhood, residing at Orlagh, took a prominent part in the investigation and prosecution of this case, and his own murder, which took place at Rosbercon, Co. Kilkenny, nineteen years afterwards, was by many attributed to motives of revenge on the part of friends or relatives of the condemned men (*See* Index).

The three Kearneys were, after conviction, brought out from town, escorted by a troop of dragoons, to the field in which the gallows had been erected, and their remains were conveyed back the same day to Kilmainham Gaol where they were buried.

It is stated that some horrible scenes took place at the execution, as the hangman was rather unskilful at his task, and that the crowd were with difficulty restrained from attacking him.

The return journey may be made by crossing Oldbawn Bridge, and either taking the road to Firhouse or continuing straight by Oldcourt Lane until the Military road is reached at a point three and a half miles distant from Rathfarnham.

In the preparation of this chapter, information has been obtained from Handcock's *History and Antiquities of Tallaght*, Dalton's *History of the County Dublin*, and *Rambles near Dublin*.

CHAPTER XX

JOBSTOWN, MOUNT SESKIN AND THE TALLAGHT HILLS

STARTING from Terenure, our route lies along the straight, uninteresting road to Templeogue village, beyond which, to the right, is Templeogue House, the ancient residence of the Domvile family, and for some time the residence of Charles Lever, the novelist. A mediaeval castle stood here until the beginning of the 18th century, when it was taken down, and a dwellinghouse erected on its site by Sir Thomas Domvile, and this in turn was replaced by the present edifice in the early part of last century. A portion of the old castle yet remains, having been so strongly built as to defy the efforts of the workmen who were employed to take it down, and it had, perforce, to be incorporated in the two dwellinghouses which successively rose over the foundations of this ancient stronghold.

The Domviles, when proprietors of this place, possessed or assumed the right of diverting the water from the old city watercourse which passed through their grounds ; and in connection with this matter, the story is told that Sir Compton Domvile, in 1738, when his nephew, Lord Santry, had been condemned to death for the murder of one of his servants, threatened, when all other means of intercession had failed, to cut off the entire water supply from the city if the sentence were carried out. This threat had the desired effect, and the noble murderer's escape was connived at by the authorities.

No doubt the threat might easily have been put into execution, but the prospect of having the whole water supply of Dublin turned into his house and grounds could scarcely have been a cheerful one for the eccentric proprietor, even though he might have had the satisfaction of driving the citizens of that day to quench their thirst with other beverages.

We next pass the village and almost vanished hill of Balrothery, a short distance from which, across the fields, will be seen the ivied ruins of Tymon Castle.

To the east of Balrothery hill is a spring well called the Limekiln well, originating a stream of water which flows into the old city watercourse. This well, in ancient times, enjoyed the reputation of supplying St. Patrick's Cathedral with water, although the only possible ground for such a claim was the fact that the city watercourse, which received the stream from the well, flowed beside the Cathedral.

A little to the west of this well there was formerly an oblong enclosure, about an acre in extent, surrounded by a fosse, and traditionally reputed to be the site of a castle and village, of which all trace has now disappeared.

On the high ground between Tallaght and Balrothery, an old thorn tree marks the site of an ancient holy well, which was destroyed many years ago by a local farmer in a fit of irritation at the injury to his fences by people drawing water from it. He carted a load of slaughterhouse refuse to the place and ordered his men to throw it into the well to spoil it, but none of them could be induced to undertake so unpopular a task, and ultimately he had to do it himself. On the way home, however, his horse ran away, and he was seriously injured by a fall from his cart—a visitation universally regarded as a punishment from heaven, due to his sacrilegious conduct.

We next enter the village of Tallaght, described in the previous chapter. Prior to the construction of the modern road to this place from Terenure, now over a hundred years ago, the coach road to Blessington, instead of entering Tallaght, passed a little to the north of it, outside the grounds of the old palace, proceeding in a straight line from the Green Hills road to the sharp angle on the tram road opposite the Protestant Church, where there formerly was a turnpike. On the side of the old road, at this point, there stood for generations a blacksmith's forge, whose long career of usefulness came to an end when the road was altered. The site is, however, easily identified by the deep deposit of cinders to be seen on raising the soil.

There is nothing further worthy of notice along the main road until we reach the small group of cottages called Jobstown, where we take the turn to the left, known as the Killinardan road, up the steep slope of Knockannavea Mountain or Tallaght

Jobstown.
(1904.)

Hill. The road becomes rougher as it ascends higher up the mountainside, and we pass between high hedge-banks of hawthorn and furze, with occasional growths of fern and the graceful lusmore or foxglove. Emerging, at length, from the enclosing hedges, our view extends over the plain and Bay of Dublin, while to the eastward will be seen Mount Pelier, Kilmashogue, the Three Rocks and Killakee Mountains; and continuing our journey, near the top of the road we meet, on the left, a narrow lane, said to be portion of an ancient track by which, in remote times, the dead were borne from the plains to be interred in the churchyards among these wild hills. On the right will now be observed a picturesque little defile overgrown with furze and stunted woods, rising over the far side of which is the hill called Lugmore, an offshoot of Knockannavea. Extending away towards Dublin will be seen the wide Blessington road, and at times may be heard the shrill whistle of the steam tram echoing among the hills, its harshness agreeably softened by distance.

We now pass a small farmhouse in a somewhat exposed position, sheltered by a plantation of elder and thorn bushes, and shortly afterwards reach the summit of the mountain called Knockannavinidee, locally known as Killinardan Hill. The road here becomes a mere bridle-track through the furze, the turf springs under our feet, and the higher mountains to the southward come into view. Mount Pelier with its conspicuous ruin lies on our left ; further to the southward is the great Military road winding like a white ribbon across Killakee Mountain ; below it is the road from Bohernabreena through Piperstown, and due south the towering summit of Seechon.

After reaching the brow of the hill, a small pond will be seen on the left ; about half a mile beyond this pond the track runs beside a rough stone wall with a double line of barbed wire on top ; keep along by this wall until it turns at a sharp angle to the left, and on the summit of the eminence to the right, about a hundred yards away, is Raheen Dhu, one of the most perfect raths to be found in the neighbourhood of Dublin.

As all this portion of the mountain is covered with heather and gorse, the rath is not easily distinguishable from the rest of the hill, but once located, its two concentric rings and the remains of the central mound can be readily traced.

From Raheen Dhu we make our way up to Knockannavea Mountain, the actual summit of which is somewhat difficult to identify, as there are a number of small eminences, all apparently about the same height, scattered over the heather-clad tract at the top. Looking westward from any of the higher points, we can see the long range of hills at the far side of the valley through which the tram road passes; directly below and glittering in the sun are the Brittas fish-ponds, over which rises Cupidstown Hill; to the right of that is Slieve Thoul, and then Knockananiller and Knockandinny.

From here we proceed due west across the mountain to the rising ground opposite, where a plantation encloses the house called Mount Seskin, properly Mone Seskin (the bog of the

Mount Seskin.
(1906.)

seskin or morass) in which form the name appears on the older maps. This house, now much dilapidated, was formerly a well-equipped country residence, and although the dwelling itself is comparatively small, it formed, in conjunction with its great array of out-offices, an extensive establishment, evidently designed to accommodate a considerable staff of servants and workmen in the old days when labour was cheap and people were glad to work for a few pence a day. The house is provided with a belfry, which, with the arched windows, at the back, gives it a somewhat ecclesiastical appearance, and the hall door, originally so large as to be out of proportion to the

rest of the building, has been reduced in size in recent years.
Dense plantations surround and shelter the place, investing
it with an air of solitude and seclusion, which is enhanced by
the deserted condition of the old coach road passing directly
in front of it. This was the only route to Blessington until
the new road through the Slade of Saggart was constructed
over a hundred years ago, down to which time a number of
coaches passed each way every day, so that the house was in a
most convenient position for communication with Dublin.

Returning along the old road towards town, in about a
mile will be seen a by-road to the left leading to a couple of
dilapidated cottages, representing the ancient village of
Corbally, according to local tradition, a place of importance
some 250 years ago, possessing a jail and marshalsea. Part of a
wall still remains which is said to have formed portion of the
town wall, and the site of the jail is also pointed out, as well
as that of the toll-house, where toll was paid in corn. Adjoining
is a field called "The Trench" or "Furrow Pit," reputed
to be the burial place of a number of the inhabitants who
died of plague about 300 years ago. The history of the locality
does not tend to bear out these traditions, which are probably
of much earlier date than that which is popularly assigned
to them.

Continuing our journey along the high road, in about three
quarters of a mile we enter a wood where there is an old farmhouse on the left, with a broken tree surrounded by a stone
seat in front. Just beside this house will be seen a disused
laneway leading to the ruins of an old country house named
Johnville, at one time the residence of Mr. Roe, of distillery
fame, who had a very pretty garden sloping up the hill, where
still remain some splendid specimens of cypress and other
evergreens. While the owner lived, the whole place was
maintained in excellent order, but after his death it was
untenanted for a long time and became greatly dilapidated.
About 1854 a Dr. Luther, hydropathist and homæopathist,
took the house and fitted it up as a hydropathic establishment,

expending a large sum in erecting Turkish, douche, and vapour baths, while outside in the grounds were mud and plunge baths, formed by damming the little stream that flows down from the mountain. The place was, however, only indifferently patronised, probably owing to the difficulty of reaching it, and after struggling for a few years it was abandoned, and has been going to ruin ever since. Scattered about through

Johnville.
(1905.)

the building may still be seen the remains of the marble mantel-pieces and hearthstones, the Portland stone staircases and ornamental work of various descriptions, all more or less broken by portions of the building which have fallen on them. The wine cellar is almost intact, and may, perhaps, still contain some of the original stock concealed beneath the accumulations of earth and rubbish.

At the rear is a well, now all but choked up with earth ; also the basin and rockery of a fountain which was supplied by a pipe from the stream at a higher level. The masonry of the open-air mud bath is still perfect, but several summer-houses which stood in the grounds to serve as a dressing-room for the guests have disappeared.

The situation of the place—on the side of the mountain overlooking the Dublin plain—is very beautiful, and it is surprising that it enjoyed only a brief spell of popularity. Now that a ready means of reaching this neighbourhood has been provided by the steam tram, such an establishment would have very much better chances of success. The by-road passing the place is not now maintained in order for general traffic, but is quite practicable in dry weather for cyclists wheeling their machines. By continuing the by-road beyond Johnville, the tram road will be reached close to the Embankment.

Pedestrians should take return tickets from Terenure to Jobstown, paying the difference if the tram is taken at the Embankment on the return journey. The distance to be walked, starting from Jobstown and returning to the Embankment, is a little over six miles.

Cyclists can ride to Jobstown, from which it will be necessary to walk with their bicycles the whole way over Tallaght Hill or Knockannavea until they reach Ballinascorney Gap. They can then ride most of the way to Brittas, from which the *old* road to Tallaght, not the tram road, should be taken, passing Mount Seskin and joining the tram road near Jobstown. The route over Tallaght Hill from Jobstown is impracticable for motors of any description.

The authorities consulted in the preparation of this chapter are :—Handcock's *History and Antiquities of Tallaght*, and Dalton's *History of the County of Dublin*.

CHAPTER XXI

BALLYMOUNT, THE TALBOTS OF BELGARD, CLONDALKIN, THE CORKAGH POWDER MILLS.

LEAVING town by either Terenure or Crumlin, we make our way to Ballymount Lane, a continuation of the Kimmage or Crumlin road from Terenure. The lane commences at the cross-roads known as Oliver's Corner, where we cross the old road from Dublin to Tallaght, used before the construction of the modern one from Terenure, and almost immediately we enter a low cutting, where formerly stood one of the green sand hills which gave name to this locality. Years of excavations have now left scarcely a trace of it, but some of its smaller companions may still be seen to the right, between us and the scattered village of Fox and Geese. After about a mile we meet another cross-roads, immediately beyond which, to the right, will be observed the ancient ivy-clad ruin of what was evidently a fortified entrance gate to Ballymount Castle. An avenue leads thence to a modern dwellinghouse named Ballymount, close to which, on the summit of a mound, is a small circular building, like the remains of a watch tower, built of limestone and brick, and enclosed by two concentric circumvallations. The appearance of the brickwork portions would suggest that they were repairs executed at periods long subsequent to the erection of the structure. This building, although commonly known as Ballymount Castle, cannot have been anything more than a watch tower of the ancient stronghold, which was probably taken down to supply materials for the erection of a dwelling-house on its site. Some portions of an old stone stairs yet remain, and traces of the fosse that enclosed this once extensive

establishment can still be discerned in places.   About a hundred
yards to the eastward is a massive wall, apparently of very
ancient date, overhung with centuries' growth of ivy.

Gabriel Beranger, who visited the place about 1780, describes
the castle as having been an extensive one, and of considerable
strength, as evidenced by its massive walls, towers, and outworks, which down to that time had remained intact.   His

Old Gateway at Ballymount.
(1912.)

description of it, as follows, is taken from Wilde's *Memoir
of Gabriel Beranger* :—

" Hearing from some cottagers that there was at a little
" distance an enchanted cave, with subterraneous wards
" extending various ways for some miles, which some men at
" different times had tried to explore, but never returned,
" I was piqued by curiosity and begged to be shown the place.

" I found a vault of good masonry, about 8 feet high and
" 6 broad ; descending this a few steps, I found at the end a
" square opening which had to be entered on all fours.   I

" procured two candles, and on offering a small reward got a
" boy to follow me. For fear of mephitic vapours and suffoca-
" tions I fastened a solid branch of tree to my cane, on which
" I stuck my candle, so that the light was about four feet
" before me.

" I then entered on my hands and feet, holding the light
" before me, followed by the boy with a candle in his hand.
" I went this way some yards, and then found two shafts—
" one leading to the right, the other to the left. I took the
" first, and advanced a good way, until I met with two more
" shafts and a very cadaverous smell. Here my boy began
" to be afraid, and I thrust my candle as far as I could in the
" two passages, but it always burned clear. Considering,
" however, that the boy would go no further, and if I went
" alone, and my candle was to be extinguished, it would be
" hard to find my way back in the dark, I prudently returned
" the way I came, observing the construction, which was of
" stone, and in good preservation. It was clearly an aqueduct
" for supplying the fortress with water, and must have been
" made at a great expense by some powerful chieftain, who
" had his residence there."

It is very unlikely that passages so large as Beranger describes
would have been constructed for the purposes of a water supply,
and it is much more probable that they led to some secret
exit, and were intended for use in troublous times.

Notwithstanding the formidable character of its defences,
Ballymount has a peaceful record, and it figures but little in
local history.

An ancient road, portions of which may still be traced,
ran from Ballymount to the Belgard road, near the cross roads
known as the Shoulder of Mutton.

As we continue our journey along Ballymount Lane we
may observe, on high ground to the left, Kilnamanagh House,
an old-fashioned country residence built on to the remains of an
ancient castle, some of the old massive doors of which remained
until recent years. There was also a monastery here, with a

church and churchyard, which probably accounts for the quantity of human bones unearthed from time to time near the house by agricultural operations. No doubt this place saw some fighting during the wars of the 17th century, when nearly all the strongholds and castles of the Pale were on their defence against enemies and marauders of every description.

From this point the lane winds in a very irregular fashion until it meets the road from Tallaght to Clondalkin, opposite the entrance to Belgard, a place of considerable historic interest, where, in a commanding position on the summit of a wooded eminence, the modern Castle of Belgard rises majestically on the site of its ancient predecessor, a structure which for 600 years withstood the ravages of time no less than the assaults of war. The locality is inseparably associated with a branch of the Talbot family, known as the Talbots of Belgard, who, so far back as the 15th century, were in occupation of the castle, and had frequently to defend it against forays by the mountaineers.

In the time of Charles the First and during the Commonwealth, John Talbot of Belgard, took sides with the Confederate Catholics, and his estates were consequently forfeited, after which he followed the adherents of the monarchy into exile and rendered distinguished service in the war in Flanders. On the Restoration the estates were restored to the family " for reason known unto the King in an especial manner " meriting his grace and favour." At the war of the Revolution, Colonel John Talbot of Belgard espoused the cause of James II., and fought at the battles of the Boyne and Aughrim, and the estates would no doubt have been forfeited a second time but for the fact that Colonel Talbot was included in the Articles of the Treaty of Limerick. As his age precluded him from going abroad with his comrades in arms, he retired to the seclusion of Belgard, where he passed his remaining years in the ease and comfort to which his adventurous and distinguished career had entitled him.

He was the last of the Talbots of Belgard, and at his death

in 1697, without male issue, his estate passed to the Dillon family by a marriage of his daughter with a great grandson of the first Viscount Dillon. Belgard subsequently passed in succession into possession of the Trant, Cruise, Kennedy, and Laurence families.

Adjoining Belgard, is Newlands, the former residence of Lord Kilwarden, Chief Justice of Ireland, who was murdered in 1803 during the insurrection of Robert Emmet.

Turning to the right opposite the entrance to Belgard, in about a mile we reach the Naas road at the cross-roads called " The Shoulder of Mutton," from an inn which stood there in old times. The low ground here, lying immediately south of the Naas road was formerly a bog known as Mone Roodan. Here we turn to the left along the main road, and after about a mile and a half, turn to the right in order to visit the once famous Corkagh Powder Mills, the explosion at which in 1787 caused such general consternation for miles around. These mills, nine altogether, erected in 1783, were regarded as an important national undertaking, and although the expectations in regard to them were not fully realised, they gave a deal of employment in the neighbourhood. One of the proprietors, named, Arabin, lived in Corkagh House, adjoining, and, being very wealthy, the house was for some years the scene of considerable gaiety, and the rendezvous of frequent hunting parties in the season.

The explosion at the mills occurred in April, 1787, and the quantity of powder stored there at the time was estimated at not less than 260 barrels. It is stated that the shock was felt even in the city and throughout a considerable area of the surrounding country. The whole building where the disaster occurred was completely torn from its foundations and hurled into the air ; ponderous masses of masonry, tons in weight, were carried five or six fields away, and one large piece was deposited close to the village of Clondalkin, while the fish in the ponds adjoining the mills were all killed by the shock, and in some cases blown out on the banks.

In *Exshaw's Magazine*, of 25th April, 1787, is the following notice of the occurrence :—" This afternoon the powder mills " of Clondalkin, belonging to Councillor Caldbeck, by some " unknown accident blew up. Two men who were at work " in the mill were destroyed, and many of the neighbouring " houses greatly shattered ; it also occasioned the sudden fall " of a stack of chimnies near Meetinghouse yard on Usher's " Quay, but fortunately no accident occurred in conse-

Round Tower, Clondalkin.
(1890.)

" quence of the same. The explosion was severely felt " in the most distant parts of the county, and even in the " County of Kildare for some miles near the banks of the canal."

The ruins of the various buildings—the grinding houses, drying sheds, and magazines—together with the ponds, mill dams and sluice gates connected with the various portions of the establishment, cover a considerable area, probably 15 or 20 acres, and the whole place is little altered from the condition in which it was left by the explosion 125 years ago. A few of the buildings have been converted into hay sheds and cattle shelters, and the little islands in the ponds present quite a picturesque appearance owing to the dense growth of trees and brushwood with which they are now covered. The water for the ponds is supplied by the River Camac, which rises in the mountains over Brittas, and flowing under the name of the Slade River through the Slade of Saggart, passes hence by Clondalkin and Drimnagh, until it joins the Liffey at Inchicore. A monument was erected on the site to commemorate the disaster, but no trace of it is now discernible, nor could any information be obtained as to its fate.

This was the second explosion of powder mills in Clondalkin, an earlier one having occurred in 1733, on which occasion a number of persons were injured, but, notwithstanding these experiences, a third mill was erected about the beginning of the last century.

Making our way from here to Clondalkin, we enter that ancient village from the south, coming at once into view of the Round Tower on the left. Brewer in his *Beauties of Ireland* (1826), thus describes this place :—" The devious street is " lined with the low cabins usual to the peasantry of this " island, but with such as rank among the neatest of their " ordinary dwellings." Since that time, however, the village has been entirely altered and rebuilt, and the paper mills of Messrs. Kynoch, together with the neat cottages erected for the employes, give the place an appearance very different from that described by Brewer.

The most interesting object in the village is the round tower, which, being the most accessible of these structures to the city, is much visited by tourists. It is 84 feet high, measures 45 feet in circumference at the base, and the walls are 3 feet thick. The door is about 15 feet from the ground, and the portion of the structure below it is solid masonry, which at a recent period was strengthened by a massive stone casing ascended by a flight of steps to the doorway.

East of the tower and now separated from it by the public road, is the modern Protestant Church, in the graveyard of which are some small remains of the ancient church, as well as an old font, rudely fashioned out of a granite boulder.

In the Gabriel Beranger portfolio in the Royal Irish Academy is a drawing of Clondalkin old church, made about the year 1770, by T. Archdeacon, which has the following note written on it :—" These old remains were demolished by the blowing " up of the powder mills in this neighbourhood sometime after " this drawing was taken."   In Grose's drawing of the place, made about twenty years later, only a small portion of one wall of the ruin is shown, from which it would appear that the remainder must have fallen during the interval.   Unless, however, the ruin was in a very dilapidated condition indeed, it seems hardly probable that it could have been " demolished " by an explosion a mile and a half distant.

An ecclesiastical establishment stood in Clondalkin in early times, but was repeatedly ravaged by Danish marauders, for protection against whom the round tower was probably erected. The Danes had a fortress here called Dunawley or Aulaff's Fort, which was burnt in the year 865 by the Irish, who slew the whole garrison.

When Archbishop Henry de Loundres, about the year 1220, established the office of Dean of St. Patrick's, he assigned for the support of the office, the church of Clondalkin, together with a portion of bog at Deansrath, about a mile from the village, for which latter concession the Dean was to pay annually one pound of frankincense at Easter to the Archbishop's Chapel at Clondalkin.

About 1326 a report on the condition of the manor of Clondalkin, defining its boundaries, describes part of it as " waste, being among the Irishry."

The circuit described in this chapter entails a journey of about 19 miles, starting from and returning to the G. P. O.

CHAPTER XXII

SAGGART, RATHCOOLE, NEWCASTLE AND CELBRIDGE.

PEDESTRIANS desirous of following the route described herein, should take the tram to Terenure, proceeding thence in the steam tram to Tallaght, and walking *via* Celbridge to Lucan, a distance of 15 miles. Cyclists, except perhaps those from the western portions of the city and suburbs, will also find the route by Terenure the best, the road therefrom to Tallaght being usually maintained in excellent order.

Leaving Terenure by the long straight tram road, we presently pass the village of Templeogue, about half a mile beyond which, on the right, is Templeogue House (*see* Index), and a few paces further, the ancient church and churchyard of Templeogue, with the old city watercourse beside it.

In front will now be seen some remains of the high ridge called Balrothery Hill, where formerly stood the old, dilapidated village of Balrothery, now entirely cleared away by the levelling of this end of the road to Tymon Castle. For many years prior to its removal it was an unsightly and conspicuous object along this road, scarcely one of the houses having been fit for habitation, besides which its exposed position must have rendered it a very uncomfortable place of residence, so that it is not surprising that its inhabitants gradually abandoned it as other accommodation became available in the neighbourhood.

It is probable that from early times a village stood here in connection with the ancient city watercourse originating at the adjoining weir on the Dodder, and the old road to this place from Green Hills village and Tymon Castle, existed for hundreds of years before the modern road from Templeogue to Tallaght was constructed.

It is worthy of note that on Duncan's *Map of the County Dublin* (1820) this hill is called "Patruddery Hill."

We next enter Tallaght, and continuing along the tram road for about a mile and a half, we turn to the right, following the telegraph wires along a narrow road leading up to Fortunestown lane—the first turn on the left. Although Saggart can be reached by the main road, this route is recommended

Saggart.
(1905.)

in preference, being more secluded, and affording rather prettier and more varied views of the hills and slade of Saggart, with occasional glimpses through the hedges of the country to the northward. Turning to the left at the end of this pretty lane, we enter the little village of Saggart, the most noticeable object in which is the fine Catholic Church, visible for a considerable distance around, while on the opposite side of the road is the burial ground marking the site of the ancient church of the locality.

In the Martyrology of Tallaght, under date of March 3rd, we find mentioned St. Moshacra of Teach Sacra ; and in the Calendar of the O'Clerys, the same Saint is referred to as

" Moshacra, Abbot of Clonenagh and of Teach Sacra, in the
" vicinity of Tallaght." About the close of the seventh century
he founded a monastery in this place, thereafter known as
Teach-Sacra (the house of the saint or priest), a name which
in time became corrupted into Tassaggard, and was subsequently abbreviated to the modern form of Saggart.

Saggart was one of the four royal manors in the County
Dublin, and lying so far out from the city, on the very border
of a wild mountainous region, suffered greatly during the
centuries of guerilla warfare between the hardy colonists
of the Pale and their resolute opponents in the hills. In
1312 the O'Byrnes and O'Tooles invaded all this district and
struck terror among the inhabitants, no less by their numbers
than by their skill in adapting the arts of warfare to the nature
of the country.

In 1359 William and George Harold (of Harold's Grange)
were granted a reward of a hundred shillings for " manfully
rescuing " some spoils which the " mountain enemie " were
carrying off, and for slaying five of these unwelcome visitors.
The reward would represent about £50 or £60 at the present
day.

In 1387 there was dug up at a place called Hogtherne,
between Saggart and Rathcoole, a ring of pure gold, which
must have been of considerable size, as its value was then
estimated at £40, and its finders, who secreted it, narrowly
escaped punishment. It was, probably, one of the gold torcs
so frequently found through the country, specimens of which
are preserved in the various museums.

Adjoining the village are the well-known Saggart Paper
Mills, giving considerable employment in the neighbourhood ;
and, nearly opposite, on the roadside, is the ruin of a small
castle, the sole memorial here of the troublous times of colonisation.

Saggart was at one time famed for its blackberries, and there
was an old saying current in the district, " To go to Saggart
" to pick blackberries."

Taking either of the turns to the right in Saggart, the road descends nearly the whole way to the Naas road, on reach'ng which we turn to the left, up the hill into Rathcoole, a village consisting of one long street, with a number of its houses in ruinous condition. Situated on the great southern highway, and a midway stage between Dublin and Naas, Rathcoole was for centuries after the English invasion, reckoned a place of considerable importance, ruled by a portreeve or governor, and maintained in a condition of defence as an outpost position

Rathcoole.
(1905.)

of the Pale. These defences, however, availed little against the overwhelming numbers of the mountaineers, and except on the occasions when a garrison was maintained in the village, the inhabitants had an anxious time protecting their lives and property.

On 26th January, 1642, Sir Thomas Armstrong was sent out from Dublin to dislodge the insurgents from Rathcoole, but, as it was held by a strong force, he was repulsed and forced to retire eastward to more open ground where the Irish again attacked him. The tide of battle then turned, but though routed, the Irish succeeded in escaping with the loss of one officer and fifty men. This engagement took place on the

Naas road at its junction with the Saggart road, and where it crosses the Slade river half a mile north-east of Rathcoole village.

A horrible occurrence took place here in the following April, as described in a letter from Colonel Mervyn Touchet to his brother, the Earl of Castlehaven, published in the Castlehaven Memoirs. It appears that in consequence of the disturbed state of the country, a number of English had taken refuge in Lord Castlehaven's house at Maddenstown, near the Curragh of Kildare, until it being considered unsafe for them to remain there any longer, Col. Touchet was directed to convey them to Dublin. This he apparently attempted without any escort, for when the party were driving in carts along the road near Rathcoole, to use the narrator's own words, " the rebels fell upon them, barbarously killed " some, and wounded others, myself and one more escaping " by the goodness of our horses. But a servant of mine govern- " ing the carts, and being an Englishman, they took, and whilst " they were preparing to hang him, Sir John Dougan's eldest " son, Walter Dougan, came forth from his father's house with " a party, and rescued him with the rest of those that were " left alive, and brought them safe to Dublin, where I was got. " In a few days afterwards the Marquess of Ormonde sent out " a party towards the place where this murder had been com- " mitted. I went with them, and coming near, we met Sir " Arthur Loftus, Governor of the Naas, with a party of horse " and dragoons, having killed such of the Irish as they met. " But the most considerable slaughter was in a great straight " of furze, seated on a hill, where the people of several villages " taking the alarm had sheltered themselves. Now Sir Arthur " having invested the hill, set the furze on fire on all sides, " where the people being in considerable number, were all " burned or killed—men, women, and children ; I saw the " bodies and furze still burning."

On the 2nd July, 1644, a small body of English were attacked and robbed of £200 by twenty Irish horsemen. The incident is referred to in a letter from the Marquess of Ormonde to Colonel Hugh Byrne.

Felix Rourke, a well-known member of the United Irishmen, was born in Rathcoole in 1765. His father was a farmer who kept the turnpike gate and a posting stage on the Naas road where Blackchurch Inn now stands. The son, Felix, fought in a number of engagements during the Rebellion of 1798, and also took part in Emmet's abortive rising of 1803, for which he was hanged on the 10th Sept. in that year, from one of the rafters of the house of the Rev. James Harold, parish priest of Rathcoole, who a short time previously had been transported for supposed complicity in the rising.

Rathcoole must have reached a low ebb in the 18th century, according to the description given by Campbell in his *Philosophical Survey of the South of Ireland* (1777) :—" The " first village I passed through, about seven miles from Dublin, " Rathcoole I think they call it, was mostly composed of clay " huts, which are sometimes, you know, both warm and neat ; " but these were so awkwardly built and so irregularly arranged, " that even Wales would have been ashamed of them. It " hurt me to see them so near the capital, where the landscape " was so prettily chequered by abundance of little white " villas, spangling the country all round, and rendering it " upon the whole very delightful."

Rathcoole at no very distant period employed a number of skilled tradesmen, and within living memory could boast of a working cutler, at a time when such a craftsman might have been vainly sought in many a more populous place.

Turning to the right, either immediately before entering Rathcoole or at the far end of it, an unfrequented road, about two miles in length, conducts us to the scattered hamlet of Newcastle, properly Newcastle of Lyons, now consisting of about a dozen houses, but formerly much more extensive. Adjoining the rectory are the remains of an ancient building of considerable strength and solidity, and within the grounds is an old yew tree, under which it is said that Dean Swift often sat and conversed with his friends. In the reign of Henry II. the lands of Newcastle were constituted into a royal manor, which in common with the adjacent districts of Saggart and Rathcoole, suffered much from the incursions of the mountain tribes. In 1535 Sir William Brereton with a strong body of troops encamped here while on the way to besiege the castle of Lord Thomas Fitzgerald (Silken Thomas) at Maynooth; and at this period of its history, Newcastle maintained a castle and garrison, and was reckoned among the " good and walled towns " of the county.

In February, 1641, the Government sent the Earl of Ormonde with a powerful army to subjugate the insurgents in the Co. Kildare, where he burned Newcastle and Lyons, plundered Naas, and devastated the greater portion of the county.

Leaving Newcastle, we take the second turn to the right at the end of the village, to reach Celbridge, and presently pass on our left Colganstown House, a quaint old residence, in the grounds of which are the ivied ruins of a castle. From here a straight, uninteresting road leads to Hazlehatch, on the Grand Canal, a station of some importance in former years when the traffic on these waterways was greater than it is at the present time. The name of this place appears on the maps of the Down Survey as " Hazelhurst," meaning a hurst or wood of hazel trees.

A short distance further, the road, by a high bridge, crosses the Great Southern and Western Railway at the pretty station of Hazlehatch and Celbridge, from which a wide road conducts us into Celbridge, formerly known as Kildrought, celebrated as the scene of the romance which has inseparably linked together the names of Swift and Vanessa. It may not be out of place briefly to re-tell here this strange and sad story. About 1709 the widow of Bartholomew Van Homrigh, a Dutch merchant, who had been Commissary of Stores for King William III. in Ireland, settled in London with her two sons and two daughters, and there made the acquaintance of Swift. The elder daughter, Esther, the " Vanessa " of Swift's romance,

who was then twenty-three years of age, read and studied with
Swift, and at length on the eve of his departure for Ireland in
1713, to take up the Deanery of St. Patrick's, confessed her
love for her teacher. Swift, expressing his surprise at her
avowal, writes :—

> " Vanessa not in years a score,
> Dreams of a gown of forty-four,
> Imaginary charms can find,
> In eyes with reading almost blind."

A few years afterwards, Vanessa's mother and two brothers
having died, she and her sister came over to Ireland to reside
at Celbridge on their estate, then known as Marlay Abbey, and
now called The Abbey. Meanwhile Swift was paying his
addresses to Esther Johnston, better known as " Stella," to
whom, there is reason to believe, he was secretly married in
1716 ; but apparently tiring of her, he resumed his attentions
to his former pupil, Vanessa, going constantly out to Celbridge
to visit her at her house. This continued for about three
years, when Vanessa, hearing rumours about her rival, " Stella,"
wrote to her to inquire the precise nature of her claims upon
the dean. This letter Stella showed to Swift, who was so much
exasperated thereat that he straightway rode out to Celbridge,
and in a furious passion strode into the presence of the hapless
Vanessa, flung down her own letter to Stella on the table
before her, and walked out of the house without exchanging
a word with her. Poor Vanessa never recovered from the
shock, and three weeks after the occurrence died of a broken
heart, in the thirty-seventh year of her age. She was buried
in St. Andrew's Church, Dublin, in June, 1723.

Vanessa's bower, where she and Swift used to sit and read
together, is still shown in the grounds of the Abbey, as well
as an old foot bridge also associated by tradition with their
memory.

In Swift's time Celbridge was called Kildrohid or Kildrought, but it is difficult now to ascertain at what precise date this name was superseded by the modern one. The name Kildrought, meaning the church of the bridge, and still the designation of the parish, was converted into the present name by the alteration of the first syllable to "Cel" and by the translation of the second into its English equivalent.

At the southern end of the village is a narrow, secluded road on the right, leading to Rathcoffey and Donadea, which is said to have acquired the curious name of Tea Lane in the following manner :—When the mill was started here, one

Celbridge.
(1904.)

of the owners brought over a number of mill hands from England, for whom he built a row of superior cottages, still called " English Row." The backs of these cottages adjoined this lane, then known as " Church Lane," and the Irish inhabitants were so impressed by the extravagant quantity of tea used by the occupants, as evidenced by the tea leaves thrown out on the road, that they gave it the name of " Tea Lane."

Adjoining Celbridge is Castletown, built by the Right Hon. William Conolly, Speaker of the Irish House of Commons about 180 years ago. From Celbridge the road should be taken to Lucan, where pedestrians can avail themselves of the Electric Railway to town.

Distances from Terenure—Tallaght, 4 ; Saggart, 8 ; Rathcoole, 9 ; Newcastle, 11½ ; Celbridge, 15 ; return by Lucan, 18¾ ; and back to town, about 28 miles. If desired, cyclists can reach town from Lucan *via* Esker and Clondalkin, which is somewhat shorter for those residing at the southern side of the city.

The following authorities were consulted in preparing this chapter :—An Article on Celbridge, by the Rev. Charles J. Graham, in the *Journal of the Kildare Archæological Society*, 1896 ; An Article on Rathcoole and Saggart, by John Sheil O'Grady, in the Journal of the same Society for 1906–8 ; Dalton's *History of the County Dublin*, and Joyce's *Irish Names of Places*.

CHAPTER XXIII

CLANE, CLONGOWESWOOD AND BODENSTOWN

TO visit the district described in this chapter, the most convenient route for cyclists on the outward journey is *via* Celbridge, which can be reached either by Lucan or Clondalkin, as may be desired. On entering Celbridge, we proceed along the village street towards the southern end, past the old mill, and keep straight ahead along the Clane road, ascending gradually for about a mile, through a well wooded country. At a distance of two miles from Celbridge, we pass, on the left, in a field beside the cross-roads, St. Patrick's Chapel, a diminutive ruined building, and a short distance further, St. Patrick's Well, enclosed and protected by stonework. This well is much resorted to for deafness, sore eyes, and other ailments, and the overhanging bushes bear ample evidence of the survival of the interesting old custom of attaching offerings. Adjoining the well is St. Patrick's Hill, rising to a height of 308 feet. A narrow and somewhat uninteresting road passes hence to Clane, through a country which evidently was at one time swampy, but has since been reclaimed by drainage.

At a distance of twenty miles from Dublin, we enter Clane, a neat village with a wide street running nearly north and south, and possessing modern churches for both the Catholic and Protestant denominations, as well as the ruins of an ancient ecclesiastical establishment. There is a legend that in the 6th century St. Ailba of Ferns, who, like Romulus and Remus, is fabled to have had a wolf for foster mother, founded a religious community at Clane ; and in 1162 a diocesan synod was held there. In this, as in other communities throughout the country, however, a complete change was effected by the advent of the Anglo-Normans—new fashions, new ceremonials, and new foreign orders were introduced, and about the year 1260 this place was selected as a settlement for the Franciscans, for whom Gerald Fitzmaurice, Lord of Offaly, built a stately abbey, the ruins of which still stand in a conspicuous position a short distance south of the village.

In the Patent Rolls, it is recorded that on the 14th March, 1391, the King granted to the Provost, Bailiffs and Commonalty of Clane, the right to impose for a period of

Clane Abbey.
(1906.)

seven years, duties upon goods entering their town, in order to provide funds for the erection of a new bridge over the Liffey or Annaliffey as it was then called. The bridge at Clane, and also that at Millicent, about 1½ miles to the south, are each built close to the site of an ancient ford, and the former of these fords having been known as Clane Ath, originated the modern name of the locality. About half a mile from Millicent bridge, down the river, is a place bearing the apparently meaningless name of Castlesize, the ancient and correct form of which, however, sheds an interesting side light on the perilous conditions of travel in former times. "Casan," meaning a path, points to the existence of a pathway down to the river, and "size"—doubtless a corruption of

" soillse," a light, would indicate that a light was, on dark and stormy nights, exhibited at some point on the river, to guide travellers to the ford. A glance at the Ordnance Map will show that the cross road from Sherlockstown is abruptly deflected from its course here, its original route having been probably in a direct line across the river by the ancient ford, close to where Castlesize House now stands.

The village of Clane doubtless originated with the Celtic ecclesiastical establishment, in later times becoming a mere appanage of the great Anglo-Norman Abbey, and the inhabitants almost wholly dependent upon the wealthy and influential community that occupied it. The geographical position of Clane on the border of the English Pale, invested it with an importance out of proportion to its deserts, and led to its incorporation in the 15th century, as a borough with a portreeve and burgesses. Its distance from the coast, though a serious disadvantage to it as an English settlement, for centuries saved it from the attentions of the Danes, their only visit to the place, in 1035, resulting disastrously to the marauders, who were overtaken near Dublin and annihilated by the exasperated inhabitants.

On January 23, 1454, the Portreeves and Commons of Clane, Naas, and some neighbouring towns, presented a joint memorial to the Duke of York, Lord Deputy of Ireland, setting forth that, " This land of Ireland, was never at the point finally
" to be destroyed sethin the conquest of this lande, as it is
" now, for the trew liege people in this partiss dar ne may
" not appier to the King's Courtes in the said lande, ne noone
" other of the trew liege people ther to go ne ride to market
" towns ne other places, for dred to be slayne, to take or be
" spoiled of ther godes ; also the mysrule and misgovernaunce
" had gone, and dayly contynued by divers gentlemen of the
" counte and your liberte of Mith, the Countes of Kildare
" and Uriell, and namly of a variance had betwixt the Erle
" of Wiltshire, Lieutenant of this said lande, and Thomas
" FitzMorice, of the Geraldines, for the title the maners of

" Maynoth and Rathmore, in the Counte of Kildare, had
" caused more destruccionne in the sayde Counte of Kildare
" and liberte of Mith within short tyme now late passed, and
" dayly doth, than was done by Irish enemys and English
" rebelles of long time before—and is likely to be fynall
" destruccionne in the sayd Counte of Kildare and liberte
" of Mith. For Henry Bonyn Knyght, with Edmond Botiller,
" and William Botiller, with ther sequie of which most part
" was Irish enemys and English rebelles, came and burned
" and distrued divers and many towns and paroche churches
" of the trew liege people, and take dyvers of them prisoners,
" and spouled ther godes. And, after the departure of the
" sayd Henry and Edmond, the sayd William, abyding in the
" sayd Counte of Kildare, by ther avice and counsaill, did so
" grete oppressionne that VIJXX townes and more, which was
" well enhabite in the feste of Seynte Michael lass passed, been
" now wasted and destrued."

Nearly opposite Clane Abbey, and on the banks of the
Butterstream, is a large block of stone, with a hollow cut in it,
supposed by some to be the pedestal of a cross, by others
believed to be what is known as a bullaun, or rock-basin, a
relic of pre-Christian times, used in certain ceremonials connected with pagan worship. The rain-water which collects
in the basin is reputed to be a cure for warts, in consequence
of which it is locally known as " The Wart Stone."

A short distance south of the village, and immediately to
the right of the road before reaching Clane Bridge, is the
Moat of Clane, traditionally reputed to mark the grave of
Mesgegra, King of Leinster, who, in the first century, was
slain in single combat with Connall Cernach, a famous warrior
of the Red Branch Knights, and champion of Ulster. At the
ford of Clane, near where Clane Bridge now stands, these two
warriors met, and after a brief combat, the Ulster champion
beheaded the ill-fated Leinster King, and carried off his head
in his chariot. Soon afterwards he met Queen Buan, the Royal
consort of Mesgegra, attended by her retinue, who, in reply

to Connall's inquiry, informed him that she was Mesgegra's Queen. Connall then told her that he had her husband's head in his chariot, whereupon she raised a loud cry of lamentation, and fell down dead. A detailed account of this tragedy is given in an old romance, entitled " The Siege of Howth," in the Book of Leinster. The moat at Mainham, a conspicuous object in the little village, about a mile and a half north of Clane, is believed to mark the resting-place of the broken-hearted Queen, who, it is recorded in the old romance, was buried by the wayside, where in time a hazel tree grew over her grave.

Clane.
(1905.)

It was in the neighbourhood of Clane that the rebellion commenced in 1798, and at the adjacent village of Prosperous, the temporary barracks occupied by the North Cork Militia and " The Ancient Britons," was attacked by the insurgents and burnt. Prosperous had been built only 18 years previously by Captain Brooke, who established there an extensive cotton factory, but ruined himself by the expenditure. Portion of Clane Parish Church was burnt during the disturbances, and about the same time all the old parochial records mysteriously disappeared.

In the early part of the last century there lived at Clane a lady of considerable literary repute—Mrs. Griffiths, wife of

Richard Griffiths, of Millicent, and mother of the Sir Richard
Griffiths, who carried out the famous valuation of Ireland
associated with his name.   Her husband, as Major of the Clane
Yeomanry, fought in the first battle with the insurgents at
Clane.

About a mile north of Clane is the well-known Catholic
College of Clongowes Wood, for nearly a century one of the
foremost public schools in Ireland.   The earliest recorded
mention of this locality is in a Roll of Henry IV., under date
of 24 Feb., 1417, assigning as portion of the dower of Anastatia
Wogan of Rathcoffey, one-third part of the " Sylva de
Clongow " (the Wood of Clongowes).   Clongowes next fell
into possession of that great territorial family, the Eustaces, who,
though at first zealous members of the Anglo-Norman garrison,
gradually became by intermarriage with Irish families, very
divided in their sympathies.   During the troubled times of
1641, when this neighbourhood was the scene of much strife
and bloodshed, James Eustace, of Clongowes, mortgaged his
estates, and fought on the side of the Irish.   A detachment
of troops, with their officer, Captain Hues, was at this time
quartered at Clongowes Wood Castle, where they were
hospitably entertained by Mrs. Eustace, a venerable old lady,
90 years of age, who was, however, barbarously murdered in
her own house by her ungrateful guests because, according
to tradition, she refused to surrender the key of a secret stronghold in the castle, retaining it in her mouth until her jaws
were broken by the soldiers.

The Eustaces, on account of the part they took in the rising,
never recovered their Clongowes estates, which were forfeited,
and many members of the family then went abroad, some of
their descendants fighting in the army of James the Second,
while others attained to positions of distinction in the service
of France.

After its confiscation, Clongowes Wood was purchased by
Sir Richard Reynell, who in 1667 sold it to the Brownes, and
by the latter its name was changed to Castlebrowne.   By

inter-marriage with the Wogans of Rathcoffey, an ancient
and distinguished Catholic family of this neighbourhood, the
Brownes became the Wogan-Brownes, who are still extant.
One of the Brownes became a Marshal in the Austrian service,
and fell in action at the battle of Prague in 1757, while another
of them—the last that owned Clongowes Wood—General
Michael Wogan-Browne of the Saxon Army—fought under
Napoleon in the Grand Army before Moscow.

Clongowes Wood.
(*The original Castle.*)

A most circumstantial story is told in the records of the family,
of the appearance of Marshal Browne at Clongowes on the
day of his death. It appears that while he was abroad, the
house was occupied by his two sisters, who, on the day in
question, were upstairs engaged with needlework. Opening off
the spacious hall of the mansion was a room, used as a laundry,
which, on account of the necessary fire there, was a favourite
resort for the servants. The door of this room, and also the
hall door were open on this occasion, when the servants
assembled there were much astonished to see enter the hall,
an officer, fully accoutred, holding his hands to his breast,

Q

from which blood was flowing and staining his white uniform. Immediately afterwards they followed him upstairs to the room where the two Misses Browne were working, but no trace of him could be discovered there, and the two ladies stated that they had seen nothing, although they at once suspected that what the servants had seen was the apparition of their brother, who, they surmised, had met his death on some foreign battlefield. So confident were they that this was the case, that they forthwith ordered mourning, had Masses celebrated, and even held a wake with all the lavish hospitality of the Irish gentry in those days. A fortnight after this incident, a communication arrived at Clongowes from abroad informing the family of the Marshal's death at the battle of Prague, on the day and at the very hour when the servants had seen his apparition.

About the year 1810 Clongowes Wood came into possession of the before-mentioned General Michael Wogan-Browne of the army of Saxony. He found the estates encumbered, and there being little inducement to return to his native land owing to the oppressive laws in force against his co-religionists, he decided to sever his connection with the place, and accordingly sold it, in 1813, to the Irish Jesuits, who, after some opposition on the part of the Government, opened it in the following year as an educational establishment. For its subsequent history, which is outside the scope of this chapter, the reader is referred to *The Story of Clongowes Wood*, by the Rev. T. Corcoran, S.J., published by the Catholic Truth Society of Ireland.

Returning to Clane, we pass at the southern end of the village, the ruins of the Abbey, a large rectangular building, bare and unattractive in appearance. Continuing along the high road, closely following the green wooded banks of the Liffey, in about two miles from Clane, we turn to the left at Castlesize, passing immediately on the right Bodenstown Church, an ancient edifice with an abundant growth of ivy, and celebrated as being the burial place of Wolfe Tone. The original tombstone marking the family resting place is supplemented by a more recent ornamental memorial, and the whole is enclosed by a massive iron cage to protect the monuments from injury or desecration.

A pretty by-road conducts us hence over the G. S. & W. Railway by a high bridge, from which on a clear day is obtained a fine view of the western fringe of the Dublin range extending into Kildare—a succession of softly rounded hills, exhibiting varied tints according to the nature of the cultivation. In the immediate foreground is the wooded hill of Oughterard, and in the distance may be seen some of the higher elevations towards the southern portion of Wicklow. Shortly after passing the railway we cross the Grand Canal by Devonshire Bridge, and at length meet a road at right angles, where turning to the right we presently reach Kill, whence our homeward journey lies along the well-known Naas road.

The total length of the circuit described in this chapter is 42 miles.

In the preparation of this article the following contributions to the Journals of the County Kildare Archæological Society have been consulted, viz. :—Vol. III., *Clane Abbey*, by the late Rev. Professor George Stokes, D.D. ; *The Moat at Clane*, by T. Cooke-Trench, Esq., D.L. ; *Clongowes Wood*, by the Rev. Matthew Devitt, S.J. ; Vol. I., *The Grave of Buan, Near Clane*, by the Rev. Matthew Devitt, S.J. ; *Notes, Antiquarian and Historical, on the Parish of Clane*, by the Rev. Canon Sherlock ; Vol. IV., Further article on same subject by the same writer.

CHAPTER XXIV

MUD ISLAND, FAIRVIEW, CLONTARF AND ITS ISLAND, DOLLYMOUNT AND THE NORTH BULL

WESTWARD of the North Strand, between Nottingham Street and Newcomen Bridge, and extending as far as Ballybough Road, was a locality of evil repute in former times, known as Mud Island, inhabited by a gang of smugglers, highwaymen, and desperadoes of every description, and ruled by a hereditary robber chief rejoicing in the title of " King of Mud Island." For about 200 years down to the middle of last century, this den of robbers was a plague spot in the district, enjoying an extraordinary immunity from molestation in consequence of what had at length come to be regarded as a sort of prescriptive right and sanctuary attaching to the locality, until at last no officer of the law durst show his nose within its sacred precincts unless backed up by an overwhelming force of military or police.

The settlement of Mud Island is said to have originated at the time of the Plantation of Ulster, when three brothers, driven out of their ancestral patrimony, came southwards and settled in the neighbourhood of Dublin, one of them taking up his abode by the sea here on what was then a waste tract of land, to which his descendants by virtue of long occupation, in time acquired a squatter's title. Then and for long afterwards, open country intervened between this place and the city, the North Strand was under water, and a rough bridle track extended along the shore some distance eastward of Ballybough Road, which was, until the building of Annesley

Bridge in 1797, the highway to Malahide, Howth, and Clontarf. In the course of time as the population of the colony increased, a considerable village of mud cabins grew up, and some of the inhabitants even departed so far from professional etiquette as to engage occasionally in honest occupations, such as carting sand, &c., when there was insufficient business in their own special line to go round.

At the time of its colonization, Mud Island was no doubt, as its name indicates, an island off the slob lands along the estuary of the Liffey, and probably accessible on foot at low water from the shore.

A hundred years ago, it was so usual an occurrence to find a dead body in one of the lanes or alleys of "The Island," that it occasioned little or no comment, and if any of the "islanders" had the bad taste to mention the matter, he would be told significantly—"'Tis a wise man that never saw "a dead one." The murdered persons were usually excisemen, bailiffs, or other limbs of the law, but be the victim who he might, the murderers were rarely brought to justice.

In the early part of last century this was a favourite landing place for smuggled goods, the contraband vessels usually lying out in Clontarf Pool or the Poolbeg; then, when night had fallen and the way was signalled clear, boats were run ashore under Annesley Bridge to what was called "The Little Sea," between the Tolka and Fairview Strand, for at that time the road from Annesley Bridge to Fairview Corner was an elevated causeway, with the sea on both sides, and Fairview Strand really deserved its name. Encounters between the smugglers and the preventive men were frequent, not unusually attended with loss of life, and even so recently as 1850, smuggling was carried on in a desultory way in this neighbourhood, although the presence of the police barrack at Fairview was a serious obstacle to the operations.

A reference to the newspapers of the 18th century will furnish ample evidence of the extraordinary lawlessness of this neighbourhood—a condition of affairs which seems to have been acquiesced in if not actually connived at by the authorities, notwithstanding the fact that murders, robberies and outrages of every description were of constant occurrence.

Crossing the Tolka at Annesley Bridge, we pass on our left the unattractive locality known as Ballybough, once an isolated village, situated on the old coast line, and washed by the sea waves when they rolled in pure and undefiled upon the open Fairview Strand. The bridge here is of rather ancient design, consisting of five plain low arches, evidently constructed more with a view to strength than elegance, and adjoining, down to a few years ago, might be seen some portions of the old sea wall originally built to protect the village of Ballybough from the inroads of the sea. Not far from the bridge is a Jewish cemetery, enclosed by a high wall, and containing a number of headstones bearing Hebraic inscriptions.

Long before the establishment of the Vitriol Works here, their site was occupied by a famous flint glass factory, where plate glass for coaches was made and polished, and so high a degree of artistic excellence attained by the artificers in the manufacture of fancy articles, that considerable demand existed for their goods, even on the Continent. This factory was established a few years after the Treaty of Limerick by Captain Philip Roche, an Irishman of good family and con-considerable property, who, in consequence of being included in the Articles to the Treaty, was enabled to retain his estates. Participating for a time in the fortunes of the Irish Brigade abroad, he at length returned to his native land, and finding himself debarred by his religion from obtaining Government employment, he turned his attention to commercial pursuits with a success beyond his expectations.

At the close of the 18th century there was an extensive iron foundry at Ballybough in which were manufactured spades, shovels, and other agricultural implements, as well as a variety of kitchen utensils, equal in quality to the best articles of the kind imported.

In early times the boundary of the City of Dublin in this

direction was defined as " running through the middle of the " road of the village of Ballybough, unto an ancient path of " an old mill," and in the accounts of the course taken by the Corporation at the annual ceremony of riding the franchises this portion of the route is thus alluded to :—

" Leaving the stone well on the left hand, they proceeded " southward until they came into the highway going into " Ballybough ; and from the gate of Ballybough they came " to the water of Tolka, by the bridge of Ballybough, there " passing over the water, keeping by the water side southward " as far as they might ride, until they came unto St. Mary's " Abbey," &c., &c.

Down to a hundred years ago Ballybough was a noted burial place for suicides, the bodies being interred in the time-honoured fashion, transfixed with stakes, in a waste plot of ground adjoining the cross roads at the bridge. Notwithstanding the widespread belief that this barbarous process of transfixing effectually prevented these unhappy beings from wandering abroad at unseemly hours and alarming the public, not a few of the inhabitants in those days would have gone a considerable round rather than pass this unhallowed spot after nightfall.

Pursuing our route across Ballybough Bridge and turning to the right, we enter upon the thoroughfare known as Fairview Strand—a name now strangely out of keeping with the place, though accurate enough in former times when the sea washed up to the road here, and the residents enjoyed a " fair view " of the bay and river, now shut off by the railway embankment.

We next pass on our left the entrance gate of Marino, with centre and wings of cut granite, surmounted by sculptured representations of the arms of the Charlemont family, and the motto " Deo duce, ferro comitante " (" With God as my guide, my sword by my side "). The house was built towards the close of the 18th century for the celebrated Lord Charlemont, who amassed here an almost unique collection of works of ancient and modern art. In the grounds is a highly embellished temple of the Doric order, originally designed and furnished as a study by its patriotic owner, who made the whole place as attractive as possible, so that he might have every inducement to live in the country of his birth.

Adjoining the grounds of Marino is the terrace known as Marino Crescent, built in 1792, where the Malahide and Howth roads diverge, and, according to current tradition in the neighbourhood, erected in this position for the purpose of intercepting the view from Marino, the builder having entertained some private grudge against Lord Charlemont. A short distance along the Howth Road, just beside Clontarf station, is a spot noted in former years for its romantic wildness, called " The Black Quarries," now enclosed within the grounds of Mount Temple.

A few paces further along the shore road, passing under the railway, we come into view of the Bay, with the Pigeonhouse and the two river lighthouses in front, to the right of these the hills of Dalkey and Killiney, the wooded country rising behind Blackrock and Kingstown, and in the background the Dublin and Wicklow Mountains in profile, their bases obscured by the smoke and haze of the city.

In 1749 a Charter School was opened at Clontarf to accommodate a hundred scholars, but, having been discontinued early in the last century, it was converted into a bathing establishment, which is still remembered by many of the inhabitants. The building may still be seen near the railway bridge over the tram road.

All this district is of great historic interest as the scene of the great battle in 1014, at which the Danes were completely vanquished by the Irish under King Brian Boru ; but this battle has been so exhaustively dealt with elsewhere as to render unnecessary any description of it here. It may, however, be mentioned that, in some of the old sagas the battle is styled " The Battle of the Fishing Weir of Clontarf," and that there is little doubt that this weir occupied the same site as the existing one near the Dublin Whiskey Distillery at Richmond Road. Around this place, consequently, the thickest of the battle must have raged, rather than in the modern district of Clontarf.

Clontarf Island, now entirely submerged at high water, stood about 150 yards off the most easterly point of the East Wall or Wharf Road, adjoining Messrs. Gouldings' Manure Works. In former times when the coastline ran by what are now the North Strand, Amiens Street and Beresford Place, the Island stood a considerable distance out at sea, and must have then been a conspicuous object in the Bay, but the reclamation of the lands along the northern bank of the Liffey, together with the gradual silting up of the estuary, enabled it in its later years to be easily reached from the shore. Its name, however, and the fact that it formed portion of the lands of Clontarf, indicates that it must at one time have been nearer to Clontarf than to any other point on the shore of Dublin Bay.

In 1538 the Prior of Kilmainham granted a lease of the lands of Clontarf with this island, to Mathew King, in whose family the property remained until the Commonwealth, when it was confiscated and granted to John Blackwell, a friend of the Protector, from whom it passed into possession of the Vernon family.

Rocque's Map (1753), shows the island to be of considerable area, and containing a residence called " The Island House."

In later times a man named Christopher Cromwell built a wooden house on the island, using it as a sort of summer residence, but in 1844 the structure was swept away during one of the greatest storms on record, when Cromwell and his son were drowned. It appears that on the night of the occurrence, a constable watching the storm from a safe point of vantage near the East Wall, saw the light in Cromwell's house go out at 10 o'clock—nothing more of course could then be ascertained, but next day the bodies of Cromwell and his son were found on the Island. The storm—a south-easterly one—carried off their boats to Annesley Bridge, while the frail wooden structure in which they were sheltering, was

swept away and dashed to pieces against the Railway embankment. (*North Dublin City and Environs*, by Rev. Dillon
Cosgrave, O.C.C.)

Clontarf Island was used as a refuge and place of isolation
during an epidemic of plague in 1650, and about a hundred
years ago enjoyed a brief popularity as a place of recreation
for the citizens. Its disappearance is partly due to the continual
carting away of its sands. At low tide it can still be distinguished by its stony surface and slightly higher elevation

"The Sheds," Clontarf.
(1905.)

than its surroundings, as well as by the remains of some wooden
structures which stood on its western extremity.

Continuing our journey along the shore road, we presently
reach the locality known as "The Sheds," adjoining which
stood the old village of Clontarf, now entirely merged in this
populous district. The name originated with some sheds or
stages erected over a hundred years ago for the convenience
of such of the inhabitants as were engaged in the curing and
drying of fish, there being at that time a considerable colony
of fishermen in the locality. About the same time a Mr.
Weekes, a local resident, built a water reservoir on the beach
for the use of the public.

In 1641 Luke Netterville and some of his adherents having seized and plundered a vessel which lay at Clontarf, the Earl of Ormonde was instructed to take retaliatory measures against them. He accordingly despatched Sir Charles Coote with some troops to the neighbourhood, where they burnt a considerable portion of the village, destroyed all the boats they could find, and burnt the house of Mr. George King, proprietor of the village and manor. The latter act was all the more remarkable, inasmuch as Mr. King had been invited into Dublin but the day before by the Government, from whom

Coastguard Station, North Bull.
(1905.)

he had received an assurance that he might safely go there " without danger of any trouble or stay whatsoever." It was, however, alleged that most of the plundered vessel's cargo was found in his house, and, true or untrue, this charge turned out a serious one for him, as he was immediately afterwards attainted, and his estates confiscated.

As we round the curve beyond "The Sheds," we come into view of the approach to the Bull Wall, where a wooden foot-bridge crosses the creek known as " Crab Lake Water." Before reaching the Bull Wall we pass, inside a wall on the left, an almost indistinguishable elevation known as " Conquer Hill," conjectured, though with little reason, to be identified in some way with the Battle of Clontarf.

The bridge leading to the Bull Wall was originally wide enough for vehicles, but was many years ago reduced to its present dimensions, since when all vehicles have had to ford the creek in order to reach the Bull.

The Bull Wall extends a distance of 3,200 yards into the Bay, forming a wide roadway without parapets, but not so strongly constructed as the great South Wall, it being much less exposed to the action of the wind and waves. The portion near tl e end is submerged at high water, and is terminated by a wrought iron lighthouse of a bright red colour, rising from a masonry base. The construction of this breakwater was carried out between the years 1820 and 1823.

The North Bull, a large sandbank island, extends over a considerable area in a north-easterly direction, and in fine weather is well worthy of exploration by the pedestrian ; it is covered in parts by a short green sward fringed by a range of sand dunes, and along its eastern shore extends a beautiful strand little known except to local residents.

In the days of duelling, the North Bull was a favourite place for these encounters.

From Dollymount and the Bull, the most conspicuous object in the view is the Hill of Howth, which, with its bright green fields, pretty villas, and patches of furze and heather, forms a pleasing and attractive picture.

Immediately beyond the approach to the Bull Wall is Dolly-mount, comprising the locality formerly known as Blackbush or Heronstown, which name survived until recently in the designation of Heronstown Road or Blackbush Lane, now known as Mount Prospect Avenue, turning inland immediately beyond Dollymount. The name of Dollymount would seem to have originated with a house bearing that title which stood on or adjoining the site of Sea Park in Mount Prospect Avenue, and which is shown in Duncan's *Map* of 1820. " Dollymount House " appears in the *Dublin Directory* up to 1836, after which it disappears, doubtless having been re-named, and in 1838 the name appears for the first time as that of a district,

under the heading of "Green Lanes, Dollymount." It is
stated that the designation was adopted in the first instance
by a member of the Vernon family as a compliment to his
wife, by name Dorothy, or Dolly Vernon.

A few hundred yards further a rivulet known as the Naniken
river, flows out on the shore at Naniken Bridge, but this, and
other local names, are gradually becoming forgotten with the
extension of the city in this direction.

From Mount Prospect Avenue an ancient roadway and
field-path leads to Raheny, passing, by a tunnel, under Lord

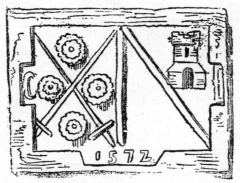

Slab formerly on house near Dollymount.

Ardilaun's grounds, and crossing the Naniken river by a ford ;
this route is, however, passable only in dry weather.

Continuing along the seashore we presently meet a road
leading to Raheny, and just at this point is a quaint old thatched
residence called Watermill Cottage, noted, by Dalton, for its
picturesque appearance, when he described it in his *History
of the County Dublin*, over seventy years ago. It was then
occupied by a Mr. Papworth, and bore in its outer wall a
tablet, of which the accompanying sketch is a representation,
containing the arms of St Lawrence impaled with those of
Plunket, the date, 1572, and the letters, C. E. The arms in
question are those of Christopher, 20th Baron of Howth,
who died in 1589, and his wife, Elizabeth, daughter of Sir

John Plunket of Beaulieu, Co. Louth ; and the initials, C. E., are those of their Christian names. Their altar-tomb may be seen in the chancel of Howth Abbey, where they are represented by recumbent figures—his effigy in armour, and that of his wife in the costume of the period.

The tablet in question was subsequently transferred to the wall of an adjacent house named " Bettyville," but has recently been removed.

The sluggish waters of the Santry river discharge themselves on the shore at this point, under Watermill Bridge, and here, in former times, stood a small mill, from which circumstance the cottage and bridge derived their names.

The extension of the tram line to Howth considerably altered the appearance of this neighbourhood, and rendered it much less secluded than formerly. A hundred years ago a road ran along the beach from here to the point known as " The Whip of the Water," where the Howth Road descends to the shore, and, although it has long since been obliterated by the action of the tides, some traces of it were visible up to the time the tram line was constructed.

A group of dilapidated cottages, insanitary, no doubt, but picturesque, as insanitary dwellings frequently are, stood on the shore near the position now occupied by the tram sheds, but were all taken down during the alterations consequent on the construction of the line. This group formed the subject of many a picture, both in public galleries and private collections ; but it is doubtful if its identity was frequently recognised.'

From the Howth road the reader can either return to Clontarf, take the train back from Raheny, or continue his journey to Howth or elsewhere as desired.

The authorities consulted in the preparation of this chapter are, Dalton's *History of the County Dublin* ; Warburton, Whitelaw & Walsh's *History of the City of Dublin* ; and for " Mud Island," two articles by " T. P. S.," which appeared in the *Irish Times* about February, 1911.

CHAPTER XXV

DRUMCONDRA, SANTRY, "BUCK" JONES
AND CLONLIFFE

ONCE an isolated village on the Great Northern road, Drumcondra now retains few vestiges of its original character, and is known to Dublin people of the present day only as a rapidly extending suburb of the Metropolis. Yet there are many residents who can remember a time when Drumcondra presented an old-fashioned and even picturesque appearance compared with its present aspect, and when it contained few houses or terraces, except those in the village and the row on the hill, which latter are said to be among the oldest dwellings in the neighbourhood

In former times Dorset Street ended at the Bethesda Chapel, and the continuation of that thoroughfare as far as the Canal Bridge was known as Dorset Lane, beyond which it was Drumcondra Lane, as far as the Tolka Bridge, and thereafter the Santry Road.

For hundreds of years this has been one of the principal highways leading out of the city, and so far back as 1634, a traveller wrote of it :—" As dainty a fine way as ever I rode, " and a most pleasant country." Even at an earlier date this road was regarded as such an important thoroughfare that in a Chancery Roll of 1450 it is styled "The Royal Way." It became the mail road from Dublin to the North after the route *via* Finglas, Ashbourne, and Duleek had been abandoned, and was traversed daily by a number of mail and passenger coaches in the early part of the last century. The milestones were placed on it in 1812 at a cost of 50s. each, and in 1823 the footpath along it was constructed as far as Swords.

Brewer, in his *Beauties of Ireland* (1826), says "Drumcondra
" or Drumconrath, although not distant more than two miles
" from the Metropolis, is marked by an air of pensive tran-
" quillity, in some measure produced by the deep shade of
" numerous trees, which embower many parts of the village."

The correct name of this district would appear to be Clonturk,
otherwise Clontolk, meaning the meadow of the boar, the
name Drumcondra having been at first applied only to the

Drumcondra.
(1906.)

village, and subsequently extended until it had superseded
the original name of the district.

In the reign of George I. some of the Dublin citizens formed
themselves into an association called "The Florists' Club,"
for the purpose of encouraging the cultivation of flowers
in Ireland. They held their meetings at the Rose Tavern
in Drumcondra Lane, where they adjudged premiums to those
who had produced the most beautiful flowers at their shows.
The Rose Tavern continued in existence until the year 1793.

Belvidere House, now St. Patrick's Training College, was
the seat of the Coghill family, for many years associated with
this locality. Sir John Coghill, Master in Chancery, resided

here in the 17th century, and on his death, his son, Marmaduke, succeeded to the estates, becoming in succession Judge of the Prerogative Court, Privy Councillor, Chancellor of the Exchequer, Commissioner of the Revenue, and representative of the University of Dublin in the Irish Parliament. It is related of him that in his capacity as judge he had occasion to adjudicate in a dispute between a lady and her husband, the latter having administered, by way of emphasising his marital authority, what is now in vulgar parlance termed " a good hiding." The judge, in delivering judgment, gravely expressed the opinion that moderate chastisement with a switch was within the matrimonial privilege of a husband, and this judicial opinion having reached the ears of a young lady to whom the judge had been successfully paying his attentions, so alarmed her that she broke off all further relations with the exponent of so ungallant a doctrine. This distinguished member of the family died, unmarried, in 1738, and was interred in the burial ground of the church erected by his sister, which contains a handsome monument to his memory. It represents him sitting in his robes as Chancellor of the Exchequer, and bears an inscription setting forth the principal events in his life, with his pedigree from the Coghills of Coghill Hall, Yorkshire. After his death, his niece and heiress, Hester, became Countess of Charleville, and she dying without issue, bequeathed her property to her cousin, John Cramer, who thereupon assumed the name and arms of Coghill, and was created a baronet in 1778.

Francis Grose, the antiquarian, was buried in Drumcondra churchyard in 1791. He was the son of Francis Grose, of Richmond, a jeweller, who acquired some temporary fame through being commissioned to fit up the Crown for King George the Second. The antiquarian was born in 1731, and early in life entered the Surrey Militia, of which he became Adjutant and Paymaster. Finding the duties unsuited to his tastes, he resigned the appointment, and after travelling through England and Wales, produced an important work

B

on the antiquities of the districts he visited. He then went to Scotland for a similar purpose, but before finishing with that country, came to Ireland, and, as the result of his travels here, brought out two large volumes on Irish antiquities, copiously illustrated. This work appeared in 1791, and soon afterwards in that year the author died of an apoplectic fit at the house of Horace Hone in Dublin.

Near Grose's grave is buried Thomas Furlong, the Wexford poet, who died in 1827.

Although such a short distance from Dublin, the district between Drumcondra and Swords for many years bore the unenviable reputation of being one of the most dangerous in the neighbourhood of the Metropolis, repeated robberies, both of mail coaches and foot passengers, as well as other outrages, having taken place in it up to the early part of the last century. The following are some of the most noteworthy instances on record :—

On 17th September, 1773, the Drogheda mail coach coming to Dublin, was robbed at the wall near Santry by two young men of good address, who, having secured all the cash and watches of the travellers, except the purse of a priest which they returned, fled on the approach of some foot passengers. About a week afterwards, one of them, named Fleming, was arrested at Stradbally, and confessed his guilt, besides informing on his comrade.

On the 24th March, 1798, the North Mail Coach on its way from Dublin, was attacked near Santry by a party of " Innocents " (insurgents), who robbed the passengers of property to the value of between £300 and £400, including all the arms which the passengers and guard had with them for their protection.

Two months later, in the same year, the Belfast Mail was stopped in Santry village by nine or ten armed men, who had previously fixed a barricade of carts across the road. They told the driver and guard that they were friends, and that the reason they stopped the coach was to prevent it from falling into the hands of a large body of the insurgents near Swords. The guard and driver believing them, dismounted, and, on being invited, entered a house, where they were detained while the coach was filled and covered with dry furze and set on fire, every portion of it and its contents being consumed, except a small remnant of the letters, which were taken back, half burnt, to the General Post Office. This outrage, however, seems to have been an act of war rather than one of highway robbery, as none of the passengers were either illtreated or despoiled of their property, and, according to the driver's account, a large crowd, estimated by him at not less than 1,000 persons, was assembled on the occasion in the adjoining fields. The Attorneys' Cavalry Corps, which happened to be patrolling in the neighbourhood, captured five men suspected of complicity in the transaction, and took them to Dublin.

On the 18th August, 1828, when the Derry Mail was on its way from town, a man intentionally drove his cart against it and broke one of the lamps. The guard gave the horse and cart with its driver into charge of the police at Santry, who, when on their way to the pound, were attacked near Coolock bridge by a party of desperadoes with the object of effecting a rescue. The police, outnumbered, fired two shots at their assailants, severely wounding two of them, whom they arrested and conveyed, with the driver of the cart, to Dublin.

In the following year a robber was shot dead on the road near Santry, and was buried in the churchyard. On another occasion a gentleman of the neighbourhood, returning on his outside car from a day's shooting, was stopped at a dark part of the road by a number of highwaymen ; he, however, offered a desperate resistance, shooting one dead, and so severely wounding another that to save the injured man's life he had to drive him into town for medical treatment after the remainder of the robbers had fled.

Besides these, many other outrages and robberies are recorded, and the numerous woods in the neighbourhood seem to have been recognised shelters for highwaymen, one of the most noted of whom, according to tradition, made his favourite lair in a hollow tree near Santry, still pointed out to the wayfarer.

Santry had, at the northern end of the village, toll-gates across the roads to Swords and Ballymun; they were removed in 1788, but the toll-house, an old red brick cottage, may still be seen at the angle of Santry demesne, and the field opposite the forge is to the present day called "The Turnpike Field."

The district around Drumcondra was, about the latter end of the 18th and the beginning of the 19th century, not only the residence, but the resort of many fashionable and distinguished people, and a number of tea houses and gardens were, during that period, established there, in the hope of attracting their patronage. After some years, however, in consequence of the extension of the city in this direction, these places came to be frequented by a different class from those for whom the originators had intended them; the amusements degenerated into rowdyism and drunkenness, and it at length became necessary to close all these resorts in consequence of the disorderly scenes enacted there.

In a poem by Thomas Dermody, published in 1806, the following reference is made to Drumcondra :—

"But ah! my dearest, let not gypsies lead,
Thy vagrant wand'ring to the rural mead,
Let dire Drumcondra e'er unheeded lie,
Though teapots, cups and saucers court the eye."

About 1819 an enterprising Frenchman named Duval, undeterred by the failure of his predecessors, rented Clonturk House and grounds, and attempted to convert them into a second Vauxhall; he had hobby horses and swings set up through the grounds, held displays of fireworks, rockets, and fire balloons, and, last, though not least, "discovered" a mineral well, in regard to which some strange stories are told.

It appears that when he took the place, this well, having been for many years in disuse, was filled up with rubbish, and Duval having got a sample of the water analysed, the expert reported that it possessed valuable chalybeate qualities. As spas were in great vogue at that time, Duval thought he saw his way to fortune, and proceeded at once to have the well cleared of all the rubbish that had lain in it so long—broken earthenware, old kettles and pots, scrap-iron, and so-forth; but at length, when it was thoroughly cleaned out, it was found that its ferruginous qualities had vanished, so, taking the hint, its "discoverers" restored the old iron, and with the adventitious aid of some well-selected chemicals, the well in a short time achieved a widespread reputation as a medicinal spa.

The time-worn and weather-beaten balustrades at Clonturk House originally belonged to Carlisle Bridge, on the demolition of which structure they were removed to their present position by the contractor for the new bridge, who then resided in this house.

Any article on this district would be incomplete without a reference to Frederick E. Jones, better known as "Buck" Jones—one of the most noted men of his time—who lived in Clonliffe House, and whose memory is perpetuated in the title of Jones's Road. The present straight Clonliffe road is a little over 100 years old, and was preceded by a narrower and more winding thoroughfare called Fortick's Lane. Clonliffe House and demesne were at this time called Fortick's Grove after their owner, Tristram Fortick, whose name may be seen embodied in an inscription on the almshouse in Little Denmark Street, endowed by him in 1765, but the original name was restored to the house by Buck Jones when he got possession of it.

Early in life, to complete his education, Jones was sent abroad, where he associated with people of rank and influence. Shortly after his return to Ireland he purchased, in conjunction with Lord Westmeath, the music hall in Fishamble Street, where he set up a theatre. Subsequently he became the lessee and manager of Daly's Theatre in Crow Street, which was then in a dilapidated condition, and he expended an immense sum in renovating it. During the troubled times of 1798 Jones became unpopular, and he was forced to close the theatre owing to the serious riots which became of almost nightly occurrence in the building. It was subsequently re-opened, but again, in 1803, for similar reasons, he was forced to close it.

Jones was considered one of the handsomest men of his day ; his manners and bearing were those of a polished gentleman, and it was said that he bore some resemblance to George IV. when Prince of Wales. In Jones's time the demesne of Clonliffe House extended as far back as the Tolka, and included what is known as " Donnelly's Orchard," and as the only means of access to Clonliffe Road was from Drumcondra road at one end and Ballybough at the other, Jones had a new road made—a continuation of Russell Street—leading by a temporary bridge across the Royal Canal, directly at right angles into Clonliffe Road opposite the entrance to his house. For long afterwards this road was universally known as " Buck Jones's road," but in recent years the name has been simplified into its present form.

Clonliffe House, a plain, well-built structure, still survives, though exhibiting, of course, some evidences of decay, and owing to the demolition of its extensive out-offices, it now presents a rather insignificant appearance. It faces Clonliffe College, and is now included within the grounds of that establishment. The house was used as a depot for the Revenue Police—a force long since extinct—from 1845 to 1857.

Jones was a man of great courage and determination, and his energetic conduct as a magistrate occasionally brought him into conflict with the criminal classes. On one occasion he nearly lost his life in consequence of his efforts to apprehend a notorious local desperado named Larry Clinch, who was known to be one of the party that burnt the Belfast mail at Santry. Clinch, so far from being intimidated by Jones's proceedings, actually had the audacity to besiege Clonliffe

House with a number of his gang.   But in this he was outwitted, for Jones, having got wind of the project, privately conveyed to his house in hackney carriages, under cover of night, an officer and guard of the Tipperary Militia.   The attack took place on the 6th November, 1806.   On that night Captain O'Reilly, who was on a visit with Jones, went to the hall-door to look out, whereupon the robbers rushed in, two of them following O'Reilly into the diningroom, where a desperate conflict ensued,   Excited by the uproar, no less than seven

Buck Jones's House, Clonliffe.
(1911.)

of the soldiers fired madly from the adjoining room, wounding their own officer, but the robbers, overawed, retired, and one of them in his flight received two bullets, from the effects of which he died during the night.   Another of them rushed upstairs, shouting " upstairs, boys, for the money and plate," to which a soldier on the first landing answered, " down stairs, boys, for the powder and ball," and, suiting the action to the word, fired, killing the robber on the spot.   The remainder of the gang were then made prisoners, and the corpses of the dead robbers, after having been exposed for a few days for the purpose of identification, and not having been claimed by their relatives, were buried in the suicides' ground, beside the cross-roads at Ballybough.

Jones's end was a sad one.   On the expiration of his patent in 1820 for the Crow Street Theatre, he failed, owing to a cabal against him, either to obtain a renewal of it or compensation for the losses entailed on him by the action of the Government in issuing a patent for the Theatre Royal (burnt in 1880), and he found himself a ruined man.   He spent a considerable time in prison for debt, and at length sank into abject poverty, his last abode having been a small cabin near where Mountjoy Prison stands.   Here, until his death in 1834, he was kept in the necessaries of life by a few faithful friends, who had known him in his better days, and who endeavoured to alleviate the old man's sorrows in his later years.

Common gossip of the locality holds that he is wont at times to revisit his whilom haunts, and there are not wanting some who aver that they have seen him, at dead of night, a tall stately figure on horseback, noiselessly riding about the neighbourhood of Jones's Road.

CHAPTER XXVI

GLASNEVIN, FINGLAS AND THE ADJACENT DISTRICT

LEAVING town, we proceed by tram or otherwise to Glasnevin, passing what is known as "Dunphy's Corner," but which about a hundred years ago was called Glasmanogue, and was then a well-known stage on the way to Finglas. At an earlier date the name possessed a wider signification and was applied to a considerable portion of the adjoining district.

Apart from the great cemetery by which the locality is now best known, Glasnevin is interesting chiefly by reason of the distinguished people who in bygone days made it their residence or resort. Of these perhaps the best known and most identified with the place is the celebrated divine, Dr. Delany, who lived here in the 18th century, and who assembled around the table in his charming house, Delville, all the Dublin wits and celebrities of his time. Doubtless the chief attraction to many of the visitors was the talented hostess, Mrs. Delany, to whose taste and refinement Delville owes much of its present interest. Swift and Stella were both in the habit of visiting the hospitable proprietors of Delville, and Swift wrote a squib jocosely satirising the grounds which he considered too small for the size of the house.

The gardens are laid out to the best advantage, and retain, in their main features, the design of their originator. They contain a number of magnificent trees and shrubs, among which are arbutus, ilex and yew, many of them of venerable appearance. A pretty stream, spanned by rustic bridges, flows through the grounds which are well enclosed, forming a delightful retreat, notwithstanding the rapid encroachment of the city in this direction.

A miniature temple, bearing the motto " Fastigia despicit urbis " (it looks down upon the pinnacles of the city), said to have been suggested by Swift, stands on a slight eminence in the grounds, and contains a medallion of Stella by Mrs. Delany.

The village of Glasnevin has, of course, been much altered since Dr. Delany's time, and is now included in the city, but a few of the older houses still remain, and are readily distinguished by their old-world gardens, with their wealth of flowering shrubs and climbing plants. It would seem to have been an undesirable place of residence in the beginning of the 18th century, if we are to believe the description given by Archbishop King in a letter, dated 1725, published in Mant's *History of the Church of Ireland* :—" Glasnevin was the " receptacle for thieves and rogues. The first search when " anything was stolen, was there, and when any couple had " a mind to retire to be wicked there was their harbour. " But since the church was built, and service regularly settled, " all these evils are banished. Good houses are built in it, " and the place civilised."

Adjoining Glasnevin are the Botanic Gardens where stood the residence of Tickell, the poet and literary executor of Addison who came to Ireland as secretary to the Earl of Wharton in 1709. Tickell, who was Clerk of the Privy Council, died here in 1740, and from his representatives the place was purchased about 120 years ago, for its present purposes, by the Royal Dublin Society.[13]

A walk of a couple of miles from Glasnevin takes us to the village of Finglas, on the old coach road to Drogheda—a road still preferred by many cyclists and motorists to that by Swords and Balbriggan. Should it be decided to go direct to Finglas, without visiting Glasnevin, the distance to be walked is two miles from where the tram leaves us at the end of the Finglas road. If this route be taken, we pass the cemetery, and

presently come into view of the steep hill descending to the
hamlet of Finglas-bridge, situated in a well wooded and
sheltered hollow formed by the banks of the Tolka. Viewed
from the encompassing heights, this little village presents
a most picturesque appearance, the blue haze of smoke from
its cottages softening the dark background of the trees, and
the buildings of Belle Vue, enclosed by their woods, in a commanding position overlooking the valley of the river.

John Dunton, the eccentric Dublin bookseller, in *The
Dublin Scuffle* (1699) refers to " the fine town of Finglas, seated
" on a hill, where I had a noble prospect of the sea and of
" all the ships in the harbour of Dublin.

" All other times I would walk through the green meadows
" from the end of Stoneybatter to the Kabragh, which is a
" village about a mile from my lodging, full of stately trees,
" which give a pleasant shade and delightful prospect. From
" thence as I came back I had the sea and harbour directly
" in my view."

When the above was written, over 200 years ago, it is possible
that the disposition of the buildings and trees may have been
such as to permit of a view of the sea from this locality, but
at the present day, although Howth is easily distinguishable,
no view of either the bay or harbour can be obtained.

Referring to this neighbourhood, Dr. Rutty in his *Natural
History of the County Dublin* (1772), page 5, sets forth his
views on what he calls the ventilation of the city of Dublin.
He explains that it lies in a valley between a lofty range of
mountains on the south and a high tableland on the north.
This, he states, causes a thorough draught, but he adds that
the advantage lies with the north side of the city, where the
land rising only to a gentle elevation enables the foul air to
escape from that side :—" A gentle breeze from the east is not
" sufficient to disperse the smoke and vapours of the city, as
" anyone will be convinced who will take a walk to Finglas,
" or any more elevated place situated to the north of the city,
" in such a state of weather, when he will see a large cloud of

" smoke interrupted by, and stagnating under the mountains
" to the south, of which the villages to the south have a large
" share, while those to the north enjoy a serener air, which
" seems to be one reason, besides the nature of the soil, for
" the preference that has been given to habitations on the
" north, to those on the south side of the river "

As regards the concluding statement, it certainly is the
case that down to about a hundred years ago, the city seemed
to be extending more rapidly on the north than on the south
side, but it is very doubtful if the inhabitants were influenced
in their choice by atmospheric considerations, and the real
cause was more probably the vague traditional fear of the
" mountain enemie " surviving until the close of the 18th
century, and handed down from early times, when Dublin
was an English colony, menaced by fierce and vengeful foes, who,
from their fastnesses in the mountains were wont to swoop
down at uncertain intervals and ravage the country even
to the city walls. This dread, operating for centuries, in
time resulted in more settled conditions both in regard to
agriculture and building enterprise, in the northern than in the
southern part of the county.

Dr. Lanigan, the learned Irish historian, resided in Finglas
for many years prior to his death and burial there in 1828,
but no memorial marked the resting-place of that genial
scholar until some thirty years afterwards, when a handsome
cross with both Latin and Irish inscriptions was erected to his
memory in the old churchyard. A commemorative tablet
has also been placed in the new church.

One of the most interesting antiquities in Finglas is an
ancient Celtic cross, which, from early times, stood to the north
of the village at a place called Watery Lane. When Cromwell's
army were passing through Finglas in 1649 on their way to besiege
Drogheda, they threw down this cross and broke it, and the
villagers, anxious to preserve it from further injury, buried it
in the churchyard, where in time it was forgotten, though
vague traditions as to its existence lingered in the neighbour-

hood. Nothing more was heard of the matter until 1816, when the Rev. Robert Walsh, LL.D., and M.D., rector of the parish, anxious to investigate the truth of these traditions, instituted exhaustive inquiries, and at length found an old man in the village who stated that he had heard his father describe the position in the churchyard which had been pointed out to him by his grandfather, as the place where the cross was buried, and on search being made, his statement was verified by the exhumation of this ancient relic after an interment of 168 years. It was then repaired by iron cramps, and erected in the churchyard near the place where it had lain so long concealed.

The name Finglas (Fion-glaiss), meaning a clear streamlet, is derived from the rivulet which flows through the village and joins the Tolka at Finglas-bridge.

In 1171 Dublin, then held by the Anglo-Normans under Strongbow and Miles de Cogan, was besieged by a great army under King Roderick O'Connor, while simultaneously a Danish fleet took up its position at the mouth of the Liffey, cutting off communication by sea. For two months the army remained inactive in camp, maintaining a blockade which reduced the garrison to great distress, but without making any attempt at an assault on the city. Despairing at last of succour, Strongbow sent out the Archbishop to make terms with King Roderick, offering to submit if he was allowed to retain the kingdom of Leinster. To this proposition Roderick returned answer that Strongbow might keep Dublin, Wexford and Waterford, but no portion of Leinster outside these three cities, and that if these terms were not accepted, Dublin would be attacked next day. This reply so much exasperated the Anglo-Normans that rather than accept the proffered conditions, they determined to make a desperate effort to cut their way through the weakest part of the encircling forces, which they judged to be that between Castleknock and Finglas. Meanwhile King Roderick, relying on the strength of his army, had become careless, relaxing discipline and neglecting matters generally to such an extent as in every way to favour the execution of Strongbow's project.

In pursuance of their resolve, a picked body of about 600 Anglo-Normans in complete armour, with some Irish allies, suddenly and silently sallied forth in three divisions towards Finglas, where they found Roderick's forces so unprepared, that at the first attack they broke up in disorder and fled

King William's Rampart, Finglas.
(1906.)

without making any effective resistance, leaving a great quantity of booty on the field, all of which fell into the hands of the attacking party. The king, who was taking a bath at the time, only escaped capture by flying precipitately from the battlefield in a semi-naked condition.

This cleverly planned sortie raised the siege of Dublin, and provided the garrison with sufficient stores and provisions to render abortive any further attempt at blockade by land or sea.

Many years ago, considerable quantities of human bones,

together with remains of antique weapons and armour, were discovered in an old quarry near Finglas wood. Dim traditions of the neighbourhood point to the place as a scene of a battle in remote times with the Danes, but as no such engagement is recorded in history, it is probable that the relics in question belonged to the battle which resulted so disastrously for the forces of King Roderick O'Connor.

In 1649 the Marquess of Ormonde encamped here prior to his overthrow at the battle of Rathmines, and obtained some successes over small parties of Parliamentarian troops near Drogheda, who had taken up positions there in order to intercept convoys of provisions coming from the north by the Drogheda and Ashbourne Road. His letters to King Charles II., written at this period, exhibit the utmost confidence as to the final issue of his operations against the city of Dublin.

In 1690 King William's army encamped at Finglas for a few days on their return from the Battle of the Boyne. Two massive structures known as " King William's Ramparts." the erection of which is ascribed by local tradition to that monarch, remain to the present day—one on the boundary of the Rectory ground, and the other, a larger one, close to the village, on the road running southward from the new church. Both have heavy growths of ivy, and present the appearance of antiquity, but the larger one is strengthened by buttresses which appear to be of recent date, and may have been added to prevent it falling out on the road.

According to tradition, St. Patrick having come to Finglas from Meath, ascended a rising ground, and viewing Dublin at a distance, blessed it, and prophesied that although then but a small village, it should one day be a city of importance, and ultimately become the metropolis of the kingdom. Possibly connected with this legend is St. Patrick's Well, standing in a field a little to the north-west of the village, and formerly held in great repute for its sanative virtues as a spa.

In early times an Abbey was founded here and dedicated to St. Canice, whose festival was formerly celebrated in the village on the 11th October. At a later date, which cannot be definitely ascertained, the church whose ruins now remain, was erected on the site of this ancient establishment, and used until 1843, when the new church was built, and the mural monuments belonging to local families moved thither from the older edifice. One of these is to the memory of the Rev. Robert Walsh, LL.D., through whose exertions, as stated, the village cross was discovered.

From some documents of the 13th century as to the rights of turbary at Finglas, it would appear that there was then a considerable supply of turf in the neighbourhood.

A hundred years ago Finglas was celebrated for its May sports, which were carried out on a more elaborate scale than at any other place near Dublin. Until about 1845 the Maypole stood in the open space near the police barrack, on the site now occupied by the pump, and although it had been, no doubt, originally decorated in the orthodox fashion with ribbons and streamers, at a later period of its existence it was painted white, with blue and red stripes encircling it like a gigantic barber's pole. During the sports it was well greased, and at the top were affixed in succession the various prizes which awaited the successful aspirants to fame as climbers. Besides the pole-climbing there was dancing, with a number of other sports and amusements, such as catching a pig, which was well shaved and soaped before being turned loose among its would-be captors, grinning through horse collars, the prize being awarded to the competitor who achieved the most fetching grin, catching a bell-ringer, his pursuers being blind-folded; foot, sack, and ass races, and improvised frolics of every description.

During this period Finglas fully equalled Donnybrook as a popular attraction, the festivities causing so much commotion and excitement in this ordinarily quiet neighbourhood that at one time it was proposed to have them suppressed as a public nuisance. Whiskey was then only a penny a glass, and the publichouses did literally a roaring trade ; the jarveys, too, reaped a rich harvest ; and if a few casualties occurred through the free use of blackthorns or an occasional car getting emptied into a ditch, these were regarded as the fortunes of war, the risks of which only added to the zest of the amusements.

These festivities began to show signs of declining in

Finglaswood House ("King James's Castle").
(1906.)

popular favour about 1820, and notwithstanding the strenuous efforts of some of the residents to revive what they called " the humours of Finglas," almost every vestige of them had disappeared by 1845.

Due south of Finglas, and situated on the green banks of the Tolka, is the conspicuous ruin of Finglaswood House, an ancient structure, which during the Commonwealth was the residence of Henry Segrave, whose possessions were forfeited to the Government. Adjoining the house, and leading up to Finglas, is a narrow, shady path known as " Savage's Lane," from a family who occupied the house about eighty years ago. The most noticeable feature in the building is a lofty square turret, the lower part of which appears to be very ancient, probably dating from the time of Queen Elizabeth, while the upper portion, constructed of brickwork, seems to be of more recent date, and is covered by a modern, slated roof. The defensive character of the original structure is indicated by the massively built turret, with its inconspicuous loopholes commanding the approach to the entrance door, and by the arched entrance at the back to an underground passage, now fallen in, which probably led to some secret exit, while inside the front wall a large well furnished the place with water. Attached to the establishment were numerous out-offices, bakehouses, and stables, with extensive walled gardens, which still contain a few of the old fruit trees, and in the western side of the house may still be seen the remains of the great kitchen fireplace.

About a hundred years ago this house was used as a tannery, and since that time has been gradually falling into decay. Over the halldoor there formerly was a stone tablet bearing the arms of the Segrave family, the ancient territorial proprietors.

The whole structure presents the appearance of a dwelling-house built on to the nucleus of an old castle, which, however, has suffered such destructive alterations in the process as to leave but little by which to judge of its original design or character.

Like many other old houses in the neighbourhood of Dublin, popular tradition assigns to this building the dubious honour of having sheltered King James on the night of the Battle of the Boyne, and although there is no historical evidence to support this belief, the ruin is in consequence almost universally known as " King James's Castle."

In addition to the authorities already quoted, an article by Mr. Wm. C. Stubbs, M.A., on the Fingal District, in the *Journal of the Royal Society of Antiquaries* for 1897, has been consulted in the preparation of this chapter.

CHAPTER XXVII

FINGAL—BALDOYLE, PORTMARNOCK, MALAHIDE AND ST. DOOLAGH'S

THE north of the County Dublin, though not possessing the same attractions in point of scenery as the mountainous district in the southern portion, yet contains many objects of deep historic interest scattered through the classic plains of Fingal. While it lacks the breezy expanses of golden gorse, the heather-clad uplands and wooded defiles of the south, it presents what is more acceptable to the practical eye of the agriculturist, a pleasantly undulating country, fertile and cultivated, and watered by numerous rivulets and streams. Towards the extreme northern portion the undulations become more marked, forming a range of gently sloping hills, anciently Slieve Breagh, extending westwards from the coast into the County Meath. According to *The Annals of the Four Masters*, the district of Fingal was bounded on the south by the Tolka, and on the north by the river Delvin, now part of the county boundary, while southwestward it extended as far as Knock Maeldoid, a small hill west of Finglas.

In the 9th century a colony of Ostmen entered Dublin and established themselves there, but being ultimately driven out of it by the inhabitants, they settled in the tract lying northwards along the coast, which thenceforth became known as *Fine-Gall*, or the territory of the Galls or strangers. Their descendants up to a recent period were known as Fingallians, and even at the present day bear traces of an origin different from their neighbours, besides being credited with the possession of distinctive characteristics and temperament.

275

We start from town by the Howth Road, and turn to the left by the road crossing the railway at Baldoyle Station, presently entering Baldoyle village, now chiefly known in connection with its horse races, but in former years a bathing resort of some note.   At one period this locality possessed an unenviable notoriety, as the resort of smugglers, highwaymen, and other undesirables, but those days are now forgotten, and the character of the inhabitants, as well as the whole aspect of the village, has altered since that time.   Some of the cottages stand on the very shore, and are often washed by the surf during the prevalence of easterly winds, the effects of which, are, however, to some extent, moderated by the adjoining peninsula of Portmarnock.

Baldoyle (*Baile-Dubhgoill*) means the town of Dubhgall or Doyle, a personal name signifying black Gall or foreigner—*i.e.*, Dane or Danar, as distinguished from Norwegians who first settled in Ireland A.D. 842 (*Irish Names of Places*, Vol. I., p. 350, and Archdall's *Monasticon Hibernicum*, edited by Cardinal Moran ; Vol. II., p. 21, *note*).

In 1369 a parliament was held in the Church of the Grange of the Priory of All Saints at Baldoyle by Sir William de Windsor, Lord Lieutenant, for the purpose of levying subsidies.   As this proceeding became the subject of popular remonstrance, a commission of inquiry was granted by Edward III. in 1373 to investigate the action of the Lord Lieutenant on this occasion, and it was found thereat " that the said Lord " Lieutenant summoned a parliament at Baldoyle where there " were no buildings except one small chapel ; and that he " chose that place for the purpose of compelling the members " of said parliament, through want of lodging and other " inconveniences, to comply with his demand ; and that " consequently the said parliament granted a subsidy of 2,000 " marks, of which 500 would be levied in the County of Meath, " whereupon the commons of said county sent Richard Bray " into England to the King."

The ivied ruins of this historic edifice, known as Grange

Abbey, may be seen in the grounds of Grange House, a mile and a quarter due west of Baldoyle village. They are situated on a slightly elevated mound enclosed by trees, quite close to and visible from the road. The building measures internally 45 feet 6 inches in length, 18 feet in width, and the side walls are about 8 feet high, from which it will be seen that the complaints as to the accommodation for the assembly convened there were amply justified (*see* Archdall's *Monasticon Hibernicum* [Moran's], Vol. II., p. 25).

At Baldoyle.
(1903.)

In 1478 on the representation of the Prior of All Saints, and Lord of the town of Baldoyle, that the inhabitants were much distressed by reason of the inordinate taxes levied upon them by the King's Admirals and their deputies, it was enacted by Parliament that the Prior should thenceforth be Admiral of Baldoyle and of all other lands belonging to the Priory in Ireland.

A short distance beyond the racecourse, the Mayne river flows out on the shore, which is here fringed by a dreary waste of salt marshes, the resort of numerous wild fowl in winter. We next come in view of the old mill of Portmarnock, a well-known landmark, unroofed and much dilapidated by the storm of 1903. A mill stood here for hundreds of years past, references to it being found in records so far back as 1663, when it formed portion of the property of the Plunkett family. At the far side of the bridge, adjoining Portmarnock House, is a small patch of land called " The Cross," on which a termon cross formerly stood to mark certain monastic bounds. Turning to the right across Portmarnock bridge, we pass a number of pretty cottages, after which will be observed, to the right of the road, the ancient church of the locality, erected in the 12th or 13th century, and used up to about 1615, since when it has been in ruins.

Between the ruin and the road lies St. Marnock's Well, formerly open, and approached by a flight of sixteen stone steps leading down to it. On its northern side grew an old willow tree long since cut down, which, according to tradition, was wont to bend over the waters on the approach of a storm, and on this account was regarded with feelings akin to veneration by the fishing folk of the neighbourhood. Beside the well was a pillar stone, now broken to fragments, some of which have been preserved, having on their angles Ogham inscriptions, and also bearing some unknown symbols, which were never deciphered or explained. It is much to be regretted that portions of this interesting relic were incorporated in the masonry of the well, when it was enclosed about 1855, and a pump erected over it, as the inscription was well defined and undoubtedly genuine.

Resuming our journey, a laneway will be seen on the left, nearly opposite the church, bearing the picturesque designation of " Blackberry Lane," and after passing the rise in the road, the shore again comes into view at the northern extremity of the Velvet Strand. Just under the point where the Martello tower stands, a small quay for landing fish was constructed about 100 years ago, when there was a much larger population along this coast than at the present time. The place was then known as Tobermaclaney, meaning Maclaney's well, and a depression in the ground near the tower marks the site of the well, the waters of which, having been disturbed by drainage operations, now spring up from the sands under the road, within a few yards of the sea waves.

The Velvet Strand, seen to great advantage from this point, is a most beautiful sight on a bright sunny day, with its wide, smooth expanse of sand, and its fringe of white surf, in striking contrast to the deep blue colour of the water. Lambay looks quite close from here, the little row of Coastguards' cottages near the harbour being easily discerned without the aid of a glass. Howth town and harbour are conspicuously in view, as also the rugged reach of precipitous cliffs on the northern side of Ireland's Eye, while to the right of Howth will be seen in the distance the Dublin and Wicklow Mountains.

After passing Tobermaclaney, the road skirts the edge of a range of low cliffs, almost within reach of the surf from the waves thundering against the dark and rocky shore. In front, at the opposite side of the creek, will be observed the Lunatic Asylum, picturesquely situated on rising ground on the Portrane Peninsula, the whole aspect of which has been altered by the building of this extensive establishment. We next pass the coastguard station, and in about half a mile further, Robswall Castle, a square edifice standing on a rock beside the shore, with a dwellinghouse built up against it. It consists of three storeys, and was strongly fortified, having been designed to command the passage of the estuary of Malahide. The ceiling of the ground storey is vaulted, and a circular staircase leads thence to the first floor, which has been entirely modernised, while off the main room is a small " garderobe." A flight of stone steps ascends to the battlements, from which a little watch tower similar to those on Dalkey and Bullock Castles, is reached. The name appears in an Inquisition in the reign of Henry VIII. as Roebuck's Wall, and is given in its present form in the notes of the Down Survey, where it is described as a thatched castle belonging to the Barnewalls of Turvey.

According to tradition this castle was founded in the 15th century by one of the de Berminghams with the object stated above, but it does not appear to have ever sustained attack or siege. We next pass on our right, the Malahide golf links—a green, undulating stretch of sand dunes, interspersed with clumps of bracken and rushes, and as Malahide is approached, we come into view of the estuary of the Broadmeadow Water—locally known by the euphonious title of Muldowney Creek—on the opposite shore of which will be seen the solitary farmhouse of Corballis.

Near Malahide will be seen, adjoining the road, a most picturesque dwellinghouse partly constructed out of a martello tower.

Malahide is a decayed watering-place which attained an ephemeral popularity about sixty years ago consequent upon the construction of the Dublin and Drogheda Railway, and although there are many good houses and terraces in the vicinity, it has, in recent years, shown little signs of revival except as a golfing resort. Two hundred years ago it was a favourite drive for the Dublin folk, and the eccentric John Dunton in *The Dublin Scuffle* (1699), says :—" Sometimes I would for " my diversion ride out a few miles either to Santry, Swords " or Malahide, a place as eminent as Billingsgate for people " going to eat oysters there."

A picture of Malahide Castle appears on the maps of the Down Survey, and in the notes is the following description of the town :—" Mallahide contains the town of Mallahide ; " there is a good stone house therein, with orchards and gardens " and many ash trees, with other out-houses in good repair ; " there are also many thatched houses and cabbins by the " seaside or bay, where fishermen dwelleth, and a mill that " goeth by ebb tides."

Malahide Castle was founded in the reign of Henry II. by Richard Talbot, who had received a grant of the adjoining lands, and was an ancestor of the present proprietor. The exterior of the building exhibits little traces of its ancient character ; the old loopholes have been superseded by modern windows, the once formidable outworks have long since disappeared, and a grassy hollow is all that now remains of the mediæval castle moat.

Adjoining the Castle are the venerable remains of "The Abbey," which consisted of a nave and chancel running due east and west, and which must have been one of the finest and largest churches in the whole district of Fingal. At the south-eastern corner of the chancel is a pointed arch door, leading to a two-storied building, probably originally intended

Malahide.

(1906.)

either as a vestry or a residence for the monks, but which for centuries past, has been used as the burial place of the lords of the manor. In the centre of the nave is a monument to the Honorable Maud Plunkett, who was maid, wife and widow in one day, her husband, son of the Baron of Galtrim, having been slain on the day of his marriage in a predatory raid in the neighbourhood. This tragic incident forms the subject of Gerald Griffin's ballad, "The Bridal of Malahide."

One of the pleasantest walks in this neighbourhood is to the top of Carrick or Malahide hill, which, although of inconsiderable elevation, affords extensive views over land and sea, from the Dublin and Wicklow Mountains to the more distant ranges of Carlingford and Mourne.

To reach this hill, take the road starting from the hotel, up a slight incline—at the end of this road a narrow pathway between high hedges turns to the left, and after passing through the fields, leads out upon the top.   From this point the northern side of Howth and the bold profile of Ireland's Eye stand prominently in view ; and between the observer and the city, which may be distinguished in the distance, is a rich wooded country of hill and dale, interspersed with villages, cottages and country seats. By continuing the pathway down the southern side of the hill, either the coast road or the inland road to Portmarnock can be reached.

If the return to town is made from Malahide, we cross the railway by the bridge at the station, whence the line runs straight across the creek and sands for a couple of miles to Donabate. We now enter upon the main Malahide road, well sheltered for a considerable distance by the dense woods of the Castle, and, counting from the railway bridge, we take the fourth turn to the right at the nearly vanished village of Feltrim, leading up by a gradual ascent to Feltrim hill, an eminence which, surmounted by its ruined windmill, forms a conspicuous object in the prettily diversified country around it.

The bricks of which the windmill is built appear to be of excellent quality, and what remains of the woodwork is still in good preservation. The view from the hill comprises the ancient district of Fingal, the expanse of the Bay, and the Dublin and Wicklow Mountains beyond it.

Malahide is quite concealed from view by the dense woods of the Castle, but Swords and its ivy-clad ruins are easily distinguishable inland.   Beyond Malahide creek, in the distance, will be seen the gently sloping eminence on which stand the massive ruins of Baldongan Castle, and in line with Swords is Garristown Hill, surmounted by its square ruin.

Feltrim Hill still retains traces of the wild character which

must have distinguished it when it originally acquired its
name of Faildruim, or the Hill of the Wolves, and the numerous
thickets of furze and brushwood scattered over it would even
now afford excellent cover for these animals. In early times
it was covered by dense forest and scrub, and was doubtless
a spot dreaded and avoided alike by natives and settlers.

The ancient and distinguished family of Fagan were long
the landed proprietors in this neighbourhood, and their

Feltrim Hill.
(1906.)

ancestral residence stood on the slopes of the hill. When the
Earl of Desmond was a State prisoner during the reign of
Queen Elizabeth he was consigned to the custody of Christopher
Fagan of Feltrim, who, magnanimously refusing to place him
under duress, allowed him complete liberty on parole. This
privilege was, however, abused by the Earl, who availed himself
of an opportunity to escape back to his own territory in
Munster. In some accounts of this incident, however, it is
stated that Fagan allowed the Earl to escape.

Returning to the main Malahide road at the point where we
left it, and continuing our journey homeward, in about half

a mile we pass through the little village of Kinsaley, with its pretty diminutive church, the predecessor of which stands a picturesque ivied ruin, a short distance to the left along the road to Portmarnock. The name Kinsaley, meaning " the head of the sea," would indicate that at some period the sea or the tidal waters of the little river flowed in as far as this point, though not within recent times, the adjoining lands having been long since embanked and reclaimed. This stream, which takes its origin near Cloghran, passes beside the village, and closely following the course of the road flows into the sea at Portmarnock bridge. That it often transgressed beyond its legitimate bounds is indicated by the name Watery Lane— the old name of the road from Kinsaley to Portmarnock— which, perhaps, originated at the time when the sea flowed in here.

Some short distance beyond this, on the right of the road, is the ancient Church of St. Doolagh's, believed to have been erected in the 12th century, and possessing many characteristics of the early Saxon churches. It has a massive stone roof of such strength and solidity that even seven centuries of exposure to the elements have made little change in its condition. Flights of stone steps lead to the several apartments, rising one above the other, and from the upper of these a ladder leads out upon the battlements. The whole building is enclosed by an ancient brick wall, outside which is a kind of raised pathway, probably marking the former level of the adjoining road.

The original walls of St. Doolagh's are about three feet thick, and of immense strength, as will be seen at the windows, most of which are now glazed, though one had to be built up owing to its exposed position. At the top of the second flight of stairs is a small recess, said to have been the penitential bed of the saint. Close to the church, but outside the enclosing wall, is a holy well contained within a circular stone basin, over which rises an octagonal building of graceful style and proportions. About the middle of the 17th century, Patrick

Fagan, of Feltrim, decorated this building, and had the walls inside covered with paintings—that on the ceiling representing the descent of the Holy Ghost upon the Apostles, while at the sides were shown St. Patrick, St. Bridget, and St. Columkille, with the patron saint (Duilech) in a hermit's garb. On the wall was a marble slab bearing the following inscription, commemorative of the curative effects of the water of the well :—

" Piscinae Solymis clarae decus efferat alter,
" Et medicas populus jactet Hebraeus aquas,
" Grata Deo patrium celebrat Fingallia fontem
" Doulachi precibus munera nacta piis ;
" Morbos ille fugat promptus viresque reponit
" Aegris, et causas mille salutis habet ;
" Scilicet aequus agit mediis Doulachus in undis,
" Angelus ut fontem, sic movet ille suum ;
" O fons noster amor ! si te negleximus olim,
" Mox erit ut nomen sit super astra tuum."

Translation (from Lynch's *Life of St. Patrick*).
" Bethsaida's sacred pool let others tell,
" With healing virtues how her waters swell ;
" An equal glory shall Fingalia claim,
" Nor be less grateful for her blessed stream.
" Thy prayers Dolachus mounted up to Heaven,
" Thence to the well the mighty power is given
" To drive the fiery fever far away,
" Strength to replace and rescue from decay,
" In every malady to life a stay,
" The cherub, wondrous moves his waters there,
" The saint behold ! who stirs the fountain here.
" Hail lovely fount, if long unsung thy name,
" It hence shall rise above the starry frame."

According to Lynch's *Life of St. Patrick*, these interesting memorials of devotion were destroyed by Sir Richard Bulkeley, presumably in a fit of iconoclastic zeal, when returning to Dublin with a party of troopers after the Battle of the Boyne.

Sir Richard, who was a hunchback, and somewhat weak minded, subsequently fell under the influence of a set of religious impostors, who, besides pretending to the gift of prophecy, undertook to change him to his proper shape and proportions. So deluded was he by their wiles that he had decided to sell his estates and divide the proceeds among them, but his death, which occurred in 1710, prevented him from carrying out his foolish designs.

A patron was formerly held at St. Doolagh's, but becoming a scene of rioting and dissipation like many others, was suppressed by the clergy in the last century.

Leaving St. Doolagh's we pass through Balgriffin, in which there is nothing of interest to notice, and continuing our journey along the high road, we pass in succession the villages of Coolock and Artane, the latter of which is memorable as the scene of the murder of Archbishop Alen in 1533 by the adherents of Silken Thomas. The unfortunate ecclesiastic, apprehensive of the resentment of the Geraldine, endeavoured to escape from Dublin by sea, but his vessel having been driven ashore near Clontarf by contrary winds, the Archbishop sought refuge in the house of his friend, Hollywood of Artane. Here he was discovered, dragged from his bed, and, notwithstanding his entreaties for mercy, brutally murdered in front of the house in which he had taken shelter. This old house or castle was taken down in 1825, and Artane House erected on its site. The scene of this unhallowed deed, now covered by the buildings of the Industrial School, is traditionally recorded as having been for generations afterwards enclosed by a fence, overgrown by rank weeds, and shunned by the people in the locality.

We next pass the small village of Donnycarney, and presently observe on the right the model Greek temple designed by Sir William Chambers, and erected by Lord Charlemont in his grounds.

A mile and a half from Artane we reach the tram road at
Marino Crescent, Clontarf, where the excursionist may be
safely left to finish the remainder of his journey.

Distances from G. P. O. for the round :—Raheny, 4¾ ;
Baldoyle, 7 ; Portmarnock Bridge, 8¾ ; Malahide, 12 ;
Feltrim Hill, 14¾ ; Balgriffin, 17 ; Coolock, 18¾ ; back to
G. P. O., 22¾ miles.

The following authorities have been consulted in the
preparation of this chapter :—An article on Fingal district,
by William C. Stubbs, M.A., in the *Journal of the Royal Society
of Antiquaries* for 1897 ; Dalton's *History of the County Dublin ;*
Archdall's *Monasticon Hibernicum* (Moran's).

CHAPTER XXVIII

FINGAL—SWORDS, GRACE DIEU, BALLYBOGHIL, CHAPELMIDWAY AND ST. MARGARET'S

PASSING through Drumcondra, Santry, and Cloghran, we enter the ancient town of Swords, consisting of a long, wide street, situated on the great northern road, at a distance of eight miles fom the metropolis. It derives its name from the Celtic word, *sord*, meaning pure, originally applied to St. Columbkille's well, which from time immemorial has been one of the principal sources of water supply in the town. This well is on the by-road to the left as we enter the village, but is now concealed from view, a pump having been erected over it during the past few years to preserve it from contamination.

One of the most notable events in the history of Swords is the funeral of King Brian Boru and his son Morrough, after the Battle of Clontarf, when the bodies of these warriors were conveyed in solemn procession from Dublin, and deposited for the night in the ancient monastery here, on the way to their final destination in Armagh.

According to the ancient records, Swords was burnt by the Danes in 1012, 1016, 1130, 1138, 1150, and 1166 A.D.; and in 1185 it was taken and sacked by O'Melaghlin, King of Meath. It must, consequently, have been a much more lively place of residence in those days than at the present time.

In 1578 a Royal mandate was issued for the better establishment of the Corporation of Swords, and for the purpose of determining the limits of its franchises and liberties. Commissioners were thereupon appointed to fix the boundaries, two miles on every side from the town.

At the commencement of the Insurrection of 1641, the Irish army assembled at Swords, and refusing to disperse in obedience to a warrant of the Lords Justices, Sir Charles Coote, with a considerable force, was sent out from Dublin to attack them. He found the entrance to the town on the Dublin side strongly barricaded, but succeeded in driving the insurgents from their positions after a sharp engagement with loss on both sides.

Swords.
(1904.)

In 1788 Richard Talbot, of Malahide, obtained an Act of Parliament authorising him to construct a canal from Malahide to the Broadmeadow Water through Swords for the conveyance of goods, in consequence of the prohibitive charges for carriage by land, but the project was abandoned owing to the death of its originator.

Swords was constituted a borough by James I., returning two members to the Irish House of Commons, and was one of the few free boroughs in Ireland (*i.e.*, not private property), the franchise having been vested in what were called, in the slang of the period, "Potwallopers," meaning Protestants who had been resident for a continuous period of six months. The last two members were Francis Synge and Colonel Marcus Beresford.

T

The most conspicuous objects in the town are the round tower, 75 feet high, which is the only surviving portion of the original monastic establishment, and the mediæval church tower, 68 feet high, belonging to a structure which was erected not later than the 14th century. The round tower is surmounted by a cross, placed there about 100 years ago. The adjoining modern church was built in the early part of the last century out of the remains of the ancient one, an illustration of which latter appears in Grose's *Antiquities*.

At the northern end of the street stands the ancient episcopal palace or castle, designed as a defence against the Danes or other marauders, and sufficiently extensive to shelter the whole population of the town and their chattels within the circuit of its formidable walls. Admission to these ruins can be obtained on application at an adjoining house. The visitor is still shown the Constable's residence, the soldiers' quarters, and the Warder's walk, as also ' St. Columbkille's Chapel," to the right of the entrance gate, with several watch towers, one of which looking north, is in excellent preservation. A full description of this ancient establishment is to be found in Alan's *Liber Niger*, and according to the inquisition recorded therein, it would appear that the place was in a ruinous condition so early as 1326.

A short distance north of the castle is an elevation known as Spital Hill, where, as the name indicates, there stood in ancient times a hospital, probably for lepers—an institution to be found in every town of importance during the period when that terrible scourge was prevalent in the country. In this connection, it should be mentioned that St. Finian, the Abbot of Swords, who was appointed by St. Columbkille in the 6th century, was himself a sufferer from this disease, and is, in fact, usually referred to as " St. Finian the Leper." The ecclesiastical establishment here was founded about 550 A.D. by St. Columbkille, who soon afterwards retired in exile to Iona, off the west coast of Scotland.

A mile and a quarter to the north-west of Swords are the ruins of Glasmore Abbey, an ancient ecclesiastical establishment which was destroyed in the 7th century by the Danes who murdered the entire community. Adjoining the ruins is St. Cronan's Well, named after the saint who fell in the massacre.

Leaving Swords by the main road, we presently cross the Broadmeadow Water, from the bridge over which is obtained a view along the estuary of that river towards Malahide. The road now passes through a dense wood—very dark in the night time—and as we ascend the height beyond Turvey bridge, to the north may be seen Baldongan castle and the low hills of Naul and Garristown, while to the south are the dim forms of the Dublin mountains in blue profile. We next pass the road to Skerries, branching off to the right, and continuing along the main road, in about a quarter of a mile we reach Corduff Bridge, where we turn to the left along the road to Ballyboghil, meeting in about a mile and a half, a grass-grown lane on the left, leading up to the site of Grace Dieu, the once-famed convent of the Canonesses of St. Augustine.

This lane, now overgrown with weeds and brushwood, and beyond the site of the convent passable only to pedestrians, is of great antiquity, as evidenced by its ancient red stone pavement, still visible in places, and the old bridges by which it crosses the intervening rivulets. It can, if desired, be followed the whole way until it reaches the main road at a distance of about a mile to the southward. The traffic along this ancient roadway must have been considerable, the convent having been a large institution, probably in constant communication with both Swords and Dublin. A short distance along the lane, a wooden gateway will be seen on the left, opening into a field containing a small pile of masonry with a low doorway, the remains probably of a small chapel in connection with the establishment, and adjoining is the ancient burial ground, long since desecrated by agricultural operations. Two horizontal tombstones still remain, one outside the building, too worn to be decipherable, and the other inside the walls, bearing the deeply-cut inscription, " Hic Jacet Johannes Hurley, cujus animae propitietur Dominus, Amen." ; no date can be traced, but from its appearance one would not suppose it to be more than 100 years old. The main convent building stood on the opposite side of

Ruin at Grace Dieu.
(1906.)

the lane, where there are now some very ancient walls which probably enclosed or formed portion of the original structure. A small mound will be seen in the adjoining field marking the position of the garden, as also some large stones where, according to local tradition, the nuns used to sit in the summertime under the shade of the trees.

Extensive orchards once surrounded the place, and although some representatives of them still survive among the adjacent hedges, they have long since degenerated into crab-trees, the delicate bloom of their rose-pink blossoms rendering them conspicuous objects in the springtime.

One of the fields to the west of the lane is to the present day called "The Avenue Field," it having been traversed by the entrance avenue to the establishment from the Brownstown road.

To the east of Grace Dieu is St. Brigit's Well, and to the south-west, Lady well, both of which supplied the establishment with water.

Grace Dieu was founded about 1190 by John Comyn, Archbishop of Dublin, and continued throughout its career to be maintained exclusively in the interests of the Anglo-Norman colonists, for the education of whose daughters it was regarded as the best institution within the Pale.

In 1539, when the suppression of the monasteries in Ireland was impending, the Lord Deputy and Council intervened " for the common weal of said land," on behalf of six important religious communities—viz., Grace Dieu, St. Mary's Abbey, Christ Church, Connal (now Great Connell), Kenlis (Kells) and Jerpoint, representing to the English Government that " in those houses commonly and other such like, the King's " Deputy and all other his Grace's Council and officers, also " Irishmen and others, resorting to the King's Deputy in " their quarters, is and hath been, most commonly lodged " at the cost of the said houses ; also in them, young men and " children, and other both of mankind and womankind, be " brought up in virtue, learning and in the English tongue " and behaviour, to the great charges of the said houses, that " is to say, *the womankind of the whole Englishry of this land* " *for the more part in the said nunnery*—[*i.e.,* Grace Dieu], " and the mankind in the other said houses " (*State Papers,* Hen. VIII.).

But greedy eyes had looked upon its fertile lands, and notwithstanding the influential memorial to the English Government, Grace Dieu was suppressed in 1539 and granted to Sir Patrick Barnewall, who thereupon made it his residence, the prioress, Alison White, being granted a pension of £6 (about £60 of our present money) a year, chargeable upon the estate and some adjacent properties. The church, however, appears to have continued in use as a place of worship up to the close of the 17th century.

There is a tradition that Turvey House, the seat of the Barnewalls, was erected out of the materials of Grace Dieu, and the complete disappearance of all the buildings of that great religious establishment would tend to corroborate this story (*see* " Turvey " in next chapter).

The site stands on high ground, commanding a distant prospect of the mountains across the city smoke, as well as a partial view of Howth.

Leaving this hallowed ground, we retrace our steps as far as the entrance to the lane, turning to the left along a high wooded road, overlooking the flat country southward, reaching at a distance of a little over two miles from Grace Dieu, the hamlet of Ballyboghil, the most conspicuous object in which is the fine church, bearing the inscription—" This Church of " the Assumption saved from ruin by the Rev. Francis O'Neill, P.P., 1900." A short distance north of the village are the ruins of the ancient church, containing monuments to members of several local families. Ballyboghil means " the town of " the crozier," and if, as stated by Dalton, this name originated with a crozier left by St. Patrick, formerly exhibited in the ancient church, it would be interesting to know what has now become of this valuable relic.

Re-crossing the bridge by which we entered the village, and taking the road at the far side parallel to the stream, in about two miles we meet a turn to the left which conducts us to the pretty, scattered village of Oldtown, with its diminutive Catholic chapel and neatly kept cottages, picturesque in their irregularity. As we continue our journey beyond the village, along a rather unfrequented road, we catch a passing glimpse on the left of Malahide, Lambay and Howth in the distance across the flat tract of country intervening between us and the sea.

At a distance of about two miles from Oldtown, we cross

the Broadmeadow Water at the entrance to Fieldstown House, in the demesne of which is an old burial ground with some remains of an ancient church dedicated to St. Catherine. This locality derives its name from the ancient family of de la Field or Feld, who came over to England with William the Conqueror, and obtained possession of these estates about the year 1200, retaining them until 1479, when they passed by marriage to the Barnewall family. The ancestral castle of the Counts de la Field stood in a pass of the Vosges Mountains in France, and its lords were owners of extensive estates in both Alsace and Lorraine. Some ruins of their ancient chateau and its chapel still remain in the Vosges—a picturesque yet melancholy memorial of this distinguished family.

About a mile further along the road we reach Kilsallaghan, where once a hamlet clustered round the village green, and where a fair was held in former times, while adjoining are the gloomy ruins of its castle, sheltered by tall trees, and presenting the appearance of having been originally an extensive edifice. In 1641 this castle having been held by Lieut.-General Byrne for the Irish army, the Earl of Ormonde was commissioned to dislodge its garrison, which he succeeded in doing after an inconsiderable engagement. About half a mile westward of the ruin is an eminence called Gallows Hill, where, according to tradition, one of these grim structures stood during the Cromwellian wars.

We next reach Chapelmidway, now consisting of a few pretty cottages, with the ancient church and churchyard enclosed by trees standing upon an eminence overlooking the hamlet. The ruin appears to be a kind of crypted appanage of the church rather than portion of the edifice itself, the foundations of which may be traced extending eastward of the existing structure. The church, which derived its name from its position midway between Kilsallaghan and St. Margaret's, is reported in an official " Visitation " as being in a ruinous condition so far back as the year 1615.

Crossing the sluggish waters of the Ward River, we continue

along the road for a mile and a half to St. Margaret's, which possesses no less than three churches—viz., the ancient church in ruins, the old church now disused, and the new church, a fine handsome structure built only a few years ago. The ancient edifice, seen on the right, approaching the village, is kept in good order, and well protected from injury or desecration by its enclosing wall. Behind the disused church is the famous tepid well of St. Brigit, which never freezes, and is said to exhale a vapour in winter.

From St. Margaret's a sequestered road leads to Finglas, passing on the way the dismal ruins of " The Old Red Lion " inn, a hostelry of some note in former times, when travellers feared to risk the perils of the notorious Santry woods after nightfall. From Finglas the excursionist may be safely left to complete his journey, according to position of his residence.

The route described in this chapter is suitable only for cycles or motors ; and the entire distance, taking the G. P. O. as starting point, is 31 miles. Energetic pedestrians may, perhaps, be disposed to walk it, but the character of the country is scarcely of sufficient interest for so slow a mode of travelling.

CHAPTER XXIX

FINGAL—PORTRANE, DONABATE AND THE BARNEWALLS OF TURVEY.

THE whole of the peninsula of Portrane has, in recent years, been altered by the erection of the great lunatic asylum in the grounds of Portrane House, a spacious mansion, now utilised in connection with this institution, and situated nearly in the centre of what was formerly an extensive deer park. The railway runs almost centrally across the peninsula, having a station at Donabate, and crosses by two causeways and bridges, the Rogerstown and Malahide creeks to the north and south of Portrane respectively. Those desirous of exploring this rather isolated portion of the county on foot should take return tickets to Donabate, while those proceeding thither on bicycles should go by the main road through Swords, turning to the right about two miles north of the latter town.

Donabate is a small scattered village, containing a handsome red brick Catholic Church, as well as the ancient church which originated the name, Domnach-bate (*i.e.*, the Church of the Ferry), and which still remains in excellent preservation enclosed within its graveyard. Adjoining and almost forming portion of Donabate is the primitive-looking village of Ballisk, consisting mostly of thatched cabins of a very poor description. A mile and a half from the railway, on the road to the Coastguard Station is the ivied ruin of Portrane Castle, a square tower standing in a field, without any trace of either bawn or outworks. At the Suppression of the Monasteries this edifice formed portion of the possessions of the wealthy religious community of Grace Dieu, all the property of which thereafter passed into the hands of Sir Patrick Barnewall, of Turvey, subsequently coming into possession of the Cusacks of Rathaldron.

Within sight of the castle, and situated almost on the sea shore, are the ruins of Portrane Church, surrounded by an embattled wall and sheltered by trees ; it was evidently at one time an extensive building, and its square ivied tower is still a conspicuous object in the neighbourhood.

Adjoining the Asylum is a modern round tower, erected on the summit of a rising ground by a former proprietor, Mrs.

Ballisk, Portrane.
(1905.)

Evans, as a memorial to her husband, whose bust is placed in the interior of the structure. This tower was formerly a very remarkable feature on the peninsula, being about 100 feet high, but is now much dwarfed by the proximity of the extensive buildings of the Asylum. The entrance door is situated, as in the ancient round towers, at such a height from the ground that it can be reached only by a ladder, and is surmounted by the armorial bearings of the Evans family. The view from the high ground adjoining, comprises Lambay Island—only three miles away—the extended distant panorama of the mountains, and to the north a fertile undulating tract, bounded by the low range of hills near the northern boundary of the county, on one of which stand the massive ruins of Baldongan castle.

Northwards, on the opposite side of Rogerstown Creek will be seen the white cottages of the town of Rush, extending along the shore.

In ancient times Lambay, when it possessed an ecclesiastical establishment, was a place of some note, and its port of embarkation, Portrane, came to acquire a sort of borrowed importance. Rechra or Rechrain was the ancient name of Lambay, and its port consequently was Port-rechrain, afterwards smoothed down into Port-rahen and Portrane.

Portrane Church.
(1906.)

On the southern side of the peninsula and facing Malahide, is Corballis, which in the 14th century was in possession of the Barnewalls, and in the 17th century was the residence of Luke Netterville, who in 1641 assembled a force of 1,200 men at Swords as a protest against the lawless conduct of some soldiery from Dublin. On the death of Netterville in 1648, the estate was granted by Parliament to Lady Harcourt, widow of Sir Simon Harcourt, who was killed at the siege of Carrickmines Castle in 1641.

An appalling shipping disaster, probably remembered by some of the older residents of Dublin, occurred off this coast in 1854. On Thursday, the 19th January in that year, the emigrant ship,

John Tayleur, a clipper-built sailing vessel of 1,970 tons, left Liverpool for Melbourne. The entire number on board was 579, of whom 460 were passengers, principally emigrants, and the vessel besides carried valuable general cargo. The accommodation and appointments were of the best description, but she was insufficiently manned, having only ten proper seamen among the crew, the rest being unskilled Lascars and Chinese, most of whom could not understand the captain's orders, and who, even if they did, were totally incapable of carrying them out.

Soon after the pilot left, a squall coming on, orders were given to shorten sail, and it became evident that the crew were entirely incompetent to manage the vessel. The mate could not get anyone to shorten sail, and for a long time the ship was at the mercy of the wind and waves. After prolonged efforts, some of the sails were taken in, but others had to be left as they were, and these continued throughout the night flapping and beating in a most alarming manner. Terribly rough weather was presently encountered, followed by a fog, which resulted in the vessel departing so much from her course that by the time she had been two days out of the Mersey, instead of being in mid-channel, she was quite close to the Irish coast. On Saturday about noon it was rumoured in the cabin that land had been seen and that the officers were afraid that the vessel would go ashore. The terror-stricken passengers crowded on deck and then saw before them the bleak and rocky coast of Lambay, against which the waves were beating furiously, while the vessel, now quite out of control, was rapidly drifting towards it. Frantic, but ineffectual efforts were made to alter her course, and as a last resource two anchors were dropped, but the cables snapped as if they had only been twine. A terrible scene of confusion now ensued, some going down to the cabin to seize their effects, some praying, and others taking leave of their friends.

The ill-fated ship soon afterwards struck with fearful force on a reef of rocks on the east coast of Lambay, between the

Seal Hole and the extreme easterly point, called the Nose. Rising on the next wave, she struck heavily a second time, the sea making a clean sweep over her amidships, and carrying away nearly everything on deck. It was soon evident that the great ship was slowly sinking by the stern, and the passengers rushed

Portrane Castle.
(1906.)

up the hatchways, men carrying their children, and women with their infants in arms, screaming and imploring help.

Forced by the waves, the ship drifted on towards the side of the creek where she struck, whereupon several of the passengers prepared to jump ashore, but the first that did so, struck his head against the rocks and sank back into the angry surf, terribly cut and injured. The next person who jumped, made good his footing and was followed by a number of the Chinese and

Lascars, who scampered away with all haste up the rocks, without waiting to give any assistance to those on board. Another of the passengers then swung himself ashore by a rope, and retaining hold of it, managed to land safely a great many more. A number of young Irishwomen who endeavoured to get ashore in this manner lost hold of the rope and fell into the sea. The ship's doctor, Dr. Cunningham, made a desperate attempt to save his wife and child, but failing, perished with them. The rigging was crowded with hundreds, who, in their terror and confusion, frustrated each other's efforts to get ashore. At length the whole ship, with a lurch, sank below water, and in a few moments the remainder of the passengers, with the exception of two in the rigging, perished. The coast-guards arrived upon the scene soon afterwards, and at once proceeded to rescue the two survivors, but succeeded with only one, the other, who was near the top, having to be left in his terrible position, notwithstanding his piteous cries to be taken off. About two o'clock next morning, however, the storm having abated, they managed to rescue him after he had been in the rigging for fourteen hours.

Of the total number on board, only 282 were saved, and of these, many were severely maimed and injured. Owing to the density of the fog and the remoteness of the locality, no help was forthcoming from the mainland, and the terrible news did not become known in Dublin until the following afternoon, when the City of Dublin Steam Packet Company's boat *Prince* was despatched with all haste to the scene of the disaster. The *Prince* anchored about half a mile off the island, and the captain despatched three boats ashore to take off the survivors, who were discovered encamped in the neighbourhood of the Coast Guard Station, in a grassy hollow, sheltered by the hill. A few had gone in the early morning by fishing boats to Malahide, whence they travelled to Dublin by train.

The losses were most numerous among the women and children, of whom, 250 in number, only three were saved. The majority of the passengers were Irish emigrants who but a short time previously had set forth on their voyage full of anticipations of a prosperous future.

The inquest on the victims, which was opened a few days afterwards at Malahide, lasted three days, two of the bodies having been carried across from the island for the purpose. About 100 of the bodies were buried in the little churchyard on the island, near the harbour, and for a considerable time afterwards, divers were employed in searching for treasure sunk with the wreck.

The bay where the vessel struck has since been known as Tayleur Bay.

Situated on the straight road between the village of Donabate and the main road to Drogheda, is Turvey, the ancestral estate of the Barnewalls, Lords Trimblestown, and Barons of Turvey. The original mansion was built by Sir Christopher Barnewall in 1565, according to a tablet which formerly stood over the west gate, but which has since been placed at the back entrance to the residence. It bears the inscription—" The arms of Sir Christopher Barnewall and Dame Marion Sharle, *alias* Churley, " who made this house in Anno 1565." According to common tradition, the mansion was erected out of the materials of the famous Convent of Grace Dieu (see Index), which had been granted to Sir Patrick Barnewall at the Suppression of the Monasteries, and some colour is lent to this story by the complete disappearance of all vestiges of that extensive establishment, which can hardly be due to the mere efflux of time. Sir Patrick Barnewall seems to have resided at Grace Dieu for some years, as appears by a letter of his dated therefrom in 1540.

The original residence was taken down in the 18th century, and the present edifice, a plain building with a terrace in front, erected on its site. It probably is incorporated with some portions of the former structure, as it contains secret hiding-places, passages and staircases, which would be unlikely to enter into the design of a building of such recent date as the 18th century. In the garden at the back of the house is a tablet with an inscription, dated 1570, in memory of Lady Barnewall, *alias* Sharle, which formerly stood on old Turvey Bridge erected by her.

This manor belonged in the 15th century to the Ormonde family, by whom it was ceded in 1556 to Sir Christopher Barnewall, above mentioned, a lawyer of eminence, and High Sheriff of the County, who died here in 1575.

The Barnewalls are an ancient Breton family that came over to England with William the Conqueror, "le Sieur de Barneville," having been one of the knights in the service of that monarch at the Battle of Hastings. About the beginning of the 13th century, according to Stanihurst, a branch of the family established themselves at Berehaven, but were all slain by the Irish septs with the exception of Hugh de Barneville, who thereupon returned to England. In 1215 King John granted him the lands of Drimnagh and Terenure, in the County Dublin, which were held by his descendants until the reign of James I., when they were ceded to Sir Adam Loftus.

In 1461 Robert Barnewall was created a baron of Parliament by Edward IV., with the title of Lord Trimblestown, and about the same time his brother, Sir Nicholas Barnewall, was appointed Chief Justice of the Common Pleas in Ireland.

In 1563, Sir Christopher Barnewall, who was the popular leader of the Irish Parliament, strongly inveighed against the constitution of the Irish House of Commons, which was largely composed of non-residents and persons elected for non-corporate towns, and, therefore, not entitled to sit in Parliament. In 1575 there died at Turvey, as already stated, this distinguished member of the family, described by Hollinshed as " the lanthorn and light as well of his house " as of that part of Ireland where he dwelt ; who, being " sufficiently furnished as well with the knowledge of the " Latin tongue as of the common laws of England, was " zealously bent on the reformation of his country." His monument, as also that of his wife, is to be seen in the church of Lusk.

In 1597 the son of Lord Trimblestown was appointed to command a contingent of Anglo-Irish assembled at Mullingar for service against Hugh O'Neill, Earl of Tyrone. Richard Tyrrell, a gentleman of English descent, was selected by O'Neill to take the field against this contingent. The result was the battle of Tyrrell's Pass, where by a feint retreat, Tyrrell lured the Anglo-Irish into a narrow pass through a bog, and then fell upon them front and rear. An utter rout followed, the Anglo-Irish force was all but annihilated, and their commander, young Barnewall, was taken prisoner and sent in custody to the Earl of Tyrone.

During the troubles of 1641, Patrick Barnewall, of Kilbrew, one of the most influential and respected gentlemen of the Pale, surrendered himself to the Earl of Ormonde and received a safe conduct to Dublin, but nevertheless, on his arrival at the Castle, he was imprisoned and put on the rack, which torture he endured, according to Leland the historian, with so steady an avowal of his innocence, supported by abundant evidence, that the Lords Justices became ashamed of their cruelty, and to make amends to this unfortunate gentleman, permitted him to reside in Dublin, and took steps to protect his estate from spoliation by the soldiery. In the same year the Barnewalls took an important part in the muster on the hill of Tara, of the Catholic gentry of the Pale, to protest against the intolerant government of Lords Justices Parsons and Borlase at Dublin Castle.

Nicholas Barnewall, of Turvey, having fled, during this period of trouble, with his family to Wales, returned in a couple of years, whereupon the King, convinced of his loyalty, as attested by many services, created him, in 1645, Baron Turvey and Viscount Barnewall of Kingsland.

In 1650, Mathias, 8th Baron Trimblestown, having been excluded from the Act of Grace and Pardon, was outlawed and attainted by Cromwell and transplanted into Connaught, although he had taken no part in the civil wars; and in 1689 King James II. ordered the issue of a warrant annulling the

U

outlawry affecting the title, but the process was interrupted by the Revolution.

In 1691, Mathias, 10th Baron, was one of the hostages from the Irish Army pending the Treaty of Limerick, and after the violation of the Treaty, he and his brother entered the service of France as officers in the Irish Brigade. Lord Trimblestown fell in action in 1692, whereupon his brother returned to his native land and recovered the family estates. Other members of the family distinguished themselves in the French and Spanish services, and rose to positions of distinction.

In 1795 Thomas, 13th Baron, who had conformed to the Established Church, sought and obtained an annulment of the sentence of outlawry promulgated by Cromwell against his ancestor, and judgment of the reversal was duly entered in the records of the Court of King's Bench, as if issued in 1689, it having been established to the satisfaction of the Court that the King had intended to grant it in that year.

Distances in miles from G. P. O.—Swords, 9 ; Donabate village, 12½ ; Coastguard Station, 15, and back to G. P. O. by same route, 30 miles. A glance at the map will suggest other routes for the return journey, any of which will, however, add to the distance.

CHAPTER XXX

FINGAL—RUSH, SKERRIES, LUSK AND
BALDONGAN CASTLE

IN this, as in last excursion, we proceed by Drumcondra, continuing along the main road for a distance of about 3½ miles beyond Swords, when a finger-post will be seen at a place called Coldwinters, indicating the road to Skerries. Here we turn to the right, and in less than half a mile, again to the right, the road rising gradually until at length we obtain a view of Rogerstown creek with its adjacent marshy lands sloping down to the water. On the opposite side may be observed Ballisk and Donabate, to the seaward Lambay Island, and in the distance to the southwards, the Dublin mountains, dimly visible through the city smoke. After passing under a railway bridge, the road descends to sea level, running along the very shore of the creek, and although this track bears obvious evidences of periodic invasion by the sea, it is generally passable for cycles the whole way to where it leaves the shore and rises on to an embankment. Close to this point is Rogerstown pier, the modern representative of the ancient port of Rogershaven. We now enter the outskirts of Rush, a town extending for a distance of over two miles along the shore, and shortly afterwards pass the ruins of an old windmill conspicuously situated on a mound to the left of the road. Rush presents the appearance of considerable prosperity, the houses, even of the poorest inhabitants being remarkable for their cleanliness and neatness. At the eastern end of the town is a small harbour, which is somewhat difficult of access, and available only for small craft, besides being greatly exposed to heavy swells of the sea when the wind blows hard from the north-east. The pier was built here in the reign of James the Second.

Rush is mentioned by Hollinshed as being one of the chief haven towns of Ireland, and in more recent times was celebrated for its fisheries, particularly of ling, which were caught and cured in great quantities by the inhabitants. Adjoining the town is Kenure Park, containing a fine mansion, formerly known as Rush House, now the residence of the Palmer family. In 1666 the manor of Kenure was granted to the Duke of Ormonde, passing subsequently to the Echlin family, who have since become impoverished, and are now represented by Sir Henry Echlin, residing in England; and from the Echlin family the estate was purchased by an ancestor of the present proprietors. The house, which is a spacious and handsome structure, contains some fine paintings as well as a rare collection of vases, and other relics from Pompeii.

The estate derives its name from the old church of Kenure, dedicated to St. Catherine, the ruins of which still remain, together with some old tombstones, one of them marking the grave of Baron Hamilton of Strabane, who died in 1668, and who married a daughter of Christopher Fagan, of Feltrim. Several of the parish priests of the 18th century are also buried there, as well as a celebrated smuggler, Jack Connor, nick-named "Jack the Bachelor," who, after a most adventurous career, died in 1772. Between the ruin and the mansion is St. Catherine's holy well.

Continuing along the main street of Rush to where the finger-post indicates the road to Skerries, four miles distant, our route thither lies along a well kept road, with the sea in view for most of the way on the right. Just halfway, a road known as Featherbed Lane, leads on the right to the pretty little hamlet and harbour of Loughshinny, while a short distance northward is an old copper mine, which was worked until about 100 years ago. In the opposite direction from Lough-shinny, where the lane crosses the railway, there was formerly

Featherbed Lane Railway Station. On the coast, near Loughshinny, is a petrifying spring, mentioned in Rutty's *National
History of the County Dublin*, which deposits calcareous
incrustations upon the rocks over which it flows. From
Featherbed Lane the road falls the whole way to Skerries, a
town which, during the last thirty years, has come greatly
into vogue as a watering place, and has considerably extended
in consequence of the increased demand for accommodation

Loughshinny.
(1904.)

by visitors. It cannot, however, be said to possess any very
striking natural or artificial attractions. The most northerly
portion of the town, containing the harbour and Coastguard
Station, is known as Red Island, it having been at one time
entirely surrounded by the sea, though now connected with
the mainland by a narrow isthmus. Due east of Red Island
are Colt Island and St. Patrick's Island, neither of which is
inhabited, the latter containing the remains of an ancient
church belonging to a monastery established there at a remote
period, and recorded in the Annals of Munster to have been
burnt by the Danes in 797 A.D. The stones of this ruin,

at the angles, the edges of the roof, and in the remains of the
groined arches in the chancel, have become honeycombed
like a sponge by centuries of exposure to the weather. Adjoining the ruin, to the southward, is the still quite discernible
site of some buildings, doubtless those of the original
monastery.

About four miles east-north-east of Skerries is the islet of
Rockabill, which, with its lighthouse towering above the
waves, forms a remarkable object in the view from all parts
of the coast of Fingal, while its brilliant flashing red light
renders it no less conspicuous in the night time. A little
to the south-east of Skerries is Shenick's Island, accessible
from the mainland at low water.

About the year 1220 the situation of the monastery on
St. Patrick's Island having been found very inconvenient, the
Archbishop of Dublin erected the parochial church on the
mainland.

In March, 1675, the royal packet was wrecked on the rocks
here on its voyage to Chester, when a number of passengers,
including Lord Meath and his son, together with the captain
and most of the crew, perished.

In 1755 the Irish Parliament granted £2,000 for the construction of a pier at Skerries, and in 1767 £1,500 more for
the same purpose. It subsequently fell into decay, but was
repaired, and extended by Hans Hamilton, an ancestor of the
present Lord Holmpatrick.

The country around Skerries is prettily diversified, and
the ruins of a few old windmills, situated on adjacent eminences,
lend a somewhat picturesque effect. As we return from Red
Island along the main street, we come to a turn on the right,
past the Protestant church, where a finger-post shows the
road to Dublin. To reach Baldongan we take this road,
being careful, however, not to take the turn to the right from
it immediately outside the town. The road is uphill most
of the way to the ruins, which are conspicuously situated on
the summit of a rising ground, about two miles from Skerries,

commanding an extensive prospect of the surrounding country. The ruins now surviving consist of the eastern and western ends of what must originally have been an extensive castle and church, the materials of which were probably utilised to build the enclosing wall around the graveyard—still used as a burial ground. The most striking feature is the great tower of the church or abbey, 70 feet high and 22 feet square,

Skerries.
(1905.)

entered by an arched doorway, leading to a flight of 53 steps to the battlements, on the eastern side of which is a two-arched bell-turret. The buildings originally formed a spacious quadrangular court, flanked by four square towers, and were erected on the site of an ancient dun or moat.

In the beginning of the 16th century this castle belonged to the de Berminghams, from whom it passed by marriage into possession of the Howth family, subsequently being held by the Barnewalls with their manor of Balrothery. In June, 1642 it was defended by the Confederates of the Pale against the Parliamentary forces, and according to a contemporary tract entitled *New Intelligence from Ireland*, dated 17th June, 1642 Colonel Trafford besieged it with cannon, and put all the garrison, about 200 in number, to the sword, while two priests who were among the defenders, were examined on the rack and afterwards deported to France.

The following more detailed accounts of the siege appear in another tract or bulletin, undated, but evidently issued within a few days of the other :—

(1) " The Lords of the Pale are besieged in Baldongan " Castle by our forces, who sent to Dublin for Ordnance to " batter it, which was sent them, guarded with 400 men, but " what they have done is not yet knowne."

" Sunday last was the day appointed for a set battle, which " (it is said) was given, but what is done is not yet knowne ; " we hope to heare by the next post."

(2) " Colonell Trafford went out from us with some 1,000 " men to forage and light upon a part of the enemy, who " betook themselves to Baldongan Castle, some 12 miles from " us who besieged them.   Two large pieces were sent to him " which came there ; ten shot two shots [*sic*] onely that night ; " and on the next day they beat down the Castle and put all " to the sword which were about 200, none of any note in it, " but two Priests that were Captaines to those Rebells, one " of them was brought home, and was examined and put to the " Racke, but confessed little ; that day 26 Priests were shipped " for France, which deserve better to be hanged."

These interesting ruins are maintained in excellent order, and are easily accessible, as the field where they stand is entered by a stile from the road.

Leaving Baldongan, we turn to the left, descending the whole way to the main road, a mile distant, where we again turn to the left, reaching Lusk at a distance of 3½ miles from the ruins.   Lusk is one of the oldest ecclesiastical settlements in Ireland, dating from early Celtic times, as evidenced by the ancient round tower incorporated in the steeple built by the Anglo-Normans in the 13th Century.   The original Celtic community continued here up to the year 1180, when the establishment was taken possession of by the Anglo-Normans, and all the Celtic monks expelled, and replaced by nominees of John Comyn, Archbishop of Dublin.

Adjoining the church, on the western side, is the steeple, a massive square building, vaulted underneath, and flanked by four round towers, one of which, belonging to the ancient Celtic establishment, is readily distinguished from the others by its greater height. The three later ones were added by

Baldongan Castle.
(1904.)

the Anglo-Normans when they built the steeple, after taking over possession of the Celtic abbey.

In 1847 the modern church replaced the ancient edifice, which had been in a ruinous condition for many years, the roof having been blown off by the great storm of January, 1839. In the aisle of the old church was preserved a hideous stone figure, traditionally reputed to be a stone idol, formerly worshipped by the Danes of the district. It consisted of a representation of a human head, without neck or body, attached to a pair of kneeling thighs and legs.

During the erection of the present edifice the workmen found the coffin-plate of the Most Rev. Dr. Patrick Russell, Catholic Archbishop of Dublin in the reign of James II. It

bore the inscription—" Here underlieth ye body of Patrick
" Russell, Rom. Cathlick Ld. Arch. Bp. of Dublin and Primate
" of Ireland, son to James Russell, of Rush, who died in ye
" 63rd year of his age, on ye 14th of July, 1692, and in ye
" 9th year of his consecration."

The most interesting memorial in connection with the church
is, however, the costly and elaborate monument of Sir
Christopher Barnewall, of Turvey, and of his wife who survived
him and married Sir Lucas Dillon of Moymet, in the County
Meath. This monument is constructed of different kinds
of stone, most of the figures being sculptured in grey Italian
marble while the lower part of the tomb is Kilkenny marble.
The deceased knight is represented in a suit of armour, his
head uncovered and his hands joined on his breast in a devotional
attitude, and his feet resting on the body of a greyhound.
His consort appears lying beside him with her hands crossed
on her bosom, and her head reposing on an embroidered pillow.
The sides are embellished with the arms of Barnewall and
Dillon. On the eastern end of the tomb is the inscription—
" This monument is made for the Right Worshipfull Sr.
" Christopher Barnewall, of Turvey, Knight, by the Right
" Worshipfull Sr. Luckas Dillon, of Moymet, Knight, and
" Dame Marion Sharl, his wife, who married herr three years
" after the deathe of the said Sr. Christopher, herr first and
" lovinge hoosbande who had issue four sonnes and fifteen
" dauchters by herr. Wish well to Dillon, 1589." On
the northern sides are names of the nineteen children,
and at the western end—" Christopher Barnewall, Marion
" Sharl."

Another interesting monument is a black marble tomb,
bearing the effigy of a knight in armour, the visor open and
sword across the left thigh, and the hands joined over the
breast in an attitude of prayer. The inscription states that
it is " the monument of James Bermingham of Ballough, and
his wife Eleanor Fitzwilliam, who died in 1637."

Adjoining it is a tomb of Kilkenny marble, erected to the

memory of Sir Robert Echlin, Baronet, of Rush, who died in 1757. It bears the lines, taken from two of Pope's epitaphs :—

" Here lies an honest man without pretence,
Blessed with plain reason and with common sense ;
Calmly he looked on either life, and here
Saw nothing to regret or there to fear ;
From Nature's temperate feast rose satisfied,
Thanked Heaven that he had lived, and that—he died."

Lusk was several times burnt during the earlier period of its history—viz., in 1069 by accident, in 1089 by a party of marauders from Munster, when 180 persons perished in the church, and in 1133 by a similar visitation. Two years later the town, abbey, and surrounding district of Fingal were ravaged and burnt by Donald MacMurrough O'Melaghlin, King of Meath, in revenge for the murder of his brother, Connor. The townsfolk, however, offered considerable resistance, and slew O'Melaghlin on the occasion.

In 1375 the officers of " the harbour of Lusk " were instructed by Government to prevent the unlicensed exportation of corn from that port, and also prevent any of the retinue of William de Windsor, Chief Governor, from leaving Ireland thence, under penalty of forfeiting their horses, baggage, &c. (Dalton's *History*). As Lusk is nearly two miles from the sea, the harbour referred to is doubtless the old port of Rogers-haven already alluded to.

In 1641, Luke Netterville and others caused proclamation to be made at the market place of Lusk, for the assembling of the Irish Confederation of the Pale at Swords.

Leaving Lusk, we reach the main road again at Coldwinters, two miles distant, and on entering Swords, take the second turn to the right, inquiring the way to Knocksedan, where there is a very remarkable flat-topped fort or rath from which the locality derives its name. Knocksedan means " the hill " of the blast," from its exposed position, it being fifty feet above the bed of the river and commanding a considerable view. As we approach this place we may observe, on the left, the extensive demesne and wooded glen of Brackenstown, variously known in former times as Bractenston, Brecknanstown, Breekneckston, and by Dean Swift as Brackdenstown. In the 16th century this estate was owned by the Burnell family; from them it passed to the Nugents, who, in the reign of James the First, sold it to one Bysse, whose son became Recorder of Dublin, and subsequently Chief Baron.

By a marriage with Chief Baron Bysse's only daughter and heiress, the estate passed into the possession of the Molesworths, who subsequently became the Viscounts Molesworth of Swords. The celebrated Drapier's letters were addressed by Swift to Lord Molesworth at " Brackdenstown." In the year 1711 a deputation of the Lower House of Convocation waited on the Lord Lieutenant to present him with an address. Lord Molesworth, who was present, made no attempt to conceal his aversion to the Convocation, which he suspected of sympathy with the Pretender, and muttered in their hearing, " Those " that have turned the world upside down are come hither." For this gross insult to the Convocation his name was struck off the list of the Privy Council.

On high ground at the opposite side of the road, and close to the cross roads, is the gaunt ruin of Brazeel House, the residence of Sir Richard Bolton, Lord Chancellor of Ireland, in the reign of Charles the First. He was a distinguished lawyer, and published the first editions of the *Irish Statutes*, as well as *The Justices of the Peace for Ireland*. In 1640 he was impeached in the House of Commons for having assisted the Earl of Strafford in the introduction of arbitrary government into Ireland. In 1661, however, all records of this transaction were voted to be expunged, " inasmuch as they " seemed to be an entrenchment upon the honour, worth, " and integrity of honourable persons, whose memory this " House cannot, in justice, suffer to be sullied with the least " stain of evil report." (Dalton's *History*).

"Edward Bolton, Esquire, of Brazille" is mentioned in the Acts of Attainder of 1689. Brazeel House was burnt early in the last century, on which occasion it is stated that a unique portrait of Sir Richard Bolton was destroyed.

In 1647 Owen Roe O'Neill and Sir Thomas Esmonde, in command of a force of Royalists, after defeating a Parliamentary force and capturing Castleknock, marched to Brazeel and encamped there that night.

The road past this place by Ballyboghil and Naul is the most direct road to Drogheda, and was the route by which many of the Jacobites retreated to Dublin after their defeat at the Boyne. On the night of the battle, the Duke of Berwick rallied 7,000 infantry at this spot, and sent word to King James (his father) who had preceded him to Dublin, to send him some cavalry to enable him to continue his retreat safely to the metropolis. The King accordingly sent nine troops of cavalry to march to the Duke's relief, and the whole force shortly afterwards broke up their camp and marched away.

Turning to the left at the cross roads, and crossing the Ward river by Knocksedan bridge, a fine, well-kept road conducts us to Glasnevin, at a distance of 8 miles from Swords.

Distances from G. P. O.—Swords, 9 miles; Rush, 15; Rush Coastguard Station, 16; Skerries, 20; Baldongan Castle, 22½; Lusk, 25½; Swords, 30½; Knocksedan, 33; G. P. O. 41.

In the preparation of this chapter, information has been obtained from an article by the late Rev. Dr. Stokes on Lusk, &c., in the *Journal of the Royal Society of Antiquaries* for 1890.

CHAPTER XXXI

HOWTH—THE OLD MAIL ROAD ; THE CASTLE, A RAMBLE AROUND THE HILL

THE road distinctively known as "The Howth Road" starts from the shore at the eastern side of Clontarf Crescent, and after passing inland for a distance of about four miles, again meets the shore at a place marked in old maps and still locally known as "The Whip of the Water," whence it skirts the coast for a mile and a half, then crosses the isthmus of Sutton in an oblique direction, and ultimately reaches Howth Town at a distance of nine miles from Dublin.

It has been the subject of remark that this road, which in width and mode of construction, presents the appearance of a great highway, is strangely out of proportion to its actual importance as a thoroughfare, and that the existence of a mere fishing village at its extremity could not have been sufficient reason for constructing it in so costly and elaborate a fashion. It should, however, be remembered that Howth, when it was constituted the mail packet station in 1809, thereby became entitled to rank as a port of the first importance, and the construction of a high road to Dublin was at once rendered necessary to enable the mails and Government despatches to be forwarded to the city with as little delay as possible. This work, which consisted mainly of improving and altering the old road, was entrusted to Telford, the eminent engineer who constructed the great Holyhead and London Road, of which the Howth Road was, for postal purposes, regarded as a continuation. The two roads were, indeed, made under the same contract, and were sometimes spoken of as " The Dublin and London Road."

There is little of interest to be seen until the village of Raheny is passed, owing to the high walls by which the road is to a great extent enclosed. At a distance of 2½ miles from the Crescent, the road dips sharply, where it crosses the valley of the Santry River, and at the head of the rising ground on the opposite side, enters the village of Raheny (pronounced *Rahenny*), anciently Rath Enna or Enna's Fort. The cir-

Kilbarrack Church.
(1903.)

cumvallations of this rath are still distinguishable in places near the old Protestant church, which is built on the site of a more ancient edifice that stood within the circuit of the rath. St. Ossan's holy well was formerly in the field between the church and the railway station, but it is now covered up, and its waters drain into the Santry River close by. A depression in the ground and a bush still marks its site.

A mile beyond Raheny, the road by a long decline reaches the shore, at " The Whip of the Water," where it meets the electric tramway, and presently passes the storm-beaten ruins of the ancient church of Kilbarrack, the most conspicuous object along the flat unbroken sweep of shore. In its lonely churchyard sleep many who, in times more perilous for sea-

farers, were cast up by the waves—some, unknown and un-
identified, passengers of stout ships wrecked upon the
treacherous shallows off the shore—others, fisher folk caught
by the tide or overwhelmed by sudden storm in their frail skiffs.

Beneath an illegible headstone in this churchyard is buried
the notorious Higgins, better known as "The Sham Squire."

In a little over half a mile beyond Kilbarrack we reach the
isthmus of Sutton, on which the Howth and Hill tram lines
intersect. On the right, as we proceed towards Howth, will
be seen the square tower known as Corr Castle, and sometimes
called "The Dane's Castle," standing in the old racecourse.
This building has been supposed to be the remnant of a more
extensive structure, but was probably only an outpost of
Howth Castle, built in this position so as to command a view
of the sea on each side of the isthmus, which would have been
a great advantage in the troublous times when it was erected.
It was formerly used as a standhouse when the races were
held here.

A mile beyond this point the road enters Howth town,
within the memory of many, a village of miserable hovels, but
greatly improved and extended in recent years.

About the beginning of the last century, when it had been
decided to supersede the Pigeonhouse as a Packet Station,
and to construct a large harbour at either Howth or Dunleary,
the relative merits of both these sites were fully discussed
and fiercely contested by the champions of the two localities.
A pamphlet on the subject was published, the following extracts
from which afford interesting glimpses of the conditions of
travelling in those days :—

" Let us ask the coachman driving the coach from the Post
" Office to Howth, would not more danger attend the
" passengers, coach, and horses going from the Post Office
" to Howth than to Dunleary ?   What would become of the
" passengers if a coach wheel broke on such a road as that lead-
" ing from Rathany to ' The Whiskey Forge ' at the foot
" of the hill ?" [14]

What, indeed! It is too dreadful to contemplate! They might have had to wait for another coach, or even to walk to Howth, a mile distant!

This worthy pamphleteer further depicts in lurid colours the perils of this terrible road :—" Let any man of common " sense travel the road from Dublin to Howth. Let him there " see what security he can find for his person or property " in a dark night. He should have a troop of horse to guard " him against land robbers ; and at high water, which at " times must be when the mail coach goes that way, he ought " to have a gunboat sailing along the strand inside of the " North Bull to prevent sea pirates from attacking him and " plundering him on the coast ! And having got his property " they need only row across the bay and share the booty in " safety."

As the average depth of the water between the North Bull and Sutton Strand is insufficient to enable one even to bathe comfortably, it is doubtful if the gunboat would have been much assistance against the "sea pirates" alluded to.

The advantages of the Dunleary road are, on the other hand, set forth as follows :—" You can throw a stone from house " to house the whole way ; there is no need to be under " apprehension of land or sea robbers attacking the mail coach, " and, at their leisure, making off with impunity. There, at " least, the expense of a troop of horse or a gunboat would " be saved."

Despite the arguments in favour of Dunleary, for which place the pamphleteer evidently held a brief, Howth triumphed, though its triumph was indeed of short duration, and the first stone of the new pier there was laid in 1807. The work was no sooner finished, however, than its worthlessness became evident, and notwithstanding the fact that over £300,000 had been spent on it, an agitation was set on foot for the construction of another harbour at Dunleary, as that at Howth was filling up so rapidly with sand and mud that it was only with considerable difficulty that sufficient depth could be maintained for the Holyhead packets.

It has been generally stated that if the harbour had been constructed a little more to the east, at Balscadden Bay, it would have fulfilled all the purposes for which it was intended.

When the steam packets commenced plying about 1818, the duration of the voyage to Holyhead was reduced to about seven hours, which was a great improvement on the speed of the sailing packets.

The earliest record we have of Howth is a reference to it on a map compiled by the Alexandrian geographer, Ptolemy, early in the second century. In this map Howth is represented as a small island called Edri Deserta, and in the Greek text Edrou Heremos, both names meaning the desert of Edar, the ancient name of Howth. Ptolemy, who never visited Ireland, and prepared his map from the accounts given to him by others, may well be excused for supposing Howth to be an island, when we consider the flat, narrow isthmus which connects it with the mainland, and, besides, we know that almost the entire shores of Dublin Bay have been rising within historic times, so that it is possible that the isthmus may have been covered, or nearly covered, at high water at least, when the Alexandrian prepared his chart 1,800 years ago.

Gerard Boate, in his *Natural History of Ireland* (1652), also notices the resemblance of Howth to an island :—" Hoath " a great high mountain, three or four miles compass in the " botom, having the sea on all sides except the west side, " where with a long narrow neck it is joined to the land, which " neck, being low ground, one may from either side see the sea " over it ; so that afar it seemeth as if it were an island. This " head may be seen a great way off at sea, for even upon the land " one may very perfectly see it, not only upon the key of Dublin, " which is six miles from thence, but nine or ten miles further " westward."

It was, indeed, at one time proposed to cut a wide ship channel across the isthmus at its narrowest part, to be called "The "Sound of Howth," and it was claimed by the projectors that the navigability of the Port of Dublin would be improved thereby.

Twiss, in his *Tour Through Ireland* (1775), states that the appearance of Howth from Stillorgan obelisk is exactly like that of the Rock of Gibraltar.

The ancient name of Howth, Ben Edar, meaning the Hill of Edar, is said to commemorate a Dedannan chieftain of that name who was buried on the hill. The modern name of Howth is a modification of the Scandinavian word Hoved, a head, which name was given to it by the Norse freebooters who settled along these coasts in early times.

Prior to 1844, when the railway was completed, Howth was a very primitive place indeed, the village consisting of wretched thatched cabins inhabited by poor fishermen. Nevertheless, a Sunday drive there on a "jingle" was one of the most popular diversions of the Dublin folk 100 years ago, while some were even hardy enough to essay a climb over the rocks and wild heather-clad hills.

A poet of the day thus describes these excursions and the primitive conveyances in which they were made :—

"Well might an artist travel from afar
"To view the structure of a low-backed car ;
"A downy mattress on a car is laid,
"The father sits beside his tender maid.
"Some back to back, some side to side are placed :
"The children in the centre interlaced.
"By dozens thus, full many a Sunday morn,
"With dangling legs the jovial crowd is borne :
"Clontarf they seek, or Howth's aspiring brow,
"Or Leixlip smiling on the stream below."

One of the principal objects of interest at Howth is the Castle, to the grounds of which visitors are generally admitted on Saturdays in summer, and on certain other days advertised by the Railway Company.

Of the original stronghold of the Howth family little information is forthcoming, either in history or tradition. The present structure seems to consist of several portions erected at different periods, but is known to have been, to a great extent, rebuilt in the middle of the 16th century by Christopher, twentieth Lord of Howth. It is an embattled building flanked by two square towers, and approached by a terrace and flight of steps leading into a spacious hall, which extends the whole length of the Castle. Among the pictures is a valuable portrait of Dean Swift, painted by Bindon in 1735, representing Wood, the notorious patentee of the base half-pennies, writhing in agonies at Swift's feet. The Dean was a frequent visitor at the Castle, to which he usually rode on horseback, and allusions to these visits are to be found in his writings. A number of antique weapons and articles of armour are also preserved in the Castle, and among them is an immense two-handed sword, said to have belonged to Sir Armoricus Tristram, the founder of the Howth family.

This Tristram was one of the Norman adventurers who came over to Ireland at the time of the Invasion, and had achieved a distinguished record for his prowess on many a hard-fought field. He and Sir John De Courcy sailed to Howth in 1177, accompanied by a chosen band of fighting men, and on landing were opposed by the inhabitants, mostly Danish pirates who had settled in this neighbourhood. A desperate battle was fought at " The Bridge of Evora," which crossed the small river, called " The Bloody Stream," flowing into the sea near the railway station, and, after heavy losses on both sides, the natives were completely defeated. This battle having been fought on 10th August (Feast of St. Laurence, the Spaniard), the Tristram family, in commemoration of the event, thereafter assumed the name of St. Lawrence. The following extract on the subject is taken from Hanmer's *Chronicles of Ireland*, but it may be observed that his account rests on no very certain authority, and that the entire circumstances connected with the landing and battle at Evora are involved in consiɑerable obscurity :—" They landed at Howth " and there fought a cruell fight by the side of a bridge, where " Sir John De Courcy, being sickly, tarried about the shippe. " Sir Armoricus, being chieftaine and generall of the field " by land, behaved himselfe most worthily. Many were " slaine on both sides, but Sir Armoricus got the victory, with " the losse of seven of his owne blood, sonnes, uncles, and

Howth and Tower Hill.
(1900.)

" nephewes ; whereupon, for his singular valour, and good " service, there performed, that lordship was allotted unto " him for his part of the conquest."

A vague tradition of this battle seems to have lingered in the neighbourhood, and is to some extent corroborated by the discoveries of human bones, antique weapons and armour, which from time to time have been made during excavations for building purposes in the vicinity of the railway station.

The most interesting object in the town, from an antiquarian point of view, is the Abbey, situated on the heights overhanging the harbour, with its burial ground, surrounded by an embattled wall. In the south aisle is the tomb of Christopher, twentieth lord of Howth, who died in 1589, and of his wife

Elizabeth, both of whom are represented by figures in high relief on the slab of the monument. Adjoining the burial ground is an ancient monastic establishment, now called " The College of Howth," which, from the character of its architecture, appears to date from the same period as the Abbey.

We now leave the town to make our way to the Old Bailey Lighthouse, but if the journey be considered too fatiguing, or the time be limited, better take the Hill tram from the Railway Station. If it be decided to walk, a choice of three routes is available—namely, the old Lighthouse road up Balglass hill, to the right of the new Catholic Church, the road to the left of the church, and the cliff path. The latter is much the most picturesque route, but it entails an addition of about a mile to the journey, and is somewhat rougher walking than the roads. To reach the path, we proceed by the road skirting Balscadden Bay, overshadowed by Tower Hill, from the Martello tower on which the submarine cable to England is carried into the sea at Balscadden Bay under the two notice boards marked " Telegraph." The cable formerly started from a station on the shore, but the entire structure was demolished one night in a storm, and the cable was thereupon removed to the Martello tower.

We next pass under the precipitous heights of Kilrock, to the summit of which there is a footpath diverging on the right from the road.

Along the road from Balscadden Bay to Kilrock quarries may be seen the stones, now utilised as kerbstones, which were used over a hundred years ago to form the roadway by which rocks were conveyed from the quarries to the shore for the construction of the harbour. Many of these stones are curiously grooved in parallel lines, probably caused by either chains or projections from the lorries carrying the rocks.

The Cliff path commences at Kilrock by a steep ascent, and then passes between wooden posts on the left, beside a small wayside hostelry. From this part of the hill there is an extensive view of the coast of Fingal as far north as Rush, whose long rows of white cottages are plainly visible to the naked eye. Malahide and Swords are concealed from view by Malahide or Carrick Hill rising above the flat, sandy shores of Portmarnock and the glistening expanse of the Velvet Strand, while to the right, forming prominent objects in the view, will be seen Lambay Island and Ireland's Eye.

Immediately on the left, as we proceed towards the old Bailey, is the precipitous headland known as the Nose of Howth, which forms the north-eastern point of the promontory, and from this the path turns nearly at right angles to the southward. A track diverging to the left leads to the Nose, but it runs perilously close to the edge of the cliffs, and is not to be recommended. Our track now skirts the edges of tremendous cliffs—jagged and bare—with the dark surging waters breaking in huge waves far below, while on the inner side is a wild tract of moorland, interspersed with heather, bracken and furze—gay in its colouring of purple and gold.

We next reach the bold headland known as the Casana Rock, a great resort of sea birds, which at times nearly cover it, their plaintive cries echoing among the cliffs and mingling with the roar of the surf. Near this point the first glimpse is obtained of the Wicklow coast, Wicklow Head being readily identified by its two old lighthouses, and to the right may be seen the long flat sweep of shore extending to Greystones, the houses of which show conspicuously in the sunshine.

This precipitous portion of the coast was the scene of a lamentable shipping disaster in 1853. The steamship *Queen Victoria*, on a voyage from Liverpool to Dublin, with about 100 passengers and cargo, struck on the southern side of the Casana rock during a dense snowstorm, between 2 and 3 o'clock on the morning of the 15th February. Eight of the passengers managed to scramble overboard on to the rocks, from which they made their way up the cliffs to the Bailey Lighthouse. The captain, without further delay, ordered the vessel to be backed, so as to float her clear of the rocks, but she proved to be more seriously injured than was imagined, and began to fill rapidly when she got into deep water. Drifting helplessly towards the Bailey, she struck the rocky base of the Lighthouse promontory, and sank in fifteen minutes afterwards, with her bowsprit touching the shore. The *Roscommon* steamer fortunately happened to pass while the ill-fated vessel was sinking, and, attracted by the signals of distress, promptly put out all her boats and rescued between 40 and 50 of the passengers. About 60, however, were drowned, including the captain.

After a protracted inquest extending over several days, the jury found that the disaster was due to the culpable negligence of the captain and the first mate, in failing to slacken speed during a snowstorm which obscured all lights, they well knowing at the time that they were approaching land. The mate was subsequently put on trial for manslaughter.

It was believed by many that if the captain had not, in the first instance, backed off the rocks into deep water, all on board could have been saved.

From the Nose to the Bailey Lighthouse the water is sufficiently deep to enable coasting steamers to keep close to the shore, and from this part of the hill may frequently be observed the operation of taking a pilot by incoming vessels. Indeed, no better point of vantage than the heights over the Bailey can be found for watching the various craft passing to and fro on this maritime highway.

Immediately beyond the Casana Rock some stupendous cliff scenery is passed, after which the path, rising higher, comes into view of Bray Head, the Sugar Loaves, Dalkey Island and the Muglins. Then the Bailey promontory, properly known as Duncriffan, green and smooth as a carpet, with the lighthouse, is seen in front, and on the opposite coast, Dalkey, Killiney, and Ballybrack hills, their green slopes dotted all over with villa residences, Kingstown obscured by its smoke, and beyond it the familiar form of Carrickgollogan surmounted by its chimney. Towering above Carrickgollogan may be seen the dark form of Douce, one of the highest mountains in the view southward.

Across the sea, eastward, will often be seen, in clear weather, Holyhead mountain, Snowdon and the Llanberis Pass, while to the southward of these will sometimes be seen the outlines of Cader Idris.

On approaching the old Bailey, which stands in a commanding position, 475 feet above the sea, it will be well to diverge

The Old Bailey Lighthouse.

from the path and ascend the heights to the right so as to reach the old lighthouse. The cottage known as the old Bailey is, owing to its white colour and conspicuous position, visible a great distance off, and consists of two portions, one of much more recent date than the other. The small massively built structure was portion of the old lighthouse, and the remainder is an addition to the older portion, to increase the accommodation after it had come to be utilised as a dwellinghouse. The circular base of the old lighthouse tower, with portion of the walls, adjoins the cottage, and the masonry is still in excellent preservation. The condition of the base, and the absence of any ruins or debris, would point to the probability

that when this lighthouse fell into disuse, after the erection
of the modern one in 1814, the tower was taken down to supply
building material for some of the adjoining cottages.

The old Bailey lighthouse is believed to have been erected
by Robert Readinge in the reign of Charles II., and, like most
of its contemporaries, was placed so high that it was often
hidden by fogs hanging around the heights when it was clear
at sea level.

The mound under the base of the tower will, if examined,
be found to consist of cinders and debris thrown down from
an old beacon tower which stood there prior to the erection
of the lighthouse in Charles the Second's time.

Early in the last century the Port authorities decided to
supersede the old lighthouse, and, accordingly, in 1814, the
existing structure was erected on Duncriffan promontory,
which up to that time bore, in excellent preservation, the lines
of circumvallation of King Criffan' fortress of 1,900 years
ago, and in consequence got the name of the Bailey, or Bally,
from the Irish bailĕ (Low Latin, ballium, a fortress). Some
portions of the fosses are yet discernible across the neck of the
promontory.

In the *Annals of the Four Masters* there is a record of King
Criffan's return, with numerous spoils of war, from an expedition
abroad, and of his death, in his fort at Duncriffan, Ben Edar,
in the year 9 A.D.

In making some excavations at the new lighthouse about
twenty-five years ago, large quantities of human remains were
found—probably relics of the battle fought here in 646 A.D.,
between Kings Conall and Kellagh, joint kings of Ireland,
and Aengus, who, as son of the previous king, disputed the
sovereignty with them.

Leaving the old Bailey, we take the road down towards the
tram station, turning to the left along the main road, which
now descends considerably, and bends towards the westward.
The Bailey lighthouse and promontory now come again into
view on the left, and as we turn the corner of the road, we

may dimly distinguish, through the overhanging smoke, the
more conspicuous buildings of the city, the tall twin chimneys
at Ringsend, and to the right, the flat, sandy reaches of Dollymount and the North Bull. We now pass a station on the
tram line appropriately called " Bay View," and from this
point the line runs along the road, on which there is little of
interest to notice until the station called " Barren Hill " is
passed, so called from the heather-clad height with that name

The Bailey Lighthouse.
(1904.)

adjoining. Immediately beyond this station will be seen a
whitewashed cottage on the right—open the iron gate beside
the cottage, and pass along by the wall to the top of the field,
where turn to the right till a path is reached. Follow this path
round the side of the hill known as Shelmartin, which lies
immediately to the right, and can be ascended from any point
along the pathway if desired.

From this part of the hill there is a fine view of the isthmus
and houses of Sutton, the peninsula and sands of Portmarnock,
and the splendid plain of Moy Bra. We now cross a stile
adjoining a cottage with pointed windows, beyond which the
pathway crosses a tract of grass and rushes, often swampy in

rainy weather. Another stile is presently reached beside a wooden gate, from which the pathway passes through a jungle of bracken often as high as one's head.

Immediately in front now appears the rocky height known as Dunhill, on the summit of which there stood in former times, before the introduction of the electric telegraph, a post office semaphore station. It may be here remarked that the semaphore system was very much more efficient than is generally supposed, and messages were often sent by it with a rapidity which would astonish modern telegraph operators. Of course its great fault was that even a partial fog paralysed the whole system.

In the summer this hill is generally one mass of purple heather—mostly the brilliant bell variety, not that known as ling.

A few hundred yards from the last-mentioned stile the pathway branches ; keep to the left and cross the stile beside an iron gate, pass along by the hedge on the right at the top of the field until a turnstile is reached. from which take the path across the field to the road and then turn to the left down Balglass hill into the town.

At the foot of Carrickmore, the precipice overhanging Howth demesne, is a cromlech of considerable size, the top of which has slipped from its supports and fallen to the ground. It is traditionally reputed to mark the burial place of a daughter of Aengus of Ben Edar, named Aideen, who died of grief at the loss of her husband, Oscar, at a battle at Gavra, near Tara, in the year 284 A.D.

This incident has been made the subject of a beautiful poem, entitled " Aideen's Grave," by the late Sir Samuel Ferguson :—

" They heaved the stone, they heap'd the cairn :
　　Said Ossian, ' In a queenly grave
　We leave her 'mong her fields of fern,
　　Between the cliff and wave.

" ' The cliff behind stands clear and bare,
    And bare, above, the heathery steep
Scales the clear heaven's expanse, to where
    The Danaan Druids sleep.

" ' And all the sands that, left and right,
    The grassy isthmus-ridge confine,
In yellow bars lie bare and bright
    Among the sparkling brine.

" ' A clear pure air pervades the scene,
    In loneliness and awe secure ;
Meet spot to sepulchre a queen
    Who in her life was pure.

      *   *   *   *

" ' When, mingling with the wreckful wail,
    From low Clontarf's wave-trampled floor
Comes booming up the burthened gale,
    The angry Sand-Bull's roar.

      *   *   *   *

" ' And here, hard by her natal bower
    On lone Ben Edar's side, we strive
With lifted rock and sign of power
    To keep her name alive.' "

      *   *   *   *

The circuit of the hill, as herein described, entails a walk of six miles ; but this can be reduced to four and a quarter miles by taking the tram from the Summit Station to Barren Hill.

The wilder portions of the hill and Ireland's Eye are dealt with in the next chapter.

The following authorities were consulted in preparing this chapter :—*The Journal of the Royal Society of Antiquaries* for 1895, containing articles on Howth by Mr. Robert Cochrane and the Rev. C. T. M'Cready ; *A Day at Howth*, by the late Mr. Huband Smith ; Dalton's *History of the County Dublin ;* Wakeman's *Old Dublin ;* and some articles in *The Dublin Penny Journal* and *The Irish Penny Magazine.*

CHAPTER XXXII.

HOWTH—ITS HILLS AND WILDS

THE Howth road and the circuit of the hill have been described in the previous chapter, and it now remains but to deal with some wilder and less frequented portions of the peninsula, which are outside the range of the ordinary excursion. We start by taking a return ticket on the tram to Sutton cross roads, whence we follow the hill tram line for about three quarters of a mile, and then turn to the right, keeping along the shore throughout. As we leave the cross roads, Carrickmore, Dun Hill, and Shelmartin look very high and precipitous—the last being prettily variegated by bright green fields along its lower slopes. Near St. Finton's Terrace, some fifty years ago, there were extensive manganese and lime works, from which dolomite or magnesian limestone was exported to England, where the magnesia was separated from the lime and converted into various valuable products. Black oxide of manganese was also found abundantly for some time, but soon became worked out.

Along the shore road we pass a number of pretty houses and villas, the builders, no doubt, having been attracted by the sheltered position, facing the sunny south-west, and protected by the hill from the harsh easterly winds of spring. The westerly gales, however, blow at times here with considerable violence, and as a result the sea undermined the road to such an extent that it has become necessary in places to have it embanked.

The road ends at the Coastguard Station, and we now take the pathway skirting the shore, presently passing a Martello tower in a dilapidated condition, situated on a point of rock

overhanging the sea. Immediately beyond this we cross a
stile, and thence keep to the right by a narrow track around
" The Red Rock," where in summer time may be observed
some splendid colour effects, the bright yellow of the furze
blossom mingling with the delicate green of its foliage, while
interspersed among the red and yellow tints of the rocks are
purple patches of heather. The pathway at length conducts
us to the very water's edge, passing a little cove and boat-
house, beyond which it crosses a low grassy tract, and at length
reaches a stile and iron gate. Ascending again, over the
rocks, and rounding Drumleck Point, we come into view
of an old wire foot-bridge on the right, constructed many
years ago for bathing purposes. The Ordnance Survey mark
on their 6-inch Map the site of a castle at Drumleck Point,
but no tradition in regard to it has ever been traced, and it is
doubtful if it ever existed. Between Drumleck Point and
The Needles is a cave, which some antiquarians claim to have
identified as one of the hiding places of Dermot and Grania.
We next pass the group of detached jagged rocks known as
" The Needles," and a short distance further, the pathway
conducts us to a field, on the opposite side of which will be
seen a notice-board bearing the words " public right of way."
Following the route indicated on the notice, we reach a well-
defined path passing through a tract of bracken, and ultimately
leading us out on the neck of the Bailey promontory. From
this point we make our way along the steep road leading to the
summit station of the hill tramway, where we cross the line
beside the station, and turn to the left along a narrow by-road.
Keeping still to the left, we at length leave the road near a
gateway on the right, and enter a delightful wilderness of
furze, bracken, heather, and sward, over which on the left
rises a precipitous height, surmounted by a carn called " The
Cross," where a cross stood down to 100 years ago. On the
summit of Carrickbrack Hill adjoining, are the remains of
another carn of considerable size. Keeping to the right in the
little defile, after a short ascent we reach the summit of Black

Linn, 560 feet high, the highest point of Howth—a distinction commonly, but erroneously, ascribed to Shelmartin, which, though it does not look it, is really 10 feet lower. Between " The Cross " and Black Linn, and extending therefrom in a westerly direction, is a heather-clad tract, known as Blackheath, traversed by a path, along which we may make our way to Shelmartin.

The view from Black Linn includes an unbroken view of the sea from Wicklow Head, with its three lighthouses on the south, to the point of land at the extremity of the long village of Rush on the north. Southward will be observed Bray Head, Greystones, the two Sugar Loaves, Dalkey, Killiney, Kingstown and the long range of familiar heights extending westward until lost in the haze and smoke of the city, while on clear days may be discerned the blue profile of the mountains of Wales. Looking towards the city, the hill with the sharp summit intercepting the view of Clontarf is Shelmartin, and to the right of that is the rocky height called Dun Hill, formerly a semaphore signal station. Between us and the harbour are the lower elevations known as the Loughoreen Hills, and under the western side of the hill is an undulating tract bearing the strange name of the Ben of Howth. Between Black Linn and Shelmartin is a slightly rising ground known as Knocknabohil.

A very ancient Celtic town of Howth was believed by Dr. Petrie and the Rev. J. F. Shearman to have existed in the Cross Garvey field, close to the Ben of Howth.

Following the path across Blackheath, we at length reach Shelmartin, which presented a dismal spectacle for some years after it was burnt in 1905, looking as bare and arid as a desert. From its summit one sees to the northward the precipitous height overhanging the demesne, known as Carrickmore, to the left of which is the isthmus, so low and narrow that it looks from here as if the sea could easily wash over it. It has been stated, though without any reliable authority, that King Criffan, who died at Duncriffan, now the Bailey promontory, in the year 9 A.D., is buried under the carn on the summit of Shelmartin.

Descending the hill, we may make our way towards the cottage on the northern side, until we meet the path skirting the rocky height of Dun Hill, by which we can return to Howth town either by taking the first turn to the left, or continuing the pathway through a picturesque tract of gorse and heather until a wooden gate is seen on the left leading into a wood. From this point a field-path conducts us to the old Lighthouse road, leading by Balglass Hill into the town, or if desired, the tram can be taken to the railway station.

As some of the visitors to Howth may be disposed to cross over to Ireland's Eye, a brief account of that island will not be out of place in this chapter. It was originally called Irish-Ereann—*i.e.*, Eria's Island, Eria being a woman's name. This in time became confounded with Erin, and the name of the island then successively assumed the forms of " Erin's Ey " (" Ey " a Danish word, meaning an island), " Ireland's Ey," and lastly " Ireland's Eye," in which meaningless designation not a vestige of the ancient name has survived.

Rabbits are found on the island, and, in ancient times it was noted for a fine breed of goshawks, which used to build their nests on its rocks. These were highly valued in the olden time, when falconry was a royal sport, and every nobleman and gentleman kept his hawks.

The ruin of St. Nessan's Church on Ireland's Eye may be fitly described as an antiquarian forgery. It was an interesting ruin in 1843, when it was sketched by the late Mr. Wakeman, but soon afterwards, it was restored without any regard to its former condition or appearance, and, as a result, it is now almost impossible to identify it with the sketches of Petrie and Wakeman. It cannot even be said that the materials of the modern ruin are those of the old church, as portions which had long previously disappeared were reproduced in the restored edition. It is stated by Petrie that the doorway of the

Y

original structure was taken down in order to utilise the stones in building the Catholic Church at Howth.

St. Nessan's Church, owing to its exposed position, was in early times constantly pillaged by Danish and English marauders, and it is recorded that Irghalach, King of Bregia, was slain in one of these attacks. It is not, therefore, surprising that, as the original ecclesiastic establishment of Howth, it was

St. Nessan's Church, Ireland's Eye, in 1843.
(*From a sketch by W. F. Wakeman.*)

for security transferred to the mainland in 1235, from which date the church on Ireland's Eye was probably allowed to fall into decay.

There cannot, however, have been any permanent monastic establishment here, as there are no indications of foundations near the church, and any stone building would have left some traces after it, seeing that the island has not been inhabited since the abandonment of the church, and has scarcely been disturbed by tillage operations.

The wild beauty of the island will amply repay one for the

trouble of visiting it ; the most interesting portion being the eastern side, where the detached rocks are of great size and fantastic shapes, and hollowed out by the action of the sea into numerous caves. On this side also is the scene of the now almost forgotten Kirwan murder—a terrible tragedy of the last century.

The view from the heights comprises, to the south—the hill, harbour, and town of Howth, with the castle embosomed in its woods ; to the right of these, the Isthmus of Sutton ; and then, in succession, Baldoyle, Portmarnock, and to the northward the fertile tract of Fingal ; while across the city haze may be discerned the rounded forms of the Dublin mountains, their summits outlined in picturesque profile, and their bases indistinct and blurred by the smoke of the Metropolis.

In the preparation of this article the following authorities have been consulted :—*The Journal of the Royal Society of Antiquaries* for 1895, containing articles on " Howth " by Mr. Robert Cochrane and the Rev. C. T. M'Cready ; " A Day " at Howth," by the late Mr. Huband Smith ; Dalton's *History of the County Dublin ;* Wakeman's *Old Dublin* ; *Irish Names of Places ;* and some articles in *The Dublin Penny Journal* and *The Irish Penny Magazine.*

The circuit described in this chapter entails a walk of between six and seven miles, which may be reduced by taking the tram back from the Summit.

CHAPTER XXXIII

KILMAINHAM, CHAPELIZOD, PALMERSTON, LUCAN AND ESKER

LEAVING town by James's Street, Mount Brown, and Old Kilmainham, we may observe among the newer buildings many quaint old houses and thatched cottages, memorials of the not very distant time when this was quite a rural neighbourhood. Near where O'Connell Road (formerly St. John's Road) crosses the railway, there stood until a few years ago, inside a niche in the wall on the western side of the road, the famous St. John's Well, ruthlessly swept away during the alterations consequent upon the building of St. John's Terrace. Its original position was, however, on the other side of the road, one hundred and twenty yards lower down the hill in the direction of the Phœnix Park. It is marked in that position on the Ordnance Survey Map of 1837, before the construction of the Great Southern and Western Railway (see also Dalton's *History*, p. 632), and the alteration in its position was probably due to the deep railway cutting here having intercepted its source, necessitating the opening of it higher up the hill, on the other side of the railway.

A pattern was formerly held here on St. John's Day (24th June), and to accommodate the votaries, a number of tents and booths used to be erected, giving the place the appearance of a fair. As might be expected, an institution of the kind so near a large city, attracted a mixed class of patrons, and the drunkenness and debauchery by which it in time became characterised, made it such a nuisance that efforts were made on several occasions, by the clergy and others, in the 18th and 19th centuries, to have it suppressed. The observances lingered

on, however, and down to about 1835, on each anniversary
there assembled in the fields adjoining the road, a number of
country carts fashioned into improvised booths in the manner
usual at the time, by blankets, patchwork quilts, &c., stretched
on arched wattles, while in all directions might be seen turf

Last appearance of St. John's Well.

and bramble fires with pots swinging over them, containing
legs of mutton, pigs' feet, bacon, potatoes, cabbage, and other
appetising delicacies for the hungry multitude. Around the
well collected the votaries with tumblers or horn goblets,
mixing whiskey with its saintly waters, or sleeping off the
effects of this irreverent mixture.

In 1538 Doctor Staples, Bishop of Meath, preached to the
multitude assembled at St. John's Well against the celebrated

Archbishop Browne, of Dublin, of which the latter bitterly complains in a letter preserved in the State Papers.

In 1710, the proceedings at this well having attracted public attention, the Irish House of Commons passed a resolution declaring that the assemblages of devotees here were a menace and a danger to the public peace of the kingdom, and prescribed fines, whippings, and imprisonments as the penalties for these " dangerous, tumultuous, and unlawful assemblies," which, as Dalton quaintly remarks, was certainly a severer penance than those persons intended to inflict upon themselves.

Even up to the time of its disappearance, the well was not without a few old pilgrims on St. John's Day, some for devotional purposes, and others to procure some of the water, which on the anniversary was believed to possess a peculiar sanctity.

A flat slab of stone in the waste plot adjoining St. John's Terrace appears to mark the recent site of this ancient well, which it is presumed has met the ignoble fate of being drained into the street sewer.

Within the wall on the opposite side of the road is the famous Bully's Acre burial ground, which from ancient times was the chief place of sepulture for the inhabitants of Dublin, and in the duelling days of the 18th and 19th centuries became the scene of numerous encounters, its notoriety in this respect quite eclipsing its historic interest. About the year 1760 General Dilks, Commander of the Forces, attempted to convert this ancient burial place into a botanic garden for the Royal Hospital, and in order to carry out this act of desecration he caused the graves to be levelled, spread a thick covering of lime over the entire surface, and enclosed the place with a high wall. The working men of the Liberties, however, exasperated at this indignity to their ancestors and relatives interred there, collected in a body one night, levelled the wall, and restored the place to its original purpose. As the only free burial place for the poor, it thereafter continued to be used until the cholera epidemic of 1832, when 3,200 interments having taken place in six months, the Government, apprehensive of pestilence, finally closed it.

According to remote tradition, an Irish chieftain who fell at the Battle of Clontarf, erroneously conjectured to be Murrough, sleeps in this graveyard beneath a tall headstone marked with curiously interlaced carvings, supposed to be the shaft of a large cross. About one hundred years ago this stone fell from its pedestal, and in replacing it, a number of Danish coins and a fine sword of the 11th century were found immediately adjoining. This weapon probably belonged to the dead chieftain, and was buried with him in accordance with ancient military custom.

When Strongbow came to Ireland, he granted the lands of Kilmainham to the Knights Hospitallers of St. John of Jerusalem, and Henry II. by charter confirmed the gift. A record of the contents of the original charter will be found in Sir John Gilbert's *Historic and Municipal Documents of Ireland*. The members of this historic order seem to have combined the functions of soldier, physician, and ecclesiastic, and to have been thoroughly proficient in the arts and duties of all three.

At the Suppression of the Monasteries this ancient body suffered the common penalty, and was dissolved by the Government of the day, all their property and estates coming into possession of the Crown.

In 1534 the citizens of Dublin having received private information that the O'Tooles were escorting to the mountains the proceeds of a foray in Fingal, sallied out to intercept them at Kilmainham Bridge, where Island Bridge now stands, but were surprised and overpowered by the spoilers at the wood of Salcock, and obliged to retire with a loss of eighty of their number.

In 1680 King Charles II. directed the building of a hospital at Kilmainham for the maintenance of aged and maimed soldiers of the army of Ireland, such hospital to be erected upon part of the lands of the Royal Park, near the old ruinous building called the Castle of Kilmainham, formerly occupied by the Knights Hospitallers. Portions of the walls of the old chapel of the Hospitallers were taken down and used as materials for the construction of the new edifice, but one mullioned window of the original structure yet remains, incorporated in the buildings of the Royal Hospital.

Adjoining Kilmainham is Island Bridge, deriving its name from an island formed by a loop in the river immediately to the west of the bridge, but now separated from the southern bank by a mill-race only, instead of by a branch of the river.

In 1535 Sir William Skeffington, Lord Deputy of Ireland, while escorting the Lord Chancellor and other officers of State returning to Dublin from Trim, had an encounter at this place with the adherents of Silken Thomas, then in insurrection against the Government. Skeffington's route from Trim lay through Castleknock to Chapelizod, and thence along the banks of the Liffey to Kilmainham Bridge mentioned above, a narrow structure across which he proposed to take his men on their way into the city. Immediately at the other side, between the Bridge and Kilmainham, was then the wood of Salcock, and under cover of this, the Geraldines had laid an ambuscade for Skeffington's force, intending to fall upon them as they emerged from the narrow bridge. The circumstances were particularly favourable for the project, for according to Skeffington's account in the State Papers of Henry VIII., a phenomenal fall of rain had caused such floods that the foot soldiers, in passing the low-lying parts of the road along the river, had to wade up to their waists in water, and in consequence, the strings of their bows had become so soaked with moisture as to be useless, while the feathers of their arrows had fallen off from the same cause, so that, had the attack been made, matters would undoubtedly have gone hard with the bowmen, as they could have done little to defend themselves. Luckily for Skeffington, however, he managed, at the last moment, to get wind of the arrangements made for his reception, whereupon he laid his guns in position beside the bridge, passed his bowmen across, and simultaneously opening fire upon the wood, cleared out the party concealed in it, thereby enabling him to bring his men safely to Dublin by the main road through what are now James's Street and High Street to the Castle.

While the use of cannon, introduced now for the first time into Ireland, had at this period become fairly general, the long bow still continued to be the principal weapon of the infantry ; and although it is not possible to state definitely when the final supersession of that historic weapon took place, there is no doubt that in England at least, where the archers attained their highest degree of perfection in the reign of Elizabeth, the bow survived the introduction of firearms by more than two centuries. It is recorded that a body of English archers were employed as mercenaries by Cardinal Richelieu at the siege of La Rochelle in 1627-8.

Neade, a celebrated authority on archery in the reign of Charles I., states that the ordinary range of the bow was from 300 to 400 yards, and that an archer could shoot six arrows in the time occupied in charging and discharging a musket. Even at so recent a period as that of the Peninsular War, the musket was regarded as utterly unreliable beyond a hundred yards, and the instructions for its use issued to the soldiers enjoined that they should not fire until they could see the whites of their adversaries' eyes.

In 1577 a new bridge was erected in lieu of that at Kilmainham, and this having been swept away by a flood in 1787, the existing fine structure was built, which in consequence of the first stone having been laid by Sarah, Countess of Westmoreland, was for many years afterwards generally known as Sarah Bridge.

Resuming our journey, we presently pass, on our left, the dilapidated locality known as Goldenbridge, so called from the original name of the bridge by which the main road crosses the Camac, a little river which rises at the head of the Slade of Saggart. After passing under the railway bridge, the Inchicore Railway Works will be seen on the left, adjoining which, near the road, are a number of the employees' cottages. Turning down the St. Laurence Road we descend into the Liffey valley, with grassy, wooded banks rising high on the left, the picturesque village of Chapelizod in front, and the Catholic church prominently in view at the opposite side of the river.

Facing the bridge, on the near side, the road up the steep hill leads to the old church and churchyard of Ballyfermot, near which formerly stood a castle whose site is now occupied by Ballyfermot House. Between the house and the road is a curious brick wall, built in a series of curves, and stated to have at one time formed portion of the enclosure of an orchard belonging to the castle. A quarter of a mile further, on the eastern side of the road, between the railway and the canal, is an old house known a hundred years ago as Ballyfermot Lodge, whose dilapidated garden walls, overhung with immense growths of ivy, testify to the antiquity of the place. A tiled roof of an old pattern on an outhouse adjoining, would suggest that the original roof on the main building was also a tiled one. If this surmise be correct, it would seem probable, from the position and appearance of this old establishment, that it is the weird " Tiled House " referred to by J. S. Le Fanu in his story of *The House by the Churchyard.*

Crossing the bridge we enter Chapelizod, once a favourite residence for Dublin citizens, and still possessing some traces of the old world respectability which characterised it at the period of which Le Fanu wrote in his famous novel. Between the two approaches from the main street to the Protestant Parish Church is an old-fashioned house, which is evidently the actual " House by the Churchyard " that plays so prominent a part in the story.

The lands of Chapelizod appear to have been among those reserved by the Crown at the Invasion, and they continued to be part of the Royal demesne up to the 14th century, when they came into possession of the family of de la Feld. In the 17th century the Crown had again acquired possession of a house and lands here which were situated to the left of the road from Dublin, on the banks of the Liffey. For some years during

the Commonwealth the house was occupied by Sir Theophilus
Jones, brother of Colonel Jones, who distinguished himself
at the Battle of Rathmines, and at a later period it was used as
a viceregal residence. A ruined turret near the river indicates
the position of the gardens of this old mansion, which was
called " The King's House," on account of its having been used
for a short time in 1690 by King William III. as a residence.

On the Liffey at Chapelizod.
(1906.)

In the 18th century it fell into decay, and was subsequently
disposed of by the Crown.

Retracing our steps and recrossing the bridge we pass through
what is now commonly accounted part of Chapelizod, but is
properly the village of St. Laurence, deriving its name from a
leper hospital dedicated to that saint in early times, when
leprosy was a common malady in the country, and closed in
1426, when its owner surrendered custody of it and its lands
to the Crown. The name of the saint is still retained in the
local nomenclature, and a fair used to be held here on St.
Laurence's Day.

A long and uninteresting stretch of road between high walls conducts us past the Stewart Institution, formerly the residence of Lord Donoughmore, into Palmerston, somewhat resembling Chapelizod in the character of its buildings. Just as the village is entered, on the right will be seen one of the old stables surviving from the coaching days, when numerous coaches for Mullingar and other towns on the great western highway used to pass daily through this place. Adjoining is a terrace, the style of which would point to the existence, in former years, of a well-to-do class of residents, while on the opposite side of the road was, until recently, a stately old mansion, now replaced by a row of small dwellings.

At the close of the 18th century this village possessed six calico printing mills, two oil mills, one dye mill, three wash mills, as well as lead, iron and copper works.

Approached by a lane from the high road is a pretty chapel-of-ease, with a small belfry bearing a clock which has long ceased to record the flying hour, and in front of the entrance is a lime tree with a circular seat around the trunk.

Beside the old stable referred to above, a by-road on the right leads to the lower and probably the original village, with the ruins of the old church of Palmerston, thickly covered with ivy, in a picturesque position overlooking the river. Adjoining is the once famed village green, where a fair used to be held on the 21st August, an institution which at one period of its existence was regarded as second only to the historic saturnalia of Donnybrook

A mile and a half beyond Palmerston, along the main road, is the little hamlet of Cursis Stream, recently improved by the erection of some handsome villa residences. There is nothing in this locality worthy of notice ; and after passing the power station of the Dublin and Lucan Electric Railway, we reach Ballydowd Hill, a considerable elevation over the surrounding country, but commanding only a very restricted view. About a mile further on we pass the long, straggling hamlet of Ballydowd, consisting mostly of neatly-kept detached cottages, and immediately beyond this **the** road branches, both routes entering Lucan by a long down hill.

At the top of the hill, where the road forks, and almost within a stone's throw of the village, a monumental slab, inserted in the wall, commemorates the murder on this spot, of Father MacCartan, of Lucan.

The inscription runs as follows :—

I.H S.

HERE

PREMATURELY FELL BY LAWLESS VIOLENCE

THE REV. JAMES MacCARTAN,

ON THE 3RD OF JUNE, 1807.

TALENTS

RICH, REFINED, AND SPLENDID,

INNATE BENEVOLENCE

AND PECULIAR URBANITY OF

MIND

DISTINGUISHED THROUGH LIFE

THIS ZEALOUS MINISTER OF THE

CATHOLIC FAITH

AND GENEROUS FRIEND OF

HUMANITY.

It appears that on the night of the murder, Father MacCartan (or McCarthy as the name is given in the newspapers of the time) dined with Lord Donoughmore's steward at Palmerston House, now the Stewart Institution, having held a station for a few days previously in the neighbourhood. When returning home about 10 o'clock he was wantonly fired at by one of a gang of robbers, who had no knowledge of him or his sacred office, and who apparently attacked him for the sake of whatever articles of value he might happen to have in his possession.

The following account of the trial is abbreviated from that in the *Freeman's Journal* of the 27th June, 1807 :—

COMMISSION INTELLIGENCE.
MURDER OF MR. McCARTHY.

Thomas Weir and Christopher Walsh were indicted for the murder of the Rev. Mr. McCarthy near Lucan, on the 3rd of the current month, for that they, instigated by the devil, &c., did murder the said Mr. McCarthy, by lodging the contents of a pistol under his left breast, of the wound whereof he died. There was another count charging the prisoners with robbing the said Mr. McCarthy of—(1) a silver watch, and (2) ten shillings English. To both these counts the prisoners pleaded not guilty.

The prisoners being asked had they any agents, Walsh announced he had no attorney but God Almighty.

James Clarke, keeper of the turnpike near Lucan, deposed that he saw deceased about 11 o'clock on the night of the 3rd June, lying on his back, dead, nearly at the top of Lucan hill, with his right hand extended, and bleeding profusely from a wound in the left breast. Witness joined in the pursuit of the murderers.

John Murphy, one of the gang, who turned King's Evidence, identified both prisoners. On the 3rd June he saw Weir with three men, named Donohoe, MacMahon, and Larkin. A meeting was ultimately arranged for that night in Thomas Street, at which the prisoners, the three men named, and witness attended, and it was there planned that they should that same night proceed to Lucan and attack the house of a man named Kenny, who, it was understood, had £180 in his possession. A car was accordingly hired by two of the party, who told the driver that they were bailiffs going out to arrest a deserter in Lucan, and they drove first to Mount Brown, where the remainder of the gang mounted the car. Witness stated that when he got to Lucan his heart failed him, and he gave his pistol to Walsh, who was a soldier in plain clothes, and who in return gave him his bayonet. When they reached Kenny's house they found there only his wife and daughter, to whom they read a document which they said was a search warrant ; they then searched the house, but, finding no money, quitted it without offering any violence to the inmates.

Memorial and scene of Father MacCartan's murder, Lucan.
(1906.)

On leaving, they divided into two parties, whereof witness and two others were the first ; Weir, Walsh, and Donohoe following at a short distance. The first party overtook and passed a gentleman in black on the road, but did not molest him ; after passing him witness looked back and observed that when the others came up, Walsh put his hand to his bosom, drew out a pistol, seized the gentleman by the throat, and fired against him. Witness saw a man fall, who he at first thought was Walsh, whereupon he immediately separated from his companions and ran away across the open country ; witness saw no more of the gang that night, and was himself arrested next morning.

On cross-examination, witness stated that his pistol was loaded with swan drops, that he did not take it out with intent to murder, and that only for the Union he would not have come so near the gallows, his trade, that of a silver plater, having been an exceedingly good one until the passing of that measure.

John White, the car driver, deposed that on the night of the 3rd June, his car was hired by Walsh and Weir to carry a party to Lucan, for the purpose, as alleged by the hirers, of apprehending a deserter.

Eleanor Burke, a servant at James Kenny's, near Lucan, gave evidence as to the visit by the party.

Major Sirr, who took the depositions of John Murphy, the King's Evidence, deposed that he took them down verbatim.

The confession of the prisoners, Weir and Walsh, was produced in evidence ; it charged Donohoe with the murder, but agreed otherwise with the evidence of John Murphy.

The jury without leaving the box, returned a verdict of guilty against both prisoners, and Judge Daly, in passing sentence of death, advised them to indulge in no vain hopes of respite. Weir begged for some time to prepare, but the judge observed that there were no circumstances in the case which would warrant any departure in the least degree from a strict compliance with the law, and sentenced the prisoners to be hanged next morning.

The murderers were executed, according to the usual custom of the time, on the spot where the crime was committed. Weir was only nineteen years of age and Walsh thirty-four. The three other members of the gang were never apprehended, and probably escaped abroad.

It may be here mentioned that the left hand road, on which the tram runs, was not in existence at the time of the tragedy.

Descending the steep hill by either road, we enter the pretty town of Lucan, picturesquely situated in the wooded valley of the Liffey at the junction with its tributary, the Griffen.

In 1758, the medicinal qualities of the spa having been discovered, this place at once came into notice, and for a number of years was quite a fashionable resort, until the proverbial fickleness of fashion consigned it to its original obscurity.

Dr. Rutty, in his *Natural History of the County Dublin*, gives

Lucan
(1903.)

a detailed account of this spa, and cites over fifty cases of various diseases which came under his observation as having been cured by taking its waters.

The Lucan demesne was originally the patrimony of the Sarsfields, the last of whom was the famous General Patrick Sarsfield, afterwards Earl of Lucan. He fell in action at the Battle of Landen in 1693, leaving a son, on whose death in 1719, the title became extinct. The estate then passed to Charlotte Sarsfield, niece of the late Earl, and she marrying Agmondisham Vesey, the property came into possession of the Vesey family, from whom it subsequently passed by a similar process into the hands of the Colthursts.

Z

Adjoining the entrance gate of the demesne, but almost concealed from observation by trees, is the ancient castle of the Sarsfields, beside which is the ivied ruin of a church containing a mural tablet to the memory of Lady Jane Butler and her husband.

Not far from the town, on the road to the Great Southern and Western Railway Station, is a hillock surmounted by a rath in excellent preservation. In the interior are several walled chambers which were formerly reached by an opening at the top, but are now inaccessible owing to portion of the entrance passage having fallen in.

Leaving Lucan by the Esker road up the steep hill, and passing the new cemetery, we presently enter the little village of Esker, more populous in former years, and once possessing a grammar school and a cotton factory. The district of Esker was one of the four ancient Royal manors of the County Dublin, the revenues of which were on occasions applied to the defence of the Pale against " the Irish Enemie." Esker means a ridge of sandhills, this place marking the commencement of the great Esker-Riada, a line of low hills which extends almost uninterruptedly to the County Galway, and was fixed upon as the boundary between the North and the South of Ireland in the 2nd century by Owen More and Conn of the Hundred Battles (*Irish Names of Places*, Vol. I., p. 402).

On the summit of one of these sand hills, and in a commanding position overlooking the little hamlet, stand the ivied ruins of the ancient church of Esker, probably dating from the 12th century. Within the hallowed circuit of its mouldering walls, a large tombstone, shattered to pieces, marks the resting-place of the murdered priest, Father MacCartan, whose tragic fate is commemorated in the following epitaph :—

" The United Parishes of Lucan and Palmerstown erected " this tombstone over the Mortal Remains of the Reverend " James MacCartan, R.C. Curate of said Parishes. As a " grateful tribute of their Respect for, and as a fitting monu-

" ment of their sincere regret for the loss of that Worthy
" Clergyman, by whose death Society was deprived of a Valuable
" Member, and Religion one of Her most zealous Ministers.
" Lamentable to add, He fell a Victim to the Sacrilegious
" Hands of a Sanguinary Banditti, by whom he was Robbed

Ballyowen Castle.
(1906.)

" and Murdered on the Hill of Lucan on the 3rd day of June,
" A.D. 1807, And in the 42nd year of his Age.
" Requiescat in Pace.
" Amen."

It is difficult to account for the mutilated condition of this
tombstone otherwise than by the supposition of malicious
injury, as from the marks on it, it would appear to have been
deliberately broken, either by dropping heavy stones upon it
or by striking it with some weighty object.

In 1248 the Manor of Esker was granted to Peter de Bermingham, whose descendants retained possession of it until
the middle of the following century. From a " regal visitation "

of 1615, it appears that the church was then in repair, but that the chancel was in ruins.

Rising out of Esker, the road is carried along an elevated ridge commanding exquisite views of the mountains in extended panorama, some bathed in sunshine, others more sombre, shadowed by passing clouds, or picturesquely wreathed in the blue smoke of the gorse fires.

A short distance further, on a by-road to the left, will be seen Ballyowen Castle, consisting of a square ivied ruin, with a modern farmhouse erected against it. Several old doorways, now built up, can be distinguished in the masonry, and the original well of the castle, in the adjoining field, is still used for drinking purposes.

This castle is somewhat different from the ordinary type, in being equipped with a lofty turret, a feature copied in the design of a modern residence in the neighbourhood. Commanding so extensive a view, this addition to a stronghold must have been a great advantage to the occupants during troublous times, in securing, to a great extent, an immunity from surprise attacks. Some traces of the old fosse which surrounded the building may be distinguished to the south of the ruin.

Returning to the main road, we presently cross in succession the Great Southern and Western Railway and the Grand Canal, half a mile beyond which we enter the village of Clondalkin. From here we ascend the long hill past Mount St. Joseph's Monastery to the Naas road, whence the return to town may be made *via* Kilmainham, Dolphin's Barn, or Terenure, according to the district desired to be reached.

The following authorities were consulted in the preparation of this chapter :—An article on Lucan and Leixlip by Mr. E. R. McC. Dix and Mr. James Mills in the *Journal of the Royal Society of Antiquaries of Ireland* for 1896 ; Dalton's *History of the County Dublin ;* Wakeman's *Old Dublin ; The Dublin Penny Journal ;* and several articles in old Dublin magazines.

Distances from G. P. O.—Chapelizod, 4 ; Palmerston, 5¼ ; Lucan, 9 ; Clondalkin, 12½ ; back to G. P. O., 19 miles.

CHAPTER XXXIV

THE STRAWBERRY BEDS, ST. CATHERINE'S, LEIXLIP, MAYNOOTH CASTLE AND OBELISK

PASSING out of the Phœnix Park by the Knockmaroon Gate, we enter upon the Lower Road, celebrated for its picturesque sylvan scenery. The northern bank of the river, rising abruptly from the roadside, forms a long range of sheltered slopes peculiarly adapted to the culture of strawberries, an industry identified with this place from time immemorial, from which circumstance originated the name of " The Strawberry Beds." On the opposite side of the river are gently sloping stretches of luxuriant meadow and woodland, while along the water's edge the trees droop gracefully into the water, intermingling their foliage with the rank growth of aquatic vegetation. The Strawberry Beds was a much more popular resort in former years than at the present day, and on fine Sundays in summer was visited by large numbers from the city. Cars used to ply between Carlisle (now O'Connell) Bridge and " the Beds " at 3d. a seat, and were so well patronised that it was not an infrequent sight to see a procession of these vehicles, amid blinding clouds of dust, extending the whole way from Parkgate Street to Knockmaroon. The outside cars, too, were longer in those days, and carried three passengers on each side without any undue compression—not to speak of two or three in the well. The strawberry vendors, pipers, fiddlers, and publicans reaped a rich harvest, the sounds of revelry filled the air, and when the shades of night had fallen, numerous involuntary dismounts were made from the cars on the homeward journey. About three miles from Knockmaroon, we pass, on the right, the entrance gate to Luttrellstown, now the seat of Lord Annaly, and formerly the ancestral home of the Luttrells, on account of whose performances there, and of the evil memories attaching to the place in consequence, the succeeding owners changed the name to Woodlands. A handsome wooden bridge erected by Lord Carhampton once spanned the river opposite the entrance gate, but was swept away by a flood in 1787.

Many pretty cottages are to be seen along the Lower Road, but they suffer considerably from the dust caused by the traffic in the summertime.

A short distance beyond the entrance gate to Luttrellstown are the Anna Liffey Mills, the successors of an edifice popularly known as " The Devil's Mill," in consequence of the legend that it was erected in the course of a single night by his Satanic Majesty. We next pass a fine bridge leading into Lucan, which, however, is outside the limits of this excursion, and we keep straight ahead until an iron gate is seen in front, through which we enter the demesne of St. Catherine's. The avenue, which, for the most part is unfit for cycling, skirts the river bank for about a mile, shaded in parts by venerable trees, and at length diverges slightly towards the north as the ruins are approached. In the spring or early summer this demesne looks its best, as the numerous cherry trees are then showing their delicately tinted blossoms, while in the sheltered glades may be seen a great profusion of wild flowers, of which the most conspicuous is the wood anemone.

The first building we pass is the ruin of a chapel, evidently modern, which bears traces of renovation in parts, and whose walls, thickly overgrown with ivy, are embattled in a fantastic manner. Nothing appears to be known as to the origin of this nondescript structure.

Adjoining is the building popularly known as " Sarsfield's " Stables," but which is more probably portion of the out-offices of the old manor house of St. Catherine's, purchased by Mr. La Touche in 1792, and dismantled by him to provide materials for a magnificent new mansion that was accidentally destroyed by fire in the early part of last century. This beautiful residence was furnished in such a manner that it was said to be " all that money could accomplish or art produce."

The sequestered locality of St. Catherine's is the site of an ancient priory, founded in 1219 by Warrisius de Peche for the Canons of St. Victor, and dedicated to the saint whose name forms the present designation. The endowment proving inadequate to maintain the establishment, the community in time became so poor and oppressed with debts that they were unable to support themselves, and accordingly, in 1323, they assigned all their property to St. Thomas's Abbey, Dublin, which continued in possession of the religious house of St. Catherine's until the Dissolution of the Monasteries. After the Dissolution it was granted to, and occupied as a residence by, Sir Nicholas White, Master of the Rolls in Queen Elizabeth's time. No trace whatever of the ancient building now survives, its site being probably covered by some portion of the modern residence called St. Catherine's.

Passing out through the iron gate adjoining the ruins, we emerge on a narrow roadway leading into Leixlip, first, however, turning to the right for a short distance, along a lane which here forms the county boundary, in order to visit the wells of St. Catherine's. Both these wells are protected by stone canopies ; the larger, provided with a wooden door and adorned with a head of modern appearance, is used for drinking purposes, while the smaller has for generations enjoyed a reputation for curing sore eyes. It is stated that neither has ever been known to run dry.

Retracing our steps to the gate we have just left, and turning to the right, we enter a picturesque avenue, shaded by lofty trees, leading into the village of Leixlip, situated in a wooded hollow, over which the Black Castle, sentinel-like, stands on a commanding eminence at the confluence of the Liffey and the Rye Water. The village presents an appearance of faded respectability—a couple of good terraces, and a few large houses testifying to its former prosperity.

O'Keeffe, in his opera of " The Poor Soldier," says :—

" Though Leixlip is proud of its close shady bowers,
Its clear falling waters and murmuring cascades,
Its groves of fine myrtle, its beds of sweet flowers,
Its lads so well dressed and its sweet pretty maids."

It cannot be stated with certainty when the castle was built, but it is believed to date from the reign of Henry II., and to have been commenced during that period by Adam de Hereford, to whom the adjoining lands had been ceded by Strongbow. In 1317 the Bruces with their army marched from Castleknock and encamped here for four days, when, according to Camden, " they burnt part of the towne, brake down the " church and spoiled it, and afterwards marched on towards " the Nas " (Naas). One of the apartments in the castle is called " King John's room," from the tradition that it was occupied by that monarch during his stay in Ireland.

Towards the close of the 15th century the castle and lands of Leixlip were granted by Henry VII. to the Earl of Kildare, but in consequence of the rebellion of Silken Thomas, an Act of Parliament was passed in 1536, whereby the manor reverted to the Crown. In 1646 the Confederate forces under Generals Preston and Owen Roe O'Neill, in their march on Dublin, took up a position adjoining Leixlip, on the Liffey. Dissensions, however, arose between these commanders, and, ultimately, O'Neill, discovering or suspecting a plot against his life, erected a temporary bridge across the river here, and made his way into Meath. The projected attack on Dublin thus proved abortive, though it might have succeeded had the commanders united.

Leixlip is a Danish name (Lax-hlaup), meaning salmon leap, and this name, which is probably a translation of an older Irish one, was in turn translated into Latin by Giraldus Cambrensis and others, as Saltus Salmonis. This Latin translation was the form used in deeds and other important documents for hundreds of years afterwards, and the scribes who prepared these documents, as a rule, used the full name, Saltus Salmonis, only at the beginning, afterwards abbreviating it into " Salt Salm," which by a further abbreviation became " Salt " simply. In this way originated the names of the Baronies of North and South Salt in the County Kildare.

The Annals of the Four Masters record that in 915 A.D. a battle took place at Ceann Fuait, said to be Confey, about a mile

Leixlip Castle.
(1905.)

north of Leixlip, between the Danes, who had settled in that place, and the Leinstermen, the latter being defeated with heavy loss. There is good reason for believing that the name of Leixlip was given to the locality by this colony of Danes who had established themselves at Confey.

In order to visit the Salmon Leap and obtain a good view of Leixlip Castle, cross the bridge at the entrance to the village, and at the far side will be seen a stile beside an iron gate opening into a pathway which leads along the river bank up to the falls ; this pathway is, however, almost impassable in damp weather. The upper or left hand pathway should not be taken, as it leads only to the mill. The Salmon Leap, once a considerable attraction in this neighbourhood, is sadly disfigured by the adjoining mills, and unless for the pretty pathway along the river, with its varied views of the picturesque surroundings, the place is hardly worth visiting.

Returning from the Salmon Leap and passing through the village street, on the left will be observed the Protestant parish church, a very old building, on the exterior of which are some carvings of heads, while the side walls exhibit traces of ancient windows. The appearance of the whole edifice is much enhanced by its ivy-mantled clock tower, which can be ascended if desired. This church stands on the site, and is possibly incorporated with some of the remains of an ancient priory, which was probably connected with the castle by a bridge across the Rye Water.

At the end of the village, the road turning sharply to the right, brings us into view of the Catholic Church, standing on an eminence in a picturesque position overlooking the village and river. Instead of taking the road to the right of the church, keep to the left of it by the pathway up the steep hill where the old road formerly passed, and take the road immediately to the left at the top of the hill. In about a mile farther will be seen on the right a remarkable conical-shaped building known as "The Wonderful Barn," built by one of the Conollys of Castletown. A rough pathway from the road leads up to the front, where will be observed over the entrance door a mural tablet bearing the inscription :—-

1743

EXECUT'D

BY IOHN GLIN.

The whole structure is built with great strength and solidity, rising by a series of floors with a trap-door in the centre of

each, through which the grain, &c., was hauled up by wind-
lasses. It stands at the north-western corner of a spacious
haggard, two of the remaining angles being occupied by smaller
structures of similar design. The windows, which are unglazed,
are triangular in shape, with oak frames, still in perfect preservation notwithstanding their exposure to the weather. A flight
of 94 steps winds round the exterior to the embattled turret,
73 feet above the base, commanding an extended view of the
surrounding pastoral country. A large well, with a substan-

"The Wonderful Barn," near Leixlip.
(1906.)

tially built stone-roofed structure over it, supplies the place
with water.

This curious edifice, in conjunction with the adjoining
buildings, was probably commenced during the severe winter
of 1741-2 to give employment to the poor, and the name of
Barn Hall, originally given to the entire establishment, has been
adopted as the modern designation of the townland in which
it stands.

About half-a-mile further, the road, by a sharp turn to the
left, conducts us to the narrow old bridge, paradoxically called
Newbridge, though really the oldest bridge on the Liffey.
Enshrined in the cloistral shade of ancient trees, this venerable
structure spans the river by a range of irregular moss-grown

arches, while beneath, the waters glide softly onward, until at length they are lost in the distance amidst the luxuriant over-hanging foliage. This quaint old bridge was built by John le Decer, Provost of Dublin, at his own expense, in 1308, and was only one of the many public works carried out by this eminent citizen of old Dublin.

Beside the bridge is the entrance to St. Wolstan's, so called because it contains the ruins of an ancient ecclesiastical estab-lishment, which, according to Archdall's *Monasticon Hibernicum* was founded in 1202 in honour of St. Wolstan, Bishop of Worcester, for the Canons of the Order of St. Victor. The ruins now surviving consist of two arched gateways, a square tower with a spiral staircase, an arched way with some apart-ments adjoining, and some ivy-clad fragments of gable walls, all carefully preserved.

In 1536, on the Suppression of the Monasteries, this establish-ment, with its extensive estates, was taken possession of by the Crown, the Prior, Richard Weston, being provided with a pension, quarters, rations, and firing, chargeable on the property. In 1538 John Alen, of Norfolk, assumed possession of the estate under the authority of a Royal Warrant, and in 1539 was appointed Lord Chancellor. St. Wolstans then became known as Alen's Court, and Sir John Alen, having died without issue, was succeeded in possession by his brother, Thomas Alen, Clerk of the Hanaper. Coming down to more recent times, we find Sir Patrick Alen, an adherent of James II., raising at his own expense a body of troops for the use of that unfortunate monarch. He became a major-general in the Jacobite army, was present at the siege of Limerick, and as a result of the terms of capitulation, was allowed to retain his estates, notwith-standing his adherence to the Roman Catholic Faith. He married twice, and had a total family of forty-two children.

The fifth son of the above, Sir Luke Alen, generally known as the " Comte de St. Wolstan," spent much of his time abroad, and was the last of the family connected with the estate of St. Wolstan's. He entered the service of France in 1735 as an officer of the Irish Brigade, served as lieutenant in Dillon's regiment, which he quitted for Lally's after the Battle of Fontenoy, was adjutant of the latter, and afterwards Adjutant-General of the French army in India. He was entrusted with the storming of Fort Sacramalous, was himself the first to enter it, and was subsequently promoted to be Commander-in-Chief in India during the siege of Pondicherry, after the fall of which he returned to France with his regiment. In consequence of taking so active a part with the French in their operations against the English, his estate at St. Wolstan's was forfeited to the Crown, and sold by the Court of Exchequer in 1752 to Dr. Robert Clayton, Bishop of Clogher. The male line of this ancient and distinguished family became extinct on the death of Captain Luke John Henry Alen at his residence in Dublin in 1879.

For about twenty years in the early part of the last century St. Wolstan's was a boarding school, an interesting memento of which is a well beside the river still bearing the name of " The Scholars' Well." A short distance from this well is a monument to Dr. Clayton and his wife, in the form of a large urn on a square granite pedestal, the sides of which bear inscriptions in Latin and English setting forth the purpose of the cenotaph.

The Marquis of Buckingham, when Lord Lieutenant, occupied St. Wolstan's as a summer residence from 1787 to 1790,

The return journey to town may be made either *via* Lucan or Celbridge, but should it be desired to include Maynooth in this excursion it is better to return to Leixlip and proceed along the main road which rises the whole way to the Midland Railway Station of Leixlip, three-quarters of a mile from the town. From the high railway bridge and the road beyond it will be seen, on the right, the green rolling banks of the Rye Water, anciently the Owenree or King's river, across the valley of which the Royal Canal and the railway are carried by an immense aqueduct 100 feet high—said to be the largest of its

kind in Ireland.   This great work, which, in its original form
cost over £30,000, is worthy of a visit, and may be easily
reached by a pathway from the railway station of Leixlip.
The remainder of the road is of little interest, running side by
side with the railway and canal, and we at length enter Maynooth at a distance of 4½ miles from Leixlip.   Maynooth is
a clean, bright-looking town, consisting principally of one wide
street, at the eastern extremity of which is the avenue leading

Maynooth Castle.
(1911.)

to Carton, the Duke of Leinster's demesne, while at the western
end is the Royal College of St. Patrick, established in 1795, to
enable persons to enter the Catholic priesthood without going
abroad for that purpose.   The spire of the church attached to
the College is 264 feet high—the highest in Ireland—and the
cross alone, although it looks so small, is 14 feet in height.
Owing to the light coloured stone of which the spire is built,
it is visible at a great distance, particularly when lit up by
sunshine.   It can be ascended by a winding staircase, and the
view well repays the trouble of the ascent.   Admission may be
obtained on application at the College.
   The most conspicuous object in the town is Maynooth Castle,

the ancient stronghold of the Geraldines, with its massive towers, walls and buttresses frowning down upon the quiet street. This castle derives a special interest from the fact that artillery was used for the first time in Ireland at its siege by Deputy Sir William Skeffington, during the rebellion of Silken

Obelisk near Maynooth.
(1900.)

Thomas in 1535. When the attack commenced, on 14th March, it was defended by one hundred men, and after having been battered for nine days by the cannon, was taken by storm, except the great keep, the defenders of which, thirty-seven in number, seeing their case hopeless, surrendered at discretion, probably expecting mercy. But their fate is best told by the Deputy himself : " Their lives [were] preserved by appoint-" ment, until they should be presented to me, your deputy,

" and then to be ordered as I and your council thought good.
" We thought it expedient to put them to execution, as an
" example to the others " (*Carew Papers*, p. 65). Local
tradition holds that they were hanged from the central arch
of the castle.

The ruins of this interesting stronghold are kept in excellent
order, and may be visited on application to the caretaker.
The place where Skeffington planted his artillery is known as
" the park hill," to the north of the castle.

We now proceed by the road to Celbridge, in order to visit
the obelisk or " folly," as it is usually called, which is so conspicuous an object in the flat country around. Crossing the
railway by the bridge adjoining the station, we take the road to
Celbridge Station, indicated on a finger-post, and, at a distance
of $1\frac{3}{4}$ miles from Maynooth, we meet, on the left, a narrow
secluded lane which leads in a few hundred yards straight up
to the obelisk. This curious edifice, which might well be
described as an architectural nightmare, stands on the summit
of a rising ground, and its lofty form, towering above the surrounding trees, is visible for nearly twenty miles around. It
was erected in 1741--2, during that remarkable season known as
" The hard frost," by Mrs. Conolly, widow of the Right Hon.
Wm. Conolly, of Castletown, to give employment to the poor,
and, like most of its contemporaries, is an ungainly nondescript
structure, devoid of grace or stability. The bulk of the monument is supported by two arches, the lower of which, if closely
observed, will be seen to be somewhat widened at the top
from the vast superincumbent weight, and from the upper one
a perceptible fissure extends upwards, while the masonry at the
extreme top of the pillar appears to be in a loose and disjointed
condition, possibly caused by lightning. The western side is
thickly enveloped in ivy, and the keystone at the back of the
lower centre arch bears the date of erection. The whole
building, from base to summit, measures 139 feet.

From the interior of the eastern arch a winding staircase
leads to the gallery over the centre, about fifty feet high,

commanding a view of Maynooth with Carton in front, and of
the whole range of the mountains at the back, but as a notice
now warns visitors against approaching the building on account
of its dangerous condition, it would be inadvisable to enter it.
From the rear, a vista of Castletown House is obtained through
the trees, which originally formed a long avenue leading up to
the monument, enabling the occupants of the house to enjoy (!)
a view of the structure.

The return to town had best be made by Celbridge, Hazel-
hatch, the Loughtown road, Milltown, and Clondalkin, so as
to afford a change from the route on the outward journey.

The authorities consulted in the preparation of this chapter
are :—An article on " Leixlip and Lucan," by E. R. McC.
Dix and James Mills in the *Journal of the Royal Society of
Antiquaries* for 1896 ; articles in Vol. II. of the *Journal of the
County Kildare Archæological Society*, on " St. Wolstan's," by
W. T. Kirkpatrick ; on " Leixlip Castle," by Lord Frederick
FitzGerald ; and on " Castletown and Its Owners," by Lord
Walter FitzGerald.

Distances from G. P. O.—Knockmaroon, $4\frac{5}{8}$ miles ; Lucan,
9 miles ; St. Catherine's, $10\frac{1}{2}$ miles ; Leixlip, 11 miles ; Maynooth, $15\frac{1}{2}$ miles ; the Obelisk, $17\frac{1}{4}$ miles ; back to G. P. O.
via Celbridge and Clondalkin, 34 miles.

A visit to " The Wonderful Barn," which is out of the direct
route, will add about 2 miles to the distance.

CHAPTER XXXV

THE FEATHERBED PASS, GLENCREE AND ITS ROYAL FOREST, LOUGHS BRAY, SALLY GAP AND CORONATION PLANTATION

THE whole of the district described in this chapter, though practicable for cyclists, is very wild and mountainous, necessitating at times walking long distances, but as the roads, on the whole, are fairly good, this will to some extent be compensated for by the long runs down hill. Unless on a motor there is no other way of exploring this wild region, as the distances to be covered are beyond the walking powers of most people, and a horse-drawn vehicle, in such a difficult country would, in point of speed, possess little advantage over walking.

Few, except those who have visited it, can form an adequate idea of this great tract of moor and mountain almost overlooking the Metropolis—a tract teeming, indeed, with busy life, but of a realm outside the sway of man's sovereignty. Traversing this dark waste of moorland, the great Military road, winding over hill and dale, like a white ribbon flung across these desert solitudes, dominates the wildness and loneliness, and forms the sole link with civilisation in this region.

The initial portion of our journey lies through Rathfarnham, Willbrook, and Ballyboden, where we cross Billy's bridge, and take the first turn on the left, known as Stocking Lane, shortly after which we must dismount and commence our long ascent of 4½ miles to the highest point of the Featherbed Pass over Killakee Mountain. Immediately now on our right is the auxiliary reservoir of the Rathmines Waterworks, and about half a mile further, we come to a level stretch of about one hundred yards, where, over a low wall to the right, is obtained the first extended view of the Dublin plain. The road now turns to the left, and at the corner is the entrance to Woodtown, built by George Grierson, King's Printer, in the 18th century.

Continuing our journey under the shade of the trees bordering the road, we pass the well-known dashed wall, so liberally inscribed with the names of excursionists. A steep ascent now conducts us past the massive entrance gate to Mount Venus, and presently on our right is seen Oldcourt road, leading by Oldcourt, Allenton, and Oldbawn to Tallaght. We are now at the foot of Mount Pelier, where the steepest portion of the road commences, with Orlagh College and its woods in the immediate foreground, and beyond these the plain extending westward into the County Kildare. A little further, and somewhat to the right of the road, is a group of farmhouses which forms a conspicuous feature in the view of Mount Pelier as seen from the country northward, and a short distance further, we pass the well-kept stables of Lord Massey, his residence, Killakee House, being at the opposite side of the road, concealed by trees. It is from near this point that the ascent is usually made to the summit of Mount Pelier. To the right of the road the green hillside rises steeply, variegated by clumps of pines, larches, and patches of yellow furze, while over the low hedge on the left will be seen Kilmashogue Mountain, the Three Rocks, and in the distance, the coast, with Kingstown, Howth, and the various familiar objects in the Bay. Presently, reaching a sharp turn in the road, we pass a small disused reservoir enclosed by a grove of trees, from which point a field path leads to Piperstown in the Glennasmole Valley.

As we continue our journey along the steep ascent, on looking back, the old ruined house on the top of Mount Pelier will be seen rising into view, while through the trees bordering the road, the dark wooded entrance to Glendoo presents a striking appearance. At the next fingerpost we turn to the right, beside one of the old danger signposts of the C.T.C., which warns the cyclist that the hill is dangerous—a very necessary warning in the old days, when brakes were all but useless, several lives having been lost through carelessness in descending this hill.

At this point, some 1,250 feet high, leaving all traces of civilization behind us, we enter upon a wild desert region, where we may well pause a few moments to look around us. Through the trees may be seen the coast and Bay, the Pigeon-house, Poolbeg, and the white sands of the Bull, and down below us the valley of the Owen Dugher, with the little hamlets of Rockbrook and Edmondstown situated on its banks. The buildings of Rathfarnham Convent form a conspicuous object adjoining the village, and with a good glass we can even discern the doings in the little village street. Whitechurch spire seems quite close, peeping above its woods, beyond which are the heights and church of Taney. We have now walked three miles, and have consequently a mile and a half more to travel before we reach the summit level of the road, and most of this also will have to be walked. Continuing our journey over bog and moor, we may observe close to the road, remains of the small square waterholes cut in the bog in former years for the purpose of obtaining supplies of ice for town, before the modern system of manufacturing it had come into vogue. The distant view of the city is very striking from here, and at night the various lights of town make a brilliant show, with their reflection in the smoke and sky. There is little to disturb the silence of this wild region, and the ear soon becomes so accustomed to the stillness that, as we stand and listen, we almost resent as intrusions the various sounds which reach us at this great elevation—the cry of a bird winging its way over the moors, the bark of a distant sheep dog, or occasionally, borne on the breeze sweeping across these desert solitudes, the faint whistle of a train, softened and mellowed by distance.

As we continue the ascent we may observe, at the opposite

side of Glennasmole, the mountains Seechon, Seefingan, and
Seefinn ; at the head of the valley is Kippure, the highest
mountain in the district, and far down below are the reservoirs
of the Rathmines Waterworks. At the upper end of the
Waterworks lakes are the few houses that remain of the hamlet
of Castlekelly, the picturesque woods enclosing Glennasmole
(formerly Heathfield) Lodge, and above these, the infant
Dodder glittering in the sunshine. Higher up, in front, may
be seen the spur of Kippure which forms the beetling cliff
overhanging Lough Bray. The dark brown slopes of Kippure
will be seen to be sharply furrowed by the mountain torrents
which swell the head waters of the Dodder in a region that,
even on the brightest day, looks gloomy and inhospitable.
We have now reached the summit of the Featherbed Pass,
1,611 feet high, and again mounting our machines, a rapid
run along a straight stretch of road through the Featherbed
Bog takes us to a sharp turn, descending to where, some hundreds
of feet below, the Reformatory stands in a commanding and
conspicuous position at the head of the Glencree valley.
Almost all ordinary trades are taught in this institution, and
the products are utilised by the inmates ; the shoemakers
and tailors supplying the boots and clothing, the younger
boys the stockings, and the bakers all the bread used in the
establishment. Besides these, there are carpenters, blacksmiths,
butchers, painters, gardeners, plumbers, and labourers, with fully
equipped workshops for the several crafts, so that the establishment is almost entirely a self-contained one.

The Reformatory is marked on the older maps as " Glencree
Barrack," having been one of the series of barracks erected
by the Government along the Military road after 1798, to
keep the inhabitants of the County Wicklow in subjection.

Looking from near the Reformatory towards Lough Bray,
the Military road may be seen in front, ascending in zig-zag
fashion the heights near the upper Lough, and sometimes
disappearing in the dark clouds which often overhang this
wild mountain region.

Scene on the Military Road on 30th January, 1910.

The Featherbed Pass on 30th January, 1910.

Leaving the Reformatory, and commencing our journey down the Glencree Valley, we traverse for some miles a bleak and boggy country with groups of cottages scattered at intervals over the barren hillsides, almost every homestead sheltered by a few stunted trees, while the characteristic odour of turf smoke from the cottages along the road reminds us that we are in a bog country. As we continue our descent, we obtain a fine view of the precipitous heights of Tonduff, with its great pine forest, at the opposite side of the valley. Almost midway is the low, rounded hill of Knockree, completely encircled by a by-road, a short distance beyond which we pass the Curtlestown Catholic Chapel and National School. Near Kilmalin is St. Moling's holy well, enclosed within the grounds of Powerscourt House, and now furnishing the water supply for that establishment. A mile beyond this point, we descend by one of the steepest hills in the county into Enniskerry, whence we can return to town by the Scalp or Bray as desired.

Glencree was in ancient times a Royal Park or preserve, almost entirely covered by primeval oak forest, and probably either wholly or partly enclosed by some description of artificial boundary to prevent the wild beasts preserved there from wandering away through the desert wilds of Wicklow. In *Sweetman's Calendar* it is recorded that in 1244 eighty deer were sent from the Royal forest at Chester to stock the King's park at Glencree, and that in 1296 the King sent a present to Eustace le Poer of twelve fallow deer from the Glencree forest.

As may be imagined, the repression of poaching formed no inconsiderable portion of the duties of the wardens or gamekeepers of this Royal preserve. Even the pious monks of St. Mary's Abbey, Dublin, who owned property in this neighbourhood, were unable to resist the temptation, as appears from the Chartulary of the Abbey in 1291, when the Abbot was attached for hunting in the forest with dogs and implements of the chase. In 1283 William le Deveneis, keeper of the King's demesne lands, was granted twelve oaks fit for timber from the King's wood in "Glincry," and a few years later, Queen Eleanor, wife of Edward I., established large timber works in the valley for the purpose of providing wood for her castle, then in process of erection at Haverford. William de Moenes (one of the family from which Rathmines derives its name) was keeper and manager of these works, and judging by the accounts of his operations in the State Papers, a very

Cottage at Lough Bray.
(1905.)

considerable thinning of the Royal forest must have been effected at this period.

The Justiciary Rolls of Edward I. in 1305 contain the entry of a complaint by Thomas de Sandely, a carpenter, to the effect that he was kept for three weeks in irons in the Castle of Dublin, at the suit of John Mathew, the Royal Forester at Glencree, who charged him with stealing timber. It appears that the culprit was caught in the act, but escaped and fled to Dublin, where he was arrested.

No further records of the Glencree forest can be discovered

after this, and it seems probable that in consequence of the
withdrawal of numbers of the English from Ireland for the
purpose of the war in Scotland, and to join Edward the First's
expedition to Flanders, the forest had to be abandoned, and
the Irish demolished it and its game. In any case it is pretty
certain that no successful attempt could have been made to
hold it during the rising of the Irish tribes and general dis-

Lough Bray
(1900.)

turbance in the country which followed the invasion of the
Bruces a few years later.

At the present day, remains of the trees which composed
this ancient forest are discovered in the bogs near Lough
Bray, as well as on the slopes of the high hills in its neighbourhood. Of course, the Glencree forest only formed a small part
of the wide-spreading forests alluded to by Holinshed and
Spenser, who tell us that the Wicklow glens were full of great
trees on the sides of the hills, and that these forests were interspersed with goodly valleys fit for fair habitations.

In the earlier days of the English occupation, when the tyrannical forest laws of the Normans were rigidly enforced, and the passion for the chase displaced all other considerations, the preservation of the natural forests became an important function of the Government. But at a later period the authorities viewed with anything but a friendly eye these great tracts of forest, on account of the shelter they afforded to the troublesome " wood kerne," and in the State Papers the woods are described as " a shelter for all ill-disposed " and " the seat and nursery of rebellion." After numerous plans had been suggested for the destruction of the woods, the Government at length adopted the surest and most profitable one, namely, the establishment of iron works in all the great forest districts.

The foregoing information respecting the Royal Forest of Glencree has been obtained from a paper on the subject by Mr. T. P. Le Fanu, in the *Journal of the Royal Society of Antiquaries for* 1893.

As an alternative to returning by Glencree and Enniskerry, the wilder and more mountainous road by Lower and Upper Loughs Bray, Sally Gap and the Liffey valley may be taken, but this route, besides being longer, will entail more walking owing to the steep ascent. A mile beyond the Reformatory, we pass a cottage from which a pathway leads to Lough Bray— a wild, gloomy tarn, 1,225 feet over sea level, believed by some to be the crater of an old-world volcano. Over its western shore rises a lofty cliff terminating the ridge of Kippure, behind which the head waters of the Dodder—the stream known as Tromanallison—takes its origin. Lough Bray Cottage, standing on a slight eminence over the northern shore, is picturesquely embosomed in a grove of trees, and commands a full view of the lake and the rugged mountain cliffs that partly encompass it. It is built in the Old English style of architecture, and was originally a gift by the Duke of Northumberland when Lord Lieutenant, to his medical adviser, Sir Philip Crampton, who had cured him of a troublesome skin disease.

About a mile further, Upper Lough Bray will be seen some distance away on the right, but it scarcely repays the trouble of a visit, as it is not so easy of access nor so picturesque as the Lower Lough. The road continues to ascend until the summit level, 1,714 feet high, is reached, 113 feet higher than the Featherbed Pass, when cyclists may again mount their machines, riding, however, with caution, as these high mountain roads receive little or no attention, and are almost always in a loose and stony condition. We next cross the infant Liffey which rises in a patch of dark bog on the left, and after a further journey of two miles through a dreary tract of heather and bog, we reach Sally Gap where the Military and the Luggela roads intersect at an altitude of 1,631 feet. At this desolate spot situated at the head of the Liffey valley, scarcely a trace of civilization is visible, and until the advent of the bicycle and motor, these roads were often left untraversed by any vehicle for many months at a time. In recent years, however, they have become so well known, that on any popular holiday during fine weather, motors, cycles, and even pedestrians may be counted by dozens.

In clear weather, Sally Gap commands an extended view of the Liffey valley, along which the road may be seen trending away for miles in the distance towards the main road to Blessington. After turning to the right, the road is rough, and almost unrideable for about a mile, and a C. T. C. danger notice warns cyclists against the danger of riding, but it is quite possible, with care, and reliable brakes, to make the descent. About a mile and a quarter from Sally Gap we pass portion of a house somewhat resembling the end wall of a church, said to be the remains of a residence in connection with the Shranamuck Iron Mines, which were worked here until the close of the 18th century. The name of Shranamuck is now all but lost, and the locality at the present day is known as Liffey Head. Immediately beyond this is Coronation Plantation, where the road passes through a miniature forest mostly of pines and larches, and where the visitor will do well to make a brief stay in order to observe the views of river, wood, and mountain. From one of the cottages on the road a pathway leads down to a footbridge across the river, near where there is a gamekeeper's cottage. Behind this cottage, and on the summit of a rising ground, is a monument, bearing on its four sides the following inscription, erected by the Marquess of Downshire to commemorate the commencement and object of Coronation Plantation :—[15]

LORDSHIP OF BLESSINGTON.
County of Wicklow.
This Plantation in the Brocky
Mountain of 500 Irish [acres]
Laid out by the
Most Honourable the Marquis of Downshire.
The fencing commenced in August, 1831.

————

It was called the
Coronation Planting, in honor of his Most Gracious
Majesty
King William IV.
The Most Noble the Marquis of Anglesey being
Lord Lieutenant of Ireland.

————

And for a future supply of useful
timber for the
Estate
And improvement of the
County and the
Benefit of the
Labouring Classes.

————

This planting
finished on the
————day of—————18—

As the concluding portion has not been filled in, it is probable that the planting was not carried out to the extent originally contemplated. Situated almost midway in the woods is Kippure bridge, crossing a tributary of the Liffey called Athdown brook, which flows down the slopes of Kippure mountain ; and close to the bridge is a shield-shaped iron tablet giving the distances in Irish measure of a number of places in the surrounding district. About a mile further will be seen, on opposite sides of the river, two groups of farmhouses, known as Scurlock's Leap and Ballysmuttan, connected by a cross road and iron lattice bridge ; and continuing our journey along the green banks of the Liffey, we presently reach Cloghleagh Bridge, a picturesque structure with stone balustrades, crossing the Shankill river. A stile across the adjoining wall leads down to the water's edge, from which there is a

Monument in Coronation Plantation.
(1890.)

pretty view of the bridge and the well-wooded banks adjoining. Not far from the bridge is a small but pretty church with a tower enveloped in ivy. At the Glen of Kilbride we enter a wood where the road forks, the road on the left leading to The Lamb, and that on the right to Brittas, from either of which the journey home lies along the well-known Blessington Steam Tram road.

Distances from G. P. O. by routes described :—Glencree, 12½ miles ; Enniskerry, 18½ ; Bray bridge, 21 ; G. P. O., 31.

Alternative route :—G. P. O. to Lough Bray, 13½ miles ; Sally Gap, 17 ; Coronation Plantation (Kippure), 21 ; Brittas, 27½ ; G. P. O., 41.

CHAPTER XXXVI

THE WESTERN HILLS, RATHMORE AND KILTEEL

LEAVING town, we make our way to Saggart by Terenure and Tallaght, turning to the right and following the telegraph line, about a mile beyond Tallaght, so as to avoid the dusty main road. Almost immediately turning to the left, we enter Fortunestown lane, a sequestered by-road, from which are obtained pleasing views of the Slade of Saggart and the adjoining hills, with occasional glimpses of the country to the northward. On entering Saggart we proceed along the village street, keeping straight ahead, past the old castle, which, with its modern windows and dashed walls, presents the appearance rather of a ruined dwellinghouse than of an ancient stronghold. A short, sharp descent brings us into the valley of the Slade—the little river that flows through the Slade of Saggart—after which we take the first turn to the right, along a gradually rising road, commanding extensive views over the flat country northward, while underneath the hill will be seen the Saggart Paper Mill, with its great wheel, and the long village of Rathcoole. As we continue our ascent, the hill of Coolmine will be seen on the left, its summit marked by a small square pillar to indicate the division between adjoining properties. About a mile and a quarter further we turn to the left, and immediately afterwards to the right, along a wild mountain road, constantly ascending, from which we obtain views of Blackchurch Hill, surmounted by its ruin, and of the wooded hills of Oughterard and Lyons. Proceeding along this road we may observe on our left the hill called Knockandinny, better known to the people around as Crockaunadreenagh, really a continuation of Knockananiller.

Our route now lies along a narrow country lane, gradually descending until a group of houses is met, where we turn to the left, up an unfrequented mountain road, which ultimately conducts us by a long ascent over Saggart Hill or Slieve Thoul, with Knockananiller, 1,110 feet high, on the left. The country here becomes wilder in character, the hedges give place to low stone walls or earthen banks topped with furze ; the shady nooks are adorned by the graceful fern and clustering violet, while the hedge-banks in spring time are illumined by the pale beauty of the primrose. We at length reach a pine plantation, where the lane becomes narrow and grass-grown, bordered by bracken and furze, and as we continue the ascent, the view extends into the plains of Kildare, over the blue range of hills far away to the westward. As we reach the summit—a truly secluded spot—1,000 feet high, we un-expectedly come into view of the mountainous country on the Wicklow side, and standing on the stile beside the iron gate we command views in both directions. Just beyond this point we meet roads turning right and left, and taking the left-hand one, which descends very rapidly, we may observe, rising immediately above us on the left, the summit of Saggart Hill. When near the bottom of the hill we turn to the right, at the cross roads, presently reaching the Blessington tram line, where we again turn to the right towards Brittas.

From Brittas we keep along the tram road for a distance of about 4½ miles, with the mountains Seechon, Seefinn, and Seefingan on our left, while a continuous line of lower elevations interposes on our right between us and the plains of Kildare. We at length come to Cross Chapel, and turning here to the right up a steep road, we take the first turn to the right up a rough laneway leading to the summit of a nameless hill, 1,153 feet high—one of the low range which forms a sort of natural border between the counties of Wicklow and Kildare. From the upper portion of this lane, in clear weather, there is a striking view over Westmeath, Kildare, King's and Queen's Counties, comprising the nearer portions of the Slieve Bloom range, the double-topped Croghan Hill in Westmeath, the Red Hills of Kildare, and the Hill of Allen surmounted by its tower, while with a glass may be distinguished Naas, Newbridge, Kildare, and many other towns and villages out in the plain. On the Wicklow side is a scene of wild mountain grandeur extending over Seechon, Seefinn, Seefingan, Mullaghcleevaun with its precipitous sides, Moanbane, and in the distance the flat summit of Lugnaquillia, frequently enveloped in cloud. A few miles away is Blessington, in the midst of a well-wooded country, and further off, in the upper Liffey valley, is Coronation Plantation, from which, with the aid of a glass, the road may be traced the whole way up to Sally Gap, the Military road being discernible thence as a line across the dark mountain side leading back towards Dublin. Retracing our steps along the lane until the road is again reached, and turning our backs on the mountains of Wicklow, we commence a long descent to Rathmore, a small hamlet, consisting of a church, a glebe house, and a few cottages.

The great rath or dun, from which Rathmore derives its name, stands prominently in view immediately north of the church. The central mound and enclosing circumvallation are still quite distinguishable, although a great part of the rath has been cut away to provide gravel for road repairs in the neighbourhood. About twenty years ago, during the progress of these excavations, a number of human skeletons were found buried within a circle of undressed limestones, and in 1894, after a landslip caused by heavy rain, there was disclosed a kistvaen, or sepulchral chamber, lined, roofed and floored with slabs of green limestone, containing a skeleton lying with the feet to the east. The floor of this chamber was 20 feet below the grass-grown surface of the rath. In the section of the rath laid bare by the excavations, a stratum of black material was observable, which, on examination, proved to be an accumulation of wood ashes, conjectured to be the deposits from culinary fires used by generations of pre-historic inhabitants. At some height above this stratum was found another layer of wood ashes, with which were mingled bones of oxen, sheep, and pigs, and broken horns of deer—the remains apparently of a settlement later than the lower one. Although, probably, not less than two thousand years had elapsed since the members of this primitive community cooked their food and warmed themselves at these fires, the ashes, when discovered, were as fresh and recognisable as though they had been extinguished but the day before.

Coming down to historic times we find that in 1229 the lands of Rathmore were granted to the Barons of Ophaly, and one of the witnesses to the deed of assignment is " Stephen de Segrave," from which family Segrave's Castle doubtless derives its name.

In 1286 Gerald FitzMaurice oge Fitzgerald, 4th Baron of Ophaly, died at Rathmore of wounds received in battle, and was buried at Kildare.

In 1356 the King sent a letter to Maurice Fitzgerald, 4th Earl of Kildare, reproving him for neglecting his manor of Rathmore, and ordering him, under penalty of its forfeiture, forthwith, to repair thither, accompanied by five esquires, twelve hobillers (horsemen), forty bowmen, and a suitable number of foot soldiers, fully armed and accoutred, to take the necessary steps for resisting the incursions of the O'Byrnes and their allies.

In 1538 the Constable of Rathmore Castle, one John Kelway, was slain by the O'Tooles under circumstances which are detailed at length in the next chapter.

On the 17th September, 1580, an encounter took place near Rathmore between a small body of cavalry belonging to the troops commanded by the Earl of Kildare and Sir Henry Harrington, and a body of the Irish, led by a brother of the redoubtable Feagh MacHugh O'Byrne of Glenmalure. The Irish had burnt Rathmore, and were returning early in the morning towards the mountains with a number of cattle taken as spoil, when, the alarm having been given, the troops set out in pursuit, and after a chase of about six or seven miles, overtook the raiders, who thereupon relinquished their prey and prepared to defend themselves. The troopers charged the party, killing several of them, at a ford, not named, but probably on the Liffey above Blessington. The survivors, rallying, made a desperate defence, killing the English officer in charge and the standard-bearer, but were ultimately overborne by the weight and numbers of the troopers, and all but two of them slain. Some fifty altogether fell in this encounter, among them being a son and two brothers of Feagh MacHugh O'Byrne. The Earl of Kildare, in his official report to the Secretary of State, testifies to the valiant manner in which the Irish fought on this occasion.

Of the ancient castle of Rathmore, so long an important outpost and stronghold of the Pale, no vestige now survives, and little information is available even as to the position of its site.

As the rath is now in charge of the Board of Public Works, and the excavations have been stopped, the preservation of this interesting relic may be regarded as assured.

At Rathmore, inquiry should be made for the road to Kilteel, as otherwise a stranger is likely to find his way to the Woolpack road, which would entail a considerable round. A short distance beyond the church is Segrave's Castle, apparently the remains of an old fortified dwellinghouse, with massive walls and a vaulted lower chamber, consisting evidently of several portions erected at different periods. It exhibits in parts luxuriant growths of ivy, and contains remains of flights of stone steps, cellars, &c. It is at present occupied as a dwelling, portion being used as dispensary for the surrounding district. Old coins, keys, and antique implements have been dug up in the vicinity.

A little over two miles from Rathmore is Kilteel, or Kilheale, where there is a fine old castle almost concealed by a grove of trees, which invest it with a gloomy appearance. According to the authority quoted at end hereof, a commandery or settlement of the Knights Hospitallers of St. John of Jerusalem was established here by Maurice Fitzgerald in the 13th century. It is recorded that in 1335 the Prior of Kilmainham appointed one Robert Clifford to be porter to the Commandery, with suitable clothing and half a mark annually for shoes, together with the use of apartments near the castle gate.

Kilteel Castle.
(1905.)

In a patent roll of the year 1541 we find an inrolment of an indenture by which " Sir John Rawson, Prior of the Hospital " of St. John of Jerusalem in Ireland, and his co-brethren, in " that the preceptory lordship or manor of Kilheale, in Kildare " County, is situated in the marches thereof, near the Irish " enemies, the O'Tholes, where resistance and defence are " required, grant to Thomas Alen and Mary, his wife, the said " lordship and all castles, messuages, &c., in Kilheale, &c., for " ever for the rent of five pounds."

In 1669 the castle was leased by the Earl of Tyrconnell to Daniel Reading, and in 1703 the property having been forfeited by the Earl, the trustees appointed to administer the forfeited estates assigned it to the Hollow Sword Blade Company, from whom it passed in 1706 to Sir William Fownes. From the Fownes family it passed to the Tighes in 1773, and from them it was purchased in 1838 by the Kennedy family, the present proprietors.

The castle consists of a single tower 46 feet high, on the north side of which is a turret containing the staircase to the upper storeys and the battlements. Adjoining and built on the side of the structure is a large arched gateway leading into a spacious courtyard, the right hand side of which is formed by a line of buildings, out-offices, &c., evidently of modern origin, but all in a more or less ruinous condition. The entrance door of the castle opens into an arched chamber, constructed with great strength and solidity so as to support the great mass of masonry above it. On ascending the winding staircase a small, round spyhole, pierced through granite, will be observed, commanding the passage to the gate. The castle consisted of three storeys and an upper chamber, the latter being arched like the basement, and a few steps from the first floor lead to the chamber over the entrance gateway. Continuing the staircase, we at length reach the battlements, from which may be seen the old projecting stone gargoyles for carrying off the rain water, still in perfect condition. The arched roof is flagged in the centre with large, flat stones, having been probably intended to be patrolled by a sentry. The staircase is lighted by the usual narrow slits, and the holes once occupied by iron bars are still discernible. Above the battlements is the turret, commanding an extended view over the mountains, a matter of great importance in the case of a stronghold situated, as this was, on the very limits of the Pale.

Behind the castle is the ancient churchyard with just a vestige of the old church, and adjoining are some blocks of an old building, said to have been a nunnery.

From Kilteel to Rathcoole, a distance of four miles, there is nothing calling for notice ; the last two miles are a continuous descent, and the concluding portion of the journey, from Rathcoole home, lies along the Naas road.

The total circuit described in this article entails a journey of about 36 miles.

In the preparation of this chapter, much information has been obtained from the following contributions to the *Journal of the County Kildare Archæological Society*, viz. :—Vol. II.—Article on Rathmore, by the Earl of Mayo. Vol. I.—Article on Kilteel Castle, by the Earl of Mayo. Vol. III.—Article on Rathmore, by Mr. Hans Hendrick Aylmer.

CHAPTER XXXVII

KILBRIDE, "THE THREE CASTLES," BLESSING-
TON, POULAPHUCA AND BALLYMORE EUSTACE

PROCEEDING along the Blessington tram road, described
in previous chapters, we can either follow the rails
to "The Lamb," or diverge from the beaten track
by taking the old coach road which turns to the left about three
miles beyond Tallaght, passing by Mount Seskin over Tallaght
Hill or Knockannavea. This route, superseded about a hundred
years ago, is less frequented than the other, and much steeper,
but commands a rather more extensive view of the Dublin
plain. *The Compleat Irish Traveller*, published in London
in 1788, thus describes this place :—" We next came to a place
" called Tallow Hill, where we employed our eyes a full hour
" contemplating as beautiful a prospect as ever Nature formed."
[Here follows a detailed description of the view.]   " In short,
" we that never saw it before were ravished with the sight.
" I own it gave me a peculiar contentment ; it looked like rest
" after fatigue. This glorious prospect is about six miles from
" Dublin, for here are roadstones marked ; but by our telescopes
" we brought it almost under the bottom of the hill."

Just at the top of the hill we pass the old country house,
Mount Seskin, described in another chapter, and in about a
mile and a half further, rejoin the tram road at Brittas. Two
miles beyond this is the place called " The Lamb," where there
is now only a tram station and ticket office, but where in former
times stood an inn with the sign of " The Lamb," which has
since left its name impressed on the locality.

Leaving " The Lamb " by the road turning off to the left
from the tramway, we descend by an undulating road fringed
with pine plantations, the rounded form of Dowry Hill being

on the left, into the romantic wooded Glen of Kilbride, situated in the valley of the Brittas River, near its junction with the Liffey. From this point Seechon, Seefinn, and Seefingan are to be seen on the left, and in front the higher elevations of Moanbane and Mullaghcleevaun. After passing the Catholic church we take the first turn on the right into a narrow, sheltered lane, conducting us to the green banks of the Liffey, with pasture lands sloping down to the water's edge. A short distance further, in a field to the right, is a square ivied ruin, called "The Three Castles," reputed by tradition to be the survivor of three, the sites of the other two being still pointed out by the people of the neighbourhood. On the southern side of the structure is what appears to have been a mullioned window, and the arched doorway on the western side is in an exceptionally good state of preservation. In the interior will be seen, still in perfect condition, the stone supports for the first floor, from which access was obtained to the battlements, now only possible with the aid of a ladder. The roof is very strongly built, arched like a bridge, and the masonry of both the interior and exterior is still wonderfully perfect. Adjoining is a large well, which furnished the water supply for the castle, and was, doubtless, included within the circuit of its outworks.

Considerable historic interest attaches to this place, which, being on the very borders of the Pale, was the scene of almost constant guerilla warfare.

About the beginning of June, 1538, John Kelway, "Constable of the King's Castell of Rathmor," was slain here by the Irish, under the following circumstances :—It appears from an account in the State Papers of Henry VIII., Vol III., pp. 18 and 27, that some short time previously this man had found "two of Tirrelagh Otoly's [O'Toole's] servauntes in "the English borders, next joynyng to the Tolys countre, "eting of meat, and for the same did immediately hang them." Tirlagh O'Toole of Fercullen (now Powerscourt) being at peace with the English Government at the time, forthwith demanded an explanation of this outrage, and accordingly, Kelway having arranged a meeting for the purpose of conferring with the Irish Chieftain, took with him, on the day appointed, a number of supporters and retainers from the adjoining districts. He probably intended treachery, but, as the sequel shows, the Irish had made ample provision for this contingency. The following letter, written to the King on the 4th June, by the Deputy, Lord Leonard Gray, from Dublin Castle, describes what took place on the occasion. (To make the letters more intelligible, the modernised spelling adopted in the article quoted at the end of this chapter has been adhered to) :—

" John Kelway, Constable of your Grace's Manor of Rath-
" more (which Manor bordereth upon the Tooles), of his own
" mind, raised certain gentlemen, poor husbandmen, and
" labourers, and went to parley with one Tirlagh O'Toole,
" with whom I was at peace, and in the parleying they differed,
" and the said Kelway chased the said Tirlagh, who took to
" flight to a certain place, where he had ambushed his kern
" [foot soldiers], and so suddenly turned, and set upon the said
" Kelway with all his ambushment, so that the said Kelway,
" and certain gentlemen of the country who were in his company
" were constrained to take [to] a small pile called the Three
" Castles, being upon the borders of the said Tirlagh's country.
" At which time they slew certain husbandmen and labourers,
" and a thatched house joining to the same pile put afire, so
" that the head of the same pile, being covered with thatch
" lacking battlement, took fire, and so all burned, so that the
" said Kelway, and such of the gentlemen as then were with him,
" were constrained to yield themselves prisoners ; and he
" being in hand with the said Tirlagh O'Toole, him slew
" cruelly. Assuring your Excellent Majesty that divers and
" sundry times I gave monition to all your constables joining
" upon the marches, to beware the train of their borderers,
" and specially to the said Kelway, who, I assure Your Grace,
" was as hardy a gentleman as any could be."

On the 5th June Sir William Brabazon, Lord Treasurer, addressed a letter, of which the following is an extract, to John Alen, Lord Chancellor, and Gerald Aylmer, whose son was at the time a prisoner in the hands of the Irish (Carew M.SS., 1515-74, No. 121) :—

" On Friday last past Mr. Kelway had parliament [conference] " with Tirloch O'Thoyll and Art besides the Three Castles ;

"The Three Castles," near Blessington.
(1905)

" who had assembled to him certain husbandmen and free-
" holders of Rathmore, Newtown, and the parish of Kill, and
" others, and would needs chase Tirloch and Art up to the
" high mountains, who there had their kerne ready, and turned
" back and set upon Kelway, and drove him to the Three
" Castles, and others with him, and set fire on the top of the
" Castle, so that they yielded ; wherein was taken Kelway and
" your young kinsman, Mr. Justice Richard Aylmer, young
" Flattesbury, Lang, and divers others ; and such husbandmen
" as the kerne met with they slew them, for they had no horses
" to flee, and as I am informed there was slain sixty house-

" holders. Thomas Lang is let forth, and Mr. Aylmer remaineth
" with them, and some others ; and after that they had Mr.
" Kelway within a while they killed him and such of the soldiers
" as was with him . . . I was never in despair in Ireland
" until now."

That the English authorities held Kelway to blame for the
entire incident is clearly shown by the following extracts, the
first from a letter written by Justice Luttrell to Chief Justice
Aylmer, and the second from a letter of Sir William Brabazon,
Privy Councillor, addressed to Thomas Cromwell, Secretary
of State—both letters having been written within a few months
of the occurrence :—

(1) " Brother Justice, I comend me unto you. Your nevue
" Richard Aylmer, it fer me shall not come forth, onles he
" pay his raunson, for so, this last day Tirlagh said playnly
" to my Lord of Ossery his messenger, and also to my servunt
" Dogherty, which chauncyed to be at Glendalach, when the
" discomfortur was made, and durst not cum from thens
" til this. Al the faut of the same mysaventur is put in
" Kelway, both by them of the Counte Kildar, that was ther
" present, and also of the Tolis [O'Tooles] as Pluncket may
" schow you. Your son, Bartholemew, scape themh apy, for
" he was there with Aylmer."

(2) " Toching the garrison of Rathmore, which Kelway
" had ; forasmuche as it is one of the chief keys of defence
" against the Tholes [O'Tooles], and that the countrie is greatly
" depopulate in thois quarters, we beseeche your good Lordship,
" that none be appointed thereunto, but sooche one as shal
" be an honest man, that wolbe resident ther, having some
" experience to governe and defende a countrie."   The
prisoners, Aylmer and Flatisbury, were shortly afterwards
released on payment of the ransom demanded.

In the *Annals of the Four Masters* under the year 1546
appears the following entry in regard to this place :—" The
" rebels were defeated at Baile-na-d-tri-g-Caislen (the town
" of the three castles) by the English and by Brian and

"Chogaidh, the sons of Terence O'Toole. The sons of
"James, the son of the Earl of Kildare—viz., Maurice and
"Henry—were taken prisoners, together with 24 of their
"people, who were afterwards brought to Dublin, and all
"cut in quarters, except Maurice, who was confined in the
'King's castle until it was determined what death he should
"receive." This Maurice was executed in the following year.

Less than a mile beyond the castle, in the townland of
Crosscool Harbour, and behind Liffey Cottage, is an ancient
burial place known as Scurlock's churchyard, enclosed by a
low wall, and sheltered by a number of lofty trees. It contains
a few recent and many old tombstones, among which may,
with difficulty, be distinguished the foundations of the ancient
church. Between the churchyard and the Liffey, and in the
low ground adjoining the latter, is a holy well under a solitary
ash tree, much resorted to in the month of June, when it is
reputed to possess special efficacy in healing various disorders.

At a distance of a little over two miles from the Three
Castles we enter Blessington by a pretty road, rising sharply
as it approaches the village, and in almost constant view of the
winding course of the Liffey.

Blessington still possesses some good houses, and the sides
of its wide street are planted with trees in boulevard fashion.

In the middle of the street, opposite the Courthouse, is a
fountain bearing the following inscription :—

"Erected on the coming of age of the Earl of Hillsborough,
"24th Dec., 1865.

"A tribute of respect from the Tenantry of the Wicklow,
"Kildare, and Kilkenny estates of the Marquis of Downshire.

"The water supplied at the cost of a kind and generous
"landlord for the benefit of his attached and loyal tenants."

Blessington is of comparatively modern origin, both town
and church having been erected in the reign of Charles II.,
by Archbishop Boyle, who presented to the church a set of
plate, as well as the fine chime of bells at present in use, the
latter bearing the date of their presentation in 1682. A

monument in the churchyard to the memory of the Archbishop, who was ancestor of the Lords Blessington, commemorates his benefaction to the village and its inhabitants. Blessington became greatly enhanced in prosperity and importance by the construction through it of the Dublin, Baltinglass, and Carlow coach road in the early part of the last century, in connection with which the great bridge designed by Nimmo was built over the Liffey at Poulaphuca in 1820, to supersede the old Horsepass bridge, about half a mile to the north-east, erected in earlier times to supersede the ford of the Horsepass. The

Blessington
(1905.)

inhabitants were incorporated in the reign of Charles II. by Royal Charter which was granted to Michael Boyle, Archbishop of Dublin, and Chancellor of Ireland, in 1669. The Corporation rejoiced in the high-sounding title of " The Sovereign, " Bailiffs, and Burgesses of the Borough and Town of Blessington," and consisted of a sovereign, two bailiffs, and twelve burgesses. The Archbishop as sovereign, was authorised by the charter to appoint a recorder, town clerk, and numerous other civic functionaries, whose salaries must have been a heavy drain upon the revenues of this Lilliputian municipality. The Borough was represented by two members in the Irish Parliament, for the loss of which representation the sum of £15,000 was awarded at the Union. This sum was paid to the Marquess of Downshire who had sustained serious loss in 1798 through the burning by the insurgents of his handsome mansion, situated with its demesne and deer park, a little to the west of the village. The house was never rebuilt, and it still remains in ruins. During the troubles of 1798 the church was used as a barrack for a garrison, temporarily maintained there for the protection of the locality.

The Compleat Irish Traveller (1788), contains the following reference to this place :—" Blessington, a pleasant place on a " rising ground. The church is very neat, and well kept, " with a sweet ring of bells, a thing not very commonly met " in this Kingdom. The town is neither large nor rich, but " its chief ornament is the seat of a worthy nobleman, that bears " the title of Lord Blessington, whose house is at the end " of an avenue to the left of the road, with a noble large terrace " walk, a quarter of an English mile in length, that leads to the " church in the town, across the road which faces the house."

Atkinson's *Irish Tourist* (1815), referring to Blessington, says :—" Though situate on grounds less picturesque than " Ballymore, it is composed of much better houses, can boast " of a more respectable population, and its position is more " elevated and conspicuous. The church, which is the most " ornamental building in the place, is seen from the vallies " and surrounding mountains, in connection with the village, " over which it lifts its modest spire, as a good object in that " dry and open landscape."

In 1815 Blessington furnished a corps of Yeomanry for the protection of that portion of the county.

To reach Ballymore-Eustace from Blessington the best route is to follow the tram rails as far as the sheds known as " The Tram Stores," where the road to the right should be taken. There is a shorter and more direct road, but being more undulating, no economy in point of time will be effected by choosing it. About 2½ miles from Blessington the road enters a dense plantation, and immediately afterwards passes

Russborough House, formerly the residence of the Earls of Milltown, situated in the centre of an extensive and well wooded park. This splendid mansion, in the Grecian style, was built after a design by Cassels, supposed to have been the architect of the Irish Parliament House, now the Bank of Ireland, and consists of a centre and two wings, connected by semi-circular colonnades of alternate Doric and Corinthian pillars. The interior is fitted up in stately fashion, and the floors of the principal apartments are constructed of polished mahogany.

About a mile beyond Russborough House we reach the tram sheds, where the road turns to the right, but, if time permits, Poulaphuca should be visited, as it is only about a mile out of the direct route.

The Liffey, which at Poulaphuca forms the boundary between the counties of Wicklow and Kildare, on approaching the fall, traverses a picturesquely wooded gorge, terminating at the bridge in a series of irregular rocky ledges, over which the river falls into a pool 150 feet below the parapet on the western side.

The name, Poulaphuca, means the pool of the Pooka, a kind of malevolent goblin peculiar to Ireland, but closely allied to the English Puck or Robin Goodfellow. All tradition of his exploits has long since passed out of this neighbourhood, and it is to be presumed that the march of modern improvements has driven him to wilder and more secluded haunts.

This locality is memorable in the annals of hunting as being the scene of the destruction of the Kildare hounds in 1813. The following description of this occurrence is abbreviated from an account, amusing for its topographical blunders, in *The Sporting Magazine* for 1832, and reproduced in the article on " Poul-a-phooka " referred to at the end of this chapter. In reading the account, it should be borne in mind that Poulaphuca bridge was not in existence at the time.

The hounds met in November, 1813, at the Tipper cross roads, near Naas, and after trying a neighbouring gorse, were trotting towards Troopersfields, when a large fox sprung up from a thicket immediately in front of the hounds, and made straight for the Wicklow mountains, over so rough a country and at such a pace that the whole field were thrown, with the exception of two, who, being well mounted, were able to keep reynard in sight.

"He passed Liffey Head, and without a check, gained the

Poulaphuca.
(1897.)

" romantic rocks, plantation, and waterfall of Pole Ovoca,
" where the river Ovoca [! !], so celebrated by Anacreon Moore,
" is precipitated over a high and rugged ridge of rocks, and
" which was then unusually swollen by a succession of rainy
" weather. In this plantation, on the other side of the Ovoca,
" was the villain's den, and, as it came in view, the hounds were
" close at its brush—a distance of twelve miles, all nearly
" against the hill, having been done in fifty-five minutes."
The fox made for a narrow part of the gorge above the fall, where

the river passed between two large rocks, and attempted to jump from one to the other, but lost his footing, and was precipitated into the torrent below. Twenty-five hounds who were leading at the time, with desperate resolution, jumped in after him, and were carried away by the flood.

When the writer of the article from which this account is taken, and Grennan, the huntsman, reached the bank of the river, fox and hounds were all in one struggling melée in the foaming eddies under the fall, some killed in the descent, others maimed but still alive, one of which latter succeeded in landing, though in an exhausted condition. The fox, the cause of all the trouble, also managed to reach the bank, though whether he escaped with his life does not transpire. Even if he failed to do so, however, it must have been a source of great consolation to him in his last moments to know that his death was being so well avenged.

" When Grennon saw the elite of his pack thus swept from " before his eyes, he stood (for assistance was impossible) for "some time like a statue ; but when he was assured, by their " lifeless remains floating in the pool below the fall, of the loss " of two particular veterans, whose names I [the narrator] " have forgotten, he could stand it no longer, but burst into " tears, and wept long and bitterly."

The route so airily described in this account is an utterly incredible and impossible one, and consisted, roughly speaking, of a run from near Naas to Sally Gap and then back to Poula-phuca. Liffey Head (adjoining Sally Gap), which is stated to have been passed on the way to " Pole Ovoca," is about 1,500 feet high, and not less than 15 miles from the meeting place, over as rough a piece of country as could be found in the County Wicklow ; and the run thither, and return to almost starting point—about 30 miles—all in 55 minutes, deserve to be classed with the exploits of Finn MacCool. Yet the writer of this amazing account was himself present at the hunt, and no doubt believed throughout that he was in the Vale of Ovoca.

Returning from the Waterfall along the road to the tram sheds, we turn to the left along the road to Ballymore-Eustace, about a mile and a half from Poulaphuca. This village, scattered over a broken piece of wooded country on the banks of the Liffey, is considerably larger than Blessington, consisting of a main street and several side streets, and is of more irregular appearance. The river is spanned here by a handsome bridge of six arches, constructed with great strength to withstand the floods from the mountains. *The Compleat Irish Traveller* thus describes this place about 1788 :—" Ballymore-

Ballymore-Eustace.
(1906.)

" Eustace is a small town on the river Liffey, with a handsome " bridge over that river. This town seems very much decayed, " though in a very pleasant situation. It was formerly of " much larger extent. The chief reason given for its decline " is that the great southern road which for ages led through " this place is now turned by way of Kilcullen bridge, which " has enriched that place and starved this, but it has much " bettered the traveller, and shortened the way, as we are " informed. Near this town is a fine large common, and it " was a very agreeable sight to see so many cattle of different " sorts pleasingly feeding on the sweet grass, as rich as any " meadow produces."

The earliest record of the ancient family of Eustace, from

2 c

which this place derives its name, is in 1373, when the Archbishop of Dublin appointed Thomas FitzEustace to be Constable of the Castle of Ballymore, with a salary of £10 a year, on condition of his residence there, and of his guardianship and maintenance of the fortress. With this appointment doubtless originated the name of Ballymore-Eustace.

Of the ancient stronghold no trace whatever now remains, though local tradition assigns for its site the eminence known as " Garrison Hill."

In 1524 Robert Talbot, of Belgard, while journeying to spend his Christmas with the Lord Deputy, was murdered at this place by James Fitzgerald, but owing to the influential connections of the Geraldines the murderer was never brought to justice.

In 1537 Robert Cowley, writing to Thomas Cromwell, Secretary of State, says :—" Ballymore and Tallagh, belonging " to the Archbishop of Dublin, stande most for the defence " of the counties of Dublin and Kildare against the O'Tooles " and O'Byrnes ; be it, therefore, ordered that the Com- " missioners shall see such farmers or tenants there as shall be " hardy marchers, able to defend that marches."

In a " Regal Visitation " of 1615, it is recorded that John Bathe was the curate of Ballymore-Eustace, and that the Irish translation of the Book of Common Prayer was in use in the Protestant church there.

In 1798 considerable skirmishing occurred both in the town itself and in its immediate neighbourhood, and the church was destroyed by the Insurgents.

The shortest way home from Ballymore-Eustace, otherwise than by Blessington, is by Rathmore and Kilteel, but it will add only a few miles to the journey to take the road leading to Naas, and turn to the right at the Watch House cross-roads into the Woolpack road, beside the Punchestown racecourse. In a field opposite the entrance to the course is a large monolith, and a short distance further, on the other side of the road, is a similar monument, about 20 feet high, inclined at an angle of about 30 degrees from the perpendicular. The list in this stone was caused, it is stated, by an attempt on the part of one of the Viscounts Allen to remove it to his mansion at Punchestown, by yoking fourteen couples of draught oxen to it. We next pass " Beggar's End," where six roads radiate, and from this point our route along the Woolpack road is very secluded, as it is very little used except during the Punchestown races. From the higher parts, extensive views are obtained over the flat, fertile plains of Kildare. At a distance of eight miles from the Watch House cross-roads we turn to the left, opposite the entrance to Johnstown House, by a short descent conducting us to Blackchurch Inn, whence our route home lies along the Naas road.

In the preparation of this chapter much valuable information has been derived from the following articles in Volume III. of the *Journal of the County Kildare Archælogical Society*, viz. :— " Rathmore " (for the Three Castles), by Mr. Hans Hendrick Aylmer, and " Ballymore Eustace and its Neighbouring Antiquities " and " Poul-a-phooka "—both by Lord Walter Fitzgerald.

Distances from G. P. O. by route described—Blessington, 20 miles ; Poulaphuca, 24 ; Ballymore-Eustace, 26 ; Punchestown, 31 ; G. P. O., 52.

CHAPTER XXXVIII

GLENNASMOLE OR THE VALLEY OF THE THRUSHES

GLENNASMOLE or the upper valley of the Dodder—
the most conspicuous glen in the Dublin range—is
well marked out by the slopes of Mount Pelier on
the east, and the towering heights of Seechon, Corrig and
Seefingan on the west, while Kippure, the highest mountain
in the view, forms the southern boundary of the valley, and
the watershed between the basins of the Dodder and the Liffey.

Pedestrians desirous of exploring this district should take the
steam tram to Tallaght, walking thence by Oldbawn bridge
to Bohernabreena and turning to the right at the chapel.
Immediately after passing Bohernabreena chapel will be seen
the entrance to Friarstown, the residence, early in the last
century, of Ponsonby Shaw, brother of Sir Robert Shaw, of
Bushy Park, Terenure. The murder of Kinlan, Shaw's gamekeeper, by the Kearneys, and the execution of the latter on
the bank of the Dodder, are described in another chapter.
Shaw spent a deal of money on improvements at Friarstown,
reclaiming and planting the grounds, which he converted
into a pretty wooded glen, with winding walks, grottoes and
miniature waterfalls. At the head of the glen he formed a lake
by damming the course of the stream, but it was hardly well
finished when it burst and swept all before it, making a complete
wreck of his work. He was so much discouraged by this mishap
that he made no attempt to repair the damage, and the place
is now in a state of wildness, which, however, invests it with a
charm it probably never possessed in its former condition.
One of the pathways leads to the bottom of the glen near a

cascade and ruined grotto, which are so densely shaded by trees that scarcely a ray of sunlight reaches them in the summer-time. This place will well repay a visit if arrangements permit.

A steep descent from the chapel leads to the picturesquely situated Bohernabreena bridge, built about 1837, across a very narrow part of the river called the Sheep Hole, a short distance beyond which is the entrance to the waterworks of

The Dodder and Glennasmole from Bohernabreena Bridge
(1902.)

the Rathmines and Rathgar township. Admission to the pathway, which is practicable for cycles, leading by the river and reservoir lakes to Castlekelly, is allowed only on production of a pass available for bearer and party, to be obtained on application to the Rathmines Commissioners. But, as will be seen further on, there is an alternative route, more direct than the waterworks pathway, in case a pass is not available.

The pathway runs close to the river, the banks of which in parts are broken and precipitous, occasionally diversified by patches of stunted wood and furze. A caretaker's cottage marks the commencement of the lower lake, and a similar cottage, sheltered by evergreens, is passed as we ascend to the level of the upper lake. The borders of these lakes have been prettily planted in places, and the whole aspect of the valley has been so much altered by their construction that if Finn MacCool could revisit the place, he would hardly recognise it as the scene of his classic exploits. As we proceed along the margin of the upper lake we can see in front the brown, furrowed slopes of Kippure, on which the head waters of the Dodder and its tributary streams, Slade Brook and Cot Brook, take their origin.

On reaching the extremity of the upper lake we emerge from the territory of the Rathmines Commissioners, and pass through the turnstile out on the public road at Castlekelly bridge, which bears an inscription stating that it was rebuilt in 1906, and that its predecessor was destroyed the previous year by a flood. In about half a mile from this we reach the secluded hamlet of Castlekelly, taking its name from an old castle which formerly defended this pass through the mountains, and whose foundations may still be traced in the masonry of some of the cottages. Eugene O'Curry visited this place in 1837, and his letters in connection with the Ordnance Survey, now in the Royal Irish Academy, afford most interesting reading as to the conditions of life in Glennasmole in the early part of last century. He obtained his information from an old man, eighty-four years of age, who spoke Irish fluently, and who stated that forty years previously, little English was spoken in this sequestered glen, the only persons having any considerable knowledge of it being the carmen whose business took them regularly to Dublin.

As an alternative to going by the waterworks pathway, Castlekelly can be reached more directly either by taking the road past Bohernabreena chapel, up the steep hill, or by entering Friarstown glen, and following the course of the stream which flows through it, until the road is met at the little hamlet of Glassamucky, situated in a deep dell and sheltered by a grove of trees Higher up the slope of the valley above this place, and on the upper road, is Piperstown, now represented by a few cottages, but more extensive in former years when the glen had a larger population.

About half a mile beyond Glassamucky was formerly St. Ann's Monastery, a small modern establishment, where some thirty years ago a quoit club used to meet and dine occasionally, the provisions being sent out from town, and the room and appointments provided in the building. Many a pleasant summer's evening was spent by the members in the pure mountain air here, the only disadvantage being the long drive from and back to the city.

A mile further, a winding pathway leads to the ruined church and holy well of St. Ann's, in a sequestered position some distance lower down the slope of the valley. This old church is properly St. Sanctan's or Sentan's, the name " Sentan " having been corrupted into " St. Ann," and the founder, one of the early saints, thereby deprived of his rightful credit and inheritance—an injustice which it is to be feared is now irrevocable. The mistake seems to have originated with the erroneous translation of the old name Killnasantan into " the Church of St. Ann," which erroneous form was adopted by Dalton in his *History of the County Dublin*, and perpetuated in the Maps of the Ordnance Survey. In Archbishop Alan's *Repertorium Viride* the name is written Killmesantan (St. Mosanctan's or Santan's Church), and in *The Annals of the Four Masters* the death is recorded in A.D. 952 of the Abbot of the Church of Bishop Sanctan. So far back as 1326 this district was described in official records as " waste by war " and " lying within the Irishry, therefore, waste and unprofitable," and the church has probably not been used as a place of worship since that time. A number of old headstones may be seen in the churchyard, and near the entrance is a holy water font carved out of a granite boulder.

An exactly similar instance of corruption of this saint's name occurs in the Isle of Man, where there is a headland called St. Ann's Head, near Santon, and four miles south west

of Douglas. Santon was known as St. Sanctan's in the 16th
century, after which it assumed in succession the forms Kirk
Sanctan, Kirk Santan, Santan, and lastly Santon, although
the parish is still Kirk Santan. The name of the headland
should, of course, be St. Santan's Head, and on some maps
a compromise is made by calling it Santon Head.

Returning to the road, and continuing our journey up the
valley, we presently reach a group of houses bearing the curiou;
name of Cunard, half a mile beyond which is Castlekelly,
already described. About half a mile further, near the confluence of Cot Brook and the Dodder, is Glennasmole Lodge,
sheltered by its woods and standing in a picturesque and commanding position at the head of the valley. This house,
which was formerly called Heathfield Lodge, was erected,
probably late in the eighteenth century, by George Grierson,
King's Printer, who was very wealthy, and who received
£100,000 as commutation of his office at the time of the Union.
After his death his three daughters, who inherited very little
from him, as he had dissipated most of his wealth during his
lifetime, resided here for many years, and altered the house
into a Swiss châlet with a thatched roof and a balcony around
of carved woodwork. They planted the gardens with many
rare plants, as well as some magnificent rhododendrons, which
still flourish there, and are the finest to be seen for many miles
around. These ladies travelled a good deal, at a time when
travelling was neither so easy nor so comfortable as it is at the
present day, and their house was adorned with curios from
many a foreign land. They endeavoured, with some success,
to introduce wood carving in the Swiss style among the people
in the valley. The house was ultimately destroyed by an
accidental fire—nothing but the stonework being left—and
the Misses Grierson were thereby reduced greatly in circumstances, as nearly everything they possessed perished in the
flames.

A Mr. Cobbe next came into possession, and re-built the
house in rather more solid fashion, with a slated roof, after

which it became known for some time as "Cobbe's Lodge."
It has changed hands several times since, and is maintained
in excellent order by the present occupiers.

Close to the boundary wall of the grounds, at the western
side, is a boulder weighing about a ton, known as "Finn
MacCool's Stone," on which there formerly was a marble
slab bearing an inscription to the effect that Finn carried

Glennasmole Lodge, formerly Heathfield Lodge.
(1905.)

the stone on his shoulder from the mountain on the opposite
side of the valley. This slab has long since been removed,
but the mark left by its insertion still remains.

The main stream of the Dodder flows immediately to the
east of the house, and those who are not afraid of rough walking,
may explore it in dry weather, for some distance towards its
source on Kippure.

The transactions of the Ossianic Society contain translations
of a number of old Irish poems relating to Glennasmole,
Finn MacCool and his bodyguard of the Fena. In one of

these—"The Chase of Glennasmole"—it is related how Finn with his famous hounds, Brann and Sgeolan, and a number of hunters and dogs met one misty morning in the glen to hunt deer They started a piebald doe, but although they hunted her all day they were unable to overtake her, and when darkness set in, they found themselves far away among the wild hills without any of their hounds, which had all become lost in the excitement of the chase. After a time, however, Brann returned in sorry plight, and, lying down before Finn, howled. Presently a beautiful woman appeared on the scene and invited the whole party to a feast, which invitation they gladly accepted, as they were hungry and fatigued. When they had satisfied themselves at the feast, a hideous witch from Greece appeared and asked Finn to be her husband, which honour he declined. She was so enraged at his refusal, that she told them she would kill them all in spite of their renowned prowess, and setting off, assembled her fleet and sailed to Howth, where she landed and fought with Goll MacMorna the Brave for three days, while fifty amazons kept guard over the enchanted Fena. Just as the witch was about to overcome Goll, the Fena broke the enchantment, and rushing to battle, Oscar drove his spear through her heart, and the slaughter of her amazon bodyguard followed.

In another poem called "The Chase of Lough Lean" (Killarney), Oisin, who had travelled to Killarney to visit St. Patrick, recounts to him at great length the mighty deeds of the Fena and their hounds, and being indignant at the inhospitable treatment he received from the saint's housekeeper, says :—"I have often slept abroad on the hills, under the "grey dew [frost] on the foliage of the trees, and I was not "accustomed to a supperless bed while there was a stag on "yonder hill." St. Patrick replies :—"Thou hast not a bed "without food, for thou gettest seven cakes of bread, a large "roll of butter [*miscaun*], and a quarter of beef every day." To which Oisin rejoins :—"I saw a berry of the rowan tree "[mountain ash] larger twice than thy roll, and I saw an ivy

" leaf larger and wider than thy cake of bread, and I saw a
" quarter of a blackbird which was larger than thy quarter
" of beef. It is this that fills my soul with sadness to be in
" thy house, poor-hearted wretch that thou art ! "

To substantiate his statement, Oisin, though he was aged
and blind, set out for Glennasmole, accompanied by a guide,
with whose assistance he found a rowan tree on which were
growing berries of a gigantic size, also some ivy leaves of
corresponding dimensions which they carefully preserved to
show to St. Patrick. On their way back to Killarney they
passed through the Curragh of Kildare, where Oisin sounded
the Dord Fian, a magic chant, whereupon a flock of blackbirds,
among which was one of immense size, answered the call.
Oisin unleashed his favourite hound Brann, which, after a
fierce and prolonged struggle, killed the gigantic bird. They
then cut off the leg, and took it with the rowan berries and the
ivy leaves to St. Patrick, who, it is to be hoped, was convinced
thereby that he should accord more generous treatment to his
guest.

In a poem called " The Finnian Hunt of Sliabh Truim," it is
related how Finn MacCool, after a victorious campaign through
the country, slaying dragons, serpents, and all kinds of monsters,
attacks and kills the terrible Arrach or dragon of Glennasmole.

Another poem called " The Adventures of the Amadan
Mor," tells how the Gruagach of the Golden Mantle, the
Amadan Mor and his lady love were passing through Glen-
nasmole :—

> " 'Twas not long till they saw in the valley,
>   A city that shone like gold,
>   There was no colour which eye had seen,
>   That was not in the mansion and many more.

> " 'Twas then the young maiden asked
>   What golden city is that,
>   Of the finest appearance and hue,
>   Or could it be betrayed or traversed ?

" Dun-an-Oir [Fort of the Gold] is its name
The strong Dun of Glen na Smoil,
There is not now of its inhabitants alive,
But myself and my wife."

" The Glen through which thou has passed,
Is always full of witchcraft."

＊   ＊   ＊   ＊   ＊

The description of the subsequent adventures of the party
in Glennasmole, with giants, " gruagachs " (hairy fellows),
and enchantments, however interesting from a mythological
point of view, is full of tiresome iteration, without any topographical allusions that would justify further quotations.

These poems probably date from about the 12th century,
though some are much older.   At that period the Glen must
have presented an appearance entirely different from its present
aspect, and wooded, as it doubtless was, to the tops of the
high hills that encompass it, while its forest fastnesses sheltered
the red deer and the wolf, it would naturally have been regarded
with superstitious fear by the simple country folk of that time.

Finn MacCool was the commander of an order of warriors
called the Fianna or Fena, who rose to great power in the reign of
Cormac MacArt in the 3rd century.   After Finn, the most
distinguished chieftains among these heroes were Oisin or
Ossian, his son, Oscar, the son of Oisin, and Dermot O'Dyna.

Finn's chief residence stood on the summit of the Hill of
Allen, near Newbridge, where its site is now occupied by a
pillar, and the whole neighbourhood, even at the present day,
abounds with vivid traditions of the brave deeds of this great
warrior and hero of the olden time.

With the passing of the heroic age, blackbirds have sadly
degenerated, and rowan berries have shrunk to the size of haws,
but the giant ivy still flourishes, and is to be found in abundance
in many parts of the Glen.   Wood sorrel, too, may be seen
growing to a gigantic size, and Oisin, had he been so minded,

might have utilised this fact also for the discomfiture of St. Patrick's housekeeper.

Above the reservoir lakes the Dodder is formed of three principal streams—viz., Slade Brook, Cot Brook, and the main stream, which latter is composed of two smaller streams, Mareen's Brook rising on the north-eastern slope of Kippure, and Tromanallison or Allison's Brook, rising on the portion above Lough Bray, in a wild and almost inaccessible region, surrounded on all sides by dreary swamps and bogs. At Castlekelly the main stream is joined by Cot Brook, and a little lower down by Slade Brook, beyond which a number of smaller tributaries flow into the reservoirs.

It is a somewhat remarkable fact that the head waters of the Liffey and the Dodder, whose courses are so widely divergent until they meet at Ringsend, are within a few hundred yards of each other, on the eastern ridge of Kippure.

On account of the number of rowan trees along its banks, and the rough and rocky nature of its course, the upper reach of the main stream of the Dodder is sometimes called "The Cataract of the Rowan Tree," a name which is, however, more properly applicable to the portion about seven-eighths of a mile above Glennasmole Lodge, where there are a couple of picturesque waterfalls. One precipitous part of the course is known as St. Mary's Cliff—the home of the giant ivy celebrated in Ossianic romance.

If the weather be dry, the return to town may be made by ascending the eastern side of the valley until the Military road is reached. This, however, entails a pretty stiff climb, and probably most of the visitors after a day's rambling about this wild country, will be satisfied to return either by the Glassamucky or Piperstown road to Tallaght, from which the steam tram can be taken to Terenure.

Distances :—From Tallaght to Glennasmole Lodge by the Waterworks pathway, 5¾ miles ; by Friarstown and Glassamucky, 5¼ miles. If the return is made by climbing the side of the valley and taking the Piperstown road back to Tallaght, the distance will be about 6 miles from Glennasmole Lodge. Returning by the Military road will entail walking to Rathfarnham, which will add about a mile to the journey. The whole of the route described is practicable for cyclists as far as Glennasmole Lodge, but a good deal of walking will be necessary.

The authorities consulted in the preparation of this chapter are :—Handcock's *History and Antiquities of Tallaght ; The Transactions of the Ossianic Society ;* Dalton's *History of the County of Dublin ;* and Joyce's *Irish Names of Places.*

CHAPTER XXXIX

THE PHŒNIX PARK, CASTLEKNOCK, CLONEE
AND DUNBOYNE

ENTERING the Phœnix Park at Parkgate Street, we proceed along what is now known as the Main Road, but which was formerly called Chesterfield Road, after Lord Chesterfield, who was instrumental in having it constructed during the period of his viceroyalty about the middle of the 18th century. It is a little over 2½ miles in length, and being nearly straight, is a more direct route to Castleknock than the old road, which it practically superseded. As constructed by Lord Chesterfield, however, it differed slightly from the existing route in deflecting to the northward between Parkgate Street and the Phœnix monument, and to the southward between that and the Castleknock gate. It was straightened out between 1840 and 1850.

In order to trace the successive steps in the process of acquisition, formation, and enclosure by the Government, of the Phœnix Park, it is necessary to go back to the 16th century, when, in consequence of the Suppression of the Monasteries by statute of 1537, the Hospital and lands at Kilmainham, where the Royal Hospital now stands, belonging to the Knights Hospitallers of St. John of Jerusalem, became the property of the Crown. For a time the place was maintained as a residence for the Viceroys, but at length becoming too dilapidated for further repairs, the hospital buildings and lands of Kilmainham, together with a large tract at the northern side of the river, were ceded to Sir Richard Sutton in 1611 in exchange for certain lands in Cornwall. Sutton sold them to Sir Edward

Fisher, who erected within the next few years a country residence which he called " The Phœnix," on Thomas Hill, now occupied by the Magazine Fort—the finest site in all the district, commanding an unrivalled view of Dublin city, the Liffey valley, and the mountains and country to the southward.

The name " Phœnix," as applied to this old manorhouse, appears for the first time in documents of the date 1619, and we have to consider what were the circumstances which led Sir Edward Fisher to adopt this name. It has been supposed by some that he chose it because the majestic appearance of the house, standing on a hill overlooking the Liffey valley, suggested the conventional attitude of the Phœnix bird rising from its ashes. The more widely accepted origin of the name, however, is that given by Warburton, Whitelaw and Walsh in their *History of Dublin* (1818), who state that it is derived from a spring called Fionn-uisge (Feenisk), which had been resorted to from time immemorial for the beneficial effects of its waters. This spring was situated on the narrow neck of land between the pond in the present Viceregal grounds and the pond in the Zoological Gardens, close to where there is now a picturesque keeper's lodge built like a Swiss châlet. Despite its merits as a chalybeate spa, it remained in an exposed and neglected condition until the year 1800, when in consequence of some cures said to have been effected through its agency, it acquired celebrity, and was resorted to by numbers of fashionable people from the metropolis. About five years afterwards it was enclosed, and an approach constructed to it by a gradual descent along a planted avenue, all traces of which have since been lost owing to alterations in the adjacent ground. Lord Whitworth having derived some benefit from its waters during his viceroyalty, had the spa covered by a small structure of Portland stone surmounted by a figure of an eagle as the emblem of longevity, while above it, on the summit of a rising ground, the Duchess of Richmond erected a rustic dome with seats around, for the accommodation of those frequenting

the spa, in the back of which structure was an entablature
bearing the inscription :—

This seat
Given by Her Grace,
Charlotte, Duchess of Richmond,
For the Health and Comfort
Of the Inhabitants
Of Dublin. August 19th, 1813.

The example set by the Duke of Richmond and Lord
Whitworth, Lords Lieutenant, in taking the waters of the spa,
was largely followed by the Dublin citizens, and during the
height of its popularity it was visited by over 1,000 persons
every week. The price charged was 5s. for the season, or
1d. a tumbler.

In after years the spa, when it had greatly fallen out of
vogue, was rented from time to time to persons who made a
precarious living, ostensibly by retailing the water to the public,
but really by the sale of more potent beverages.

As Warburton, Whitelaw and Walsh give no authority for
their statement that this spa was the original Fionn-uisge,
and as it does not appear to be mentioned by any earlier writer,
it is possible that their information was derived from the
common tradition at the time. Dalton, in his *History of the
County of Dublin* (1837), follows their statement, as also the
author of *The Picture of Dublin or Stranger's Guide*, &c. (1843),
and other writers.

It seems probable, therefore, that the Fionn-uisge or
Feenisk spa originated the name of the lands on which the
Phœnix manor house was built by Sir Edward Fisher, who
naturally adopted the same name in selecting a title for the
house. These lands formed the earliest portion of the Park
subsequently known as the Phœnix, a name so closely resembling
" Feenisk " that it was substituted for it as the nearest English
equivalent, as happened in the case of the river Finisk, a
tributary of the Munster Blackwater, which has been corrupted

2 D

into " Phœnix " by at least one historical writer on the district. The stone covering erected over the well by Lord Whitworth was in time replaced by a rustic thatched structure which was accidentally burnt about 1877. There then remained only some stone steps and jambs, on the removal of which soon afterwards, the site was levelled and sown with grass. For some time prior to its obliteration, the well, becoming neglected, had degenerated into a mere puddle, and there seems to have been a suspicion that, owing to the construction of two main drains in its vicinity, the water had become contaminated.

Near the Phœnix column, and just outside the Viceregal grounds, behind the gate lodge, is a beautifully clear spring which has been supposed by some to be the original Fionn-uisge.

The Government, being without any official residence for the Irish Viceroys, in 1618 repurchased the Phœnix lands with the new house which Sir Edward Fisher had built thereon, and from that time until the Restoration, the Phœnix manor house was the principal viceregal residence, Strafford, Ormonde, and Henry Cromwell being among its occupants during that period. About 1670 a new residence for the viceroys, subsequently known as "The King's House," was acquired at Chapelizod, but the Phœnix house continued in occasional use by viceregal functionaries until 1734, when it was demolished to make room for the present Magazine Fort of which Swift sarcastically wrote :—

> " Behold a proof of Irish sense,
>   Here Irish wit is seen,
> When nothing's left that's worth defence,
>   We build a magazine."

The Crown lands held with the manor house after its purchase from Sir Edward Fisher in 1618, cannot have exceeded 400 or 500 acres, and this being considered inadequate for a viceregal demesne and deer park, additional lands were at intervals acquired at Chapelizod, Grangegorman, Castleknock, and Ashtown, as well as the land extending to the site of the present Viceregal Lodge, the cost in all amounting to over £40,000. The Phœnix Park, as thus constituted, was of considerably greater area than at present, including as it did, the lands of Kilmainham and Chapelizod, and a connecting strip between them on the south of the river. About 1660 the limits of the Park having been sufficiently extended, the Government considered it advisable to enclose it, and, accordingly, the sum of £6,000 was expended on the erection of a boundary wall, but the contractor proved to be little better than a swindler, and in the absence of proper supervision the work was executed in sorry fashion.

In 1680 a Royal Warrant having been issued for the erection of the Royal Hospital, and for the appropriation to its use of 64 acres from the lands of the Park, it became necessary to re-adjust the southern boundary, and opportunity was at the same time taken to detach all the lands at the south side of the river from the Park, which thereupon assumed its modern shape and dimensions.

Within the past few years the strips of land along the river between Islandbridge and Chapelizod have been acquired by the Crown as a technical addition to the Phœnix Park, which, therefore, extends now as it did of old to the south side of the Liffey. The immediate purpose of this acquisition was, however, to prevent the disfigurement of the view from the Park by the erection of unsightly buildings along the river.

While the original conception of the Park would appear to have been that of an appanage and game preserve of the Viceregal residence, the public from an early date seem to have been admitted to it, and by the beginning of George the Second's reign it had come much into vogue as a fashionable resort. Improvements by successive viceroys added to its attractions and popularity, but no name has been so closely associated with the Park in the public mind as that of the Earl of Chesterfield, who, during his viceroyalty, ornamentally planted and laid it out, constructed the Main Road, and erected the Phœnix column, besides opening the greater portion of it to the public.   The Phœnix monument was, of course, designed in complete ignorance of the true etymology of the name of the Park, which, if ever recognised, must have been completely lost on the abandonment and subsequent demolition of the old Phœnix manor house and the transfer of the viceregal residence to Chapelizod.

This graceful monument bears on two opposite sides of the pedestal the inscriptions :—

Civium oblectamento
Campum rudem et incultum
Ornari jussit
Philippus Stanhope
Comes de Chesterfield
Prorex

Impensis suis posuit
Philippus Stanhope, Comes
De Chesterfield, Prorex.

[*Translation.*]

Philip Stanhope, Earl of Chesterfield, Lord Lieutenant, ordered this wild and uncultivated land to be ornamented for the pleasure of the citizens.

Philip Stanhope, Earl of Chesterfield, Lord Lieutenant, erected [this column] at his own expense.

The monument, which was erected in the years 1745-7, is beginning to show the effects of time, and the portion above the plinth has taken a perceptible list to the northward.   It would greatly add to its interest if a tablet were affixed, setting forth the circumstances under which the Park acquired its name, and explaining the misconception under which the column was erected by Lord Chesterfield.

It may be mentioned that in bright warm weather a remarkable mirage is at times visible on approaching the Phœnix monument from the Dublin side. The road on these occasions assumes the appearance of a pool of water in which reflections of passing objects are seen. This phenomenon has appeared only since the road was treated with tar to mitigate the dust raised by motor traffic, and is caused by refraction resulting from the heating of the layer of air next the road surface, the tar on which is easily heated by the sun.

The King's House at Chapelizod, acquired about 1670, as already stated, falling into decay in the 18th century, the Irish Viceroys ceased to use it, and about 1758 it was finally abandoned as a viceregal residence. For many years afterwards, the viceroys had to find quarters for themselves, as had other officials on appointment here, but this proving inconvenient and unsatisfactory, negotiations were opened for the acquisition of a suitable residence, and in 1781 the Government purchased the house of Mr. Robert Clements, then a plain brick structure, which, with the additions made by Lord Hardwicke, the Duke of Richmond and Lord Whitworth, developed into the present Viceregal Lodge.

The Main Road is the usual route to Castleknock, but is not nearly so picturesque as the more circuitous road skirting the southern boundary and commanding a succession of views of the fertile valley of the Liffey, the more prominent objects in the southern portion of the county, and the mountains extended in the distance. Proceeding by this road, which diverges from the Main Road a short distance from the Park Gate, we pass on our right the site of the old Star Fort, an extensive fortified enclosure which was never completed. We next pass the Wellington Testimonial, 205 feet high, the most conspicuous object in the Park, and presently the Magazine Fort, about a mile beyond which is the Royal Hibernian Military School, situated on the heights over Chapelizod. Leaving the Fifteen Acres on our right, we take the first turn to the left, leading to the Furry Glen and passing out of the Park at the

Knockmaroon Gate, where instead of descending the steep hill down to the riverside, we keep to the right, up hill, to reach Castleknock. About three-quarters of a mile further is a cross-roads, close to which will be seen two somewhat similar hills, each surmounted by a ruin. That on the right is Windmill Hill, and the ruin on its summit was originally designed as a small observatory. To the left, and partly concealed by the south-western wing of Castleknock College, is the " knock " or hill from which Castleknock derives its name, prettily planted with tall trees and crowned by the ruined castle of the Tyrrells. The hill and ruin are maintained in excellent order, and visitors desirous of seeing them are admitted on application. From the summit of the hill an excellent view is obtained of the surrounding country when the trees are not in full foliage.

Local tradition avers that a vast treasure is buried in Windmill Hill—a type of tradition which is, however, quite common in the neighbourhood of ruins throughout the country.

Towards the close of the 12th century Strongbow made a grant of the lands of Castleknock to his friend, Hugh Tyrrell, a distinguished warrior, who, on taking up possession, built a castle and assumed the title of Baron of Castleknock, held by his descendants for three hundred years. In 1317 King Robert Bruce and his brother Edward, with an army of 20,000 men, encamped here, intending to besiege Dublin, but owing to the energetic measures adopted by the citizens, who burnt all the houses and buildings outside the city walls, the besiegers, deprived of all shelter, abandoned their project and marched on Limerick instead. In 1642 Colonel Monk, afterwards Earl of Albemarle, with a body of Parliamentarians, took the castle by assault, some eighty of the defenders being slain, and many more hanged on surrender. In 1647 Owen Roe O'Neill and Sir Thomas Esmonde, in command of a Royalist force, retook the castle from the Parliamentarians after defeating a strong force of cavalry sent to the assistance of the garrison. The castle fell into decay about the time of the Restoration, and has never since been repaired. In one of the walls is a window, of which Stanyhurst (1584), wrote :—" Though it " be neither glazed nor latticed, but open, yet let the weather " be stormy, and the wind bluster boisterously on every side " of the house, and place a candle there, and it will burn as " quietly as if no puff of wind blew. This may be tried at " this day, whoso shall be willing to put it in practice."

Half a mile further is the village of Castleknock, where an

Castleknock.
(1905.)

old tradition avers there is a spring well innocuous to human beings, but poisonous to all the lower animals. No information is now available as to its position, and it remains for some investigator to achieve the fame of its re-discovery by experiment. Adjoining the church is a holy well dedicated to St. Brigid, the patron saint of the parish. A short distance to the north-east of the castle is a vein of lead ore, where a mine was opened in 1744 by a Mr. Edward Ford.

A mile beyond Castleknock is Blanchardstown, near which the road crosses the Midland Railway and the Royal Canal by a high bridge affording extended views along the green banks of the Tolka. Three hundred years ago there was a wood known as the Great Wood of Blanchardstown or Scald Wood, in the possession of the Luttrells, and a considerable portion of it still remains to the north and east of the village. Continuing our journey, after a mile and a half further, we enter the hamlet of Mulhuddart, situated on the right bank of the Tolka and traversed by one of its tributaries. A little over half a mile to the north-east is the ruin of the old church, close to which is Our Lady's Well, enclosed by a stone covering with two niches for statues.

In an account of " A Journey from Dublin to the Shores of Lough Dergh," written by Isaac Butler about 1741, it is stated in regard to Mulhuddart Church, that " Ye Church, " at present in ruins, is situated on a hill and dedicated to ye " Virgin Mary ; from it appears a most extensive and delightful " prospect into ye County of Dublin and Meath ; in it was " committed a most barbarous and infamous action by some " of ye neighbouring Inhabitants in September, 1690, a Com- " pany of Colonel Foulkes men in their march to Dublin by " stormy and rainy weather, retreated into ye Church for " Shelter, but were all of them murthered in cold Blood before " ye morning, some of ye wretches were afterwards executed " in Thomas Street, Dublin, among ym Pat Moore, And. " Cannon, Ph. Strong, Jhn. Cummin, &c., others made their " escapes."

" About midway ascending to ye Church is an excellent Well ; " it is carefully walled, and several large trees about it. Here " on the 8th September, a great patron is kept with a vast " Concourse of all Sexes and Ages from many miles, upwards of " eighty Tents are pitched here furnished with all kinds of " Liquors and provisions for ye Reception and Refreshment " of ye Company."

From Mulhuddart the road follows the course of the Tolka through a somewhat uninteresting country, and after a couple of miles enters the County of Meath at the village of Clonee in which there is little of interest to notice. From Clonee, we continue along the main road, taking the first turn to the left to reach Dunboyne, which comes into view at this point.

Dunboyne has a wide street and a village green, on which the fair is annually held on the 9th July. In the graveyard adjoining the village is the ivied tower of the old church. In the reign of Henry VI. a writ was issued, dated 28th July,

Lady's Well, Mulhuddart.
(1906.)

1423, ordering the Portreeve and Commons of the town of Dunboyne with the able men of their bailiewick to proceed to Trim and aid in its defence. In 1534 the village was sacked and burnt by Silken Thomas immediately before the siege of Maynooth Castle, and in 1798 it suffered considerable damage, the church and many of the houses being burnt. Turning to the left at the end of the village, we keep straight ahead for about two miles, where we again turn to the left, and after a mile and a half, once more turning to the left, we meet a road on the right crossing the Midland Railway and leading into the town of Leixlip by a very steep hill. Before crossing the railway will be seen on an adjoining eminence, a structure bearing the euphonious title of Knockmulrooney Tower, over the entrance door of which is a slab with the inscription " Rd. Wilson, 1812." From the summit of the hillock, which is difficult of access owing to the fencing, a fine view is obtained of the surrounding country.

Leixlip has been described elsewhere, and we proceed home by the main road through Lucan and Chapelizod or by Lucan and Clondalkin if the southern suburbs are to be reached.

Distances from G. P O. :—Castleknock, 5¾ miles, Mulhuddart, 6¾ miles ; Clonee, 10½ miles ; Dunboyne, 12 miles ; Leixlip, 16¾ miles ; and back to G. P. O. by Palmerston and Chapelizod, 27 miles. If the lower road be taken from Lucan, it will add somewhat less than a mile to the journey.

Authorities consulted :—An article on " The Phœnix Park, its origin and early History," by the late Mr. C. Litton Falkiner, published in the *Proceedings of the Royal Irish Academy for* 1901 ; *Rambles Near Dublin ;* Dalton's *History of the County Dublin ;* Warburton, Whitelaw and Walsh's *History of Dublin ; Journals of the Royal Society of Antiquaries,* &c.

CHAPTER XL

THE ENGLISH PALE

AFTER the first waves of Anglo-Norman invasion had
subsided, and the new settlers had securely established themselves in Dublin, their next care was to
set about clearing the natives from the country immediately
outside it, with a view to carrying on, without molestation,
the arts of agriculture and husbandry upon which the colony
depended for its food supplies, as in any emergency the colonists
could not count upon speedy succour from their kinsfolk
across the sea ; for England was, in those days, to all intents
and purposes, as remote from Ireland as is America at the
present day.

Towards the close of the reign of Edward I, there seems to
have been a general tendency on the part of English settlers
throughout the country to congregate in the district around
Dublin, which thence became known as " The English Land,"
while those English who resided outside it were said to be
" inter Hibernicos," *i.e.*, among the Irish. This district was
limited, roughly speaking, by the great mountain tract of
Wicklow on the south, by the Carlingford and Mourne
Mountains on the north, and by the Westmeath shore of the
Shannon on the West, whence the border ran by Edenderry,
Rathangan, and Kildare to the Barrow, following the course
of that river to the sea. It was not until a full century after
this, that the English land became known as " The Pale,"
from which period it showed a general tendency to shrinkage
on account of the encroachment of the natives, until by 1515
it included only portions of the four counties, Dublin, Kildare,
Meath, and Uriel (Louth).

About the year 1364 the power of the Kavanaghs and other native chieftains had grown to such an extent that the outlying portions of the Pale had to be abandoned, and the settlers generally had to fall back from the border extending southward by Kildare and Carlow to the sea. These chieftains exacted a tribute called " Black Rent," from the English settlers along the borders, guaranteeing in return, immunity from molestation by the Irish ; and this tax became at last so intolerable an impost that an Act was passed in the 24th year of Henry VIII (1533) forbidding any further payments of this description. That this enactment, however, failed in its object is shown by the complaint of the Irish Council in 1599 that the English subjects still paid most oppressive " black rents."

With the view of anglicising such Irish as lived within the Pale, it was enacted in 1465 that every Irishman dwelling among Englishmen, in the Counties of Dublin, Meath, Louth and Kildare, " shall go like to one Englishman in apparel, and " shaving off his beard above the mouth, and shall be within " one year sworn the liege man of the King, and shall take to " him an English surname of one town, as Sutton, Chester, " Trim, Scrine, Cork, Kinsale ; or colour, as white, black, " brown ; or art or science, as smith or carpenter ; or office " as cook, butler, &c., and he and his issue shall use this name " under pain of forfeiting his goods yearly."

By an Act of a Parliament held at Drogheda in 1488, the boundary of the Counties (Dublin, Meath, Kildare, and Uriel or Louth), constituting the Pale, is defined as extending " from Merrion inclusive to the waters of the Dodder, by the " new ditch to Saggard, Rathcoole, Kilheel [Kilteel], Rathmore, " and Ballymore [Eustace] ; thence to the County of Kildare, " into Ballycutlan, Harristown, and Naas, and so, thence to " Clane, Kilboyne, and Kilcock, in such manner that the " towns of Dalkey, Carrickbrennan [Monkstown], Newtown " [Blackrock], Rochestown, Clonken, Smethistown, Ballyboteer " [Booterstown], with Thorncastle [between Booterstown " and Blackrock] and Bullock, were in Dublin Shire." This

last proviso meant that the coast from Dublin to Bullock was
included in the Pale, although detached from the main portion
of it.   From Kilcock the boundary ran by the Rye Water and

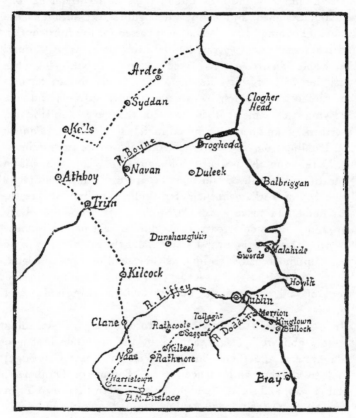

The Pale according to the Statute of 1488.

Ballyfeghin to the parish of Laracor, thence to Bellewstown
by the Boyne—" and so far as the Blackwater runneth from
" Athboy, and so, to Blackcawsey by Rathmore to the Hill
" of Lyde, and then to Muldahege and the parish of Tallen
" and Donaghpatrick, Clongell, and so, to Syddan, and so, down

" to Maundevillestown, by West Ardee, and so, to the water
" of Dundugan, and so, as that water goeth to the sea."

So far, there appears to have been no fence or boundary to
mark the limits of the Pale, but in 1494, at a Parliament convened at Drogheda by Sir Edward Poynings, the author of the
famous "Poynings' Law," an act was passed for the construction
and maintenance of a great double ditch or rampart, around
the whole district. This Act ran as follows :—" As the
" marches of four shires lie open and not fensible in fastness
" of ditches and castles, by which Irishmen do great hurt in
" preying the same ; it is enacted that every inhabitant,
" earth tiller, and occupier in said marches—*i.e.*, in the County
" of Dublin, from the water of Anliffey to the mountain in
" Kildare, from the water Anliffey to Trim, and so, forth to
" Meath and Uriell, as said marches are made and limited by
" the Act of Parliament held by William Bishop of Meath,
" do build and make a double ditch of six feet high above
" ground at one side or part which mireth next unto Irishmen,
" betwixt this and the next Lammas, and the said ditches to be
" kept up and repaired so long as they shall occupy said land,
" under pain of 40s. ; the lord of said lands to allow the old
" rent of said lands to the builder for one year, under said
" penalty."

In 1537, Justice Luttrell refers to the Pale as extending
" from Dublin to Tallaght, and so, by the mountain foot into
" Oughterard, and thence into St. Wolstan's [near Celbridge]
" and to Leixlip, and thence to the Barony of Dunboyne,
" Rathangan, and so, as the highway extendeth thence to Trim
" unto Athboy, and from Athboy to Ardbraccan, and from
" Ardbraccan to Slane, and from Slane to Mellifont and to
" Drogheda, and so, as the sea extendeth to Dublin." This
shows a considerable shrinkage as compared with the limits
defined by the Act of 1488.

In the 34th year of Henry VIII. (1543) the vexed question
of the boundaries of the Pale was again the subject of an enactment, by which it was laid down that "The English Pale

" doth stretche and extend from the town of Dundalk to the
" town of Derver [Darver] to the town of Ardee, always on the
" left side, leaving the march on the right side, and so, to the
" town of Sydan, to the town of Kenlis [Kells] to the town
" of Dengle [Dangan] to Kilcocke, to the town of Clane, to
" the town of Naas, to the bridge of Kilcullen, to the town
" of Balimore [Eustace], and so, backward to the town of
" Ramore [Rathmore], and so, to the town of Rathcoule, to the
" town of Tallaght, and to the town of Dalkey, leaving always
" the marche on the right hand from the saide Dundalk,
" following the saide course to the saide town of Dalkey."

This enactment seems to have been a mere assertion of
authority on the part of the Government, as at the time large
portions of the district on the south, adjoining the mountains,
were practically in possession of the Irish.

The lands immediately outside the Pale constituted a sort
of neutral ground, such as we nowadays call a " hinterland,"
and were known as the March lands or the Marches. These
districts were occupied sometimes by English and sometimes
by Anglo-Irish, but almost invariably by old soldiers and
men accustomed to the use of arms, and being the scene of
unceasing raids and guerilla warfare, were generally in a waste
and desert condition. The Marches are sometimes referred
to in old records as " the land of war," and the conditions of
life there closely resembled those in former times existing on
the Scottish border.

The favourite ambition of Richard II. was to drive the Irish
out of Leinster, and in this he would probably have succeeded
but for two great natural obstacles. One of these was the
dangerous and impenetrable district now known as the Bog
of Allen, at that time partly covered by primeval forest, and
held by the O'Connors, Princes of Offaly. The other was the
wild mountainous tract extending for over forty miles south
and south-west of Dublin, and over twenty miles in width,
which remained unsubjugated and even unexplored by the
English up to comparatively recent times. Into neither of

these districts durst the armoured and mail-clad Anglo-Norman troops venture, as their elaborate and cumbersome equipment would only prove their undoing, and facilitate their destruction by the agile and light-footed Irish kerne, who were as much at home in these trackless forests and treacherous swamps as the snipe and the woodcock that inhabited them. For centuries afterwards, these two districts defied all efforts at conquest, and in the case of Wicklow, it may indeed be said that the long struggle ended only 100 years ago, after the construction of the Military roads, and the erection of barracks at Glencree, Drumgoff, and Aughavanagh.

How the English colonists, looking forth from the battlements of their wall-girt city at the neighbouring mountains, must have fumed and fretted at these natural obstacles to their dominion, is indicated by the querulous letter of Sir George Carew in 1590, in which he states that " those that dwell even in the " sight of the smoke of Dublin are not subject to the laws."

Campion thus speaks of the Pale in his *History of Ireland* (1571) :—" An old distinction there is of Ireland into Irish " and English Pales ; for when the Irish had raised continual " tumults against the English planted heere with the Conquest, " at last they coursed them into a narrow circuite of certain " shires in Leinster, which the English did choose as the fattest " soyle, most defensible their proper right, and most open to " receive helpe from England. Hereupon it was termed " ' their Pale ' as whereout they durst not peepe. But now " both within this Pale, uncivill Irish and some rebells do dwell, " and without it countreyes and cities English are well " governed."

Gerard Boate in his *Natural History of Ireland* (1652) makes the following interesting allusion to the Pale, entirely, of course, from the colonist's point of view :—" There is yet " another division of Ireland whereby the whole land is divided " into two parts, the English Pale and the land of the mere " Irish. The English Pale comprehendeth only four counties, " one whereof is in Ulster—viz., Louth, and the other three

" in Leinster, to wit, Meath, Dublin, and Kildare ; the
" original of which division is this. The English at the first
" conquest, under the reign of Henry II., having within
" a little time conquered great part of Ireland, did afterwards,
" in the space of not very many years make themselves masters
" of almost all the rest, having expelled the natives (called
" the wild Irish, because that in all manner of wildness they may
" be compared with the most barbarous nations of the earth)
" into the desert woods and mountains. But afterwards
" being fallen at odds amongst themselves, and making several
" great wars, the one upon the other, the Irish thereby got
" the opportunity to recover now this, and then that part of
" the land, whereby, and through the degenerating of a great
" many from time to time, who, joining themselves with the
" Irish, took upon them their wild fashions and their language,
" the English in length of time, came to be so much weakened,
" that at last nothing remained to them of the whole kingdom'
" worth the speaking of, but the great cities and the forenamed
" four counties, to whom the name of the Pale was given,
" because that the authority and government of the kings
" of England, and the English colonies or plantations, which
" before had been spread over the whole land, now were
" reduced to so small a compass, and as it were, impaled within
" the same. And although since the beginning of this present
" age, and since King James's coming to the Crown of
" England, the whole island was reduced under the
" obedience and government of the English laws, and
" replenished with English and Scotch colonies ; neverthe-
" less, the name of the English Pale, which in the old
" signification was now out of season, remained in use, and
" is so still, even since this last bloody rebellion [1641]
" wherein the inhabitants of almost all the Pale, although
" all of them of English descent, have conspired with the
" native Irish, for to shake off the government of the
" Crown of England, and utterly to extinguish the reformed
" religion, with all the professors thereof, and quite to root

" them out of Ireland." (A typical example of an English writer of the period on Irish matters.)

Of the double-ditch constructed in pursuance of the Act of Poynings' Parliament in 1494, some portions still remain or remained till recently, that " from Merrion inclusive to the " water of the Dodder," having been doubtless the old double-ditch and pathway running through the fields south of Aylesbury road, from old Merrion Churchyard to Seaview Terrace near Anglesea Bridge over the Dodder. This was the route taken by the Corporation in ancient times, when riding the franchises or boundaries of their municipal jurisdiction, which, naturally enough, were, in the neighbourhood of the city, coincident with the limits of the Pale. Although this ancient passage has now been closed for many years past, and its original mearing is nearly all levelled, its course can still be traced from Seaview Terrace down to Nutley Lane. Indications of it are again discernible in the grounds of Nutley, behind the boundary wall of St. Mary's Asylum until it joins the lane leading by Old Merrion Churchyard, out on the Rock Road. At this point stood Merrion Castle, the ancient stronghold of the Fitzwilliams, who, as territorial proprietors, were relied upon to keep inviolate this portion of the English settlement against the incursions of the mountain tribes, for which reason probably this place was selected as suitable for the commencement of the rampart of the Pale.

From where Anglesea Bridge now stands, " the water of the " Dodder," probably formed the boundary as far as Firhouse or Oldbawn, above which it would have been perilously close to the mountains. Of " the new ditch " which ran to Saggart, Rathcoole, and on to Ballymore Eustace, and which may have been an earthwork constructed at an earlier period for the same purpose, I am not aware of any portion now surviving, nor of any trace of the rampart of 1494, until we come to Clane, where a portion commences about half a mile north-east of the village, running northward for half a mile until it is lost in the lawn of Clongowes Wood College. It re-appears just beside the College farmhouse, immediately north of the main buildings, and continues for about a quarter of a mile northward, almost reaching the by-road that leads to Rathcoffey House. A further portion may be seen about three miles north of the College, to the right of the road to Kilcock, continuing for over a quarter of a mile, and forming portion

The Rampart of the Pale at Clongowes Wood.
(1905.)

of the boundary dividing the parishes of Clane and Kilcock. All these portions retain their original dimensions, and although the rampart must have presented but a trifling obstacle to the Irish, who were described as being " so swift of foot, that like " unto stags they ran over mountains and valleys," yet it must have afforded a valuable protection to the settlers against cattle raids, which formed the principal motive of most of the Irish incursions into the Pale.

The responsibility for the maintenance and repairing of this great earthwork devolved upon the Wardens of the Marches,

the stern realities of whose life are vividly depicted in the
spirited reply of Garret, Earl of Kildare, Lord Deputy, to
charges preferred against him in 1524 by Cardinal Wolsey :—
" As touching my kingdom (my lord) ; I would you and I
" had exchange kingdomes but for one moneth, I would trust
" to gather up more crummes in that space than twice the
" revenues of my poor earldome ; but you are well and warme,
" and so hold you, and upbraide me not with such an odious
" storme. I sleepe in a cabbin when you lye soft in your bed
" of downe ; I serve under the cope of heaven, when you
" are served under a canopy ; I drinke water out of a skull
" [helmet], when you drink [wine] out of golden cuppes ;
" my courser is trained to the field, when your jennet is taught
" to amble ; when you are begraced and belorded, and crowched,
" and kneeled unto, then I finde small grace with our Irish
" borderers, except I cut them off by the knees."

It is possible that along the line of border defined by the
Statute of 1488, there may still remain many other portions
of the Rampart besides those described herein, and it is to
be hoped that the matter will be further investigated by
persons living in the several localities.

In the preparation of this chapter valuable information has
been derived from the following articles in *The Journals of
the County Kildare Archæological Society*—viz., " The Rampart
of the Pale," by the Rev. M. Devitt, S.J., in Vol. III. ; " The
Pale," by the late Rev. Denis Murphy, S.J., in Vol. II.

CHAPTER XLI

CANALS AND CANAL TRAVELLING IN THE LAST CENTURY *

A PERUSAL of the journals and pamphlets of the period when the various projects for canal construction were under discussion, would lead one to the belief that the many ills and misfortunes from which this country suffered, would be speedily exorcised by an elaborate system of inland navigation. The dark and gloomy bogs would be drained into these new waterways and transformed into smiling expanses of cornfield and meadow, the turbulent rivers would no longer overflow their banks, but be kept within bounds by a similar disposal of their superfluous waters, commerce would be extended into the remotest districts, and the whole country, the whilom scene of poverty and strife, would be henceforth the abiding home of peace and plenty.

By dint of such optimist writings, frothy speech-making, and skilfully-manipulated statistics, the public were at length worked up to the necessary pitch of enthusiasm, and induced to subscribe their money in the confident belief that they were on the high road to fortune. The shares went up and down like other speculations, but mostly downward, people talked of " going into the canals," just as their descendants now speak of investing in railways or trams ; and the only question was whether it was to be " Grands " or " Royals."

Once launched, the scheme was carried out on a scale of the utmost extravagance, not to say magnificence ; hotels built

* This special article appeared in *The Weekly Irish Times* of the 13th January, 1906, and is reproduced, with some alterations, by permission of the proprietors of that paper.

out of all proportion to any reasonable estimate of the traffic, canals twice the width of those constructed elsewhere, boats to match, uniforms for the officers, and so much money lavished on bridges, aqueducts, culverts, and other incidental works, that the capital was spent long before the conclusion of the undertaking.

The Grand Canal was commenced in 1755, and in 1807 the depot for passenger traffic was established at Portobello, where a palatial hotel—now a hospital—was erected for the thousands of passengers, who, it was anticipated, would be constantly going and returning by the boats; while James's Street Harbour was as now, the headquarters of the Company and the goods traffic. At the Bog of Allen this canal divides into two branches, one going to the Barrow at Athy, and the other to the Shannon near Banagher. Near Sallins it crosses the Liffey by the Leinster Aqueduct, which was constructed at a cost of £7,500.

Some forty years later, work was commenced on the Royal Canal, which was really an offspring of the other, originating in a dispute among the directors. Both canals were rather unfortunate at their inception, having been, as stated, constructed on too expensive a scale for the amount of traffic. One of the most costly items in connection with the Royal Canal was the great aqueduct over the valley of the Rye Water at Leixlip, which cost no less than £30,000, and by the time the canal had reached Kilcock, only 20 miles from Dublin, about £200,000 had been spent! More capital had then to be raised, and, as in the case of the Grand Canal, the difficulty of paying interest on the total amount drove the directors to levying tolls so high as to constitute a severe check upon the commercial success of the undertaking.

The following description by the Rev. Cæsar Otway in 1839 sets forth the facts with the common sense and breezy humour which characterise his writings :—

" Rising out of Leixlip the road leaves the line of the Liffey " and runs parallel to the small stream of the Rye Water,

" over which is thrown, at an immense expense, the largest
" aqueduct in Ireland, constructed by the Royal Canal Com-
" pany, a speculation got up by an angry capitalist to rival
" the Grand Canal Company, from whose direction he had
" retired in disgust, and whose vanity and pique was the
" cause of this great absurdity, and of loss and bankruptcy
" to thousands. It is said that the enormous cost of this
" aqueduct was gone to in compliment to the late Duke of
" Leinster, who desired that the canal should pass by *his*
" town of Maynooth ; it certainly would have been more
" advantageous to the commerce of the kingdom and the

Passenger Boat in Portobello Harbour.
(*From " The Picture of Dublin,* 1811.)

" prosperity of the company had they not deflected here to the
" south, but rather kept northward through the plains of
" Meath, made Lough Sheelan instead of Lough Owel, their
" summit level, and met the Shannon more towards its source,
" rather than run their line parallel, as it now does, at only
" a few miles distance from the Grand Canal, each starving
" and interfering with the other, and acting like two rival
" shopkeepers, who instead of setting up at remote districts
" of the town, frown balefully at each other from opposite
" sides of the same street."

A copy of the time-table of the boats, with rules and regulations for passengers, issued by the Grand Canal Company
about the beginning of the last century, affords interesting
and amusing reading. From it we learn that three boats
plied each way daily between Dublin and Tullamore, that the

speed averaged between three and four miles an hour, and that the fares were 10s. 10d. 1st cabin, and 5s. 11½d. 2nd cabin, with proportionate charges for intermediate distances. Meals were served on board in very homely fashion, the dinner almost invariably consisting of boiled mutton and turnips, and the charges set out in the time table are as follows :—

First Cabin.

	s.	d.
Breakfast, including eggs..................	1	1
Dinner, with small beer..................	1	7½
Porter, per bottle........................	0	5
Cyder	0	10
Pint of port............................	1	4
Do. sherry	1	7½
Do. claret	1	7½

Roast dishes never figured on the menu, as there was no means of roasting on board, and the meat dinner was served up every day in the week, Fridays included, whether the passengers comprised priests, parsons, Protestants, Catholics, or vegetarians. No wine was sold to passengers in the second cabin, and the charges for meals there were somewhat lower.

The odd amounts charged both for fares and meals are explained by the fact that they are the equivalents in Irish currency for even amounts in English money.

The maximum number of passengers was 45 1st class and 35 2nd class, " and should any persons above that number " force themselves into the boat, the boat-master is not on " any account to proceed until they are removed."

These passenger boats were constructed somewhat like the conventional Noah's Ark, but much longer in proportion. The cabin extended nearly the whole length of the vessel, and was divided into two parts, 1st and 2nd class, each having two rows of seats with a table between, on which meals were served and games were played by the passengers. The roof of the cabin was flat so as to form a deck, which, being railed around and furnished with seats, something like the top of a modern tram-car, was in fine weather much the pleasantest part of the vessel. Only first-class passengers were allowed on the deck.

Resuming our perusal of the " regulations," we find that wine was sold only in pints, " and not more than a pint to any " one person, nor to those who do not dine on board—nor to " children—nor is the allowance of wine to one person, without

Passenger Boat entering Harcourt Lock, near Rialto Bridge.
(*From an aquatint by J. J. Barralet in the National Gallery, Dublin.*)

" his or her express desire, to be transferred to another." The precise meaning of this last proviso is not quite clear, unless it was intended to prevent the forcible appropriation of one person's drink by another.

A praiseworthy desire on the part of the Company to uphold the notions in vogue at the time as to tobacco, is evidenced by the rule that " No smoking of tobacco is to be permitted " in any part of the boat." Fancy how modern travellers would relish the prospect of being deprived of the solace of " the weed " during a journey of twelve or thirteen hours' duration !

We further learn with interest that " Dogs in each cabin " are to be paid for as passengers," and in order to preserve inviolate the sanctity and aristocratic atmosphere of the first-

class, " No servant in livery is to be admitted," " Nor is any
" second-class passenger to be admitted on deck on pain of
" paying as for first cabin." To prevent any interference
with the navigation of the boat, " It is requested that no person
" will stand on the deck so as to intercept the view of the
" helmsman," and it was further laid down that there was
to be " No gaming on Sundays under penalty on the boat
" master of two guineas for each offence "—a rather curious
method, it may be observed, of punishing offenders.

Passengers who became refractory either from drink or other
cause, and refused to conform to the regulations, were frequently
put ashore by the boat's officers, or, as we say nowadays,
marooned, and there left to the mercy of the natives, to make
the best terms they could with them till the arrival of the
next boat.

The rule, " No spirit, mixt or plain, to be sold on board,"
was on the whole a wise one, when we consider how limited
was the accommodation, and how uncomfortable even one
intoxicated passenger could make all the rest in the small
cabins.

These great waterways in time became a favourite mode of
travelling to the larger towns in the interior of the country,
although not to a sufficient extent to make them a commercial
success, and general traffic became much extended by means
of coaches, caravans, and other conveyances in connection
with the boat service.

Notwithstanding the fact that in its earlier stage this means
of conveyance was slow, many people much preferred the canal
boat with its " State cabin " and pleasant deck, to the dusty,
hot, and jolting stage coach, with its closely-packed " six
insides ; " and the canal boat had the additional advantage
that if one got tired of sitting, it was always possible to get
out and walk. Indeed, if the Companies' advertisements
were to be believed, the advantages of this mode of locomotion
were numerous and surpassing. The facilities for viewing
the country were greater, although, truth to tell, canal scenery

is not generally of an exciting character. Then the passengers were not delayed for their meals, and, in addition, the travelling was sure to be soothing to the nerves, the motion being nearly as imperceptible as the progress ; while the leisurely rate of speed afforded such opportunities for observation as to make the journey as pleasant as a walk among the meadows and green pastures through which the canal passed. Finally, it was set forth as an overwhelming advantage over land travelling, that the passengers were safe from molestation by robbers ! This appears to have actually been the case, although why, it is not now easy to explain, and when one considers the number of well-to-do passengers, who must have carried money and valuables with them, it seems surprising that this method of travelling did not bring into existence a specialised variety of pirates to prey on the canal traffic. There are numerous parts of both canals, far removed from houses or locks, where four or five determined men might easily have held up a boat, and after leisurely plundering the passengers, made their escape without difficulty. In the boardroom of the Grand Canal Company are still preserved, as interesting relics of the past, a number of fine blunderbusses and heavy pattern pistols with which the officers of these boats were armed to repel any predatory attacks by land or water.

In the course of years a demand having arisen for more expeditious travelling, the companies designed a new pattern of boat called a " fly-boat," lightly built and sheeted with iron, very narrow, and towed by three or four horses galloping at the rate of nine miles an hour. In Mr. and Mrs. Hall's *Ireland* (1845) such a boat is described, but it is stated that it was by no means a pleasant kind of conveyance, as on account of its narrowness the passengers were painfully cramped inside. This is the experience of many old people, still alive, who travelled in these fly-boats, and who say that comfort was to a great extent sacrificed to speed. Furthermore, it was found impossible to provide accommodation for cooking on board, and short intervals had to be allowed at the companies' hotels for the necessary meals, while, owing to the narrowness of this type of boat, there was no deck over the cabin, as the weight of passengers there would have rendered it top-heavy.

Dr. James Johnston, an observant English visitor, in his *Tour in Ireland* (1844), describes the busy scene at Portobello between 6 and 7 o'clock on a summer's morning, passengers of all descriptions, with their luggage constantly arriving on foot and on vehicles at the harbour. This writer states that in fine weather passengers sat on the railed deck over the cabin, but on passing a lock, all hands had to be sent below, and the doors closed, to prevent the spray from coming in, while a cascade of water splashed all over the forecastle, and he adds that " the dress of the postillions, the measured canter or " gallop of the horses, the vibrations of the rope, the swell " that precedes the boat, and the dexterity with which the " men and horses dive under the arches of the bridges, without " for a moment slackening their pace, all produce a very curious " and picturesque scene such as I have never seen equalled in " Holland on any of its canals."

The following advertisement from *The Sligo Journal* affords an interesting glimpse of " expeditious travelling " in the year 1823 :—

" Royal Canal.—Cheap, secure, and expeditious travelling " to and from Dublin to Sligo. A boat will leave Dublin " every day at three o'clock p.m., and arrive at Tenelie (or " 39th lock) at nine o'clock the following morning, whence " a most comfortable caravan starts and arrives in Boyle that " evening at 5, passing through Longford, Rouskey, Drumsna, " and Carrick-on-Shannon. The following morning a car " will leave Boyle for Sligo and return to Boyle the day after. " The fares of the boat, caravan, and car from Dublin to Sligo, " a distance of 110 miles (Irish), is only sixteen shillings."

That this mode of travelling was actually considered thoroughly satisfactory is shown by the following interesting extracts from Warburton, Whitelaw and Walsh's *History of Dublin* (1818) :—" The many advantages, comforts and con-

" veniences which the traveller finds by the establishment of
" clean and commodious passage boats, constantly moving
" along the various lines, passing at stated hours from stage to
" stage, uninterrupted by any change of weather, and with a
" rapidity and security which, added t● the reasonable terms
" of accommodation, affords one of the most pleasant, com-
" fortable, and expeditious modes of travelling to be found
" in any part of the world.   Of these there are at present ten
" plying on the Barrow and Shannon lines of the Grand Canal,
" and with such expedition that the passage from Dublin
" to Shannon Harbour, 63 Irish miles or above 80 English
" miles, is performed in one day between the hours of four in
" the morning and 10 in the evening, and at an expense exclusive
" of entertainment, of 21s. for the first cabin and 14s. 1d.
" for the second . . . The passage to Athy of over 54
" miles takes 12 hours and 35 minutes. . . .   In passenger
" boats of both canals the entertainment is excellent, and the
" price of every article, so as to prevent imposition, hung up
" in the cabin. There is no charge for attendance, and to
" preserve sobriety and decency of manners, the use of spirits
" is prohibited."

" Before the Rebellion of 1798, vast quantities of military
" stores were conveyed to different parts of the kingdom by
" the Grand Canal, and when the French landed at Killala,
" the Marquess Cornwallis embarked a considerable number
" of troops at Dublin and Sallins, and proceeded with them
" 56 English miles to Tullamore, where they arrived in a few
" hours fresh and fit to proceed on their march to Athlone."

The accompanying reproduction of a time-table issued by
the Grand Canal Company about the year 1800, for the original
of which the writer is indebted to the courtesy of the Company,
is headed with an illustration of a passenger boat, towed by
two horses, about to pass under Rialto Bridge, South Circular
Road, at the fiery speed of three miles an hour.   The passengers
may be seen, mostly standing on deck, apparently admiring
the scenery, and it will be observed that an individual is fishing

at the bow, while three others, probably officers, as one of them is holding the tiller, are represented in consultation at the

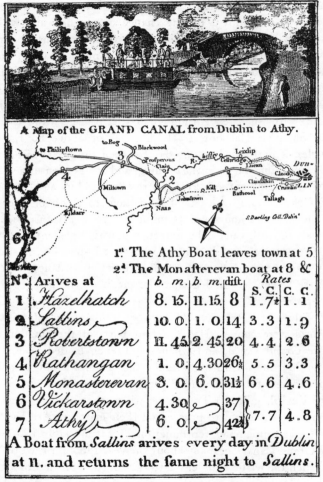

Nᵒ	Arives at	b. m.	b. m.	dift.	Rates S. C.	C. C.
1	Hazelhatch	8. 15.	11. 15.	8	1. 7½	1. 1
2	Sallins	10. 0.	1. 0.	14	3 . 3	1 .9
3	Robertstown	11. 45.	2. 45.	20	4 . 4	2 .6
4	Rathangan	1. 0,	4. 30	26½	5 . 5	3 .3
5	Monasterevan	3. 0.	6. 0.	31½	6 . 6	4 .6
6	Vickarstown	4. 30		37	7. 7	4 .8
7	Athy	6. 0.		42½		

1ˢᵗ. The Athy Boat leaves town at 5
2ᵈ. The Monsterevan boat at 8 &

A Boat from *Sallins* arives every day in *Dublin* at 11. and returns the same night to *Sallins*.

Timetable of Canal Boats
(About 1800.)

stern. It cannot be any anxiety about the weather which engages the attention of these mariners, as the appearance of the sky and distance would indicate that the good ship was going to have a calm voyage, so we may assume that they are beguiling the time by spinning the usual yarns accredited to the nautical profession.

It will be noticed that there is an uninterrupted view of the mountains from the canal bank, and that all the surroundings which are now so well built over, are represented as quite rural, the only building coming into the view being a house beside the bridge, apparently connected with the traffic. A lordly individual canters past on horseback, heading for town, while a pedestrian placidly contemplates the inspiring scene from the opposite bank.

A map of the canal system to the Barrow is given underneath, together with the distances, the hours of arrival at, and departure from the several stations, and the fares for the " state cabin " and 2nd cabin. It will be seen on referring to these particulars, that the rate of speed, in some cases, works out at less than three miles an hour. In this matter, however, there was a steady improvement as the years rolled on, until by the establishment of the fly-boats, a speed of nearly nine miles an hour was attained.

In connection with the elms along the banks, shown in the illustration as quite juvenile, and still surviving, though their ranks are now much gapped and attenuated, it may be mentioned that these trees were originally planted along the canals near Dublin with the object of providing a supply of timber to renew the city water-pipes as they became decayed. Long before it became necessary to make use of them, however, wooden water-pipes had everywhere become superseded by those of earthenware or iron, and consequently most of these trees have been allowed to live to a hoary old age. The great storm of February, 1903, laid many a veteran among them low, and to reduce the risk of any further obstruction to the traffic, a number of the survivors have been lopped to such an extent as considerably to reduce their dimensions.

The supersession of the horse by mechanical traction—a process in steady progress all over the civilized world—has commenced on the Grand Canal, and at the present time the Company have five boats propelled by 15 h.p. "Bolinder" internal combustion engines, while it is expected that in the course of a few months the number will be considerably increased. As their introduction has so far proved a success, both as regards cost of working and economy of time, and as a speed, inclusive of stoppages, of about four miles an hour with a full cargo can be obtained, it is highly probable that the present generation will see the last of the horse on this service.

As the railway system gradually extended through the country, passenger traffic on the canals decreased ; now one district and then another was tapped by the railways, until by the middle of the last century nearly all the passenger boats had ceased plying, and for years afterwards they were to be seen lying neglected and forgotten in the docks, their once trim decks and cosy cabins discoloured from age and decay. Whatever their ultimate fate—and let us hope it was a kindly one—they formed a most interesting link between the good old go-as-you-please times, and the modern age of hurry and bustle, when, instead of being satisfied with sixty miles in a day, people are beginning to grumble at sixty miles an hour.

These long tedious journeys were not without some counter-balancing advantages, for they afforded opportunities for observation of and acquaintance with, one's fellow-passengers, not possible in modern conveyances, and many a friendship thus formed, long survived the manner and the means of its origin.

Peace to your timbers, ye quaint old boats—ye were the very embodiment of the times to which ye belonged !—ye knew not the storm nor the stress of modern life, the feverish hurry of our present-day existence ; and if we now in our vaunted superiority feel disposed to laugh at your primitive design and leisurely progress, let us pause and consider whether we are after all, so much the better and so much the happier for the improvements in travel and communication with which the present scientific age has provided us.

CHAPTER XLII

MARTELLO TOWERS

MARTELLO towers, which are so plentifully studded along many portions of the English and Irish coasts, were built in Ireland by the military authorities under "The National Defence Act" of 1804. There were originally fifteen between Dublin and Bray, but some six or seven have either been taken down, or have fallen, in consequence of the erosion of their sites by the sea. They cost on an average about £1,800 each, and usually took some six months to build. The ordinary number of men in occupation was only three, but sometimes, as at Sandycove, where the tower was reinforced by a battery, there was a larger garrison.

The tower on Dalkey Island was built in the summer of 1804, and on its completion, the signalling station at Dalkey was transferred to it from the semaphore tower on the top of Dalkey Hill (*see* p. 63). Sandymount Martello tower—a well-known landmark on the shore of that suburb—was erected in 1806, and was, some years ago, sold to the Dublin Tramways Company.

The name Martello is said to be a corruption of Mortella, and to have originated with the celebrity acquired by a fortified tower in Corsica, in consequence of the extraordinary resistance it offered to an attack by a British force in the French Revolutionary wars. In 1793 Corsica was in insurrection against the French, and the British Government, as a matter of policy, decided to support the insurgents. It was arranged to begin operations by taking a tower, held by the French, in a strategic position on Cape Mortella, a headland dominating the only safe anchorage in the Gulf of San Fiorenzo. This structure was armed with one 24 pounder and two 18 pounders. Accordingly, in September, a British squadron of three ships of the line and two frigates went to the assistance of the insurgents, and the two frigates were ordered to capture this tower. After a comparatively short bombardment it was abandoned by its little garrison and occupied by the British. Some short time afterwards, the French recaptured it, and profiting by their previous experience, considerably strengthened its defences and armament.

In the following year, 1794, a further attempt was made by the British to support the Corsican insurgents. On the 7th February, a party of 1,400 troops was landed and a determined attack made on the tower next day. Simultaneously with the attack by land, two ships, the *Fortitude* and the *Juno*, bombarded it for two and a half hours, without effect, and then retired, the *Fortitude* being on fire and having 62 men killed and wounded. The shore batteries continued the attack, but their fire was equally unsuccessful until at length red-hot balls were tried, one of which set fire to the bass junk with which the massive parapet was heavily lined, and the garrison of 33 men then surrendered. The captors were much surprised to find that the armament consisted of only three pieces—two 18 pounders and one 6 pounder.

At this period all England was in constant apprehension of an invasion by the French, and the remarkable defence offered in this case by so small and lightly armed a garrison, greatly impressed the military authorities with the suitability of such towers for coastal defence. Accordingly, we find Martello towers being built in great numbers along the shores of England, especially the south and east coasts, where whole stretches are studded with them at short intervals. Their erection was strongly denounced by Cobbett and others at the time, as unjustifiable extravagance. They are nearly all of the same type, consisting of solid masonry with vaulted rooms for the garrison, an ammunition store underneath, and a platform on the top for one or two or even three guns firing over a low parapet. The entrance was usually by a door about 18 or 20 feet from the ground, access to which was obtained by a movable ladder.

Similar towers were subsequently erected by Austria on the shores of the Adriatic, and were called Maximilian towers.

"Mortella" in Italian means "myrtle" which grows abundantly on Cape Mortella and originated its name.

"Martello Tower" is used occasionally by contemporary writers in a figurative sense, to signify a position of great strength or security in any political or public question.

The *Encyclopædia Britannica* (11th Edition) from which the details of the above action have been obtained, derives the name, as stated, from Cape Mortella, and on this point most authorities agree. A few, however, give the derivation as being from the Italian "martello," a hammer, because, it is alleged, such towers were originally equipped with a bell, which was struck with a hammer on the approach of an enemy. Defensive towers were erected on the coast of Southern Italy ot the close of the 18th century, and, it is stated, were called "Torri di Martello," but whether this name, if authentic, was adopted from the English, or the English from the Italian, is not now easy to determine.

CHAPTER XLIII

THE OLD CITY WATER SUPPLY

EARLY colonists landing at the mouth of the Liffey, would naturally select as their headquarters, the highest point that rose above the last place where the river was fordable, before it joins the sea. Such a position would mean safety and support combined with facility of offence or defence. What is now known as Cork Hill fulfilled these conditions, and there is good reason to suppose that on this site rose the primitive stronghold that in time became the nucleus of Baile-Atha-Cliath—the ancient town-of-the-hurdle-ford.

Almost the first care of the colonists would be to secure an abundant supply of water. The Liffey was close at hand, but owing to floods and other causes was unsuitable; and so it came about that its tributary, the Poddle, a clear stream rising at the foot of the Tallaght hills, became at an early date the source of the citizens' water supply. This arrangement sufficed down to about the year 1200, when the city had grown to such an extent that it became necessary to seek some additional source. Accordingly, in 1244, Maurice Fitzgerald, Justiciary of Ireland, ordered an Inquisition to be held for that purpose. As a result, it was determined to supplement the waters of the Poddle by constructing a watercourse to it from the Dodder. This watercourse, still in existence and maintained, starts from a weir at Firhouse, flows across the fields and under the Tallaght road, thence by the old churchyard at Templeogue, through the grounds of Templeogue House, then flowing northward, joins the Poddle at a slightly lower level, about $\frac{1}{4}$ mile north of Mount Down House near Whitehall cross-roads. From this point the united streams flow by Kimmage cross-roads to Larkfield

Mills and on to " The Tongue " at Kimmage. Here the
waters are divided by a wedge-shaped stone or tongue, two-
thirds flowing by the original course to the city *via* Green-
mount, under the Canal to Goodbody's factory and thence
to Blackpitts, New Row, Patrick Street, past St. Patrick's
Cathedral, turning east at Ross Road, through the Castle
and Palace Street to Wellington Quay, where the waters

" The Tongue ' at Kimmage

may be seen flowing into the Liffey, the outfall usually
attracting a large assemblage of sea fowl. The other branch
(one-third), diverted north at The Tongue, flows to Dolphin's
Barn and thence by the elevated rampart known as " The
Back of the Pipes " or " The Pipes," to the old City Basin
near James's Street. A branch starts from the first portion
at Goodbody's factory, flows alongside " The Back of the
Pipes," Marrowbone Lane, Pimlico and Ardee Street to
Warrenmount, joining the main stream at Fumbally's Lane.
The urban portions of these streams are now, of course,
almost entirely underground, and seldom seen or heard of,
but in former times they frequently gave trouble by inun-

dating the low lying parts of the Liberties, and even invading the precincts of St. Patrick's Cathedral, where, it is recorded, considerable damage was done by the floods.

The great monastic establishment of St. Thomas's Abbey, or, to give it its correct title—the Abbey of St. Thomas the Martyr—which stood on the site now occupied by Thomas's Court, claimed or arrogated proprietorial rights over the portion diverted by Dolphin's Barn and "The Pipes," and disputes in consequence arose at times between this powerful community and the civic authorities. This establishment, which was really an English institution, was under the patronage of the King, and its abbots, who were appointed and held office subject to royal approval, were *ex officio* members of the Irish Privy Council and peers of the Irish Parliament, besides which they exercised judicial functions at the court in the Abbey. It suffered the common fate of all the monasteries at the Dissolution.

At an early period a reservoir or conduit stood outside James's Gate, and it is recorded that in 1254 water was first supplied from it to the citizens. Important people were allowed to have independent supplies brought into their houses by pipes, and it was usually stipulated that the diameter of such pipe should not exceed that of a goose quill. In the cases of private supplies, there was no tap, and the water was constantly flowing into a tank or suitable vessel to receive it. In 1323 the rent for such service was 6*d*. a year, and for a subsidiary supply from another person's cistern, the charge was 1*d*. a year.

As may be imagined, it was a serious offence to pollute the water supply, and one of the statutes dealing with the matter prescribes a fine of 12*d*. for " washing puddings and tripes " therein.

The original conduit or cistern near James's Gate was supplemented in 1308 by the erection of another at Cornmarket through the munificence of John Le Decer, an eminent Dublin citizen, and in 1670 the original one was replaced by a larger structure.

It is recorded that in 1573 the inhabitants of Thomas

Street were ordered to pave their street as far as the water-course channel, from which it would appear that the supply flowed in an open course—probably in wooden troughs—along the street, whence it was conveyed in leaden pipes to the various houses specially supplied.

In 1573 and again in 1689, serious trouble was caused in the city in consequence of interference with the water supply by the Talbots of Templeogue, through the grounds of whose residence it flowed. In 1738 Lord Santry having been convicted for the murder of one of his servants, was sentenced to death, and would have been executed but for the action of his uncle, Sir Compton Domvile, then residing at Templeogue Castle, who when all other means of inter-cession failed, threatened to cut off the city water supply if the sentence were carried out. The threat was effective, and the noble murderer's escape was connived at by the authorities.

Some yeoman of standing residing in the neighbourhood of Tallaght or Templeogue, was usually entrusted with the supervision and maintenance of the watercourse from the Dodder to the Tongue, the remaining portion being looked after by a corporate official appointed for the purpose. The old water supply seems to have been superseded about the beginning of the last century, and is now used only for industrial purposes.

" The Tongue," which is a well-known landmark in the Kimmage neighbourhood, giving name to a townland, is approached by a field-path from the Dark Lane adjoining the Lower Kimmage road.

It is now almost impossible to identify the original course of the Poddle owing to the numerous drains and watercourses with which it is connected, but what would appear to be the principal stream takes its rise near the foot of the Tallaght Hills, passes the Aerodrome and flows about ¼ mile north of Tallaght, thence across the fields to the Fairy Well near Tymon Castle and on to Kimmage.

The addition of the watercourse from the Dodder must have afforded an appreciable measure of relief to the thirsty citizens of 700 years ago, as it contains a much larger volume of water than the original Poddle, and is besides, much more swiftly flowing. The old watercourse is still widely known and spoken of as " The City Water."

In the preparation of this chapter much valuable information has been obtained from an article on the subject by Dr. Henry F. Berry, M.A., in the Journal of the Royal Society of Antiquaries for 1891.

CHAPTER XLIV

THE ASHBOURNE ROAD AND DUNSOGHLY CASTLE

THE great highway known as the Ashbourne road, runs from Finglas, almost straight in a north-westerly direction, to Ashbourne and Slane in the Co. Meath. It was constructed about the beginning of the last century, and is marked on Taylor's Map of the Co. Dublin (1816) as " Great Slane Road and Londonderry " [road]. It is also marked on Duncan's Map (1821), but only " Ashbourne Inn " appears on the site of the village of Ashbourne. Although an intolerably monotonous road for a pedestrian, it is fairly pleasant for the more rapid locomotion of the cycle or motor.

Two miles beyond Finglas, on the old Duleek road to the right, are the dismal ruins of the Red Lion Inn, a hostelry of some note in former times, where wayfarers overtaken by night were wont to stay, rather than risk the dangers of the journey to Dublin in the darkness.

At the crossroads beside Kilshane bridge, some three miles from Finglas, the turn to the right leads to Dunsoghly Castle, a structure of imposing appearance and in such good preservation that it can hardly be termed a ruin. It consists of a square building with a projecting tower at each angle, one of which contains a winding staircase to the battlements, while the others are fashioned into small apartments. The external walls are from 4 to 5 feet thick. On entering is seen what was the large vaulted kitchen, to which a somewhat modern entrance has been constructed ; thence a wooden staircase leads to the first floor consisting principally of the drawing-room, once a fine wainscotted apartment. A further flight of steps leads to where stood the second floor, and another to the upper floors and roof, the latter being

slated and evidently modern. Most of the windows have
been modernised and glazed, and the fireplaces are also of
modern date. The upper parts of the towers are entered by
short flights of steps from the roof, and were doubtless intended to serve as watch towers. Traces of outworks remain,
as also of a fosse which was filled from a neighbouring stream.

Dunsoghly Castle

The modern house adjoining is believed to occupy the site of
the original " dun."

Although the height is only about 80 feet, the view from
the roof and towers is surprisingly extensive. To the northward are Garristown hill with its square ruin, Baldungan
Castle, Loughshinny and Lambay; east and south are
Ireland's Eye, Howth, Dalkey and Killiney, the Sugar Loaf
and the rounded outline of the Dublin mountains with their
continuation westward in the line of low hills extending into
the County Kildare. Nearer will be seen St. Margaret's
and its ruins, the woods of Santry, and the city enveloped
in its smoke and haze.

The castle appears to have been built in the 15th century, about which time the property came into the possession of Sir Rowland Plunkett, youngest son of Sir Christopher Plunkett, Baron Killeen, who was Lord Deputy in 1432, and it has since continued in the possession of the family and its descendants.

Adjoining the castle is a small chapel, in the side of which, facing the main structure, is a slab over a low carved doorway, bearing a representation of the Cross and the accompaniments of the Crucifixion, excellently carved in full relief. Underneath is the inscription : " J.P.M.D. D.S. 1573 " (Johannes Plunkett Miles de Dunsoghly, 1573).

To the northward of the castle are the remains of a small brewery—a usual accessory to an important residence in the olden time.

Not far from Dunsoghly and one mile due east of the village of St. Margaret's, at Dunbro, there stood towards the close of the 13th century, a stately mansion which vied even with the Castle of Dublin, in its magnificence. This great establishment was the residence of Stephen de Fulebourne, Chief Governor of Ireland, a distinguished ecclesiastic and a brother of the Order of St. John of Jerusalem. No description of the building has survived, but its site was probably identical with or adjoined that of the modern Dunbro House. For the foregoing information in regard to it, I am indebted to Dr. Ball's recent publication " Southern Fingal."

Returning to the main road, at a distance of 4½ miles from Finglas, we reach the Ward crossroads, the centre of a great hunting district, and origin of the name of the Ward Hunt. After passing the Ward will be seen the ruin of some stables used for changing horses in the coaching days.

At a distance of 9½ miles from Finglas we enter Ashbourne, a village in which there is little to notice. It was all built at the one time—about 1823—by Frederick Bourne, a local landed proprietor. The old turnpike house, which is older than the village, is a prominent object on entering the street. On the left will be seen what is called " Castle Street," a rough grass-grown lane, with remains of the massive stone pillars of an entrance gate, which evidently belonged to Killegland or Ashbourne Castle, an extensive quadrangular structure which stood here up to about eighty years ago, when it was demolished for the sake of its building material. No traces of it are now discernible, but the site is pointed out by the inhabitants.

Near Ashbourne, on a rising ground slightly south of the road to Donoughmore is a monument bearing the inscription :

ERECTED AS A LASTING TESTIMONY TO
CHARLES BRINDLEY
BY HIS MANY FRIENDS
IN AFFECTIONATE REMEMBRANCE OF
HIS FAITHFUL SERVICES AS HUNTSMAN
FOR THIRTY-FIVE YEARS TO THE
WARD HOUNDS
JANUARY 1880

The monument is of grey sandstone and is handsomely embellished with appropriate hunting representations, together with a mounted figure of the famous huntsman whom it commemorates. The carving has suffered considerable injury in places.

The return journey may if desired be made by Swords, following the course of the Broadmeadow Water.

The distance from G.P.O. to Ashbourne is 12½ miles, thence to Swords 8½ miles, and from Swords to G.P.O. 8 miles.

CHAPTER XLV

DONNYBROOK FAIR

(*Air*—" The Sprig of Shillelagh ")

" Whoe'er had the luck to see Donnybrook Fair,
    An Irishman all in his glory was there
With his sprig of Shillelagh and Shamrock so green !
His clothes spick-and-span new without e'er a speck,
A neat Barcelona entwined round his neck,
He goes into a tent and he spends half a crown,
He meets with a friend and for love knocks him down,
    With his sprig of Shillelagh and Shamrock so green ! "

FEW of the present generation have any idea of what a source of demoralisation Donnybrook Fair was to Dublin. Every year on the approach of Fair time (26th August), large sums of money were withdrawn from the savings banks in Dublin to be squandered in drunkenness, gambling and other dissipations ; all business was in a state of partial suspension for weeks together : every anniversary was signalised by numerous cases of personal injuries if not by actual loss of life, and in some instances even epidemics were ascribed to the Fair. Servants, mechanics, shop assistants, tradesmen and clerks visiting the place, were drawn into the vortex of dissipation, and losing their money, their situations and their characters, swelled the numbers of the unemployed in the city, and drifted thence into crime. The city magistrates made no secret of their opinions that when such an abomination was permitted in a civilised community, it was a reasonable ground for mitigating the punishments incurred by yielding to its numerous temptations.

About a week before the Fair commenced, a number of

dealers and tent owners resorted to the green, and proceeded to erect the various tents and shows, causing much excitement in the ordinarily sleepy village.   These tents were mostly constructed in a very primitive fashion by driving a number of wattles into the earth in two parallel rows, and then turning down and tying together the tops like an arbour in a garden. Having thus constructed the framework, it remained but to clothe it in a suitable manner.   Those who could afford such a luxury, used canvas, but they were the minority, and in most cases the impecunious proprietors had to utilise for the purpose any kind of rags and coverings in their possession at the time.   These comprised sacks, bedclothes, winnowing sheets, rugs, old clothing and other miscellaneous articles cut into various shapes and sizes, patched on each other and quilted together, producing in combination, colour effects rivalling those of an Oriental bazaar.

The booth when completed was adorned with a tall pole or flagstaff, having attached, some gaily coloured rags and streamers whose fantastic irregularity became in time enhanced by the action of the wind and rain.

The interior was furnished by laying a number of doors and planks on mounds raised along the middle, so as to form a continuous table, and planks were similarly laid along the sides at a lower level, forming seats.   On these benches the company sat, eating, drinking, singing and watching the evolutions of the dancers who amused them, until one by one they dropped off their seats and sank below in blissful unconsciousness, whereupon the proprietor, seeing that there was nothing more to be got from them, bundled out the whole lot to make room for a fresh company.

In the case of those tents which boasted of a cuisine, or, as it was usually expressed, " neat victuals " or " entertainment," it was the custom to have suspended from a triangle over a fire, a large well stocked pot, which ' like a hell-broth boiled and bubbled,' and by its fragrant and appetising odours, excited the hunger of the passing votaries of pleasure.

Of merchandise there was practically none,. the principal articles being food and drink—mostly the latter.   The food usually consisted of Dublin Bay herrings, corned beef, potatoes, bacon and cabbage, while in the better class booths joints of meat were served in a superior style to suit the more fastidious tastes of their customers. The drink was mostly whiskey made into punch, porter and ale not as yet having come into popular favour, and the whiskey was only about a penny a glass. Seats were in some cases placed outside the tents, where those too poor to participate in the joys of the interior, were regaled at a reduced price in the open air.

Some of the pots contained promiscuous edibles broken up into small portions—pigs' and sheeps' feet, potatoes, turnips, beef and mutton bones, etc. The proprietors then invited the public to try their luck at fishing out whatever they could with a long-handled fork, at the rate of " three prods in the pot for a penny." A roaring trade was usually done at this branch of the catering, which afforded great amusement to the onlookers.

On the densely crowded portions of the fair green a scene of tumultuous excitement prevailed. On all sides might be heard the sounds of drums, bells, toy trumpets, brazen-lunged hawkers extolling their wares, mingled with a caco-phonous medley of fiddling, bag-piping and singing. Not infrequently perhaps a dozen fiddlers and pipers would be found in close proximity, each playing away vigorously and independently to his own company, producing a maddening discord of sounds, which, accompanied by the shouting, singing and confused din, rendered the place a veritable pandemonium.

Every day during the continuance of the Fair, the road from town was from an early hour crowded with vehicles of all descriptions, principally outside cars, which in those days accommodated three on each side comfortably, not to speak of one or two in the well, and the stream of traffic, in dry weather, kept up a continuous cloud of dust the whole way from town. The charge on the cars was usually 2d. a head, but in times of unusual briskness, it was advanced as high as 4d.

The equine portion of the Fair, the ostensible reason for its existence, was at one time a source of much amusement to the thousands who attended it. It was a recognised custom that no horse was to be offered for sale until the owner jumped it across a mud wall and ditch specially constructed for the purpose, and the falls and vicissitudes of these amateur jockeys, as they mounted again and again, battered and torn, on their unfortunate mounts, were greeted with noisy enthusiasm. Many of these miserable quadrupeds were in reality more fitted for the glue factory or the cats'-meat man than the steeplechase, though occasionally, when goaded to madness by a drunken rider, one of them would develop amazing energy, running amuck, scattering the people in all directions, and sometimes even capsizing tents, causing endless uproar and confusion among the inmates—horse, rider, tent, musicians and all becoming tangled up together in one mad medley.

Numerous were the varieties and types of beggars that attended—crutched, wooden-legged, blind, deaf and dumb, and deformed—many of them artfully faked up for the occasion, who contrived, so long as they had the sense to keep sober, to deceive the unpractised eye and draw largely on the generosity of the public. Few of them, however, were proof against the temptations that everywhere confronted them, and thus it was not an unusual sight, towards evening, to see one of these worthies who erstwhile had been hobbling about on crutch or wooden leg, now using it with disastrous effect upon his adversaries in one of the shindies.

As evening approached, the conduct of the multitude became less restrained—wilder shouts and laughter proceeded from the swings, the singing grew more discordant and the dancing more disorderly, and the conduct of the crowd became more and more uproarious and broke out into numerous brawls.

From an early hour in the evening, the road to town became crowded with those returning, and night was made hideous with drunken shouting and singing, both from the pedestrians pursuing the uncertain tenor of their ways, and the more exalted revellers returning on the cars. Some, too drunk to go home at all, slept out in fields, gardens and ditches on the way, waking next morning with stiffened joints and aching heads.

At hours varying according to their individual tastes, but generally between 11 *p.m.* and 2 *a.m.*, the jaded tent-owners ejected or carried out their most tenacious patrons, and closing up their tents for the night, snatched a few hours of troubled rest till the re-commencement of the saturnalia next morning.

The tents and booths usually bore the proprietors' names and addresses, with the object of attracting patrons from the same locality, and to indicate the class of goods sold, signs and symbols, similar to those of the old inns, were displayed, such as a cooked ham, a pot, a leg of mutton, or a whiskey bottle.

One sign showed a young fellow, gaily attired, dancing with a pretty girl, while underneath was a scroll bearing the inscription :—

> " Here Paddy comes to have a swig,
> A better one he never took,
> And now he'll dance an Irish jig
> With Dolly Dunne of Donnybrook."

Another with a picture of a bee-hive, for which symbol of industry no justification was discoverable in the interior, exhibited the following invitation :—

> " In this hive we're all alive,
> Good whiskey makes us funny,
> So don't pass by, but stop and try
> The sweetness of our honey."

The fighting which unfortunately became the leading characteristic of this remarkable festivity, was in many cases quite aimless, or became so after the first bout or two had been fought off and the number of combatants had increased. " Every man for himself " then became the

2 G

watchword, and most of the company being in a condition incapable of distinguishing friend from foe, struck out wildly at anything, even the rounded protuberance on the outside of a tent produced by the head of some reposing reveller inside, being too tempting a target to pass without a whack. All this, however, occurred without any spite or ill-feeling whatever—for the mere love of fighting in fact.

However Donnybrook Fair may have amused visitors, and furnished themes for satirical humorists, it is beyond question that in Dublin at least, it came to be regarded by all the decent classes as a gigantic nuisance and national disgrace. As the confines of the city extended, it became more and more a menace to the peace and well-being of the community, who looked forward to it each succeeding year with increased feelings of apprehension, until at last degenerating into a mere drunken orgy, it was felt to be no longer endurable, and the inhabitants took vigorous concerted action to rid themselves of the incubus. A public committee was formed, a campaign commenced against it in the Press, a subscription list opened, and finally, in 1855, the Patent was purchased for the sum of £3,000 from the family into whose possession it had fallen, and the Fair allowed to lapse. For some years afterwards a publican in the village with a field attached to his premises, persisted in holding a miniature fair on his grounds, but in 1859 even this *simulacrum* of the original was stopped by the refusal of the magistrates to renew his licence.

The Sunday immediately preceding Fair week, which commenced on 26th August, was called " Walking Sunday," and for some years after the suppression of the Fair, a number of people from the city used to assemble at the Fair Green and do the round of the public houses in the village, but nothing like the scenes of former years were enacted, and in time even this practice fell into disuse.

CHAPTER XLVI

THE HISTORY OF THE DUBLIN AND KINGSTOWN
RAILWAY

EARLY in the last century, proposals were made to connect the Port of Dublin with Kingstown by ship canal, but the project was abandoned when railways were introduced into England, and a number of Dublin merchants recognising the value of the new mode of transit, resolved to run a railway to deep water at Kingstown. For this purpose a company was formed, with a capital of £200,000, and the necessary Act of Parliament (1 & 2 Wm. IV, Cap. 69) received Royal assent on 6th September, 1831.

From the outset the project was most unpopular; it was met by every possible kind of opposition, and everything that could be said or done, appears to have been tried to defeat the proposal. The directors, notwithstanding, had raised over three-fourths of the estimated cost, and in May, 1832, they approached the Board of Works for a loan of £100,000, but that body, which appears to have had the support of popular opinion in its action at the time, refused the loan, stating that " it did not appear to them that the construction of a " railroad from Dublin to Kingstown for the purpose of " expediting the conveyance of passengers between these " places, would be a work of sufficient public utility to " warrant them in recommending the issue of so large a sum " by way of loan from the funds placed at their disposal." The directors, undaunted, continued the agitation, making themselves still more unpopular, but their belief in the line never wavered, and as one discouragement after another was met, they only became more determined to succeed. The whole project was decried as a huge piece of dishonesty—the directors were denounced as if they were a pack of swindlers,

and a further application for a loan was met, as might be
expected, by another refusal.   The directors on this occasion,
however, succeeded in getting a hearing, by means of a
deputation to the Board of Works, and ultimately, in August,
1832, a loan of £75,000 was obtained.

In the contract was the somewhat unusual provision that

The Building of Clarence Street Bridge.
(*From "The Dublin Penny Journal,"* 1834)

the contractor, Dargan, was to give his whole time to the
undertaking, though, in view of the time allowed, it would
seem to have been an unnecessary condition.

It was stipulated in the specification that the retaining
walls of the embankments were to be of stone from the
Donnybrook quarries, also that " every part of said railway
" and works shall be ready to be opened for the public con-
" veyance of goods and passengers over the entire line thereof
" on or before 1st June, 1834 "—thus allowing for the entire
execution of the undertaking, a period of only about eighteen
months from the date of the contract.

As a result of this undue haste, for which there appears
to have been no adequate reason, much of the masonry was

of an inferior character, and in the section from Westland Row to Barrow Street, the retaining walls, when the embankment was filled in, exhibited such ominous symptoms of yielding outwards, that heavy iron tie-rods with cast iron washers had to be inserted at frequent intervals to prevent absolute collapse. These pins may still be seen along this portion of the line. Several of the bridges, too, proved unsatisfactory, and within ten days of the opening of the line, the one over the Dodder where Lansdowne Road station now stands, was swept away by a flood. A temporary bridge was erected in its place, and was replaced, in 1847, by the existing iron structure.

It was originally intended that each of the bridges over streets should consist of a single semi-elliptical arch, but the Wide Streets Commissioners interposed and insisted on having two small side arches for foot passengers added in all the principal thoroughfares.

To obtain water supplies for the engines at Westland Row, a well was sunk at Sandwith Street, where water was obtained in plenty, but of such bad quality that it was deemed unfit even for locomotive consumption.

The line was formally opened for traffic on 17th November, 1834, and trains were run at intervals during the day, but no constant service was maintained until the following January, when trains were run on week days, every half hour, both ways, from 9 o'clock *a.m.* till 5 o'clock *p.m.*, while on Sundays trains ran every 20 minutes, with the exception of an interval from noon till 2 o'clock *p.m.* The single fares were 1*s.*, 8*d.* and 6*d.* for the three classes.

This, the first railway in Ireland, seems to have been constructed more with a view to the conveyance of goods than passengers, but as happened under similar circumstances, with several of the early English railways, it was, almost from the outset, swamped with passenger traffic.

As the Kingstown railway became more and more used by the public, so the road fell into disuse, and a great change soon became noticeable in that ancient highway. Formerly presenting a most animated appearance, traversed as it was by a succession of outside and "low-backed" cars and "jingles," with their jovial jarveys and passengers, it now became comparatively deserted, and used mainly for the conveyance of goods—the merry sound of the hoofs and wheels was replaced by the roar of the adjacent trains, and the humours and traditions of the Rock Road, told in many

Train passing over Sandwith Street Bridge.
(*From "The Dublin Penny Journal"* 1834)

a song and story, ended with the advent of the usurping locomotive.

The first sleepers supporting the rails were made of granite but it did not take long to discover the unsuitability of this unyielding material for the purpose, and they were soon changed for wooden ones. Some of these granite sleepers may still be seen in places along the line.

Connection between the engine and carriages was at first by means of chains, which as may be imagined, produced very unpleasant results when starting or stopping—the carriages crashing together again and again before they came to rest. The spring buffer to some extent remedied this, but it took some time before a silent and satisfactory method of coupling was evolved.

" The Dublin Penny Journal " of 25th October, 1834, gives
the following description of the opening runs : " On Saturday,
" the 8th instant, the first trial of the steam engine ' Vauxhall '
" with a small train of carriages filled with ladies and gentle-
" men, was made on the line of railway from Dublin to the
" Martello tower at Williamstown. The experiment is said to
" have given great satisfaction, not only as to the rapidity
" of motion, ease of conveyance and facility of stopping, but
" the celerity and quickness with which the train passed, by
" means of the crossings from one line of road to another.
" The distance was about two miles and a half [Irish ?] which
" was performed four times each way at the rate of about
" thirty-one miles an hour. The controul over the machinery
" was complete, the stopping and reversing the motion
" was effected without a moment's delay."

" On the 9th instant a train of carriages, crowded with
" ladies and gentlemen, proceeded the entire length of the line
" from the station-house at Westland Row to Salt-hill.
" There were eight carriages attached to the train ; one of the
" first class, three second, and four of the third class. The
" first trip was made by the locomotive engine called the
" Hibernia, and with the many disadvantages attendant on
" a first starting, the trip to the station-house at Salt-hill
" was performed in fifteen minutes and a half ; and back to
" Dublin in twenty-two and a half minutes."

.   .   .   .   .   .

" Having joined in one of these trips we were delighted
" with the perfect ease and safety with which it was per-
" formed ; there is so little motion perceptible even when
" going at the quickest rate, that we could read or write
" without the slightest inconvenience."

The illustrations accompanying the articles in " The
Dublin Penny Journal " for 1834, some of which are reproduced here, are of great interest at the present time,
showing, as might be expected, considerable changes in the
district since the line was constructed, 88 years ago. The
bold cliff scenery appearing in the view at Blackrock, has
all but disappeared as a result of the alterations in the coast-

line at the Public Park, while the tract enclosed between the
embankment and the Rock Road, shown in the picture as
under water, is now dry and grass grown.   This tract became
in time a very objectionable feature in the neighbourhood,
and caused much annoyance to the inhabitants by the foul
odours proceeding from it, its normal condition being that
of a salt swamp.

What seem now, curious notions as to speed, persisted for

Train passing Merrion on its way to Kingstown.
From " The Dublin Penny Journal" 1834)

some time after the beginning of the railroad era, and one
eminent authority writing on the subject, expressed the hope
" that he would not be confounded with those hot-brained
" enthusiasts who maintained the possibility of carriages
" being driven by a steam engine on a railway at such a
" speed as twelve miles an hour."

" The Quarterly Review " for March, 1825, in reference to
the line proposed to be constructed between London and
Woolwich, sagely remarked " What can be more palpably
" absurd and ridiculous than the prospect held out of loco-
" motives travelling *twice as fast* as stage coaches ! We
" should as soon expect the people of Woolwich to suffer
" themselves to be fired off upon one of Congreve's *ricochte*

" rockets as trust themselves to the mercy of a machine
" going at such a rate. We will back old Father Thames
" against the Woolwich Railway for any sum. We trust
" that Parliament will, in all railways it may sanction, limit
" the speed to eight or nine miles an hour, which we entirely
" agree with Mr. Sylvester, is as great as can be ventured on
" with safety."

The prejudice against railway travelling long survived its

View from Blackrock, looking towards Merrion.
(*From " The Dublin Penny Journal"* 1834)

introduction, and when at length it was proposed to popularise
it by means of cheap 3rd class fares, the measure was opposed
in Parliament by ministers of the Crown, on the ground
that " it would only encourage the lower orders to wander
aimlessly about the country."

The first carriages were called coaches, and in appearance
were really coaches bolted to wooden platforms supported by
flanged wheels, in some cases several coach bodies being fixed
to one long platform, but this early type of carriage never
made its appearance in Ireland. The persistence of the
coach idea in the designs of railway carriages would afford
an interesting field for research, and even at the present day

some of the features of the old horse coaches are quite discernible in the carriages of certain companies.

In the early days of the Dublin and Kingstown, and of other railways also, a man sat in a box seat on the front carriage, in a similar position to that of the driver of a horse omnibus, immediately behind and over the engine tender, but diligent inquiries have, so far, failed to elicit information as to the duties of this mysterious functionary. It has been averred in some quarters that he carried a whip, but of this allegation, confirmation is lacking. Of his existence, however, there can be no doubt, as apart from the evidence of old people who have seen him, several illustrations in the author's possession, apparently issued with the sanction of the Railway Company and dating about 1845–50, show this officer *in situ*.

When one considers that these men were without any kind of protection except the clothes they wore, that they must have received a goodly share of smoke and smuts from the engine, and that they were driven at 30 to 40 miles an hour in all weathers, times and seasons, it would not be surprising to learn that promotion in this branch of the Company's service was rapid.

After the determined opposition to the construction of the Dublin and Kingstown Railway, it might reasonably have been expected that similar hostility would have been shown to the Atmospheric Railway, an extension of the former line, and a further innovation, but strange to say, the project received every encouragement, apart from the opposition of the engineering experts who discredited the " Atmospheric " system.

The Dublin and Kingstown Railway though still preserving its separate identity as a Company, is incorporated in the Dublin and South-eastern Company's system, of which it has formed a part since the extension of the original line to Bray.

CHAPTER XLVII

THE ATMOSPHERIC RAILWAY—1843-1854
(Kingstown to Dalkey)

THE great success of the Dublin and Kingstown Railway, constructed in the years 1832–4, naturally resulted in numerous schemes for other railways all over the country. That which was considered to have the first claim, however, was for the extension of the Kingstown line southward towards Bray, and this would, no doubt have been carried out, but for a new system of propulsion championed by the eminent engineer, Brunel, known as the Atmospheric system, in which the engine supplying the power was stationary, and the train was drawn along by the suction of a plug or piston through a tube. This system was emphatically denounced and opposed by Stephenson, the great locomotive engineer, and for a time, public opinion was much divided and puzzled by the claims of the rival systems as advocated by their two great protagonists. Ultimately, James Pim, an eminent Dublin citizen of his day, wrote a pamphlet or petition in favour of the Atmospheric system which attracted such widespread attention and support, that commissioners were appointed to inquire into and report upon it. Their report having been favourable, a loan of £25,000 was granted for the construction of a line to Dalkey, and land for the purpose was granted by the Harbour Commissioners, adjoining their line, locally known as " The Metals," for the haulage of granite from the Dalkey quarries for the Kingstown harbour piers. The working of the line was entrusted to the Dublin and Kingstown Railway Company, and it was opened for traffic in July, 1844, after it had been running experimentally for some months previously.

The following is the plan on which the system was worked, and which had been tried for short distances in England. A pipe, 15 inches in diameter was laid between and on a level with the rails, and the air in this was exhausted from one end by a powerful steam-driven air pump, forcing a travelling piston along the tube by the pressure of the atmosphere. A rod or plate connecting the piston with the train, travelled along the pipe in a slit covered with soft leather flaps which opened and closed again as the rod passed along. The piston consisted of an airtight plug connected with and followed by a metal framework seven yards long, closely fitting but not airtight in the tube, to give stability of direction to the plug, and the rod connecting the piston with the train was well *behind* the front of the piston, by which arrangement, leakage was reduced to a minimum as the train passed along. The slit, as stated, was covered by leather flaps, which were greased with a composition of wax and tallow, and after this slit was opened by the connecting rod, a wheel behind it attached to the train, pressed it down again, while a copper heater following, filled with burning charcoal, was supposed to melt the composition and seal it down again. This latter contrivance, however, proved ineffective, as its rate of movement, 30 to 40 miles an hour, was entirely too rapid to enable it to melt the composition.

In time it was found necessary to supplement these arrangements by employing an attendant to follow each train and to press down and further grease the leather flaps.

Notwithstanding the mechanical disadvantages of the atmospheric system, the line seems to have worked well, continuing in use for nearly eleven years, and all experts seem agreed that the workmanship and execution of everything connected with it were of the highest class.

The engine house where the great air pump was worked by a steam engine, stood on Atmospheric Road, on the site now occupied by the house called "The Bungalow." With its tall chimney it formed a conspicuous object in the then sparsely inhabited neighbourhood, and the great fly-wheel possessed a fascinating interest for the juvenile residents. A small reservoir adjoining, supplied water for the engine, and immediately beyond this was the old Dalkey station, about five minutes walk from the village. Portion of the masonry connected with the engine house, may still be seen on the railway cutting, adjoining the site.

For a short period prior to the supersession of the atmospheric by the locomotive system on this line, both systems worked concurrently, and at one stage of the transition period when some difficulties arose which necessitated the stopping

The Engine House at Dalkey.

of all traffic, John Wilson, the well-known owner of the "Favourite" fleet of Dublin omnibuses, came to the rescue, and supplied the missing link between Dublin and Dalkey.

In appearance the carriages were similar to those on the Kingstown railway at the time, and the front one, which carried the connection, was called the piston carriage. The fares were : 1d. 3rd class and 2d. 2nd class—there was no first. The line commenced immediately beyond Kingstown station, and passengers walked from one platform to the other. The speed was pretty much the same as the locomotive driven trains—from 30 to 40 miles an hour.

The pipe ended about 100 yards before reaching Dalkey, the momentum carrying the train into the station, and a look-out man at the power house stopped the pumping engine when he saw or heard the train approaching. The pressure was shown at the power house by a special barometer in connection with the tube.

As the line was uphill the whole way to Dalkey, the return journey was performed by gravity, and before leaving Dalkey station, an attendant lifted the piston by means of a lever, and hooked it up under the train, so as to run clear of the tube.

On one occasion a serious explosion occurred at the power or engine house, which so deranged the machinery, that the trains had to submit to the indignity of being towed along by one of their hated rivals, a locomotive engine.

The Atmospheric Railway was a great attraction in the district, and brought numerous visitors there, besides which engineering experts were sent by many foreign governments to inspect and report on the working of the system. In fact, during the period of the railway mania, the attention of half Europe was focussed on this little line, descriptions of it appeared in many foreign papers and magazines, and " The Illustrated London News " of the 6th January, 1844, contains an illustrated article on the subject.

The line, which was exactly 9,200 feet in length, was identical nearly the whole way with the course of the modern railway, but at Castlepark Road, the old Atmospheric track diverges from and forms a loop with the modern line, and the old granite bridge which crossed it may still be seen adjoining the bridge over the railway.

An experimental telegraph line for signalling purposes was carried on supports projecting from the embankment along the line, but it is stated to have been a failure.

The principal cause which led to the supersession of the atmospheric by the locomotive system was the difficulty of keeping the leather flaps air-tight, which proved greater than was anticipated, and added considerably to the cost of working, as attendants had to be employed for the duty. Trouble was also caused by rats gnawing the leather for the sake of the grease.

There are many still living who have travelled on this

interesting little line, and its memory is perpetuated in the title of " Atmospheric Road " which adjoins the cutting from Castlepark Road to Barnhill Road.

For detailed technical information on this subject, see " Stephenson on the Atmospheric Railway system, 1844 " ; " Mallet, Kingstown and Dalkey Atmospheric Railway, 1844 "; and " Bergin, Atmospheric Railway, 1843 "—all in National Library, Dublin.

CHAPTER XLVIII

LAMBAY ISLAND

THE island of Lambay which is so conspicuous a feature off the north Dublin coast, lies three miles due east off Portrane Point, and is about a square mile in area. In the early part of last century it maintained a population of about 100 who eked out a precarious livelihood by husbandry and fishing, but they gradually died out or left the island, until in recent years there were only some two or three families and the coastguards residing there. Near the shore, on the western side, is the chapel, a small whitewashed building, where Mass is celebrated twice or three times a year by a priest from the mainland.

Almost concealed by the grove of trees near the landing place is the castle—a curiously designed building with thick walls and loopholed angle towers, the splayed walls of which give the structure a polygonal appearance. When or by whom it was erected, is not known for certain, but if we allow for some alterations, it probably represents the castle which the notorious John Tiploft, Earl of Worcester, was commissioned to erect, while Lord Deputy, for the defence of the island against the king's enemies.

In a field to the south, and still quite distinguishable, is a bank or ditch, believed to be the remains of the fortification which Thomas Challoner, who leased the island in the 16th century, constructed, as a condition of his tenure, for the defence of the inhabitants in any emergency.

Nearly in the centre of the island is Trinity well, surrounded by shrubs and bushes, where in former years a patron was held on Trinity Sunday. Rising above this and to the north is Knockbane, 418 feet high, the greatest elevation on the island.

The small harbour on the western side affords fair shelter except when the wind blows hard from the west.

The eastern coast of Lambay is the scene of the terrible shipping disaster, the wreck of the *John Tayleur* in 1854—fully described at page 299 *et seq*.

Lambay was formerly spelt Lambey (Lamb ey) meaning lamb island, a name which probably originated with the practice of sending ewes over from the mainland in the spring and allowing them to yean on the island and remain there with their lambs during the summer. The ancient name of Lambay was Rechru in the oldest Irish documents, and in more recent ones Reachra and Rechra. In a grant to Christ Church, in the 14th century, the island is called Rechen, and the parish on the mainland to which it belonged, Portrahern, which after 700 years, is still quite recognisable in its modern representative, Portrane. The point of land at that place was the port of embarkation for the island, and the tradition of this has survived to the present day—(Joyce's " Irish Names of Places," Vol. I, p. 111).

In the time of Pliny and Ptolemy, Lambay was known by the name of Limnus or Limni.

In the State Papers of Henry VIII, the Lord Deputy, in his report to the King, objects to the Navy being allowed to lie at Lambay " when the Frenchmen and Scots both have " knowledge of your said navy and where they lie, and so " may pass between the said Lambay and the Hollyhead, " which is three-score or four-score miles, without danger of " the same your navy."

In 1691, after the surrender of the fort of Ballymore in Westmeath to General Ginkle, the officers who were taken prisoners were removed to Dublin, but the men, over 1,000 in number, were sent to Lambay where they were confined until the Treaty of Limerick ; all persons being prohibited from passing over to the island under heavy penalties. When the Treaty was signed, however, emissaries were sent by the Irish Government to discourse with the prisoners, without disclosing to them that their release was a condition of the Treaty, and to acquaint them that if they would take the oath of allegiance and promise to go to their respective habitations, they would be set at liberty and permitted to live quietly at home. (Story's Impartial History, p. 91, and Harris's Life of William III, p. 351.)

In the reign of Queen Elizabeth the island became the property of Sir William Ussher, and his descendant, archbishop Ussher, stayed there for some months in 1626 while under treatment by his physician, Dr. Arthur.

Lambay Island has been for some years past the property of the Hon. Cecil Baring who has put some of the land adjoining the castle into cultivation, added a wing to the old building, and made the island a sanctuary for wild birds and animals.

An interesting account of the island, principally from a naturalist's point of view, appears in " The Irish Naturalist " for January and February, 1907, which can be seen at the National Library, Dublin.

CHAPTER XLIX

OLD MAPS OF DUBLIN AND ITS DISTRICT

THE old maps of Dublin and its neighbourhood are not so numerous as one might expect in view of the political importance of the Irish Metropolis from an English point of view. One of the earliest and best known is Speed's map of the city, dated 1610. Besides this he published a map of " The County of Leinster," but owing to its small scale, little detail is shown, and it is not of much topographical interest. Next come the maps of the Cromwellian Survey, commonly known as " The Down Survey," carried out by Sir William Petty in 1655–6. This survey was in connection with the distribution of the Forfeited Estates in Ireland ; detail, as might be expected, is rather scanty, and the roads are generally indicated by dotted lines. The map of the Dublin District contains some points of interest, but the scale is too small to admit of identification of more than general features.

Brooking's map of the City, 1728, is a well engraved and accurate map of the city as it then was, but shows nothing outside it.

John Rocque's maps of the City and County, in several editions, *circa* 1756–1770, are excellent maps, showing such an advance on their predecessors, that it is quite possible to identify most of the main roads and many of the by-roads. They were issued in various scales. On the 1762 edition the Grand Canal is shown as " Part of the New Canal." Very little is shown in Rathmines and Rathgar, but Rathgar Avenue and its continuation as far as the Dodder, now known as Orwell Road, appear as a high road. The Dodder was then crossed by a ford near this point. The site of the modern Sandymount village is occupied by " Brickfield Town," and Lord Merrion's brickfields extend thence along the shore to Merrion. Sandymount Avenue and Serpentine Avenue are recognisable, as also Simmonscourt Road. Many of the mountains are shown with their present names, but the southern side of the Two-rock Mountain is called " Black Mountain "—a name which now appears to be quite lost.

Brownrigg's Map of the district along the Grand Canal from Dublin to the Barrow at Monasterevin, with views, elevations, etc., scale about 1 inch to the statute mile, was published in 1788, and appears to have been mainly intended to show the country adjoining the canal, then a work attracting considerable interest.

Allen and Archer's Map of the City of Dublin, published in 1797, includes the urban area only.

The first really detailed maps of the County were those published by John Taylor, of 8 Upper Baggot Street, in 1816, and by William Duncan, principal draftsman to the Quartermaster General's Department in Ireland, in 1821. Both of these maps are beautifully engraved. Taylor's map is occasionally inaccurate in the drawing, but is a great advance on anything that preceded it. Five years afterwards, Duncan produced his splendid map, which is quite a masterpiece of accurate detail, and it, to a great extent, superseded Taylor's. It must have taken years of patient work, and entailed an immense amount of travelling at a time when conveniences of locomotion were few. It is a large map and was usually sold in a roller and mahogany case, to hang on a wall. The scale is 3 inches to an Irish mile, equivalent to $2\frac{5}{14}$ inches to a statute mile. Detailed tables of distances are given, as also the system of triangulation on which the map was based. For many years afterwards, it was the standard map of the County Dublin used in public offices and departments, even after the Ordnance Survey maps of 1837 had come into general use.

Not the least interesting feature in this map is the view, which is partly incorporated in the title scroll, of Kingstown and the Bay from a point adjoining Martello Avenue, about a hundred yards north of Sandycove Railway bridge. It bears no title, but is readily identifiable by anyone familiar with the locality. No buildings of any kind are represented on the road between the observer and Kingstown, but conspicuously in view on the left is the rock surmounted by its

half-moon battery, which originated the name " Stoneview "
(*see* p. 48)—the title of a detached house which stood on an
adjoining site.

The principal object in this view is a Martello tower which
stood on the rising ground at Martello Avenue. An enclosure
with low walls adjoins the tower, and in the immediate foreground is a pool with some rocks beside it. Open country
extends from the tower to Kingstown, and no buildings inter-
vene between the main road and the sea except a few small
cottages on the shore, where there appears to be a rough

Kingstown in 1821
(*From Duncan's Map of the Co. Dublin*)

track leading towards Newtownsmith. A heavy wagon,
drawn by one horse, is being led by the driver along this
roadway, and another solitary vehicle of the same description
is represented on the main road, proceeding to Kingstown.
Only one pier—the east—is shown in the picture, and in the
distance may be observed the squat form of the old Poolbeg
Lighthouse (*see* p. 14). The Royal Hotel appears in the course
of erection, with its attendant scaffolding, and beyond and
to the left, are the houses of Patrick Street.

Howth is so accurately drawn and so true to elevation—a
rare virtue in an artist of those days—that we may safely
assume that the whole drawing is equally accurate—probably drawn by Duncan himself, whose trained draftsman's
eye would be unlikely to indulge in the exaggeration and
idealism so common in pictures at that period.

The following are some of the features of interest in these two maps :—

DUNCAN'S MAP—1821

Considerable spaces of open country are shown in this, as also in Taylor's map, both on the north and south sides of the city, within the compass of the Circular Road. Two villages appear at Clontarf—Clontarf and Clontarf Sheds. A lake is shown south of Sandymount Tower, on the low ground south of and adjoining the present Sydney Parade Avenue. Rathmines Road has " Mt. Anthony " and " William's Park," and Rathgar Road—then new—has no buildings shown on it. A building, however, is shown at the top of Rathgar Avenue, probably " The Thatch " (*see* p. 171). Castlewood Avenue extends only a few hundred yards in length from Rathmines Road. " Three Rocks " are marked at the summit of the Three-rock Mountain, the Two-rock Mountain is called " Three Rock Mountain," and its south-eastern side is called " Black Mountain." Leopardstown is correctly given as Leperstown, the original form, which is no doubt a translation of the Irish, Ballinalower. On the line of road now known as Bath Avenue and Londonbridge Road, only one house is shown—the Umbrella House (*see* p. 22). The present Londonbridge was erected in 1857, and was preceded by a wooden bridge, a water-colour drawing of which by Du Noyer may be seen in the National Gallery, Dublin. This road was laid out in 1800. In De Gomme's map of 1673, its site is all covered by water. No thoroughfare beyond Mount Street bridge over the canal is shown on Duncan's Map, and the road from town to Ballsbridge was Baggot Street and the present Pembroke Road.

TAYLOR'S MAP--1816

" Quay " is marked beside Tobermaclaney martello tower at Portmarnock. Belmont Avenue is called " Coldblow Lane." Oakley Road (formerly Cullenswood Avenue) is called " Dunville Lane," and at its southern extremity is shown a row of houses extending from about the site of

Annesley Park to the Railway, called "Dunville Place." These houses survive to the present day. On Rathmines Road, "Tourville" appears near Williamspark, and Castle-wood Avenue is a *cul-de-sac*. Rathgar Road is called "New Road." The Yellow House is shown in its present position beyond Rathfarnham. The Naniken river, flowing out on the shore about ¼ mile south of Watermill Cottage beyond Dollymount, is called "Ballyhoy stream." The Griffen river which flows into the Liffey at Lucan, is called "Racreena river" at Milltown, near Lucan, and "Esker river" at Esker.

All the maps mentioned in this chapter can be seen at the National Library, Dublin.

At Lucan, near the entrance to St. Catherine's

NOTES

NOTES

1 (p. 6). The immense mass of granite required for the South Wall—greater even than that required for Kingstown Harbour—was obtained from the quarries at Dalkey Hill and from the foreshore between Bullock and Kingstown. To facilitate the conveyance of the material, the Ballast Board rebuilt the harbours of Bullock and Sandycove, and acquired a lease of Bullock Castle for many years.

2 (p. 18). The name of Richard Cranfield is commemorated in the title of Cranfield Place which runs from Tritonville Road to the site of the Baths on the shore.

3 (p. 19). Sandymount Avenue was formerly Sandymount Lane. the name having been changed some 70 or 80 years ago when the neighbourhood became a residential one.

4 (p. 26). The old city gallows is shown on one of Rocque's maps as standing at the intersection of Lower Baggot and Fitzwilliam Streets.

5 (p. 32). Along the road between Merrion and Williamstown may still be seen, now high and dry, the old sea wall which served to protect this portion of the coast against the ravages of the sea, prior to the construction of the Railway.

6 (p. 60). The following poem on Killiney Hill by my friend, Mr. S. S. McCurry, appears in his book, " The Ballads of Bally-tumulty." He now lives in London, and the plaintive verses show that he, like many of his countrymen, does not take kindly to being " An Exile of Erin."

KILLINEY HILL

To other lands, to other skies,
  With restless feet we stray,
While Erin stands with tearful eyes,
  Inviting us to stay.
" Are not my hills and valleys fair,
  " For thee to roam at will ? "
" Has earth a picture to compare
  " With sweet Killiney Hill ? "

There proudly was I wont to climb,
  For summers twenty-five,
And gazing round me felt each time,
  'Twas good to be alive,
God's bounty over sea and plain,
  Would care and envy kill,
And all the ways of men seemed vain
  On fair Killiney Hill.

When Spring with rosy fingers dressed
    The trees in tender green,
'Twas bliss along the slope to rest,
    To watch the living scene ;
I've heard her stealing o'er the sod
    At eve when all was still,
More fragrant turf she never trod
    Than fair Killiney Hill.

When Summer held the sultry air,
    Mid Glenageary trees,
How glad was I to wander there,
    To catch the evening breeze.
When Autumn brought the pensive mood
    I lingered in the chill,
To think of God and all things good
    On fair Killiney Hill.

Not Winter's weird, unwelcome blast,
    Could turn my steps away,
Watching the rain-clouds as they passed
    Across the mountains grey.
Each changing season of the year,
    With fresh delight could thrill,
To make remembrance yet more dear
    Of fair Killiney Hill.

But passing are the joys of earth,
    As all our lives we prove,
And tears too often wait on mirth,
    And loss aye shadows love ;
Now cast upon a distant shore,
    Dim fears my bosom fill,
That seldom I may visit more
    My own Killiney Hill.

                                S. S. McCurry.

7 (p. 77). See further notice of Donnybrook Fair herein.

8 (p. 122).   Carew O'Dwyer bought Orlagh in 1836 from Nathaniel
    Caldwell, Governor of the Bank of Ireland, and rebuilt it, adding
    spacious rooms, and stables.   He also laid out new gardens and
    pleasure grounds and introduced song birds, no gun being allowed
    near the place.
        The large banqueting hall was hung with tapestries brought
    from Paris when Louis Philippe altered the rooms in the Tuileries
    which Marie Antoinette had occupied.
        The drawing-room was adorned with pictures of special interest,
    including a life-like portrait of Lord Edward Fitzgerald, one of
    Thomas Moore painted by Jackson, another of Curran and many
    others of well-known personages.
        In the oratory was a window of 15th century stained glass.
    Father Thomas Burke, the distinguished Dominican preacher,
    often celebrated Mass there.

9 (p. 134). Quite close to the Three Rocks, on the northern side, are
    the foundations of a small rectangular building of which nothing
    is known.

10 (p. 157). This tablet was removed in June, 1912.

11 (p. 172). When Rathgar Castle came into possession of the Cusacks early in the 17th century, there were in its neighbourhood only two high roads—one leading to Harold's Cross and Rathfarnham, and the other following the route of Rathmines Road and Upper Rathmines to the Dodder and Milltown. It is obvious, however, that so important a residence must have had some means of access to the main throughfares, and so we may assume that there were accommodation roads or bridle tracks leading from it to both these main roads. One such track, now represented by Rathgar Avenue, was doubtless the route to the city *via* the Rathfarnham road, and the other probably coincided with the modern Highfield Road. In regard to Rathgar Avenue, the quarries on Orwell Road may have been working prior to the erection of Rathgar Castle, in which case a track would already have existed for the conveyance of the material to the city. The roads now known as Terenure and Highfield Roads, leading from Palmerston Park to Terenure, were constructed in the latter half of the 18th century to open up communication with the Rathfarnham Road, probably through the influence of Chief Justice Yorke who then lived at Rathmines Castle, on the site of Palmerston Park. The Rathgar Road was then laid out about 1800, to join up Rathmines Road with these.

On Orwell Road, about 80 yards from the tram track, are the massive pillars of a gateway leading to some cottages. From the style and appearance of these pillars, it is evident that they are much older than any of the adjoining buildings, and as no structure necessitating such a gateway has stood on the site of Rathgar Castle since the disappearance of its ruins over a hundred years ago, it is not unlikely that these pillars are the remains of a gateway in connection with the out-offices of this old mansion.

A large rectangular building, apparently facing westward, is shown on Taylor's map (1816) on the site of the castle, and as the same building is shown on Rocques' map of the County, dated 1762, there is little doubt that it represents the ruins of Rathgar Castle.

12 (p. 183). The following description of " The Bleeding Horse " in about 1710, is taken from Le Fanu's book " The Cock and Anchor " as quoted by Miss A. Peter in her interesting book : " Old Dublin."

" Some time within the first ten years of the 18th century,
" there stood at the southern extremity of the city, near the
" point at which Camden Street now terminates, a small, old
" fashioned building, something between an ale-house and an
" inn. It occupied the roadside not unpicturesquely. One gable
" jutted into the road, with a projecting window which stood out
" from the building like a glass box, held together by a massive
" frame of wood, and commanded by this projecting gable and a
" few yards in retreat, but facing the road, was the inn door,
" over which hung a painted panel representing a white horse,
" out of whose neck there spouted a crimson cascade, and under-
" neath, in large letters, the traveller was informed that this was
" the genuine old ' Bleeding Horse.' Old enough in all conscience
" it appeared to be, for the tiled roof, except where the ivy
" clustered over it, was crowded with weeds of many kinds, and
" the boughs of the huge trees which embowered it, had cracked

" and shattered one of the cumbrous chimney stacks, and in
" many places it was evident that but for the timely interposition
" of the saw and axe, the giant limbs of the old timber would in
" the gradual increase of years, have forced their way through
" the roof and the masonry itself."

Within the author's recollection this inn exhibited a pictorial
representation of its title " The Bleeding Horse," by which name
it is still known. It would seem probable that this old hostelry
was in existence at the time of the Battle of Rathmines.

13 (p. 266). Addison was an intimate friend of Tickell, and often
stayed with him at his residence which stood almost on the site
of the Superintendent's house, Botanic Gardens. The Yew tree
walk is traditionally associated with his memory, and is still
called " Addison's Walk."

14 (p. 320). " The Whiskey Forge " stood at the point of land immediately north of the Claremont Hotel.

15 (p. 380). I regret to see that Coronation Plantation is now (1920)
being cut down, and I fear that Glendoo is likely to meet the
same fate.

EQUIPMENT

BOOTS, ETC.—For walking in the country there is nothing so comfortable as a pair of old, well-cared boots or shoes, with thick soles kept soft and waterproof with dubbin. For cycling in warm dry weather, canvas shoes are very cool and light on the feet.

A pair of light anklets are very useful in wet weather or in boggy country, and throw off a good deal of the rain which falls from a waterproof. They should be of soft pliable material to enable them to be rolled up and carried in the pocket when not required.

GLOVES.—The only really satisfactory protection for the hands in very cold weather is a pair of woollen gloves inside leather ones—the latter, of course, must be a large size. Some prefer the wool outside, but my experience is that the gloves are warmer and wear better with the leather outside. Mittens (without fingers) if thick enough, are the warmest of all, but are rather clumsy.

WATERPROOFS.—A light cycling cape is the most convenient and portable protection against the weather, and can be had light enough to carry in the pocket. Also—a square of waterproof cut from an old mackintosh is very useful as a seat in damp weather, and when folded takes up little room.

MAPS.—It is recommended that this book should be read in conjunction with some good map of the District. The best is the Ordnance Survey map of the Dublin District, 1 inch to the mile, mounted on fabric, price 3s. It extends from Portrane on the north to the southern slopes of Bray Head on the south, and to near Naas on the westward. A smaller scale is of little use except for cycling or motoring on the main roads.

CAMERA.—If you are a photographer, do not encumber yourself with a heavy camera—you will be tempted either to leave it at home or else to use it recklessly so as to have some value for the trouble of carrying it. A camera should be of such size and weight as can be carried for a whole day without inconvenience, should no opportunity arise for using it. Most of the photographs reproduced in this book were taken with a folding Kodak, fitted with an ordinary lens, and weighing little over a pound. Even with the smallest cameras, very pleasing mementos may be obtained of places or persons, and enlargements made therefrom up to half plate size.

If a camera be taken on the carrier of a bicycle, which is not to be recommended, it should have a thick padding of felt, at least half an inch thick around it. A frame bag is, however, a much better way of carrying it. It goes without saying that a camera for the pedestrian or cyclist should be of the film variety.

GLASS.—A glass of some kind is a pleasant companion in a country ramble. The best, of course, are the prismatic kind, but they are now very expensive. A magnifying power of 6 will be found the most generally suitable. In the case of the old style of glass (Galilean) a higher power than $4\frac{1}{2}$ is not advisable on account of the smallness of the field. Do not buy an inferior glass of any description—they are injurious and uncomfortable.

INDEX

INDEX

SUPPLEMENTARY INDEX